A GLOBAL AGENDA

Issues Before
the 51st
General Assembly
of the
United Nations

A GLOBAL AGENDA

Issues Before the 51st General Assembly of the United Nations

An annual publication of the United Nations Association of the United States of America

John Tessitore and Susan Woolfson, Editors

Rowman & Littlefield Publishers, Inc.
Lanham • Boulder • New York • London

ROWMAN & LITTLEFIELD PUBLISHERS, INC.

Published in the United States of America
by Rowman & Littlefield Publishers, Inc.
4720 Boston Way, Lanham, Maryland 20706

3 Henrietta Street
London WC2E 8LU, England

ISBN: 1057-1213

ISBN 0-8476-8369-9 (cloth : alk. paper)
ISBN 0-8476-8370-2 (pbk. : alk. paper)

Printed in the United States of America

Cover by Scott Rattray

 The paper used in this publication meets the minimum requirements of American National Standard for Information Sciences—Permanence of Paper for Printed Library Materials, ANSI Z39.48–1984.

Contents

Acknowledgments *vii*

Contributors *ix*

I.   **Making and Keeping the Peace** 1

    1. Beyond Peacekeeping *1*
    2. The Former Yugoslavia *11*
    3. Haiti *24*
    4. Africa *30*
    5. The Middle East and the Persian Gulf *52*
    6. The Former Soviet Union *64*
    7. Cambodia *75*

II.   **Arms Control and Disarmament** 83

    1. Nuclear Proliferation *84*
    2. Nuclear Arms Control *88*
    3. Nuclear Testing *92*
    4. Chemical and Biological Weapons *96*
    5. Transparency in Armaments and Conventional Arms Control *98*

III.   **Economics and Development** 105

    1. The Global Economy *105*
    2. Development Outlook *115*
    3. World Trade *126*

IV.   **Global Resource Management** 135

    1. Environment and Sustainable Development *135*
    2. Food and Agriculture *150*
    3. Population *159*
    4. Law of the Sea, Ocean Affairs, and Antarctica *167*

V.   Social and Humanitarian Issues   173

    1. Human Rights   *173*
    2. Refugees and Internally Displaced Persons   *210*
    3. The Status of Women   *219*
    4. Drug Abuse, Production, and Trafficking   *229*
    5. Health   *233*
    6. Crime   *237*
    7. Children and Youth   *241*
    8. Aging   *247*
    9. Disabled Persons   *250*
  10. Habitat II   *253*

VI.   Legal Issues   261

    1. The ILC, the International Criminal Court, and the Draft Code of Crimes   *262*
    2. War Crimes and U.N. Ad Hoc Tribunals   *282*
    3. The International Court of Justice   *289*
    4. Space Law   *291*
    5. Other Legal Developments   *295*

VII. Finance and Administration   303

    1. U.N. Finance   *303*
    2. U.N. Administration   *321*

Index   333

Acknowledgments

The production of this volume was very much a team effort. Indeed, it is perhaps more accurate to say that *A Global Agenda* is the product of two teams, and each deserves our acknowledgment and thanks.

First, of course, are the contributors, whose names and brief biographies are listed in the following pages. These talented men and women from a wide variety of professional backgrounds accepted their assignments knowing full well the difficulty of meeting our publication deadline as well as the hardship of taking on yet another project in addition to existing burdens. Such cooperation and sacrifice comes from a deep personal commitment to *A Global Agenda* in particular, and to the work of the U.N. system in general.

Almost as essential as the authors themselves was the cadre of volunteer interns who provided research and editorial assistance to the contributors and editors alike. These young people, who gave so generously of their time and energy over the spring and summer months, have made an invaluable contribution to this volume. Whether fact checking, hunting down documents, proofreading, or—as in some instances—actually drafting subsections on U.N. social issues, these future leaders brought their infectious enthusiasm and good cheer to an editorial process that often seemed overwhelming. To Carin Abrahamsohn, Yaron Ben-Zvi, Rajesh De, Jenny Engström, Adam Howard, Elizabeth Madigan, Andrew Su, and Cristian Winder go our profound thanks and our very warm wishes for the great years ahead.

John Tessitore
Susan Woolfson

Contributors

Carin Abrahamsohn (Health) served as a UNA-USA Communications Intern while completing her degree at Barnard College, where she majored in political science.

Ricardo Alday (Haiti) is U.N. correspondent of the Mexican News Agency.

Frederick Z. Brown (Cambodia) directs Southeast Asian studies at the Paul H. Nitze School of Advanced International Studies of Johns Hopkins University.

Erika H. Burk (The Former Soviet Union) is the producer of *America and the World* on National Public Radio and Assistant Director of Media Projects for the Council on Foreign Relations.

J. Lee Byrd (Refugees, with Kanya D. Tampoe Sanders) is a consultant for the Washington-based Refugee Policy Group.

Jenny M. Engström (Children and Youth), a UNA-USA Communications Intern, is completing a master's degree at Columbia University's School of International and Public Affairs, where she is specializing in conflict resolution and humanitarian affairs.

Gordon M. Goldstein (The Former Yugoslavia) is director of Security Council and Nonproliferation Affairs at UNA-USA.

Shareen Hertel (The Status of Women) is a New York-based independent consultant on economic development, currently working with the Council on Economic Priorities and the Mission of Chile to the United Nations.

David Isenberg (Arms Control and Disarmament, with Kathryn R. Schultz) is a senior research analyst at the Center for Defense Information in Washington, D.C., where he specializes in the international conventional arms trade, military counternarcotics efforts, and U.S military force structure and readiness issues.

Jules Kagian (The Middle East and the Persian Gulf) covered the United Nations and the American scene for a number of Middle Eastern newspapers and radio and TV stations during more than two decades. He is currently U.N. correspondent for *Middle East International* (London).

Gail V. Karlsson (Environment and Sustainable Development; Habitat II) is a New York-based attorney specializing in international environmental law. She attended Habitat II as UNA-USA's press representative.

Lee A. Kimball (Law of the Sea, Ocean Affairs, and Antarctica) is a specialist in treaty development and international institutions relating to environment and development issues. She works as a consultant in Washington, D.C.

W. Andy Knight (Legal Issues) is an assistant professor of political studies at Bishop's University, Quebec. Co-Editor (with Keith Krause) of *State, Society, and the U.N. System: Changing Perspectives on Multilateralism* (United Nations University Press, 1995), he serves on the Executive Committee of the journal *Global Governance.*

Craig Lasher (Population) is a senior policy analyst and legislative assistant at Population Action International, a private nonprofit organization that works to expand the availability of voluntary family planning services worldwide.

David A. Lynch (Economics and Development) is an assistant professor of political science at Saint Mary's University, Minnesota.

Elizabeth K. Madigan (Drug Abuse, Production, and Trafficking), a UNA-USA Communications Intern, will be attending the Paul H. Nitze School of Advanced International Studies of Johns Hopkins University in fall 1996.

Stephen P. Marks (Human Rights) is director of the United Nations Studies Program at the School of International and Public Affairs of Columbia University, where he teaches international law, U.N. peace operations, law and politics of the United Nations, and human rights and economic development. He represents the Geneva-based International Service for Human Rights at the world body.

Martin M. McLaughlin (Food and Agriculture) is a consultant on food and development policy.

Bhaskar Menon (Beyond Peacekeeping) is editor of *International Documents Review,* a weekly newsletter on the United Nations.

W. Ofuatey-Kodjoe (Africa) is professor and executive officer of the Ph.D. program in political science at the City University of New York Graduate School and University Center, where he specializes in peace-keeping and in human rights.

Kanya D. Tampoe Sanders (Refugees, with J. Lee Byrd) is a consultant to the Washington-based Refugee Policy Group.

Kathryn R. Schultz (Arms Control and Disarmament, with David Isenberg) is a senior research analyst at the Center for Defense Information in Washington, D.C., where she specializes in nuclear weapons, nuclear proliferation, ballistic missile defenses, and European security issues.

Deborah Scroggins (Finance and Administration) is assistant political editor at the *Atlanta Journal and Constitution.*

Andrew H. Su (Aging; Disabled Persons), a UNA-USA Communications Intern, is completing a master's degree at Columbia University's School of International and Public Affairs, with a concentration in human rights and humanitarian assistance and in East Asia.

John Tessitore (Co-Editor) is Executive Director of Communications at UNA-USA.

Cristian B. Winder (Crime), a UNA-USA Communications Intern, is completing a master's degree at Columbia University's School of International and Public Affairs, with a concentration in economic and political development.

Susan Woolfson (Co-Editor) is Managing Editor of Communications at UNA-USA.

I
Making and Keeping the Peace

1. Beyond Peacekeeping
By Bhaskar Menon

On the 32nd floor of the U.N. building, along a carpeted corridor of the Situation Centre of the Department of Peacekeeping Operations (DPKO), there hangs a photograph of a bearded, rough-hewn soldier in a blue beret. On his protective hand is perched a tiny sparrow. Stan Carlson, the Canadian head of the Situation Centre, stops before the picture after giving a journalist a tour of the facilities. "Look carefully" he says, "under the bird." There, on the muscular hand, is a pool of guano. "The situation, exactly," says Carlson, leading the way to the elevators. He is laughing, but there is a slight edge in his voice.

Among peacekeeping staff at the United Nations, the sense of being unappreciated despite honorable effort and achievement is palpable. Media coverage of the performance of U.N. peacekeepers in Bosnia-Herzegovina was a regular topic of bitter comment by U.N. spokesmen. As Secretary-General Boutros Boutros-Ghali noted in speaking to a meeting of representatives of regional organizations at U.N. Headquarters on February 15, 1996, there is "an imbalance in the manner in which tasks are assigned to the U.N. and regional organizations." In Bosnia, a "small and lightly armed U.N. force was sent as peacekeepers into a continuing war." This, in turn, was replaced by "a massive and well-armed NATO combat force" to monitor a signed peace agreement.

A December 1995 booklet from the newly established **Lessons Learned Unit of the Department of Peacekeeping Operations** noted a number of reasons for dissatisfaction with the way things had turned out for the U.N. Operation in Somalia (UNOSOM II). "The Operation's mandate was vague, changed frequently during the process and was open to myriad interpretations," it said. The changing mandates were "in many respects contradictory." The original directive to protect the delivery of humanitarian assistance changed "to encouraging and assisting in political reconciliation, to establishing and maintaining a 'secure environment' to

1

capturing a leader of one of the factions at one stage and, later, to encouraging negotiations with the same leader."

These changes "were decided upon with little explanation to member States, troop contributing countries, the humanitarian community operating in Somalia or the Somali people. As a result, UNOSOM was bedeviled with disagreements among the various players—between troop contributing countries and the Secretariat, contingents and NGOs, senior UNOSOM officials and the humanitarian community, UNOSOM and U.N. agencies—which, in the end, even led to clashes between UNOSOM and some elements of the Somali community." The booklet noted the discrepancy of the resources provided to the Unified Task Force (UNI-TAF)—the original multinational force led by the United States—and UNOSOM II. The former was "given wide power, ample resources and a limited mandate" to deal with the situation in part of southern Somalia. UNOSOM II, which took over from UNITAF, was given "far less authority . . . a much broader mandate" and "was supposed to cover the entire country."

Trajectory of Change

During the first four decades of the United Nations, peacekeeping operations were few and far between—13 in all—and were run out of the Office for Special Political Affairs. In general, once an operation was in place, situations tended to be static, for U.N. intervention was preceded in most cases by cease-fire agreements. All this changed after the end of the Cold War. With the permanent members of the Security Council working cohesively, the potential for U.N. peacekeeping seemed virtually unlimited. In 1988 and 1989 five new operations were established, doubling in two years the number of extant operations. In the 1991–93 period, there were 15 new operations (16, if you count Operation Desert Storm, which the Security Council authorized but did not control). Since 1994 there has been a decline, despite the fact that on paper seven new missions were established.

The appearance of growth is deceptive, because four of the new operations (UNPREDEP, UNMIBH, UNMOP, and UNTAES) replaced parts of the larger U.N. Peace Forces in the former Yugoslavia (UNPROFOR). The Aouzou Strip Observer Group lasted only a few days, and the mission in Tajikistan consisted of fewer than 50 observers. Only UNAVEM III, the third and largest incarnation of the Verification Mission in Angola, represented a substantial addition, with a strength of over 6,500 troops. Eight years after the boom in U.N. peacekeeping began, few people at the United Nations today foresee a return to those "glory days."

The post-Cold War trajectory of changes in U.N. peacekeeping can also be described in terms of **money spent and the number of personnel**

Table I-1
Peacekeeping Operations Past and Present

UNTSO	U.N. Truce Supervision Organization	June 1948–present
UNMOGIP	U.N. Military Observer Group in India and Pakistan	January 1949–present
UNEF I	First U.N. Emergency Force	November 1956–June 1967
UNOGIL	U.N. Observation Group in Lebanon	June 1958–December 1958
ONUC	U.N. Operation in the Congo	July 1960–June 1964
UNSF	U.N. Security Force in West New Guinea (West Irian)	October 1962–April 1963
UNYOM	U.N. Yemen Observation Mission	July 1963–September 1964
UNFICYP	U.N. Peacekeeping Force in Cyprus	March 1964–present
DOMREP	Mission of the Representative of the Secretary-General in the Dominican Republic	May 1965–October 1966
UNIPOM	U.N. India-Pakistan Observation Mission	September 1965–March 1966
UNEF II	Second U.N. Emergency Force	October 1973–July 1979
UNDOF	U.N. Disengagement Observer Force	June 1974–present
UNIFIL	U.N. Interim Force in Lebanon	March 1978–present
UNGOMAP	U.N. Good Offices Mission in Afghanistan and Pakistan	April 1988–March 1990
UNIIMOG	U.N. Iran-Iraq Military Observer Group	August 1988–February 1991
UNAVEM I	U.N. Angola Verification Mission I	January 1989–June 1991
UNTAG	U.N. Transition Assistance Group	April 1989–March 1990
ONUCA	U.N. Observer Group in Central America	November 1989–January 1992
UNIKOM	U.N. Iraq-Kuwait Observation Mission	April 1991–present
UNAVEM II	U.N. Angola Verification Mission II	June 1991–January 1995
ONUSAL	U.N. Observer Mission in El Salvador	July 1991–April 1995
MINURSO	U.N. Mission for the Referendum in Western Sahara	September 1991–present
UNAMIC	U.N. Advance Mission in Cambodia	October 1991–March 1992
UNPROFOR	U.N. Protection Force	March 1992–January 1996
UNTAC	U.N. Transitional Authority in Cambodia	March 1992–September 1993
UNOSOM I	U.N. Operation in Somalia I	April 1992–April 1993
ONUMOZ	U.N. Operation in Mozambique	December 1992–December 1994
UNOSOM II	U.N. Operation in Somalia II	May 1993–March 1995
UNOMUR	U.N. Observer Mission Uganda-Rwanda	June 1993–September 1994
UNOMIG	U.N. Observer Mission in Georgia	August 1993–present
UNOMIL	U.N. Observer Mission in Liberia	September 1993–present
UNMIH	U.N. Mission in Haiti	September 1993–present
UNAMIR	U.N. Assistance Mission for Rwanda	October 1993–March 1996
UNASOG	U.N. Aouzou Strip Observer Group	May 1994–June 1994
UNMOT	U.N. Mission of Observers in Tajikistan	December 1994–present
UNCRO	U.N. Confidence Restoration Operation (Croatia)	1995–1996

Table I-1 (continued)

UNAVEM III	U.N. Angola Verification Mission III	February 1995–present
UNPREDEP	U.N. Preventive Deployment Force (former Yugoslavia)	March 1995–present
UNMIBH	U.N. Mission in Bosnia and Herzegovina	December 1995–present
UNTAES	U.N. Transitional Administration for Eastern Slavonia, Baranja and Western Sirmium	January 1996–present
UNMOP	U.N. Mission of Observers in Prevlaka	January 1996–present

involved in operations. The annual peacekeeping budget at the end of January 1988 was $230.4 million. By January 1992 it had grown to $1,689 million. By December 1994 it was $3,610 million—some three times the regular budget of the Organization. But then a period of decline began. In 1995 the peacekeeping budget was about $3 billion. The midyear estimate for 1996 was about half that.

The **number of military, police, and civilian personnel deployed** in U.N. peacekeeping operations on the three dates mentioned above were 11,121 in January 1988, 13,856 in January 1992, and 77,783 in December 1994. The number of U.N. peacekeepers in the field in mid-1996 was below 28,000.

Major Issues

The difficulties faced by U.N. peacekeepers point to larger issues central to the concept and efficacy of the United Nations. Unlike any other international organization, the United Nations is empowered to act along the entire continuum of conflict resolution. It can address the economic and social seeds of war, engaging issues before they become disputes. It can relate developments at the national, regional, and global levels to the welfare of the individual and to international security. It has wide scope for pacific settlement of disputes, and if all else fails, it has the capacity to unite states in the use of armed force in the common interest. The synergy and range of action envisaged in the U.N. Charter reflect the lesson the founders of the United Nations learned from the failure of the League of Nations: that international security cannot be maintained by political agreements among major powers if the economic and social arrangements that underpin world order are unstable, unjust, and prone to conflict.

During the four decades of the Cold War, progress toward the Charter model for international cooperation was fitful, at best. Since the end of East-West confrontation there has been a major effort, despite a welter of crises and huge imbalances in international power relationships, to rectify distortions, to revive the vision of the Charter, and to reform the instruments that can advance it. The process has not been—and cannot be—tidy, for the tasks at hand range from the reform of unwieldy and nonfunctional parts of the United Nations to such conceptual and political challenges as refashioning the Security Council and establishing a valid role for the United Nations in the areas of economic and social development. **Five working groups of the General Assembly** have been focusing on various aspects of this reform effort, and the expectation is that some overall blueprint for reform will emerge.

The challenges of redefinition in the area of peacekeeping are particularly great, for the concept is nowhere mentioned in the Charter and there was, till the 1990s, no written framework of definitions. The Secretary-General pointed out in a report to the Security Council in March 1994 [S/26450] that there was as yet no fully developed permanent system of U.N. peacekeeping, only an ongoing series of ad hoc operations established on a case-by-case basis. The first peacekeeping operation—the U.N. Truce Supervision Organization—resulted from ad hoc arrangements for unarmed military observers, made in May 1948 by the U.N. Mediator for Palestine, Count Folke Bernadotte. It set the pattern for "traditional" peacekeeping operations, involving the use of unarmed or lightly armed military personnel to separate combatants with their prior consent—a reversal of the concept of enforcement action contained in the Charter.

In response to the Secretary-General's report, the Security Council in May 1994 issued a statement on peacekeeping operations that for the first time in U.N. history acknowledged its important role in maintaining international peace and security. Specifically, the statement set out criteria for the *Establishment of operations, On-going review, Communication with non-members of the Council (including troop contributors), Stand-by arrangements, Civilian personnel, Training, Command and control, and Financial and administrative issues.*

The statement was seen as establishing some ground rules for peacekeeping, but Security Council practice has defied tradition as well as some commonsense rules. In each of the following cases, the Council action was unprecedented:

- In Cambodia, the entire administration of a sizable country was effectively supervised by the United Nations.
- In the aftermath of the breakup of Yugoslavia, the Council sent a peacekeeping force and then mandated it to undertake enforcement action.
- In Somalia, the Council invoked the enforcement provision of the U.N. Charter to mandate a humanitarian mission that had as one of its aims the overall political reconstitution of a member state.
- In Haiti, the U.N. mission was mandated to create secure condi-

tions in the country after a military junta had been replaced with the legally elected President.

- In the former Yugoslavia and in Rwanda, the Security Council invoked the enforcement provision of the Charter to establish International Tribunals to try those guilty of war crimes or massive violations of human rights.

The General Assembly considers peacekeeping every year in one of its main sessional committees and in a **34-member Special Committee**, which usually meets in the spring. While affirming the importance of peacekeeping activities, the General Assembly has adopted a nuanced position on the matter, putting it in the context of the pacific settlement of disputes and emphasizing the need to respect the national sovereignty and territorial integrity of states. In addition to overall policy aspects, the Assembly is in charge of appropriating funds to pay for peacekeeping. One of the problems it faces in that capacity is the **decision by the U. S. Congress** that it will cap contributions to peacekeeping budgets at 25 percent, lowering the level unilaterally from a little over 30 percent.

Intrastate Conflicts

An extremely significant factor in the evolution of U.N peacekeeping is the increase in intrastate conflicts. Of the five peacekeeping operations that existed in early 1988, four (UNTSO, UNMOGIP, UNIFIL, and UNDOF) had resulted from efforts to stop interstate wars and only one (UNFICYP) had been in response to an intrastate conflict. Of the 21 operations established since then, only 8 deal with interstate disputes (UNGOMAP, UNIIMOG, UNTAG, ONUCA, MINURSO, UNO-MUR, UNIKOM, and UNASOG). The others are intrastate, though some, like the conflicts in the former Yugoslavia, have distinct interstate dimensions.

The Security Council got past the specific Charter injunction not to intervene in the internal affairs of states using a loophole the Charter itself provides. Article 2, paragraph 7 reads: "Nothing contained in the present Charter shall authorize the United Nations to intervene in matters which are essentially within the domestic jurisdiction of any state or shall require the Members to submit such matters to settlement . . . but this principle shall not prejudice the application of enforcement measures under Chapter VII." The Security Council has invoked Chapter VII repeatedly over the past few years in order to address issues that would otherwise be judged to lie within the jurisdiction of sovereign states. The Somali civil war, the intransigence of UNITA in Angola and of the military junta in Haiti, the need to bring to justice the perpetrators of war crimes in the former Yugoslavia and Rwanda, all were seen by the Council as grounds for invoking the enforcement powers of the U.N. Charter.

The Secretary-General in his 1992 report *An Agenda for Peace* affirmed that the "foundation-stone of the work of the United Nations must remain the State," but qualified that statement significantly. The time of "absolute and exclusive sovereignty" had passed, if in fact it ever existed, he said. At the national level there was need to balance the needs of good internal governance with the requirements of an ever more interdependent world. He also put a damper on new claims of sovereignty: "When commerce, communications and environmental matters, among others, transcend the administrative borders of older, multicultural and polyglot States, it makes little sense to draw new ones based on narrower claims to ethnic, religious or linguistic identity. If every such group in the world claimed statehood, there would be no limit to fragmentation. Peace, security and economic well-being for all would become ever more difficult to achieve."

New Challenges

In dealing with conflicts that involve militias and armed civilians with little discipline and undefined command structures, the United Nations has had to deal with fluid situations in which civilians are primary targets of violence. **Some 80 percent of those killed in current wars are civilians, and about half of them are children.** Because of this, humanitarian emergencies have been commonplace, and the combatant authorities—insofar as they can be called authorities—are frequently unable to cope.

The **number of refugees** (including people displaced within countries by war and human rights abuses) has multiplied in recent years. The Office of the U.N. High Commissioner for Refugees (UNHCR) had 13 million recipients of aid at the end of 1987; in April 1996 that figure had risen to 27 million. Conceptually, the new humanitarian situations have brought forth the controversial claim that the United Nations has the right to humanitarian intervention.

As the **abuse of human rights** has been a central feature of many of the conflicts facing U.N. peacekeepers, special arrangements for investigation, confidence-building, monitoring, and verification have had to be made. In El Salvador, a Commission on the Truth helped expose abuses and recommended corrective action. In the former Yugoslavia and Rwanda, International Tribunals to prosecute those guilty of massive human rights abuses are at work.

The **organization of national elections and the recasting of state institutions** has been a feature in a number of recent operations. In Cambodia, El Salvador, and Mozambique, U.N.-supervised elections resulted in functional governments. In Angola, elections monitored but not organized by the United Nations led to renewed war, and the United Nations was central to the subsequent process of recovery and stabilization. In Western Sahara, a referendum seeking to ascertain the wishes of the majority—independence or union with Morocco—has been stalled for years for political reasons.

Recent peacekeeping operations have proven increasingly dangerous, and this is reflected in the **rising number of U.N. staff and peacekeepers killed and wounded**. In 1992 one U.N. staff member was killed on average every month; in 1993 that figure doubled. The overall death toll of U.N. peacekeepers, which stood at 772 in June 1990, had risen to 1,444 as of January 1996. After the Secretary-General underlined these issues in *An Agenda for Peace*, the Security Council dealt with the matter in a Presidential Statement on March 31, 1993. Recognizing that U.N. forces were increasingly being deployed in situations of real danger, the Council called on all states and other parties to various conflicts to take all possible steps to ensure the safety and security of U.N. forces and personnel. The General Assembly, which had been considering the matter in its Special Committee on Peacekeeping Operations, moved to formalize the legal basis for the protection of U.N. personnel. In 1994 it adopted a Convention on the matter.

In a 1993 report on the security of U.N. operations [S/26358], the Secretary-General also flagged another security problem: Some troop-contributing governments were making arrangements to support and, if necessary, extricate their troops if their position should be judged untenable. While such concerns were understandable, they tended to weaken the overall security of the operation. Any security precautions must cover *all* its personnel and not just one or two contingents, he pointed out.

Support Problems

Peacekeeping operations are only the most visible part of complex political efforts to resolve situations of conflict. Political support is also much needed; and where such support has been intact and strong, as in Namibia, Cambodia, and Mozambique, peacekeeping operations have achieved significant success. Where it has been weak, or where the political interests of powerful states have been at cross-purposes, as in the Balkans and in Angola, there have been severe difficulties.

A form of political support that has become increasingly important to the United Nations in recent years has been that of **regional organizations and arrangements**. The United Nations has benefited from institutionalized consultation with regional organizations, it has received diplomatic and operational support (from the Organization of American States in Haiti), it has "co-deployed" forces (with ECOMOG in Liberia and with the Commonwealth of Independent States in Tajikistan), and it has undertaken joint operations (with the OAS, to monitor human rights in Haiti).

U.N. peacekeeping is entirely dependent on material support from states. More than 70 states were contributing troops and equipment to U.N. peacekeeping operations in 1996 (see Table I-2), and 55 of them expressed a willingness to participate in "standby" arrangements for peacekeeping operations. Three (Denmark, Jordan, and Ghana) signed formal agreements to do so. As the demands of U.N. peacekeeping have

Table I-2
Monthly Summary of Troop Contributions to Peacekeeping Operations as of December 31, 1995

No.	Country	Strength	No.	Country	Strength
1	United States	2,851	40	New Zealand	82
2	India	2,078	41	Malaysia	81
3	Bangladesh	2,029	42	Italy	78
4	Russian Fed.	1,731	43	Kenya	75
5	Pakistan	1,468	44	Guyana	61
6	Canada	1,163	45	Trinidad & Tobago	56
7	Brazil	1,143	46	Jamaica	55
8	Nepal	1,142	47	China	45
9	Ghana	1,061	48	Hungary	44
10	Norway	1,057	49	Senegal	40
11	Finland	1,032	50	Spain	39
12	Poland	947	51	Bahamas	37
13	Uruguay	928	52	Belize	35
14	Zimbabwe	900	53	Benin	35
15	Romania	891	54	Australia	33
16	Austria	855	55	Guinea Bissau	29
17	Ireland	744	56	Switzerland	29
18	Indonesia	742	57	Bulgaria	28
19	Belgium	691	58	Togo	28
20	Ukraine	660	59	Barbados	27
21	Fiji	634	60	Germany	26
22	Slovak Republic	614	61	Algeria	23
23	Argentina	507	62	Turkey	20
24	France	475	63	Guinea	18
25	United Kingdom	475	64	Congo	15
26	Zambia	370	65	Greece	12
27	Denmark	324	66	Tunisia	9
28	Portugal	278	67	Thailand	7
29	Korea, Rep. of	255	68	Chile	6
30	Netherlands	253	69	Singapore	6
31	Sweden	236	70	Chad	5
32	Nigeria	230	71	Guatemala	5
33	Djibouti	220	72	Tanzania	5
34	Mali	192	73	Cuba	4
35	Czech Republic	188	74	Venezuela	3
36	Egypt	154	75	El Salvador	2
37	Malawi	146	76	Albania	1
38	Honduras	132			
39	Jordan	131		Total	31,031

grown in recent years, there has been "donor fatigue" among troop-contributing countries. This has constrained U.N. operations, with tragic results in the former Yugoslavia and Rwanda. In Rwanda, the lack of logistical support prevented the United Nations from fielding a force that could have played a critically important role during the genocide of 1994. In the former Yugoslavia, the problem was endemic. When, for instance, the Security Council was considering the implementation of "safe areas," and the Secretary-General asked for 34,000 troops [S/25939], the Security Council preferred to start implementation under a light option requiring 7,600 troops. Even that minimum requirement was not met for months.

The only way the United Nations can pay for peacekeeping operations is by apportioning the cost among members. Under the Charter, states are obliged to pay their share, but a large number do not. Among the major offenders have been the United States and the Russian Federation. In April 1996 the unpaid dues to U.N. peacekeeping budgets totaled $1.8 billion.

Recent experience has highlighted the **importance of information** in successful U.N. operations. It is important to know when a situation is deteriorating to a point where international intervention will be necessary. Information is also critical to the making of appropriate and effective decisions and to their implementation. The U.N.'s information-gathering mechanisms are fairly undeveloped. There are plans to link existing early-warning networks concerning environmental threats, the risk of nuclear accident, natural disasters, mass movements of populations, the threat of famine, and the spread of disease.

Information is also important in operational theaters, to explain to the public what peacekeepers are doing and why. The United Nations now normally pushes for the inclusion of radio broadcast facilities in negotiating status of forces agreements with governments, but in almost every case there has been official reluctance.

A key issue in almost all peacekeeping operations is **micro-disarmament**. There has been an enormous proliferation of automatic assault weapons, antipersonnel mines, and small arms of every description in areas of conflict, fed by an illicit arms trade that is estimated to be about a third of all arms flows. U.N. peacekeepers have been directly involved in the work of micro-disarmament most successfully in Central America, where weapons have been collected and destroyed. In Namibia and Mozambique the cantonment and demobilization of embattled forces was effectively done. In other areas, particularly Angola, Liberia, and Somalia, efforts at implementing arms embargoes and getting the rival parties to disarm have proved difficult to implement.

New Capacities

The scope, number, and complexity of post-Cold War peacekeeping operations required the United Nations to make quantum improvements in its capacity to plan, prepare, launch, and sustain them. The Department of Peacekeeping Operations (DPKO) was established in 1992, a high-tech Situation Centre was set up the next year, and the Lessons Learned Unit held its first analytical seminar in June 1995. Other important improvements are an expanded Military Advisor's Office, reformed U.N. procurement arrangements, and a new annualized budgeting procedure. But much of what had been built up during the peak years of peacekeeping activity was at risk in 1996, in the wake of the precipitous declines in budgets and operations.

Following the withdrawal of U.N. forces from Somalia and Rwanda and the reduction of the U.N. presence in the former Yugoslavia, the question of what to do with the improved peacekeeping capacities at Headquarters assumed some urgency. For budgetary reasons, there is a strong push to dismantle some of the structures of DPKO.

Under-Secretary-General Kofi Annan, who heads DPKO, favors retaining them. Speaking to the General Assembly's Special Committee on Peacekeeping Operations on April 1, 1996, Annan noted the declining trend in U.N. operations but pointed out that the unpredictability of world politics makes it hard to know what will happen in the medium term. Whatever the trend, he did not foresee any change in the types of conflicts and circumstances in which peacekeepers would be called into action: Most conflicts would continue to be within states rather than between them. The collapse of state institutions, the breakdown of law and order, and humanitarian emergencies would continue to be attendant crises. Negotiated peace settlements, when accomplished, would have to cover a wide range of military, political, humanitarian, and other civilian matters. If they were to endure, support would have to be provided through long-term programs addressing the root causes of conflict.

Annan says he was asked by a delegate what DPKO would be doing in the event there were few operations to field and watch. "I said we would do what NATO had done in all the years before it put the Implementation Force into Bosnia. We would prepare for action when it became necessary."

2. The Former Yugoslavia
By Gordon M. Goldstein

By the time the U.N. engagement in the former Yugoslavia finally ended in December 1995—after the ghastly massacre of thousands by Serbs within the U.N. "safe haven" of Srebrenica, after the lightning strikes by the Croatian army to recover the disputed Krajina region, and after fierce NATO airstrikes on Serb forces followed by the grueling American diplomacy that yielded the Dayton agreement—the mission had assumed a resonant and deeply humiliating historical symbolism. "Bosnia had become for the United Nations what the Vietnam war was to the United States," writes journalist David Rieff. The dénouement of the U.N. debacle signified the end "of an operation whose passing virtually no one in Bosnia and few even inside the U.N. itself speak of with anything except relief" [*The New Republic*, 2/12/96]. During a torturous three-and-a-half years in which the United Nations Protection Force (UNPROFOR) was alternately ignored, harassed, detained, robbed, bombed, taken hostage, and cynically deployed as human shields to ward off air attacks, the cumulative damage to the credibility of the United Nations was indeed massive, and perhaps even irreparable. The end of the UNPROFOR mission not only closed a painful chapter in the history of peacekeeping, it may well have defined through its failure the future of such U.N. operations deep into the next century.

Intensifying Slaughter, Changing Fortunes

The summer of 1995 saw stunning military developments in the battle for territory in the former Yugoslavia. Taken together, the extraordinarily brutal massacre at Srebrenica, the seizure of the Krajina, and the contest for supremacy over Sarajevo changed the course of the Balkan war.

Srebrenica

In a June 26 report circulated in New York and in Western capitals, General Rupert Smith, the top U.N. military commander in Bosnia, warned of the extreme danger faced by the inhabitants of the U.N. safe haven in Srebrenica, which was then defended by 450 lightly armed Dutch soldiers. Despite Smith's warning of an imminent Bosnian Serb attack, the lightly armed UNPROFOR contingent in Srebrenica was not reinforced. On July 11 the onslaught commenced, and confusion ensued. Fleeing civilians delivered reports of rape, murder, corpses dumped along the side of the road, bodies hanging from trees, and smoldering houses torched by Serb soldiers, in some cases while residents hid in them [*Newsweek*, 7/24/95].

According to an investigation by four *New York Times* reporters, "the killing was chillingly methodical, part mass slaughter, part blood sport." The massacre at Srebrenica was "the worst war crime in Europe since World War II: the summary killing of perhaps 6,000 people." According to the *Times* account, the top military leadership of UNPROFOR indirectly facilitated the mass killings: "**General Bernard Janvier, the United Nations Commander for Bosnia**, vetoed the air strikes that Dutch peacekeepers in Srebrenica requested to defend the town. United Nations officers said he had little enthusiasm for protecting an enclave widely viewed as an indefensible impediment to ending the war."

On July 10, 24 hours after Bosnian Serbs began to attack "with shells sometimes falling every minute," Janvier convened a meeting with his top military advisors. "It was a tense meeting, repeatedly interrupted for updates from the Dutch troops," reports the *Times* investigation. "The general asked for advice. The response was nearly unanimous: air strikes. . . . General Janvier was unpersuaded. He announced that he would sleep on it. He left his aides 'aghast,' as a United Nations official put it."

After repeated requests Janvier finally approved airstrikes at 2:40 p.m. on the afternoon of July 11. Four planes were involved, and they damaged one Serb tank. "It was far too little, too late," concluded the *Times* account. "The Bosnian Serbs brushed off the largely symbolic attack." That evening, the systematic massacre of the Bosnian Muslims of Srebrenica commenced [*New York Times*, 10/29/95].

The scope of the massacre, still not finally determined, is staggering. Some 5,200 captured Muslim men were herded with their hands bound behind their backs into a sports stadium in Bratunac. From there small groups of the prisoners were taken by truck to an adjacent field, where they were forced to lie down and then murdered with Serb machine gun fire. "Srebrenica was militarily indefensible," wrote journalist Charles Lane, "but only because the U.N. military deterrent operated under ambiguous and unwieldy rules designed less to protect Bosnians than to avoid Western casualties and obscure the accountability of Western governments." **Under the command of General Ratko Mladic,** a Serb force of 1,500 men and tanks overwhelmed the Dutch peacekeepers, who were outnumbered four to one [*The New Republic*, 8/14/95].

Compounding the atrocious nature of the crimes, Dutch peacekeepers were turned into unwitting accomplices. Serb troops seized U.N. armored personnel carriers and UNPROFOR uniforms. Dressed as Dutch troops and driving U.N. vehicles, they tricked fleeing Muslims into leaving their hiding places. According to various eye-witness accounts, the Serb troops, clad in UNPROFOR's blue helmets, abducted dozens of Muslims and slit their throats or shot them in the back or the head [*The New Yorker*, 9/4/95]. About 7,000 people believed to be in Srebrenica when it fell on July 11 were still unaccounted for two weeks later [*New York Times*, 7/25/95]. Continuing their ethnic cleansing of U.N. safe areas in late July, Bosnian Serb troops captured the town of Zepa, easily rolling over 79 Ukrainian soldiers. The Bosnian Serbs demanded that all men from the age of 16 to 55 be surrendered as prisoners of war [ibid.].

Krajina

Less than a month after the Bosnian Serbs routed Muslims in Srebrenica and Zepa, the Croatian army launched a lightning strike on Knin, the 13th-century fortress that had served as the ethnic Serb breakaway capital for four years. Knin was just one of the towns the Croatian army captured back from rebel Serbs who had been occupying the so-called Krajina region.

Prior to the Croatian offensive **Yasushi Akashi, the U.N. special envoy to the former Yugoslvia,** spent 72 hours engaging in frenetic but fruitless shuttle diplomacy between Brioni, a luxury resort island in the Adriatic, where Croatian President Franjo Tudjman was vacationing, and Knin, headquarters for the Krajina Serbs [ibid., 8/1/95]. In contrast to Akashi's efforts, the Croatian military strikes were formulated with the tacit acquiescence of the Western powers. "The United States and Germany had been sympathetic to a military action by Croatia, but they wanted it to be quick and clean," wrote reporter Raymond Bonner. "The operation has been quick, but not clean" [ibid., 8/6/95].

During three days of rapid military conquest, Croatian soldiers forced Danish peacekeepers and captured rebels to act as human shields during army advances. The United Nations reported "significant looting" in Knin by Croatian soldiers and estimated that between 60,000 and 100,000 Serbs from the Krajina fled as a result of the attack [ibid., 8/7/95]. After viewing themselves as victors against Muslims and Croats for four years, the sudden reversal of fortune was a shock for the retreating Serbs. "Many of them brought with them the bitter realization," wrote Jane Perlez, "that they were suffering the same kind of ethnic cleansing that the Serbs had carried out, with the winners of territory forcing members of opposing ethnic groups to leave the area." Compounding the losses suffered by the Krajina Serbs, the leadership of the Bosnian Serb military began to fray, as **18 generals ignored a vote of the Bosnian Serb parliament and vowed to stand by General Ratko Mladic, who had been dismissed by Dr. Radovan Karadzic, the Bosnian Serb leader**. The public split between the two men followed several weeks of losses by Bosnian Serbs to Croatian forces [ibid.].

Sarajevo

The suffering of Sarajevo, a modern and once beautiful European city, had over the years come to signify the acuteness of Bosnia's agony. Death in Sarajevo came principally in two forms. Randomly and continually, Serb soldiers picked off local residents as they sought to navigate the treacherous "sniper's alley," a boulevard through the heart of the city. That measure of death was delivered in small numbers, often with weeks separating single acts of punctuated murder. The more explosive expressions of violence took the form of artillery shells targeted on large clusters of civilians, such as the gruesome blast of February 5, 1994 that killed more than 68 people and wounded more than 200 who had gone shopping on a sunny winter afternoon at the outdoor Markale marketplace. After the marketplace attack, NATO succeeded in stopping the Serbian bombardment by threatening airstrikes on gun positions near the city. That threat deterred a similar attack for more than a year. But by the summer of 1995, the credibility of NATO's resolve had eroded.

On July 2, the target was the United Nations itself, as a mortar shell apparently fired by rebel Bosnian Serbs hit U.N. headquarters in Sarajevo, showering shrapnel on the compound and the U.S. Embassy next door. The attack culminated two days of rising violence against civilians and peacekeepers, as shells fired by Serbs killed 13 civilians and wounded 81 others [ibid., 7/2/95]. By August 1, following the Serb attacks on Srebrenica and Zepa, the NATO allies were prepared to extend the protection of Western air power to all of the safe areas in Bosnia, including Sarajevo. The allies promised that attacks on the enclaves would meet a "firm and rapid" bombing campaign [ibid., 8/2/95].

On August 22, UNPROFOR stood by helplessly as Bosnian Serb attacks killed 6 people and wounded 38 in Sarajevo, one of the so-called safe areas. Explaining that the attack on civilians came in response to a Bosnian army attack on an ammunition factory in Serb-held Vogosca, U.N. spokesman Alexander Ivanko dismissed the notion of U.N. military action to defend Sarajevo from further bombardment. "What happened today was a firefight between two armies," he said. "It makes a very shaky case for an impartial force to get involved in something like that" [ibid., 8/23/95]. That policy proved much harder to justify following the next, more devastating Serb assault on August 28, when two shells slammed into the central Sarajevo market area, killing 37 people and wounding 80 in the most devastating single attack on the Bosnian capital since the Markale massacre 18 months before [ibid., 8/29/95].

UNPROFOR's Impotence, NATO's Strength

The late summer attack on Sarajevo proved to be a turning point in the protracted Balkan crisis. After 40 months of tentative and halting engagement—and **the loss of 10,000 civilian lives in Sarajevo alone**—NATO decisively entered the conflict, unleashing five waves of airstrikes on Serb targets throughout Bosnia. The breadth and intensity of the airstrikes stood in stark contrast to the cumulative record of sporadic and ineffectual military action orchestrated under the aegis of U.N. forces and the notorious **"dual key" arrangement**, which provided the U.N. civilian leadership a veto over NATO military action.

The August 30 airstrikes involved more than 200 sorties of NATO planes, including 48 American aircraft, the largest military action undertaken by the Western alliance since it was established in 1949. The objective of the bombing campaign was not only to eliminate the Bosnian Serbs' capacity to shell Sarajevo by taking out their gun positions, ammunition dumps, command posts, and radar installations but also to force them, even against their will, to the bargaining table [ibid., 8/31/95].

The determined NATO air campaign followed a Security Council decision made earlier in the summer to supplement UNPROFOR's 22,500 peacekeepers with an additional 12,500 troops, in the form of a rapid reaction force [S/Res/998, 6/16/95]. The troop increase for UNPROFOR was supplemented by a decision for the first time to deploy German troops in a support capacity in Bosnia [*New York Times*, 6/26/95]. U.N. leaders also agreed to scrap the cumbersome dual key arrangement, which had given a de facto veto over airstrikes to Yasushi Akashi, chief of the U.N. mission to the former Yugoslavia [ibid., 7/7/95].

It took the shelling of civilians in Sarajevo—now coupled with the very real specter of a costly, militarily dangerous, and politically humiliating withdrawal of UNPROFOR—to mobilize a response from the Western powers. That response would seek to circumvent the United Nations; the robust application of NATO military power, supported by active American diplomacy, would define a new phase in the Balkan war.

American Diplomacy: The Road to Dayton

Responding to the catalyst of suddenly assertive U.S. leadership, beginning on August 30 **NATO air forces flew 750 strike missions against 56 Serb target complexes**. Meeting in Belgrade two weeks later with Serbian President Slobodan Milosevic, **U.S. special envoy Richard Holbrooke** was presented with a surprise proposal to end the siege of Sarajevo in exchange for the cessation of NATO's bombing campaign. Marking a turning point in the Balkan crisis, Serbian strongman Milosevic had delivered the Bosnian Serb leadership, which was in disarray politically and eviscerated militarily [*Time*, 9/25/95].

The path to securing Bosnian Serb acquiescence was arduous and episodic. Following the initial four-day blitz of airstrikes, NATO paused for negotiations, which were ultimately fruitless. On September 5 the allies resumed bombardment of the Bosnian Serbs, determined to persuade them to withdraw about 300 artillery pieces to a distance of 12.5 miles from Sarajevo [*New York Times*, 9/6/95]. On the eve of crucial U.S.-led talks among the three warring parties in Bosnia, NATO expanded its campaign on Serb-held positions, bombing bridges, ammunition dumps, communications centers, and air defense radars [ibid., 9/7/95].

Meeting in Geneva with Holbrooke as bombs rained down on Bosnian Serb positions, the three rivals took the first step toward peace, and the Bosnian Muslim government, for the first time since the war began in 1992, agreed to recognize an autonomous Serbian entity. In exchange, Serbia and Croatia accepted the legal existence of Bosnia and endorsed a formula that would leave the Bosnian government and its Bosnian Croat allies with 51 percent of the contested land [ibid., 9/9/95].

As the first meaningful progress evolved on the diplomatic front, the Bosnian Serbs were embroiled in a deteriorating effort to maintain their position on the battlefield. NATO expanded its bombing campaign to northwest Bosnia, using 13 cruise missiles to attack heavily fortified Serb air defense networks. For the first time in the allied air war the Serbs of Bosnia had lost important military assets [ibid., 9/11/95]. At the same time, Bosnian government and Bosnian Croat forces scored territorial gains in western Bosnia, swelling the number of Serbian refugees to an estimated 50,000 [ibid., 9/15/95].

Finally, the Bosnian Serbs around Sarajevo folded, succumbing to the collective pummeling of NATO air power, an invigorated Bosnian army, and the heavy political leverage of Serbian President Milosevic, who had been transformed by Holbrooke from a pariah and war criminal to a Balkan statesman. **On September 15 the Serbs of Bosnia took the first steps to lift the siege of Sarajevo,** beginning the removal of tanks and artillery and reopening roads and the airport. Warning of renewed air attacks if the Serbs reversed their retreat from positions around Sarajevo, President Clinton told reporters: "Let me emphasize: if the Bosnian Serbs do not comply with their commitments, the air strikes will resume" [ibid.].

On September 21, U.N. and NATO commanders announced that Serb forces had completed the pullout from positions around Sarajevo and, as a result, NATO planes would not resume bombing attacks [ibid., 9/21/95]. Five days later the Foreign Ministers of Bosnia, Croatia, and the Serb-dominated Yugoslavia endorsed a two-page statement calling for a group presidency, a parliament, and a constitutional court [ibid., 9/24/95]. As the framework agreement was initialed, military developments on the ground had created a territorial balance close to the roughly 50–50 partition of Bosnia that negotiators fruitlessly sought through diplomacy for two years [*Christian Science Monitor*, 9/22/95]. In light of the two breakthrough Bosnian accords, NATO decided that a heavily armed, U.S.-led peacekeeping force backed by tanks, artillery, and air power should replace the U.N. Blue Helmets for a year once a final peace settlement was reached [*New York Times*, 9/30/95].

The successful American strategy of brokering an end to the siege of Sarajevo and the outline of a peace settlement was a classic example of coercive diplomacy, the combined and entwined exercise of military and political power. "This is the application of force married to diplomacy that we always talked about but never did," said one White House official. "This is policy matching rhetoric." In respect to UNPROFOR, the strategy had only to ensure that no peacekeepers would be taken hostage before beginning an aerial campaign against the Serbs. In practical terms this meant that the British had to complete their pullout of troops from the eastern enclave of Gorazde, which they did on August 30, the day the airstrikes began [*Washington Post Weekly*, 9/18–24/95].

The European Union, like vulnerable UNPROFOR units, was also eased out of the picture. A month before the United States revived its own Balkan diplomacy, Washington scuttled a proposal by the EU special envoy, Carl Bildt, to lift U.N. sanctions against Serbia if President Milosevic formally recognized Bosnia. Calculating that far more could be extracted from Belgrade in return for easing punitive economic measures enacted by the Security Council three years earlier, the United States dismissed a plan that was supported by Britain, France, and Russia [*New York Times*, 8/4/95].

The United States also clashed with Russia over continuation of the airstrikes. As the bombardment of Serb forces continued, so did Russian displeasure at the spectacle of their Slavic brethren being hammered into submission. On September 12, Russian frustration spilled over at the United Nations, where Moscow tried to get the Security Council to call an immediate halt to the NATO bombing campaign. A Russian draft resolution citing "excessive use of force" won little support in the Council. China was the only permanent member to line up behind Moscow, and a total of 10 of the Council's 15 members reportedly opposed the measure.

In meetings with European leaders around the time of the failed Council resolution, Russian President Boris Yeltsin complained that NATO had been ignoring Moscow's opposition to the air offensive. Yeltsin, of course, was absolutely correct. Russia *was* being ignored—quite deliberately—and the Security Council itself had been eclipsed by the vigorous revival of U.S. leadership. While the dual key arrangement with the United Nations had been essentially dissolved, it had one important vestigial characteristic: The decision to end the bombing campaign could not be made by the United Nations alone; the airstrikes could only be halted by mutual consent of the United Nations *and* NATO. Thus the bombing campaign was controlled by NATO, and policy within that institution was largely directed by the United States [ibid., 9/13/95].

The American coercive diplomacy strategy continued into October, as the U.S. Balkan negotiator Richard Holbrooke sought to solidify a nationwide cease-fire while NATO persisted with the threat of military pressure. NATO warplanes, for example, bombed three Bosnian Serb SA-6 surface-to-air missile batteries after the sites locked their radar on the NATO planes flying overhead [ibid., 10/5/95].

After several fits and false starts, the warring parties declared a 60-day cease-fire on October 12 and agreed to travel to the United States to negotiate a final settlement of the conflict [ibid., 10/13/95]. **The negotiations would be conducted under Washington's auspices and involve the presidents of the three dominant parties:** Franjo Tudjman of Croatia, Alija Izetbegovic of Bosnia, and Slobodan Milosevic, who as leader of the rump

Yugoslavia had been a catalyst to the war but would now negotiate on behalf of the Bosnian Serbs. The political rehabilitation of Milosevic, who had so efficiently exhorted his followers to seek an ethnically pure "Greater Serbia," was viewed by the Clinton administration as a necessary compromise in the pursuit of a Balkan settlement [ibid., 10/31/95].

As the momentum of U.S. diplomacy increased, the U.N. leadership sought to capitalize on the changed conditions and extricate itself from an operation that contributed to its financial crisis and severely damaged its credibility. In a statement that coincided with the first reports of an imminent cease-fire, a spokesman for Secretary-General Boutros Boutros-Ghali confirmed that the United Nations would begin a withdrawal of nearly a third of its troops, including units from Bangladesh, Britain, Canada, the Netherlands, and Pakistan [ibid., 10/6/95]. Concurrent with the announced reduction of the U.N. role in the former Yugoslavia, the Secretary-General also recalled his top representative in Zagreb, Yasushi Akashi, and replaced him with Under-Secretary-General Kofi Annan, who had previously been responsible for all U.N. peacekeeping operations. The move was welcomed by the United States [ibid., 10/11/95].

The Dayton Diplomacy Process

For 21 grueling days in November, the enemies of the war in the former Yugoslavia fought their battles not in the contested fields and valleys of Bosnia, but across a negotiating table and in often sharply blunt exchanges with their American hosts and interlocutors. Ensconced in the sealed atmosphere of Wright-Patterson Air Force Base in Ohio, the leaders of Bosnia-Herzegovina, Croatia, and Serbia engaged in the diplomatic equivalent of shock therapy, finally yielding a peace accord that had teetered on the edge of collapse up until the final moment of agreement.

In the concluding, sleep-deprived hours of the marathon negotiations, it was the credible U.S. threat to scuttle the talks that helped spur the Balkan antagonists to a series of crucial concessions and, finally, an imperfect but desperately needed peace. On Sunday, November 20, the United States said it would shut down the talks whether or not the parties resolved their remaining differences. It was a high-stakes gamble to end the nearly four years or war and terror, and it worked [ibid., 11/21/95]. Fearful that a precious moment of opportunity to end the crisis was slipping away, the three leaders signed off on a bewildering settlement that created two distinct self-governing units—a Muslim-Croat federation and a Serb republic—overseen by a rotating collective Bosnian presidency, a federal parliament, a constitutional court, and other central institutions. The Bosnian state envisioned in the Dayton accord has two armies: that of the Serbs and that of the federation. It has three administrations: that of the Serb republic, that of the federation, and that of the central government.

The panoply of outstanding and viciously contentious **disputes over territory** were resolved through a series of complicated deals. The Bosnian-Croat federation would have control of 51 percent of the territory and the Serbs would have 49 percent. Within that mix the Bosnian Muslims won control over the capital of Sarajevo and the Serb-held suburbs of the city. The eastern Muslim enclave of Gorazde would be connected to the rest of the Bosnian government territory by a narrow corridor that Milosevic agreed to expand after downing a large glass of whiskey and observing the three-dimensional topography of the area on a virtual-reality computer map. Eastern Slavonia would be returned to Croatia by the Serbs after a transitional period, and the fate of the contested Serb-held town of Brcko would be decided by arbitration [ibid., 11/22/95].

The Dayton Accord and the United Nations

The principal consequence of the Dayton accord for the United Nations was that its role in the former Yugoslavia would be limited to civilian police assistance, humanitarian relief, and the judicial processes of the War Crimes Tribunal for the former Yugoslavia. Authority for international military forces was transferred from the French Commander of UN-PROFOR to the U.S. Commander of the Implementation Force (IFOR). The 60,000 troops that compose the IFOR were drawn from NATO and assorted non-NATO states, including many of the contingents already on the ground as part of the UNPROFOR operation. IFOR has been subject to the control and direction of the North Atlantic Council, which is composed of NATO's 16 member states.

All civilian aspects of the post-Dayton Bosnia mission have been put under the authority of Carl Bildt, the former Swedish prime minister who had represented the European Union in the Bosnian peace negotiations. Bildt was appointed the head of a Steering Board of international organizations, which pointedly did *not* include the United Nations. Responsibility for relief and refugee assistance was vested in the U.N. High Commissioner for Refugees (UNHCR), and a force of 1,700 U.N. police monitors was put under the authority of the U.N. International Police Task Force. The International Criminal Tribunal for the Former Yugoslavia is also under the aegis of the United Nations.

The formal transfer of U.N. authority began on November 30, when the Security Council moved to limit the presence of the peacekeeping force in Bosnia to two more months and to just 45 more days in Croatia. Only in Macedonia, another former republic of Yugoslavia, did the Council extend its peacekeeping mandate for six months, the duration previously applied. A U.N. contingent of 1,105 soldiers, nearly 500 of them American, is stationed in Macedonia as a preventive deployment—the first of its kind—to preclude the kind of ethnic warfare that engulfed

Bosnia and Croatia [*New York Times*, 12/1/95; see also *International Documents Review*, Vol. 46, No. 43]. The mission in Macedonia has been a quiet but substantial success both for the proposition of preventive diplomacy and for the potential role U.S. forces might play in such operations [*Christian Science Monitor*, 10/19/95]. The Macedonia mission has been overshadowed, however, by other aspects of the U.N. engagement in the former Yugoslavia and by the massive NATO mission that is the progeny of U.S. diplomacy to broker a peace accord.

The NATO Mission

For the first year of its existence the cumbersome, politically variegated state entity created at Dayton will be ensured by a heavily armed 60,000-member NATO contingent, fortified by 20,000 U.S. troops. Securing approval for U.S. participation in the mission from the Republican-controlled Senate proved to be a formidable task for the Clinton administration, but one it ultimately achieved. The President benefited enormously from the reluctant but influential support of Majority Leader Bob Dole, who helped rally passage of a Senate vote by a margin of 69 to 30 [*New York Times*, 12/14/95].

Proponents of the deployment noted the stability provided by an ample number of troops, the liberal rules of engagement, and the clearly delineated NATO command structure. Some critics of the NATO deployment focused on an element of the policy that ironically reassured others: the declared one-year limit for U.S. participation in the mission. "The very idea of creating a stable Bosnia in one year is ludicrous," asserted General William E. Odom, the former head of the National Security Agency [ibid., 12/5/95].

By most measures the NATO mission thus far has been highly successful. In early January 1996, under mounting pressure from the United States and NATO, Bosnian Serb officials released 16 Bosnians who had been detained while traveling through Serb-controlled suburbs of Sarajevo [ibid., 1/4/96]. Despite Moscow's initial wariness, Russian troops—taking orders from a Russian general at NATO headquarters—arrived in Tuzla to participate in the peacekeeping operation, the first time Russian and American soldiers have been in the same European theater of operations as allies since World War II [ibid., 1/12/96]. And despite isolated incidents of vandalism and violence, the transfer of Serb-held suburbs in Sarajevo to Bosnian control has been continuing [ibid., 2/26/96].

Although the strength and cohesion of the operation has not been seriously challenged, the future of the NATO mission in the former Yugoslavia is by no means assured. In February 1996, NATO officers raided a building near Sarajevo that had been used as a terrorist training center. Ten men were arrested, including three Iranians [ibid., 2/17/96]. When, late in the winter, adherence to the accord appeared shaky, Secretary of State Warren Christopher and a team of European diplomats reconvened a meeting of the top Balkan leaders to extract a renewed commitment to the terms of the Dayton accord [ibid., 3/18/96]. And while the United States has made clear its determination to quit the peacekeeping operation after one year, warnings have mounted that the fragile Bosnian peace could collapse without the presence of American and other NATO troops [ibid., 3/21/96].

The political pressure to extract U.S. forces from Bosnia by the end of 1996 has produced palpable anxiety within a risk-averse Clinton administration. By mid-June the White House predictably looked toward the November presidential election as the lodestar for policy decisions. When Secretary of Defense Perry acknowledged the obvious eventuality that U.S. troops may have to remain in Bosnia well into 1997, the White House spokesman—and the President himself—were quick to shrug off the Pentagon chief's incautious speculation [*New York Times*, 6/13/96]. A few weeks later, on the heels of a historic decision by the U.N. Ad Hoc Tribunal at The Hague to define rape as a war crime [ibid., 6/28/96], the United States and NATO appeared to retreat from a threat to reimpose economic sanctions on Serbia if Radovan Karadzic, the Bosnian Serb leader, did not leave power [ibid., 7/1/96].

U.N. Sanctions and the Arms Embargo: A Pattern of Evasion

The practical impact of U.N. sanctions and the arms embargo is not clear. Both measures were the subject of persistent evasion. Although sanctions certainly disrupted Belgrade's economy, the punitive economic measures intended to isolate the rump Yugoslavia were systematically circumvented by Serbs and Russians laundering hundreds of millions of dollars through the offshore banking system of the Mediterranean island of Cyprus [ibid., 9/15/95]. In respect to the arms embargo, it was an open secret that Croatia was a porous point of entry for smuggled weapons bound for the Bosnian government. In April 1996 it also became clear that the United States had given Zagreb tacit approval for arms transfers from Iran, a revelation that sparked sharp criticism from Congress [ibid., 4/14/96]. Both the sanctions regime and the arms embargo have been discontinued. With the negotiation of the Dayton accord, the Security Council voted for the phased lifting of the 1991 arms embargo [S/Res/1021, 11/22/95] and the suspension of economic sanctions [S/Res/1022, 11/22/95; see also *International Documents Review*, Vol. 6, No. 42].

Human Rights and War Crimes

The enforcement of human rights has itself been a casualty of the Balkan war. In July 1995, as he resigned in protest from his position as Special

Rapporteur on human rights in the former Yugoslavia, Tadeusz Mazo-wiecki, a former Prime Minister of Poland, made no effort to hide his disgust. "I wondered," he said, "if the train I was on was that of the United Nations or the League of Nations" [*Foreign Affairs*, 5–6/96]. Mazo-wiecki, on a visit to Tuzla, watched sadly as people turned away from him after learning that he was a U.N. human rights envoy.

At roughly the same time as Mazowiecki's resignation, the **International Criminal Tribunal for the Former Yugoslavia** indicted the Bosnian Serb leader, Radovan Karadzic, and the commander of the Bosnian Serb military, General Ratko Mladic. The charges against both men include persecuting, shelling, killing, and deporting civilians throughout Bosnia; sniper attacks against civilians in Sarajevo; and taking U.N. peace-keepers hostage and using them as human shields [*New York Times*, 7/26/95].

The Security Council, hampered throughout the Bosnian crisis by a fundamental inability to implement its resolutions, nonetheless condemned violations of international human rights and demanded Serb compliance with international humanitarian law. The resolution also asked the Secretary-General to prepare a report on human rights atrocities in the former Yugoslavia [S/Res/1019, 11/9/95]. The resulting document from Boutros-Ghali was unusually strong, asserting that Bosnian Serbs had engaged in "a consistent pattern of summary executions, rape, mass expulsion, arbitrary detentions, forced labor, and large scale disappearances" [*New York Times*, 11/30/95]. Just two weeks earlier, six Bosnian Croat leaders were charged with war crimes and crimes against humanity in connection with the deaths of scores of civilians in Muslim towns and the burning of whole villages in central Bosnia [ibid., 11/14/95]. The record of enforcement of the indictments, however, has been lackluster. As of March 1996, 53 people had been indicted: 7 Croats, 3 members of the Serbian Army, and 43 Bosnian Serbs. Yet only two—both Bosnian Serbs—have been apprehended and sent to The Hague to stand trial. The majority of other suspected war criminals are being sheltered by governments and militaries in the former Yugoslavia [ibid., 3/7/96].

The Role of the Secretary-General

The Secretary-General told the besieged citizens of Sarajevo on December 31, 1992 that they should be grateful for their plight. "You have a situation which is better than ten other places all over the world," Boutros-Ghali explained. "I can give you a list of ten places where you have more problems than in Sarajevo" [*Foreign Affairs*, 5–6/96]. Professor Fouad Ajami of Johns Hopkins observed that "the Bosnians and their cause were a great irritation to this Secretary-General." Why? "The Bosnians refused to do him the favor of a quiet surrender," noted Ajami. "Grant Boutros-Ghali the virtue of consistency: from the time he dismissed Bosnia as a 'rich people's war,' compared with the 'orphan conflicts' he cares so much about, he showed the Bosnians a steady measure of indifference. They stood in the way of his stewardship of the world body, of the new, exalted language he had begun to peddle about a world outgrowing the nation-state and the rules of the Westphalian system" [ibid.].

The Legacy of the Balkan War

As the UNPROFOR mission ended in late December 1995, "after repeated humiliation and the death of 107 of its soldiers," as one reporter noted, "the blue and white flag of the United Nations was stained with the blood of thousands of civilians it had vowed to protect." There was such a profound gap between the pretense of protection as it was ordained in New York and its operational reality in Bosnia that the former UN-PROFOR commander, General Francis Briquemont of Belgium, disclosed prior to his premature departure that he did not even bother to read Security Council resolutions anymore. The incoherent pattern of professed "impartiality" in the face of repeated violations of Council decisions gradually eroded UNPROFOR's credibility, until nothing was left but a multinational chess board upon which all U.N. players were merely pawns.

An era that began in 1990 with a luminous although atypical triumph of cooperation to reverse the Iraqi invasion of Kuwait ended amidst the mass graves of Srebrenica. Those unfortunate enough to depend upon the protection of blue-helmeted guardians as the Serbs advanced are buried in shallow graves in that infamous enclave, with slit throats or riddled with bullets. The Orwellian perversity of the U.N. "safe-haven" in Srebrenica, where outnumbered and out-gunned peacekeepers became mute witnesses to a living horror, will likely mean that the imprimatur of the United Nations will not in the future be so recklessly applied. If another Bosnia should erupt—and it is safe to assume one will—the world community will likely not hide behind the pretense of U.N. protection.

3. Haiti
By Ricardo Alday

The flawed first round of legislative elections in June 1995 and several postponements of the runoff set the scene for a difficult and tense summer in Haiti, where voting was perceived as the first real test to the country's transition to democracy and the dress rehearsal for the presidential balloting scheduled for December. Contrary to widespread feelings among U.N. and U.S. officials, who feared that violence might erupt to historical levels during campaign and election days, Haitians were generally peaceful, with U.N. and OAS troops and police looking on. The main problem turned out to be mismanagement, disorganization, and lack of electoral experience. Growing protests from the opposition, death threats, and scattered violence followed, as the date of the final round was moved from July to August to September. Major rival parties threatened to boycott the runoff ballot, claiming that the Electoral Council was botching the elections and favoring the Lavalas Movement, a three-party coalition endorsed by President Jean-Bertrand Aristide. The Electoral Council denied any wrongdoing and said the problems were caused in part by a weak organizational structure, but also by U.S. and U.N. pressure to rush the process.

At local and national levels Lavalas candidates were far more popular than were representatives from the 26 other political blocs, mainly due to the charismatic influence of their leader. But several foul-ups in the first and make-up voting stages provided some legitimate grounds for the opposition's claims, thus complicating the scenario and endangering the country's fragile political stability. After spending a great deal of political capital to return democratic rule and the hope of long-term stability to the impoverished Caribbean nation, both the United Nations and the United States had a lot at stake in completing parliamentary voting. With major problems in many of its missions around the globe—particularly in the former Yugoslavia and various places in Africa—the United Nations could not afford a failure in Haiti. As for the United States, President Clinton needed a successful parliamentary process in Haiti to justify at home the widely unpopular policy of sending thousands of U.S. troops to restore to power a left-leaning priest-turned-politician who had denounced U.S. policies until they worked in his favor.

In early August, Clinton dispatched U.S. Deputy Secretary of State Strobe Talbott to Port-au-Prince with an eight-point plan to try to revitalize the political process [*New York Times*, 8/30/95]. The strategy demanded some concessions and political reform from Aristide, who, despite the pressure, didn't deliver and preferred to put some distance between himself and Washington. Secretary-General Boutros Boutros-Ghali then made his own try, instructing his Special Representative in Haiti, Algerian diplomat Lakhdar Brahimi, to organize a dialogue with the Haitian government and opposition parties to promote broad participation in the forthcoming elections. The results, however, were the same. "Although a series of discussions took place, a solution could not be found and virtually all non-Lavalas parties decided not to participate in the second round, reruns or complementary elections," Boutros-Ghali told the Security Council [S/1995/922, par. 23].

The turnout at the September 17 runoff election was about 30 percent. Twenty-two of 27 parties boycotted the process, and the result was largely as anticipated: a sweeping victory for Lavalas candidates, who obtained a majority in both chambers of Parliament. Thus, Aristide held overwhelming political control. The results, although disturbing to some because of the problems that surrounded them, came as a fresh and deep breath to the United Nations and the U.S. government. "The mass appeal of the president and the robust presence of UNMIH [United Nations Mission in Haiti] provide a strong deterrent to undemocratic action by disgruntled elements, including former members of the Haitian Armed Forces," Boutros-Ghali told the Security Council [S/1995/922]. The security situation in the country continued to improve in general terms, but public unrest over economic issues was on the increase. Neither the return of the elected president nor the U.S. and U.N. presence was able to produce the economic miracle the Haitians had expected.

The government faced great structural problems in its attempt to address massive demands. The conflict between U.S. pressure to move quickly with a program of economic reform and, on the other side, growing discontent among political leaders (including members of the presidential cabinet) and trade unions who denounced the plan to sell state-owned enterprises to the private sector left Aristide navigating in difficult waters, though in the end he decided to go with nationalistic winds. An anti-privatization committee was established to protest negotiations by government officials with the International Monetary Fund (IMF) and the World Bank for a structural adjustment loan. Talks stalled, and so did the urgent disbursement of funds from other international sources.

On October 10, 1995, Prime Minister Smarck Michel, leading negotiator with the Bretton Woods institutions, presented his resignation, and the incipient privatization process was also interrupted [ibid.]. Aristide was identified by some of his close aides—including Michel—as one of the main obstacles to privatization, which created unnecessary friction with donor countries. Economic problems remained at the top of the nation's agenda, and although some U.N. agencies and the Inter-American Development Bank (IDB) were actively estimating infrastructure projects and private investment was growing, the needs were and still are more far-reaching.

UNMIH and the joint U.N.-OAS International Civilian Mission to Haiti (MICIVIH), charged with verifying full observance of human rights, stressed the importance of accelerating development activities, the completion of a fully operational National Civil Police, and the training of personnel in the judicial and penal systems, if Haiti was to solidify its democratic institutions. On October 15, 1995, the Secretary-General and U.S. Vice President Al Gore led celebrations in Port-au-Prince to commemorate the first anniversary of the return of President Aristide to power. Both Boutros-Ghali and Gore took advantage of the occasion to reaffirm support of the Haitian democratic process, to appeal to all political forces to participate in the upcoming presidential elections, and to prepare for the departure of UNMIH in February 1996. Three days later the new Parliament was sworn in, and on October 23 the Lavalas-controlled legislative body had no objections to Aristide's proposal to appoint then-Foreign Minister Claudette Werleigh to succeed Michel as Prime Minister.

As the presidential election grew nearer, the security situation began to worsen and to seriously threaten the whole transition process. In early November an outbreak of street violence and politically motivated assassinations caught everyone off-guard, but even more surprising was the response of Aristide who, after losing a cousin and political associate in an attack, urged his followers to "go to the neighborhoods where there are big houses and big weapons" to help the police disarm wrongdoers [*New York Times*, 11/19/95]. Before a crowd of astonished diplomats and U.N. officials, he also blasted the U.N. Mission for failing to disarm hostile paramilitary groups, which he blamed for the new wave of violence. "Dear friends of the international community, I know you need me just as I need you," he said, showing a side of himself that had not been seen since his return to power. Aware of his vast grass-roots popularity and his influence over the civilian population, he switched his appeal of tolerance, peace, and reconciliation for one of vigilantism and revenge. At least seven people were killed and dozens of homes of suspected Aristide opponents burned in the week following his unprecedented call. This response from average Haitians was a dramatic reminder from the President to everyone in Haiti of his vast powers.

Further exacerbating tensions, a day after meeting with U.S. National Security Advisor Anthony Lake, and nine days after having hand-picked René Preval as the Lavalas candidate for president, Aristide suggested on November 24 that he might not step down in February when his tenure expired [ibid., 11/25/95]. The Haitian Constitution prohibits two consecutive presidential terms, but many Lavalas members have argued that Aristide should be allowed to remain in office to make up for the three years he spent in exile after being ousted by a military coup in 1991. Sudden tensions with Washington and Aristide's inability or unwillingness (or both) to go ahead with the privatization of nine state enterprises resulted in a freezing of the disbursement of financial aid. Under enormous U.S. pressure Aristide ended his ambivalence over stepping down, but not until the White House assured him the return of more than 150,000 pages of documents seized from the military rulers by U.S. troops when they invaded the country a year before.

On December 15 the U.N. General Assembly approved a resolution that stressed the importance of the upcoming presidential elections and expressed its readiness to consider the extension of MICIVIH beyond its expiration date of February 7, 1996, when the new President was to be sworn into office [A/50/L.53]. Two days later, after a short three-week campaign with no serious debate, the elections took place as scheduled, this time with better organization and a complete supply of ballots. As expected, Lavalas' René Preval, a 53-year-old agronomist, won easily over 13 other candidates, taking 87.9 percent of the votes [S/1996/112] in a contest boycotted by the main opposition parties. Turnout was low, with less than 30 percent of the 3.7 million potential voters going to the polls. No major violence was reported. Security was guaranteed by the newly established National Civilian Police and the 6,000 UNMIH members.

The newly elected leader faced formidable tasks. The economy was still moribund, social unrest and political violence were latent, and more than $120 million of foreign aid was still frozen because of the privatization dispute. Security and the disarmament of paramilitary forces also remained a major challenge. Still, Preval had started to build bridges well before his inauguration, such that by the end of 1995 he had already met with all the major foreign players affecting his country's fate. On January 5 he asked the United Nations and the United States to support an extension of UNMIH for at least six more months, until August 1996, because the National Civilian Police was not fully prepared to maintain the secure and stable environment recognized by U.N. resolutions as a prerequisite for a fully democratic transition. The Clinton administration, which promised Congress that all 2,800 American members of UNMIH would leave Haiti shortly after Preval's inauguration, said it would back such an extension but without U.S. troops.

In the last week of January 1996 the President-elect met with representatives of international financial institutions and discussed loans and aid, as well as the link between development and security. U.N. peacekeeping forces started their gradual withdrawal. On February 7, Aristide—who had married a Haitian-American lawyer days before—handed over the presidency to Preval in the first peaceful transition of democratic power in more than 190 years of the nation's history. No foreign dignitaries attended the ceremony, with the exception of Taiwan's Vice President Li Juan-zu, whose visit—given China's position vis-à-vis Taiwan—proved to be a headache for U.N. Security Council members as well as for the Caribbean nation.

On February 10 the Clinton administration decided to continue $13 million in aid to Haiti in an effort to avoid any delay in the withdrawal of U.S. troops and the disruption of crucial development programs. This was done despite conditions imposed by Congress in response to growing political violence within Haiti, and after learning that one of the very last acts of the Aristide administration was the reestablishment of relations with Cuba. Secretary-General Boutros-Ghali officially recommended on February 14 a six-month extension of UNMIH, with a reduced force of 2,500 members, including 1,600 peacekeepers and 300 combat support troops [S/1996/112].

In his report to the Security Council, the Secretary-General said the work of UNMIH provided Haiti with an opportunity to build up the public security service and the judiciary, and to create the other conditions needed for economic and social development. "Much remains to be done before it can be said that democratic rule is secure in Haiti and its people have embarked irreversibly on the road to peace, tolerance and prosperity," he added [ibid.]. But China, infuriated by the presence of Taiwan's Vice President at Preval's inauguration, indicated that the recommendations of the Secretary-General were too extensive given the financial situation of the United Nations. Beijing, which did not contribute troops to the Haiti operation and which bore less than 1.0 percent of the cost of the mission, now threatened to veto the proposed six-month extension in a transparent effort to punish Haiti for its ties to Taiwan. In a compromise move, the operation was extended for a period of four months with a contingent of 1,200 troops and 300 international civilian police—far less than what the Council wanted. A last-minute Canadian offer to pay for an additional 700 troops closed the gap.

After the new government began to function and a continued U.N. presence was assured, all the main players inside and outside Haiti assessed their roles with expectations of a smooth transition. On March 4, 1996, the Secretary-General appointed Venezuelan diplomat Enrique Ter-Horst to succeed Lakhdar Brahimi as the head of UNMIH, after the Algerian diplomat decided to step down. A week later the General Assembly extended the presence of U.N. and OAS observers of MICIVIH until August 31 [A/50/L.67]. And on March 12 the last U.S. troops in Haiti left the country.

By the end of March, rumors of a serious split between Preval and Aristide were widespread, although both men denied them. Preval had to govern in the shadow of his predecessor, who as a common citizen took a more vocal position against privatization. Aristide's opposition threatened the ability of the new government to unfreeze economic assistance and eroded the unity of the Lavalas Movement. Some observers suggested that after being the center of attention for five years, Aristide found the second row uncomfortable.

At the beginning of May 1996, UNMIH's chief, Ter-Horst, said in New York that the security situation was slowly improving, but a further six-month mandate of the mission was indispensable to cement the democratic process and to allow the National Civilian Police to be fully prepared for its duties. He invited members of the Security Council (during China's monthly presidency of the body!) to visit Haiti so they could be convinced of the urgency of a such a mandate.

On June 28 the Security Council formally extended the mission for another six months, but to satisfy objections from China it agreed to limit the U.N. component to 600 troops, in addition to 600 civilian police

[S/Res/1063]. However, at the insistence of Canada, the agreement also calls for U.N. member states to supply an additional 700 soldiers who will not be part of the official U.N. contingent. These troops would come primarily from Canada, with some from Pakistan and Bangladesh. No U.S. troops would be involved, but the United States agreed to pay a substantial share of the costs for the troops not under U.N. command [*Washington Post*, 6/28/96].

4. Africa
By W. Ofuatey-Kodjoe

Some of the conflicts that have led the United Nations to launch peace-keeping operations in Africa are remnants of the decolonization process. The operation in Western Sahara addresses one of these. Many more of the conflicts receiving U.N. attention in Africa have surfaced relatively recently, but so tangled are their causes and effects that they challenge the U.N.'s traditional thinking about peacekeeping. Contributing to the challenge is the fact that these are primarily internal conflicts, often characterized by a particular viciousness born of near-primordial hatreds and intensified by competition for economic resources. To deal with challenges of such complexity, the U.N. Security Council has expanded the scope of its operations to include such nontraditional activities as monitoring cease-fires, assembling troops in designated areas and disarming them, mediating disputes, monitoring elections, protecting refugees, and rehabilitating the national infrastructure, both economic and physical.

These efforts have met with mixed success. In Angola the end of a 15-year civil war and a unified national army look like real possibilities; and in Mozambique, where the world organization successfully monitored the first multiparty elections, the country is now scheduled for a massive reconstruction exercise in which the United Nations plays a major role. Somalia and Liberia, on the other hand, seem to be sinking back into the morass of interethnic warfare; and in Rwanda and Burundi, although mass killing has subsided, there are ominous signs of future ethnic violence. In Western Sahara the United Nations may be on the verge of withdrawing after 15 years of civil strife and a six-year cease-fire.

In dealing with these complex emergencies, the United Nations has found it useful to act in concert with a number of other groups: regional bodies, nongovernmental organizations in the security field, and humanitarian relief agencies. The U.N.'s experience here offers lessons—not least about the variety of collaborative arrangements that can help the world community carry out the work of conflict resolution and protection of human rights.

Western Sahara

The question of Western Sahara has been before the United Nations since 1966, when the General Assembly asked Spain to acknowledge that the region was a non-self-governing territory and that the United Nations would be responsible for its administration. Madrid refused to comply, maintaining that the territory was a province of Spain. In the early 1950s there had emerged a clandestine anticolonial movement in the territory of Western Sahara among the indigenous population known as the Saharawi. An uprising against Spanish colonialism in 1957–58 was ruthlessly put down. When Spain agreed to hold a referendum on self-determination in 1975, the anticolonial elements decided to come together (in the words of the Polisario manifesto) "as the unique expression of the masses, opting for revolutionary violence and the armed struggle as the means by which the Saharawi Arab African people can recover its total liberty and foil the maneuvers of Spanish colonialism" [quoted by Tony Hodges, "The Western Sahara File," *Third World Quarterly*, vol. 6 (1), 1991, p. 84]. Thus was born the **Popular Front for the Liberation of Saguia el-Hamra and Rio de Oro (the Polisario Front).**

Enter Morocco and Mauritania, claiming the right to occupy the territory themselves. Whereupon the General Assembly asked the World Court for an Advisory Opinion on the matter [A/Res/3292, 12/13/74]. The Court failed to detect "legal ties of such a nature as might affect" the decolonization of Western Sahara or application "of the principle of self-determination through the free and genuine expression of the will of the peoples of the Territory" [ICJ, *Advisory Opinion on Western Sahara*, 10/16/75, p. 25].

In defiance of the ICJ ruling, King Hassan of Morocco announced that he would lead a "Green March" into the Sahara to recover the territory. The U.N. Security Council responded by deploring the march and calling for the withdrawal by Morocco of all participants [S/Res/380, 11/6/75]. Within the year Spain decided to exit the territory, but not before signing the so-called **Madrid Accords** that partitioned the area between Morocco (the northern two-thirds) and Mauritania (the southern third). It was at this point that, as a counter move, the Polisario established an independent state, the **Saharan Democratic Arab Republic (SDAR) with a government in exile.** Mauritania eventually withdrew from the territory, leaving the conflict to **the Saharawi**—who claimed to be a national liberation movement struggling to exercise the right of self-determination and maintain the independence of their territory—and **Morocco**—which claimed to be exercising its legitimate authority over dissident subjects [A/Res/4278, 12/4/78].

Between 1976 and 1984 the **Organization of African Unity (OAU)** made several attempts to resolve "the question of Western Sahara," but was unsuccessful in the main. The OAU [AG/Res/104 (XIX)] did develop the formula that was to serve as the basis of U.N. efforts in this arena: a cease-fire, followed by a free and fair referendum on self-determination by the people of Western Sahara, to be conducted under the auspices of the United Nations and the OAU. In 1985 the General Assembly invited the Secretary-General and the Chairman of the OAU to try convincing the two sides "to negotiate in the shortest possible time . . . the terms of a cease-fire and the modalities for organizing the said referendum" [A/Res/40/50]. A devastating war had broken out in the meantime, and there were renewed efforts in the United Nations by Secretary-General Javier Pérez de Cuéllar, who decided in 1986 to shift U.N. involvement into high gear through personal mediation efforts. He did this with the cooperation of the OAU, but the bulk of the effort came in his meetings with Morocco and the Polisario between 1986 and 1988, producing the basic **Settlement Plan**.

When the Security Council created the **United Nations Mission for the Referendum in Western Sahara (MINURSO)**, the matter was expected to be resolved within the year [S/Res/690, 4/29/91]. An informal cease-fire had already been in effect for two years, and Morocco and the guerrilla-backed Polisario Front had agreed to submit to a popular vote their dispute over control of the former Spanish colony. The **Identification Commission** and a **Referendum Commission** that were to advise the Special Representative of the Secretary-General got down to work, and the process of drawing up a timetable began. On September 6, 1991, a formal cease-fire went into effect, and a referendum was scheduled for January 1992.

Then came mutual accusations of cease-fire violations and disagreements about the encampment of troops and the return of refugees. But what actually derailed the proceedings was the question of **who was eligible to vote** in the referendum. It had been determined in the 1988 Settlement Plan, which had been accepted by both sides [A/43/680], that the voting list would be based on the Spanish census of 1974, updated by the Identification Commission. The latter was asked "to calculate the real growth of the Saharan population . . . taking into account . . . (i) births and deaths [and] (ii) movements of the Saharan population, and consult with the tribal chiefs" [S/23299, 12/19/91]. The voting list provided by the Secretary-General, based on these guidelines, was unacceptable to the two sides.

Fast forward to March 1994. Impatient with the continued failure of the parties to resolve long-standing differences on the exact criteria to be observed in determining voter eligibility—even after intensified mediation efforts by the U.N. Secretary-General—the Security Council directed [S/Res/907, 3/29/94] that actual registration for the referendum proceed according to a U.N. compromise proposal of 1993 [see *A Global Agenda: Issues/49*, p. 59]. Accordingly, it instructed the Identification Commission (appointed by the Secretary-General to verify the eligibility of individual applications for voting cards) to begin actually registering voters, with a view to holding the referendum by the end of 1994. The Security Council went on to threaten the scuttling of the entire mission if the Secretary-General could not report any progress here. The operation opened officially on August 28, 1994, the Secretary-General established a benchmark of 25,000 registrations a month, and the Security Council approved an expansion of the Identification Commission. It also extended MINURSO's mission, to May 1995 [S/Res/973, 1/13/95].

The **identification operation** did not make much headway in the early part of 1995: The Commission had too few resources to handle the volume of applications, many of the Saharan tribes failed to present their leaders to testify on the credentials of prospective voters, and there were disputes between Morocco and the Polisario about OAU participation in monitoring the referendum. A mission dispatched to the area in June 1995 concluded that the parties could have solved all technical problems (tribal testimony and the like) if only they had the political will to do so [S/1995/498, 6/21/95]. When, on June 23, 1995, the Polisario announced that it was suspending participation in the identification project, hopes for the success of the project dimmed considerably [*U.N. Chronicle*, 6/95].

The Security Council took a series of actions to push the referendum process forward. It reasserted its confidence in the identification plan and the participation of the OAU [S/Res/995, 5/27/95], called on both sides to cooperate [S/Res/1002, 6/30/95], and extended the mandate of MINURSO—initially through September 1995 [S/Res/995, 5/27/95] and then (in the expectation of a referendum in February 1996) through January 31, 1996 [S/Res/1017, 9/22/95]. History records the optimism of that view, and no progress toward a referendum was made during the spring of 1996. **By its Resolution 1056 of May 29, the Security Council suspended the identification process.** Although it extended the mandate of MINURSO until November 30, 1996, it reduced its numbers from 288 to 230. The Council also reminded the parties that unless they made significant progress, the United Nations would consider other options, including further reductions in MINURSO's strength.

Angola

During the 1960s many political groups and movements within Angola struggled for independence against Portugal—and often against each other—and by 1970 three of these liberation movements had emerged as the most powerful. The **Popular Movement for the Liberation of Angola (MPLA)**, under the leadership of Agostinho Neto, had most of its support among urban groups, intellectuals, and the Kimbundu tribe; the **National Front for the Liberation of Angola (FLNA)**, led by Holden Roberto, had its base among the Bakongo people of northern Angola;

and the **National Union for the Total Independence of Angola (UNITA)**, led by Jonas Savimbi, had its stronghold in the central and southern rural areas inhabited by the Ovbimbundu and other tribes.

In the climate of the Cold War, their rivalry invited external intervention: The United States supported the FNLA, the Soviet Union the MPLA, and China both the FNLA and UNITA. Portugal's attempt to unify the three movements and establish a single transitional government to rule the country until independence failed. When the Portuguese left the country in November 1975, civil war broke out immediately.

By 1980 the MPLA was established in Luanda as the government of Angola, backed by Soviet military and economic aid and Cuban troops. The FNLA had retreated to Zaire, and UNITA controlled much of the southern third of the country. Between 1981 and 1988, **fighting between UNITA and the MPLA** escalated dramatically, as did the encounters between the South African Defense Forces (SADF) and the MPLA (and between the SADF and the Namibian liberation force, the South West Africa People's Organization). The issue of **linking South African withdrawal from Namibia with the withdrawal of Cuban troops from Angola** was first raised by the United States in 1982, when a new U.S. administration decided take advantage of an impasse in the Namibian negotiations to reduce Soviet and Cuban influence in southern Africa. South Africa quickly took up the call for withdrawal of Cuban troops as a precondition for its own withdrawal and the implementation of Security Council Resolution 435 on the independence of South West Africa (Namibia). According to the U.N. Secretary-General, the linkage issue now became the main obstacle to the implementation of 435 [S/15943, 8/29/83] and his attempts to move the independence process forward were for naught. It was not until 1988 that war weariness on the part of all factions and an easing of Cold War tensions brought a new willingness to negotiate a regional settlement.

A series of negotiations based on **diplomatic initiatives by the United States** (largely outside the framework of the United Nations) led to the adoption of the "**Principles for a Peaceful Settlement in Southern Africa**" on December 13, 1988, which was to serve as the basis of a tripartite agreement among Angola, Cuba, and South Africa. The agreement called for the withdrawal of 50,000 Cuban troops within a 30-month period, in exchange for the withdrawal of South African support for UNITA and the implementation of Resolution 435. The Security Council gave its endorsement [S/Res/626, 12/20/88].

The **U.N. Angola Verification Mission (UNAVEM)** was created to monitor the phased withdrawal of Cuban troops [ibid.]. Pursuant to this resolution, the Secretary-General deployed a team of 70 military observers under the command of Brigadier General Pericles F. Gomes of Brazil.

UNAVEM became operational on January 3, 1989, and completed its work on July 1, 1991—36 days ahead of schedule [S/22644 Annex, 5/28/91].

Efforts by President Kenneth Kaunda of Zaire, by several African heads of state together, and by Portugal to mediate the conflict between the Angolan government and UNITA failed to produce a peace agreement in 1989. Not until September 1990, when another negotiating session was held at the urging of the two superpowers, was there any progress toward a settlement. On December 13, representatives of the MPLA, UNITA, and Portugal, under the leadership of the United States and Russia, hammered out a peace plan. The plan, which called for a cease-fire but set no date, was repudiated by the MPLA before it could take effect.

As a result of **vigorous efforts by Portugal and the two superpowers**, UNITA and the MPLA did work out the terms of a cease-fire (**the Escoril Accords**, May 1, 1991), and on May 31, 1991, President José Eduardo dos Santos and Jonas Savimbi signed the **Bicesse Accords**, ending the civil war. These called for a multiparty system, demobilization of the rival armies and formation of a new national army (Forces Armades de Angola, or FAA), termination of outside military assistance, and U.N.-monitored free and fair elections, to be held in September 1992. On the eve of the signing, May 30, the U.N. Security Council voted to enlarge and prolong the mandate of UNAVEM, renamed **UNAVEM II**, to help verify compliance with the terms of the cease-fire and the monitoring of elections [S/Res/696, 5/30/91]. UNAVEM II was made up of some 700 military and civilian personnel (among them, 350 military and 126 police), to be withdrawn from Angola at the end of November 1992. The cost of the 18-month mission was an estimated $132.3 million [U.N. press release SC/5279, 5/30/91; and *Africa Recovery*, 6/93].

More than 90 percent of the registered voters participated in the **elections of September 29–30, 1992,** under the gaze of 800 or so international observers, including 400 U.N. observers. Despite assurances from U.N. Special Representative Margaret Anstee and others that the elections were free and fair, **Savimbi refused to accept an unfavorable outcome**. Throughout October, UNITA withdrew its forces from the FAA. It also launched attacks against government forces and several major cities, breaking the cease-fire. Due to postelection violence, UNAVEM II was reduced to 500 military, 18 police, 11 paramedics, and 50 international civilian staff. (It was not returned to full strength until October 1994.)

Although efforts by Anstee to broker a new cease-fire produced no lasting agreement, the U.N. Security Council voted to extend the mandate of UNAVEM II past the November 30 deadline. As the violence spilled into 1993, however, U.N. Secretary-General Boutros Boutros-Ghali recommended that the U.N. force in Angola be reduced to about 80 observers and that all be withdrawn on April 30, 1993, if the fighting had not stopped [S/25140, 1/21/93].

U.N.-sponsored negotiations—in Addis Ababa (January 27–30, 1993) and Abidjan (April 12–May 21)—failed to produce a new cease-fire, although at Abidjan the government did agree to a set of terms for one. On June 1, 1993, the Security Council unanimously condemned UNITA for rejecting the election results, resuming warfare, endangering the peace process, and rejecting the cease-fire terms accepted by the government at Abidjan the previous month [S/Res/834]. On September 15, the Security Council took concrete action, voting to place an embargo on military and petroleum products to areas held by UNITA and threatening other sanctions unless UNITA agreed to an effective cease-fire, to the implemention of the peace agreement, and to comply with all Security Council resolutions [S/Res/864]. On October 25, with the newly appointed U.N. Special Representative to Angola, Alioune Blondin Beye, as chair, new U.N.-sponsored peace talks between UNITA and the government got under way in Lusaka, the Zambian capital. As these talks went on, the Security Council postponed additional economic sanctions against UNITA [S/Res/890, 12/15/93] and, in support of the progress made on the peace process, agreed to several extensions of UNAVEM II [S/Res/903, 3/16/94; S/Res/922, 5/31/94; S/Res/932, 6/30/94; S/Res/945, 9/29/94; and S/Res/952, 10/27/94]. The issues of UNITA troop withdrawal from occupied territory and power-sharing in a new government and legislature had stymied the U.N.-brokered talks for many months, but on October 31, 1994, the parties initialed the **Lusaka Protocol** [S/1994/1241, 11/3/94], **a follow-up to the Bicesse Accords** that had paved the way for U.N.-monitored elections back in 1992—and renewed civil war. The formal signing was set for November 15.

Despite an intensification of the fighting, the Protocol was signed on November 20, 1994, and a cease-fire went into effect on November 22. The Security Council stamped the occasion with a brief statement and the next month extended an enlarged UNAVEM mission through February 8, 1995 [S/Res/966, 12/8/94]. On that date the Security Council, at the advice of the Secretary-General, unanimously authorized the formation of **UNAVEM III** [S/Res/976, 2/8/95]. The 7,000 troops and military observers had a wide array of duties: supervise the separation of government and UNITA forces, monitor the cease-fire, and oversee the demobilization of rebel troops and their integration into the national army; provide assistance for the encampment of troops and for the clearance of some 10 million landmines; supervise the integration of 5,500 UNITA personnel into the Angolan National Police; chair the Joint Commission on the integration of UNITA into the national administration; and provide for the delivery of humanitarian assistance to an estimated 3.5 million Angolans—about 35 percent of the population [ibid.].

On March 28, 1995, Blondin Beye reported that the first stage of troop disengagement had been completed. On May 6, Savimbi formally recognized Dos Santos as President of Angola (in August Savimbi would accept the post of Vice President); and on May 31 the first contingent of UNAVEM III arrived in the country. Encouraged by these developments, the Security Council agreed to extend the mission to February 8, 1996 [S/Res/1008, 8/7/95]. The peace process was briefly delayed when UNITA decided to suspend its encampment of troops, alleging government breaches of the cease-fire, among them the use of mercenaries from South Africa [*Keesings World Report*, 11/20/95, p. 40,888].

Resolving the dispute with the government in January 1996, UNITA promised to encamp 16,500 of its 62,500 troops by the February 8 termination of UNAVEM III. The Secretary-General suggested a six-month extension of UNAVEM to speed the completion of the entire process; the Security Council agreed to three months [S/Res/1045, 2/8/96]. The UNITA encampment process proceeded steadily after that, and by February 28, 1996, 16,000 UNITA troops had been encamped [*Keesings World Report*, 2/28/96, p. 40,939]. In the spring of 1996, UNAVEM III was extended for two additional months [S/Res/1055, 5/8/96], expiring July 8.

Somalia

Somalia's ongoing civil war has roots in a complex and rigid clan system. Years ago the six major clans (Darod, Digil, Dir, Hawiye, Isaaq, and Rahanwein) and an abundance of subclans clashed over territorial and water rights; more recent clashes have grown out of competition for state-controlled resources and political power. In fact, the chain of events leading to all-out civil war began with the development of clan-related opposition to the regime of General Mohammed Siad Barre in 1988. Although the regime crushed this rebellion led by the Somali National Movement (with its strong base in the Isaaq clan), it was at this point that other clan-based armed groups and political factions began to emerge.

When Barre fled to exile, **Ali Mahdi Mohammed of the United Somali Congress** (USC, based in the Hawiye clan) claimed leadership of Somalia's provisional government. He was challenged by other groups, which led to large-scale violence in Mogadishu and other parts of the country and, by the end of 1991, to full-blown civil war. The main contenders were two subfactions of the USC: Ali Mahdi's own and the one led by **General Mohammed Farah Aidid**. By then, 300,000 Somalis had been killed and over a million of the 7 million inhabitants had fled the country. Twelve months of fighting had also resulted in widespread hunger and the breakdown of central administrative authority—in fact **the complete absence of a national government.**

The U.N. Security Council first took up the matter of Somalia in January 1992, adopting a resolution that called on the Secretary-General to increase humanitarian assistance to Somalia and work with the Organization of African Unity and the Arab League to achieve a cease-fire

[S/Res/733, 1/23/92]. The lateness of the international response to the civil war and the devastation wrought by the fighting itself hampered the ensuing efforts to restore stability and delivery emergency aid to a country that was already among the world's poorest and least-developed.

The **earliest mediation efforts** involved a visit to Somalia by U.N. Under-Secretary-General James Jonah and talks with representatives of several Somali factions at U.N. Headquarters. Aidid and Ali Mahdi did sign a cease-fire agreement, and on March 17, 1992, the Security Council adopted a resolution calling upon the various Somali factions to abide by it [S/Res/746]. The Secretary-General's reports at the time characterized the situation in Somalia as **"extraordinarily complex"** and **resisting "conventional solutions,"** and he requested strong action. The Security Council, in response, created the **U.N. Operation in Somalia (UNOSOM)**, involving a 50-member cease-fire monitoring group and **a 550-strong security force "in principle"** [S/Res/751, 4/24/92], which would have the job of protecting U.N. relief workers, equipment, and supplies within Mogadishu and escorting relief convoys through the city and its immediate environs. Meanwhile, the OAU, the Arab League, and other international organizations, such as the Islamic Conference, made their own further attempts to mediate the conflict.

On June 23, 1992, the Secretary-General announced that the principal warring factions had agreed to the initial deployment of what would become by year's end **the largest and most complex U.N. peacekeeping operation to that date**. The 50 cease-fire monitors, however, were not fully deployed until July 23, three months after the establishment of UNOSOM, and the Secretary-General was unable to announce agreement on the deployment of the 500 "security personnel" approved "in principle" until some months later.

Continued fighting in Mogadishu and elsewhere, increasingly desperate humanitarian conditions, and further prodding by the Secretary-General persuaded the Security Council to authorize an urgent airlift of relief supplies in July [S/Res/767, 7/27/92] and increase the size of UNOSOM to 3,500 in August [S/Res/775, 8/28/92]. It also **expanded the mandate of UNOSOM to enable it to protect humanitarian convoys and distribution centers throughout the country**. Despite these plans on paper, it was not until September 14 that 500 Pakistani troops arrived in Mogadishu—the first UNOSOM contingent. Not surprisingly, this force was inadequate to contain the fighting, however sporadic, and bands of protection-racket "technicals" continued to make the delivery of food and other relief items difficult if not impossible.

In October 1992 the United Nations launched its **"100-Day Action Programme for Accelerated Humanitarian Assistance for Somalia."** According to this initiative, the World Food Programme (WFP) and the International Committee of the Red Cross (ICRC) were to provide

50,000 tons of food a month to the central and southern regions; UNICEF was to step up its feeding programs for children; and other U.N. agencies and some nongovernmental organizations were to join these efforts. Philip Johnston of CARE-USA was appointed Operational Manager of the program, which was to be supervised by Jan Eliasson, Under-Secretary-General for Humanitarian Affairs.

In fact, however, the entire security situation in Somalia deteriorated badly during October and November as the civil war intensified, and many relief personnel were forced to evacuate. In the latter month, the death rate due to disease and starvation increased from about 60 a day to 300, and on December 3 the Security Council authorized the Secretary-General to use "**all necessary means** to establish as soon as possible a secure environment for humanitarian relief operations in Somalia" [S/Res/794], **citing Chapter VII of the U.N. Charter, "Action with respect to threats to the peace."**

This action paved the way for the creation of a **Unified Task Force (UNITAF), led by the United States**, to protect the delivery of food and other emergency supplies. The first contingents of UNITAF arrived in Somalia on December 9, 1992, and secured the port and airport of Mogadishu.

During the opening months of the new year, U.N. officials found reason for cautious optimism. Fourteen Somali political groups attending a U.N.-sponsored meeting in **Addis Ababa**, January 4–15, agreed to a cease-fire, disarmament of their troops, and a reconciliation conference. Gathering again in the same city on March 15 and 27, the 14 agreed to form a transitional government (although one faction, the United Somali Congress [USC], headed by Mohammed Farah Aidid, did not sign the agreement, raising doubt about its value). U.S. officials were heartened too, the relative success of Operation Restore Hope having lent credence to the idea that the "[United States] could go into Somalia quickly, get out quickly and turn it over to the U.N." [Newsweek, 6/21/93].

On March 4, 1993, the U.N. Security Council approved the Secretary-General's plan for **creation of a second U.N. operation in Somalia (UNOSOM II) to take over from UNITAF** [S/25354, 3/3/93]. This plan detailed the deployment of an extensive and expensive peace-enforcement operation, the first of its kind under U.N. command, with a broad mandate and unprecedented U.S. participation. Authorized under Chapter VII and not subject to the approval of any Somali faction, UNOSOM II would combine the humanitarian mandate of UNITAF with more general security functions. In addition to protecting U.N. and NGO personnel, facilities, and equipment, UNOSOM II was to monitor compliance with the cease-fires called for under the January Addis Ababa agreements; respond with force if necessary to violations or threatened violations; seize small arms of irregular forces; and assist in repatriation activities and the removal of landmines (estimated at anywhere from 100,000 to several million). The 20,000-member military component of the operation would oversee the implementation of the disarmament provisions of those Addis Ababa Agreements by securing the heavy weapons surrendered by organized militias and establishing "transition sites" for the fighters and separate "cantonment sites" for their arms. UNOSOM II would also be assisting "the people of Somalia to promote and advance political reconciliation, through broad participation by all sectors of Somali society, and the re-establishment of national and regional institutions and civil administration." The actual deployment of UNOSOM was approved three weeks later [S/Res/814, 3/26/93], and the transfer of administrative and budgetary control from UNITAF to UNISOM II took place on May 1. The transfer of the military command was completed on May 4.

The operations of the United Nations moved into a new phase on June 6, when the Security Council, meeting in emergency session, called for "the arrest and detention for prosecution, trial and punishment" of those responsible for **the killing of 23 Pakistani troops** on the previous day. On June 17 the Secretary-General's Special Representative, Admiral Jonathan Howe, issued an **arrest warrant against General Aidid** [S/26022, 7/1/93]. Over the next five months the attempt to capture Aidid dominated the UNOSOM II agenda.

The U.N. Secretary-General emphasized in his August 17 report to the Security Council that "the overall situation in Somalia [had] undergone a major transformation" and had "stabilized," at least in the southern part of the country. Under the Addis Ababa Agreements, which provided for a cease-fire, disarmament, and political reconciliation, Somalia's clan leaders—excluding Aidid—had made meaningful progress in reestablishing governmental institutions for the proposed two-year transition period, including the formation of a quarter of the projected 92 district councils. Relief and rehabilitation programs were also beginning to show results in terms of the eradication of mass starvation, the reopening of schools, and a steady increase in such economic activities as livestock export and commercial shipping [S/26317, 8/17/93]. In August 1993, as the Secretary-General prepared his report, deployment of UNOSOM II in the central and northern regions of Somalia was still pending, due to logistical and financial difficulties associated with fielding so large a force, and Aidid's stronghold of South Mogadishu remained "tense" [ibid.]. By September, UNOSOM had 26,000 of the 28,000 troops it had been authorized and a civilian staff of 2,800, who had begun to establish the humanitarian, political, and security operations called for at Addis Ababa.

The Secretary-General went on to stress the importance of **restoring peaceful conditions through nonmilitary means**. In September the Security Council approved his proposals for reestablishing Somali police, judicial, and penal systems under U.N. supervision [S/Res/865 Part B, 9/22/93].

This same resolution set March 1995 as the completion date for UNOSOM II, at which time responsibility for the reconciliation and re-habilitation process would be passed on to a duly elected Somali govern-ment. (According to the Secretary-General's plan, interim courts and a partial prison system would begin functioning by October 31, 1993; and some 10,000 police would be trained and deployed by the end of 1994 [S/26317, Annex I, 8/17/93].)

It was on October 3, 1993, that the United States mounted the major raid to capture Aidid's commanders that resulted in the **death of 18 and the wounding of 75 U.S. troops** and led Washington to **redefine the U.S. role in Somalia**. Some two weeks later General Thomas Montgomery, the highest-ranking U.S. officer with the American troops, stated that "the primary mission of U.S. forces in Somalia would be to defend U.N. troops and their military compounds, as well as protect food deliveries if fighting erupted again in the city" [*Facts on File*, 787E1, 1993]. In mid-November the Se-curity Council called off the attempt to apprehend Aidid [S/Res/885, 11/16/93]. In December, President Clinton announced the complete **withdrawal of U.S. forces by March 31, 1994.**

With Aidid off the "most wanted" list, he declared a unilateral cease-fire on October 9, 1993 [*Facts on File*, 72E1, 1994]. Encouraged by this turn of events, the Security Council adopted Resolution 878 [10/29/93] extending the mandate of UNOSOM II until November 18, 1993 (later extended to May 31, 1994 [S/Res/886, 11/18/93]). The Security Council in February 1994 unanimously adopted a resolution calling for a scaling-down of UNOSOM to 22,000, enforcement of the Addis Ababa cease-fire, and mediation of the conflict by the Secretary-General [S/Res/897, 2/4/94]. The new Special Representative of the Secretary-General, Ambassador Lan-sana Kouyate, brokered a **national reconcilation agreement** between Aidid and Ali Mahdi just two days before the last U.S. forces departed the country. This March 24 agreement called for a meeting to discuss a Legislative Assembly and for convening a National Reconciliation Con-ference on May 15, 1994.

Disputes among the various factions postponed the initial meeting three times, fighting broke out among rival militias, and on April 25 a splinter group announced the formation of the "independent state of So-maliland," postponing the preparatory meeting for a national reconcilia-tion conference for a fourth time.

The Security Council, at this point, was mainly engaged in winding down the U.N. operation, which was scheduled to terminate in March 1995, and it voted four extensions of the UNOSOM mandate to bring it to that date [S/Res/923, 5/31/94; S/Res/946, 9/30/94; S/Res/953, 10/31/94; and S/Res/954, 11/4/94].

As the **withdrawal of UNOSOM contingents** began in early 1995, Somali clans were fighting fiercely for control of the Mogadishu airport, and a multinational force called "Operation United Shield" sailed near the coast to protect the withdrawal and lend symbolic strength. By the time the withdrawal was completed, chaos reigned. Since March 1995, Somalia seems to have sunk back into unrelenting clan-related violence. When Aidid declared himself President in mid-June 1995, he sought to consolidate his hold on the country by launching attacks on regional capitals. As of spring of 1996, heavy fighting continued in Mogadishu [*New York Times*, 4/6/96].

Liberia

For quite a while the Security Council seemed intent on staying out of the civil war in Liberia, which began in December 1989 when **guerrilla forces under Charles Taylor** invaded the country from the Côte d'Ivoire and toppled the regime of Sergeant Samuel Doe. Doe, who had sought to transform his government from a military dictatorship into an "elected" presidential dictatorship, used all sorts of measures to eliminate the opposition and consolidate his power. Those who opposed him—in fact, the pressure for a return to civilian rule began barely a year after the coup that brought him to power in 1980—represented a variety of groups in society, but the issues, and the fighting, have assumed an ethnic and tribal character [D. Elwood Dunn and S. Byron Tarr, *Liberia: A National Polity in Transition*, Metuchen, N.J.: Scarecrow Press, 1988, p. 124].

A first attempt by then-Secretary-General Javier Pérez de Cuéllar to bring the Liberian conflict to the attention of the Security Council, on May 28, 1990, met with no success; and a **peace plan for Liberia** submitted to the Security Council on August 8, 1990, by the **Economic Community of West African States (ECOWAS**, a subregional organization) failed to generate even a resolution acknowledging its efforts. The components of the ECOWAS plan were an immediate cease-fire, the establishment of a peacekeeping force and an interim government, and preparations for free and fair elections within 12 months under international supervision. A **seven-nation Military Observer Group (ECOMOG)** was set up during that summer of 1990 to assist the **ECOWAS Standing Mediation Committee (SMC**, established the previous spring) in supervising the cease-fire, and ECOMOG did manage to establish a 20-kilometer "security perimeter" around Monrovia, the capital, and to install an **interim government**, although Taylor had declared himself President of Liberia and his National Patriotic Front of Liberia (NPFL) controlled more than 90 percent of the country by then. The Security Council simply requested that the Secretary-General send a Special Representative to observe the situation and sit in on negotiations conducted by the SMC (composed of Nigeria, Gambia, Ghana, Mali, and Togo) [*West Africa*, 3/16–22/92, p. 449].

By mid-1991 there were five contenders for power in Liberia: Charles Taylor and his NPFL; the Interim Government of National Unity (IGNU) created by ECOWAS and its President Amos Sawyer; some remnants of Doe's Armed Forces of Liberia (AAFL), with Brigadier General David Nimley as Acting President; Prince Johnson, who had broken with Taylor and in February 1990 established the Independent National Patriotic Front of Liberia (INPFL); and the United Liberation Movement for Democracy in Liberia (ULIMO), founded in Conakry, Guinea's capital, in May 1991 and generally believed to be "a mixed bag of people, most of whom were members of the Krahn tribe and former officials of the Doe government" [ibid., 6/24/90, p. 1035].

From November 1990 through October 1991, ECOWAS engaged in a number of diplomatic efforts, the last of a long line of which did bring a compromise of sorts (the **Yamoussoukro IV Accord**)—on a separation of forces and preparations for national elections [ibid., 11/11–17/91, p. 1991]. As armed clashes between ULIMO, NPFL, and ECOMOG forces became more frequent, however, attempts at implementation were derailed.

On October 15, 1992, while fighting ULIMO elements, NPFL forces opened fire on ECOMOG forces, violating the cease-fire and triggering full-scale warfare with ECOMOG and ULIMO. (Taylor's siege of Monrovia, eventually broken by ECOMOG, would last until February.) A month after this widening of hostilities the Security Council imposed an **arms embargo** on Liberia [S/Res/788, 11/19/92] and affirmed its "belief that the Yamoussoukro IV Accord . . . offer[ed] the best possible framework for a peaceful resolution" of the conflict [ibid.]. The embargo and significant military gains by ECOWAS and ULIMO led Taylor to sue for peace; and joint U.N./OAU/ECOWAS diplomatic efforts brought an agreement between IGNU, ULIMO, and NPFL, which was signed in Geneva on July 17, 1993, and ratified at Cotonou, Benin, on July 25. The war had already claimed the lives of 150,000 Liberians and created 750,000 refugees—a third of the population and the **largest per capita refugee flow in the world** [*Washington Post*, 11/3/93].

The **Cotonou Agreement** had a military component and a political one. It called for an immediate cease-fire—effective August 1, 1993—to be followed by the disarmament, encampment, and demobilization of the warring factions. These actions were to be monitored by a **Joint Cease-fire Monitoring Committee** composed of equal numbers of representatives of the three factions, ECOMOG, and an advance team of U.N. observers. This Committee was eventually to be replaced by a monitoring group consisting of an expanded ECOMOG (with additional troops from outside West Africa) and a U.N. observer mission.

According to the Agreement too, each of the parties would remain in control of territories it held at the time of the signing but had to remove all road blocks and release all prisoners and detainees to the United Nations or the International Red Cross. The U.N. embargo on NPFL-held areas would remain in effect, to be lifted upon ECOWAS certification that the terms of the cease-fire were being met.

The political aspect of Cotonou called for the formation of a transitional government of six months' duration, to be followed by free and fair elections. The executive branch of the transitional government would consist of a five-member Council of State (three from the warring factions and two chosen from a group of nine eminent citizens nominated by the three factions). The legislature would be composed of 13 people each from IGNU and NPFL and 9 from ULIMO. The judiciary would remain as presently constituted, but with the addition of a ULIMO nominee to fill a vacancy on the supreme court. (Still to be decided was the distribution of 17 cabinet posts.) None of the heads of the three factions would be eligible to participate in the transitional government, which would sit down with the electoral commission to work out the modalities of general elections. Members of the transitional government could not run for office in these elections, to be held within seven months.

ECOWAS and the OAU were to ensure that the agreement was fully implemented, while the United Nations was to monitor the implementation process to verify its impartiality. The seven-month **U.N. Observer Mission in Liberia (UNOMIL)** approved by the Security Council had the mandate to investigate and report to the Violations Committee alleged violations of the cease-fire; monitor compliance with the arms embargo, border closings, and provisions for disarmament and demobilization of combatants; observe and verify the election process; aid in the coordination of humanitarian assistance in the field; report major violations of international humanitarian law; train ECOMOG engineers in mine clearance; and coordinate ECOMOG's nonenforcement activities [S/Res/866, 9/22/93].

Lack of agreement on the distribution of cabinet posts had delayed the scheduled start of the disarmament process, and this led in turn to a delay in the swearing in of the transitional Council [*Keesings World Report*, 11/93, p. 39,719]. In the meantime, there were violations of the cease-fire by all sides.

The pace of progress on military and political fronts picked up after a meeting of the three parties on February 15, 1994, in Virginia on the outskirts of Monrovia. With the assistance of the Secretary-General's Special Representative for Liberia, Trevor Gordon-Somers, the interim government and the rebel factions agreed to supply ECOMOG and UNOMIL with data they had requested to facilitate disarmament—numbers and locations of troops, weapons, and the like. The United Nations and ECOWAS announced plans to complete the deployment of their respective forces and commence disarmament by March 7, and the parties agreed to swear in the transitional Council of State on that date.

This so-called "**Triple Seven Agreement**" set elections for September 7, 1994 [S/1994/187, 2/17/94].

On March 7 as scheduled, and with considerable fanfare, the **Liberian National Transitional Government (LNTG)** was sworn in and the disarmament and demobilization of combatants began. But the information about troop strengths and locations was not immediately forthcoming and the exercise proceeded very slowly. By mid-April only about 2,500 of an estimated 40,000 troops had been demobilized, and there was heavy fighting in western Liberia between two ULIMO factions and, in the southeast, between NPFL and the breakaway Liberian Peace Council (a group with links to ULIMO). These skirmishes not only slowed the disarmament process but **increased the number of internally displaced Liberians, which now stood at 800,000** [*Issues/50*, p. 50]. The renewed fighting also had the effect of putting UNOMIL observers at personal risk, with the result that they were deployed only in the relatively peaceful 15 percent of the territory—the portion under IGNU control [S/1994/588, 5/18/94].

Disturbed by the "limited progress" in implementing the Cotonou Agreement, the Security Council called on the LNTG, ECOWAS, and the OAU to convene a meeting with the factions by July 31, 1994, to discuss the issue of disarmament. The U.N. Secretary-General was instructed to report back on September 2 [S/PRST/1994/33, //13/94].

In his report to the Security Council, the Secretary-General noted that by late August, UNOMIL had withdrawn its forces completely from the western region and from two of nine monitoring sites in the north, the scene of yet more fighting by another new faction. Meanwhile, the situation had deteriorated drastically—mostly due to unorganized violence and increases in banditry and in the harassment of civilians. On October 21 the Security Council denounced the **kidnapping of 43 UNOMIL observers** [S/Res/950, 10/21/94].

On September 7, 1994, the **Chairman of ECOWAS, President J. J. Rawlings of Ghana,** convened a meeting of the Liberian faction leaders. The **Akosombo Agreement** of September 12 reaffirmed the Cotonou Agreement and called for a nationwide cease-fire, followed by encampment, disarmament, and demobilization. Three months later the Liberian factions met again in Accra, where, on December 21, 1994, they signed the "**Accra Agreement.**" This one called for a nationwide cease-fire by December 28, 1994, a new Council of State, elections on November 14, 1995, and the formation of a new government on January 1, 1996. The Secretary-General's next report to the Security Council was guardedly optimistic. The cease-fire seemed to be holding, and the Security Council extended the mandate of UNOMIL for another three months [S/Res/972, 1/13/95].

As usual, this optimism was short-lived. By March 20 the cease-fire had broken down completely (although the Security Council continued to vote extensions of the UNOMIL mandate [S/Res/985, 4/13/95, and S/Res/1001, 6/30/95]). **Adding teeth to the embargo** in April, the Council established a committee of the whole to monitor compliance and recommend "appropriate measures" against violators. A continued U.N. presence in Liberia, it warned, was dependent on the reestablishment of an effective cease-fire and the receipt of sufficient contributions to ECOMOG by troop contributors [S/Res/985, 4/13/95]. Desperate, ECOWAS Chair Rawlings convened a meeting of Liberia's factions at Abuja, Nigeria, where, on August 16, 1995, agreement was reached on a comprehensive cease-fire and on holding general elections on August 20, 1996. The Security Council welcomed the signing of the "**Abuja Agreement**" and extended the mandate of UNOMIL to January 31, 1996 [S/Res/1014, 9/15/95].

Fighting broke out again between ULIMO factions near Tubmansburg at the beginning of 1996 and had spread to Robertsport by mid-January. The agreement was unraveling quickly; and although Taylor and Kromah (head of one of the wings of ULIMO) had declared themselves a "**collective presidency**," the heavy fighting in Monrovia continued unabated, attended by the usual looting and seizure of hostages. By April 1996 the fighting had spread throughout the country and ECOMOG seemed powerless to do anything about it. On April 14 the United States evacuated 500 U.S. and 1,100 other nationals from Monrovia [*Facts on File*, 4/20/96, p. 289]. On May 31, 1996, the Security Council extended the mandate of UNOMIL until August 1996 at reduced strength, and requested the Secretary-General to keep it informed of the situation in Liberia [S/Res/1059].

Rwanda and Burundi

U.N. involvement in the crises in Rwanda and Burundi dates back to 1993, when officials in both countries requested assistance from the Security Council to defend the government against armed insurrection. The violence that has beset these sister countries has its roots in their ethnic composition and colonial history. In each, **animosity between the two main ethnic groups, the Tutsis and the Hutus,** dates to pre-colonial times when the former ruled over the more numerous Hutus (85 percent), enforcing a rigid caste system (*ubuhake*). This bitterness was reinforced by the Belgian colonials' support of Tutsi privilege through a combination of land awards, Western education, and judicial appointments.

By the early 1950s the Hutus were not only engaged in anticolonial agitation but had begun to direct their animus at the two Tutsi monarchies of Ruanda and Urundi, through which the Belgian government administered the trust territories that had been in its care since World War I. There were sporadic acts of violence by the newly formed Parti de l'Emancipation du Peuple **(Parmehutu)** in Ruanda and Parti de Liberation du Peuple Hutu **(Palipehutu)** in Urundi, and in 1959 came a Hutu uprising that led to large-scale civil war in the two kingdoms. The Parmehutu won U.N.-supervised elections in 1961 and declared the independence of Rwanda, with Jouvénal Kayibanda as the first President. The Tutsi aristocracy of Urundi, however, retained power during the transition from colonial rule to an independent Kingdom of Burundi under the Tutsi-dominated Union pour le Progrès National (Uprona), with Pierre Buyoya as President. **By 1962, Rwanda had emerged as a country dominated by a Hutu elite and Burundi as one dominated by a Tutsi minority**, both governments taking the form of military dictatorships. In Rwanda, attempts to break the Tutsi economic stranglehold led to renewed civil war in 1963, in which approximately 20,000 were killed and 160,000 (mainly Tutsis) fled into Burundi and Uganda. The violence was less widespread under Tutsi rule in Burundi.

Thirty years later, both governments continued to struggle to maintain their authority over opposition from ethnic rivals. In Rwanda, Juvénal Habyarimana, President since 1988, had managed to set up a government of national unity, but the promised political reform was delayed by the 1990 invasion of the Uganda-based **Tutsi-dominated Rwandan Patriotic Front (RPF)**, which sought to overthrow the regime and repatriate the Tutsis who had fled to Uganda. In May 1992, Habyarimana negotiated a cease-fire with the RPF in Arusha, Tanzania, and tried to work out a power-sharing scheme, including the integration of RPF elements into the national army. The cease-fire broke down two months later and the fighting intensified. In February 1993, Rwanda and Uganda sent letters to the United Nations requesting the deployment of military observers along their common border. In March, the RPF and the government reinstated the cease-fire of 1992 and reopened peace negotiations under the auspices of the OAU in Arusha.

Meanwhile, in Burundi in May 1990, Major Pierre Buyoya abolished the military government, announced plans for the formation of a democratic constitution cum one-party government, and established a unified government with himself as President and a Hutu as Vice President. This was designed to achieve national conciliation between Hutus and Tutsis. Later that year the Tutsi-dominated ruling Uprona abolished the Military Committee for National Salvation and transferred its functions to an 80-member central committee with Buyoya as chairman and a Hutu, Nicolas Mayugi, as secretary-general. This new government was strongly opposed by the Hutu nationalist group, Palipehutu, then operating out of Tanzania. Despite ethnic violence throughout the country in late 1991, Buyoya put together a **new coalition government** based on the new constitution, and the first presidential election was held on June 1, 1993. Melchior Ndadaye of the Front for Democracy (Frodebu) emerged as the winner—

Burundi's first Hutu President. To provide ethnic balance he chose a Tutsi, Sylvie Kinigi, as Prime Minister and included seven Uprona members in his cabinet. Now Buyoya and Uprona became the opposition. Then, in October, came the Tutsi-inspired coup in which a number of Hutu officials—including Ndadaye—were massacred and 300,000 Hutus fled across the border to Rwanda, Tanzania, and Zaire. A regional summit held at Kigali on October 28 requested the United Nations to establish an "international force for stabilization and the restoration of confidence" in Burundi [A/48/567, 11/2/93].

The initial U.N. response to these two requests was minimal. In the case of Rwanda the Security Council authorized the formation of the 105-member **U.N. Observer Mission Uganda-Rwanda (UNOMUR)**, to be deployed on the Uganda side of the border [S/Res/846, 6/22/93]. Its 81 military observers were to verify the compliance of the Tutsi-dominated RPF with the RPF's pledge to cease the transport of weapons, ammunition, and military equipment into Rwanda. Soon after the authorization of UNOMUR, the **Organization of African Unity**'s three-year effort to settle the Rwandan conflict bore fruit. The August 1993 **Arusha Peace Agreement** it brokered between the Rwandan government and the RPF called for verification of the cease-fire, a broad-based transitional government, and elections in the fall of 1995. Although the 132 members of the **OAU Neutral Military Observer Group (NMOG)** had been monitoring compliance with the cease-fire since July 1992, the Arusha Agreement required the deployment of a much larger "neutral international force" to oversee the integration of the armed forces of the opposing side [see *Issues/49*, pp. 37–38]. The OAU appealed to the United Nations, and on October 5 the Security Council created the **U.N. Assistance Mission for Rwanda (UNAMIR)**, incorporating UNOMUR and integrating members of NMOG into the operation, whose mandate included contributing to the security of Kigali, monitoring the cease-fire and establishing a demilitarized zone, investigating instances of noncompliance with the Peace Agreement, assisting in mine clearance and in the coordination of humanitarian assistance, and monitoring the return of refugees [S/Res/872, 10/5/93].

In the case of Burundi, the United Nations dispatched on a fact-finding mission in early November 1993 Special Representative of the Secretary-General James Jonah, who commented to reporters afterward that, given the financial and logistical burdens associated with 16 ongoing peacekeeping operations, the Security Council could not be expected to take on any new ones [*Washington Post*, 11/3/93]. By mid-November the conflict had produced 659,000 refugees and 150,000 displaced persons—some 15 percent of the population. Moderate elements of the army managed to put down the October coup, and in January 1994 the National Assembly elected a Hutu moderate, Agriculture Minister Cyprien Ntaryamira, to head a **government of national consensus** [*Keesings World Report*, 1/12/94, p. 39,805].

On April 6, 1994, **Presidents Habyarimana and Ntaryamira** were killed in an airplane bombing over Kigali en route from a regional summit sponsored by the OAU. In Rwanda, pandemonium broke out at the news of the President's death, and in what many believe to have been a pre-planned campaign, the **Presidential Guard organized Hutu militias and civilians to massacre Tutsis and government opponents.** By late April, between 200,000 and 500,000 people, mainly Tutsis, had been killed and over 2 million Rwandans displaced. Although there were no killings of this magnitude in Burundi, the violence, if sporadic, was widespread and principally between members of the Hutu-dominated Frodebu and the Tutsi Uprona.

As the slaughter continued in Rwanda, the Security Council convened at U.N. Headquarters in New York and, in what has been called one of the most tragic nondecisions of that chamber, failed to reach consensus on the need to stop the massacre or reimpose order [UNA-USA, *A Report on the Fifth Annual Peacekeeping Mission*, 1995]. **The Council did not want to upgrade UNAMIR from a Chapter VI to a Chapter VII operation**, and no country would make further troop commitments. In fact, on April 21, 1994, at the height of the killing in Rwanda, the Security Council agreed to **decrease the size of the U.N. force** to 270. The "new" mandate of the drastically reduced force would be solely to act as an intermediary between the parties in the attempt to secure a cease-fire [S/Res/912, 4/21/94]. By the middle of May, with the bulk of the forces withdrawn, the death toll had reached an estimated 500,000 [UNA-USA, *A Report on the Fifth Annual Peacekeeping Mission*, 1995].

After a number of desperate pleas by the Secretary-General, and pressure generated by CNN's 24-hour coverage of the **Rwandan genocide**, the Security Council decided to dispatch a 5,500-member force, **UNAMIR II**, still under Chapter VI but with a broader mandate than the previous mission: to police Kigali airport, create "safe areas" for refugees, monitor an arms embargo, and "contribute to the security and protection of displaced persons, refugees, and civilians at risk" [S/Res/918, 5/17/94]. But **staffing this mission proved difficult**, owing to the lack of resources (and prominently of troop contributions). Under these circumstances, the Security Council decided to endorse the launching of a **French-led interim force** to pacify the area and protect civilians. Now acting under Chapter VII of the U.N. Charter, the Security Council authorized "**Operation Turquoise**" to use whatever means necessary to fulfill its mandate within two months [S/Res/929, 6/22/94]. The force entered Rwanda on June 23, 1994, and established a safe area in a triangle of land between Cyangugu, Kibuye, and Gikongoro [S/1994/798, 7/6/94]. There it was able to offer protection to some 850,000 Hutus in 50 camps [ibid.].

Having won the civil war, the **Tutsi-led Rwandan Patriotic Front (RPF)** had strengthened its hold on the country. The Parmehutu government, and indeed most **Hutus, fearing reprisals for the massacre of Tutsis of April 1994, had fled across Rwanda's borders** [*U.N. Chronicle*, 12/94]. The RPF set about establishing a government of national unity composed of its own members and members of other groups but definitely excluding such Hutu organizations as the Parmehutu. Pasteur Bizimungu was installed as President and Faustin Twagiramungu as Prime Minister. (UN-AMIR was expected to take over from Operation Turquoise by August 21, 1994, but it took until the end of November for the mission to reach its authorized strength [UNA-USA, *A Report on the Fifth Annual Peacekeeping Mission*, 1995].)

In Burundi the search for a viable successor to the Ntaryamira regime also presented problems. A compromise **"Convention on Government"** signed on September 10, 1994, by 10 of the 13 political parties, called for a four-year transition period, a 25-member cabinet (55 percent Hutu), a prime minister from the opposition, and a likewise ethnically divided National Security Council. A week later they approved a procedure for the selection of a president by the National Assembly; and on September 30, Sylvestre Ntibantunganya, a Hutu, was elected as that interim head of state [S/1994/1152, 10/11/94; and see *Issues/50*, pp. 37–38]. By year's end this power-sharing agreement had begun to fall apart, and incidents of interethnic violence began to increase.

Since denouncing the attempted coup of 1993, the Security Council had been monitoring events in Burundi with the aid of briefings from the U.N. Secretariat. The Secretary-General, for his part, had appointed a Special Representative, Ahmedou Ould-Abdallah, and dispatched a two-man **fact-finding mission** to investigate the coup and subsequent violence, although their report, prepared in May 1994, had not been released or shared with the Security Council as much as a year later [*Issues/50*, p. 36]. In August 1994 the Security Council directed **two other fact-finders** (earlier dispatched to Mozambique) to travel on to Burundi for a two-day visit, and it sent out **yet another mission** in February 1995 [S/1994/1163, 10/15/94], both under Ambassador Ibrahim Gambari of Nigeria. Gambari's reports [S/1994/1039, 9/9/94 and S/1994/1163] called attention to the general breakdown of law and order and to "a culture of impunity" from prosecution, and he called for **U.N. action to avoid a repetition of the recent tragic events in Rwanda**. The Security Council condemned those opposed to power-sharing in the new Burundi government but took no action on the matter [S/PRST/1995/13, 3/29/95].

From Burundi in April came reports that some **Hutu extremists** had formed a National Council for the Defense of Democracy and were arming themselves for an all-out war with the government. Interim President Ntibantunganya warned that the country was on the brink of war and genocide, and the call was taken up by all 27 relief agencies operating in the country as well as by the Pope, the European Union, and the OAU [*Keesings World Report*, 3/16/95, p. 40,439].

However, calls on the Security Council to take action to forestall imminent disaster were largely ignored. As a result of the Secretary-General's July 16, 1995 visit to Burundi, the Security Council decided to **lift the arms embargo on both Rwanda and Burundi** [S/Res/1012, 8/17/95]. Subsequent actions by the Security Council in the late winter and early spring of 1996 took the form of admonitions—to use "restraint," to put "an end to the violence," to arrive at a "negotiated settlement," to find "a diplomatic solution" [*Keesings World Report*, 1/25/96, p. 40,891; *New York Times*, 1/30/96 and 3/6/96]—as the fighting continued. March's toll was 100,000 people killed and 56,000 more Burundians in flight from their homes [*New York Times*, 4/5/96].

There was an already **enormous concentration of refugees in the region** in late 1994 when the Security Council decided not only to extend UNAMIR for an additional six months but also to expand its responsibilities to include the monitoring of the treatment and repatriation of refugees [S/Res/965, 11/30/94]. For the new Tutsi regime in Rwanda the issue of repatriation and refugees was important in two respects. For one thing, 400,000 or so of their ethnic kin had fled Rwanda during the genocide and later remained in neighboring countries. For another, Hutu ex-government leaders and soldiers in refugee camps were organizing militias for a reinvasion of Rwanda [S/PRST/1994/75, 11/30/94]. The **security situation in these camps**—especially the three north and south of Lake Kivu at the Zaire-Rwanda border—had deteriorated markedly. Bandits, soldiers, and gangs had established control over the distribution of food and relief to the 1 million mostly Hutu refugees here, ruling through extortion and intimidation.

To facilitate the repatriation of refugees, the government created **"Operation Retour,"** and by February 1995, UNAMIR (now fully deployed) was cooperating with the RPF operation. But the pace of repatriation was slow, and by mid-1995 the Secretary-General reported that there were still 1.1 million Rwandan refugees in Zaire, 600,000 in Tanzania, and 240,000 in Burundi [S/1995/304, 4/14/95].

In June 1995 the Security Council extended UNAMIR's mandate once again, but now the government of Rwanda requested a reduction in the force level, from 5,500 troops to 2,330, by September 8 and to 1,800 by October 8 [UNA-USA, *A Report on the Fifth Annual Peacekeeping Mission*, 1995] due to its growing level of confidence in dealing with the problem of security within its territory.

The **Ad Hoc International Criminal Tribunal for Rwanda**, established by the Security Council in November 1994 at Rwanda's request [S/Res/955, 11/8/94], opened formally on November 27, 1995. With so many potential defendants in custody, however, there is little prospect of quick indictments or trials (and the very real possibility that defendants will be abused or even killed before the trial can take place) [see *Issues/50*, pp. 252–53; and see also the "Legal Issues" chapter of the present volume]. On December 12, 1995, the first indictments were issued, and by May 30, 1996, only 11 had been handed down. The first trial is scheduled to begin on September 19 [*New York Times*, 5/31/96].

5. The Middle East and the Persian Gulf
By Jules Kagian

Iraq

After nearly a year of rejecting Security Council Resolution 986 (1995) that would allow Iraq to sell limited amounts of oil to obtain humanitarian supplies for its suffering people, Baghdad notified Secretary-General Boutros Boutros-Ghali in January 1996 that **it was ready to begin these talks without prior conditions** [*Washington Post*, 1/17/96]. Iraq's Deputy Prime Minister, Tariq Aziz, was quoted as saying Iraq still objected to the terms of the Council's measure with "no change in our stand" toward a document Baghdad had already rejected [*Financial Times*, 1/18/96].

Specifically, the resolution would allow Iraq to sell $2 billion worth of oil over a six-month period in what is known as an **"oil-for-food" deal.** Under the plan, to be strictly supervised by the United Nations, 30 percent of the proceeds would be used to compensate Kuwait and other victims of Iraq's aggression. Modest sums would be diverted to pay the expense of U.N. arms inspection programs and to compensate Turkey for the use of its pipeline. The remainder would be spent on food, medicine, and other humanitarian goods for the Iraqi people. Specifically, the resolution provides for $150 million out of every $1 billion of oil sold to be used by the United Nations to pay for its relief program in three predominantly Kurdish northern provinces that have broken away from Baghdad and are under the military protection of the Gulf War allies [*New York Times*, 4/24/96]. It was made clear from the outset that the **terms of the resolution were not negotiable** and that all aspects of the operation would be strictly handled by the United Nations.

During talks in early 1996 at U.N. Headquarters in New York, the Iraqis demanded a role in monitoring the revenue and the distribution of humanitarian supplies, especially in the north, on the basis of reasserting Baghdad's sovereignty. The talks were temporarily suspended after three rounds, and the Iraqi delegation complained to newsmen on April 22 that British and U.S. intervention led the Secretary-General to make changes in "almost every paragraph" of an accord that was close to completion [ibid., 4/24/96]. U.S. and British diplomats maintained that they wanted an agreement on the issue, but one that would not weaken existing economic sanctions against Iraq or allow Saddam Hussein to improve his position in any way. In particular, the United States and Britain wanted funds reserved for Iraq's Kurdish provinces funneled through the existing U.N. assistance program there. They questioned the fairness of Iraq's rationing system to handle food distribution. They also objected to Iraq's choosing the bank into which oil payments were to be made and from which letters of credit would be issued to pay for essential supplies. The Iraqi delegation to the oil talks was headed by **Ambassador Abdul Amir al-Anbari**, who headed Iraq's Mission to the United Nations during the Gulf War, while Hans Corell, the chief legal counsel, led the U.N. team.

On May 20, after months of negotiations, **Iraq accepted Security Council Resolution 986.** Secretary-General Boutros-Ghali hailed the agreement as a great U.N. victory. He said the resolution was based on one of the most important objectives of the United Nations, which is to alleviate the problem of poverty. **Madeleine Albright**, the chief U.S. delegate, said it was an excellent day for the people of Iraq, who have not been able to get the required amount of food and medicine because of President Saddam Hussein's priorities. She said it was a great day for the United Nations, which stands in charge of the whole operation; and it was a great day for the United States, the author of Resolution 986. Ambassador Albright **stressed that the agreement leaves the sanctions regime intact.**

The agreement would add about 700,000 barrels a day of Iraqi oil to world supplies at current prices. The plan requires that Iraqi oil must pass from Iraq's Mina Al-Bakr oil terminal and through the Kirkuk-Yumurtalik pipeline across Turkey to the Mediterranean. Before Resolution 986 can be implemented, some finetuning has to take place. Abdul Amir al-Anbari, Iraq's negotiator, said oil exports could begin in as little as a month, but U.N. officials believed it might take longer.

The oil-for-food agreement is the most important development between Iraq and the United Nations since the end of the Gulf War. The Secretary-General must certify every 90 days that Baghdad has complied with the terms of the Security Council resolution. Indeed, the process received a major setback on July 1, when the United States rejected Baghdad's plan for its implementation. A decision by the Secretary-General to go forward with the plan was awaiting a review by U.N. legal experts and other officials [*Washington Post* and BBC, 6/2/96].

Weapons of Mass Destruction

In its report [S/1996/258] of April 11, 1996, the **U.N. Special Commission set up to oversee the destruction of weapons of mass destruction in Iraq said it was still not satisfied** that Iraq had eliminated all such weapons. The Commission said it was still concerned about Iraq's germ warfare, chemical, and ballistic capabilities. The Commission also said it wondered about Iraq's failure to account fully for the number of long-range missiles it produced. The Commission accused Iraq of **concealing information and equipment** related to its weapons programs, and reported that, although large parts of Iraq's weapons programs had been accounted for, gaps remained. There is also concern that Iraq may still be engaged in forbidden activities, and the report expressed concern about Iraq's decision in 1995 to import missile guidance systems in violation of U.N. sanctions.

Although the report did commend the authorities in Baghdad for their cooperation in some areas, it warned that recent standoffs between Baghdad and U.N. inspectors, which were reported to the Security Council, give the impression that Iraq still has something to hide. **Rolf Ekeus, Executive Chairman of the Special Commission**, told a Senate subcommittee on permanent investigations that his team believes that Iraq has hidden between 6 and 16 ballistic missiles [*Washington Post*, 3/21/96]. He said this helps explain the recent confrontation of the inspectors with Baghdad authorities when they were denied immediate access to government buildings suspected of harboring launchers or other evidence related to the missiles. **CIA Director John Deutch**, who also appeared before the subcommittee the same day, said that if such delays become routine, Iraqi officials will have "ample opportunity to destroy relevant material and ultimately prevent the U.N. from attaining a full and complete accounting" of Iraq's weapons' efforts [ibid.].

Following the defection of two of Saddam Hussein's key lieutenants to Jordan on August 10, 1995 (they were subsequently murdered after returning home), Iraq felt compelled to lift the veil of secrecy on its weapons of mass destruction program to an unprecedented degree. One of the defectors was Lieutenant General Hussein Kamil, who was in control of Iraq's nuclear, chemical, and biological programs for almost a decade. Ekeus and his team were given 147 boxes and two containers filled with documents, which were still being assessed as of May 1996. Ekeus had already established that, in violation of Iraq's treaty obligations and previous statements, **Saddam had amassed a huge biological warfare capability** that was available for use against allied forces in the Gulf War [*Wall Street Journal*, 5/30/95]. Appearing before the Near East and South Asian Affairs Subcommittee of the Senate Foreign Relations Committee, U.S. Permanent Representative to the U.N. Madeleine Albright said that America's position on Iraq's sanctions has been consistent, principled, and based on a realistic and hard-won understanding of the nature of the Iraqi regime. She said the administration's policy will not change until and unless Iraq does everything the U.N. Security Council says it must [Federal Press Service, 5/3/95].

In mid-June 1996 a new crisis developed between Iraq and U.N. weapons inspectors, when they were barred from sites suspected of holding banned weapons material. Acting under Chapter VII of the U.N. Charter, the Security Council adopted Resolution 1960 (6/12/96) deploring Iraq's refusal to allow access to selected sites and demanding that the government of Iraq allow all U.N. inspectors "immediate, unconditional and unrestricted access" to any and all areas. Subsequently, chief arms inspector Rolf Ekeus was able to reach an agreement with Baghdad that conformed with the latest Security Council resolution. However, Ekeus told correspondents that he believes that President Saddam Hussein's regime continues to hide banned arms and other material that the Iraqis promised to destroy [*Washington Post*, 6/25/96].

The Arab-Israeli Conflict and the Peace Process

On September 28, 1995, Israel and the PLO initialed the "Israel-Palestine Interim Agreement on the West Bank and Gaza Strip." This accord, also known as the "Taba Agreement" or, more popularly, "**Oslo II**," details the mechanisms and the limitations of Palestinian self-rule beyond the Gaza Strip and Jericho to significant portions of the West Bank. The accord is the second stage of the process that began when Yitzhak Rabin and Yasser Arafat shook hands on the White House lawn on September 13, 1993, having signed the "**Declaration of Principles**" that ended 26 years of total estrangement and set a timetable for a permanent disengagement of Arabs and Israelis. The first stage, initiated in May 1994, established Palestinian self-rule in the Gaza Strip and Jericho in the West Bank. The final and most crucial stage, which was scheduled to begin in May 1996, will be the "permanent status negotiations" over the fate of Jerusalem, Arab refugees, Jewish settlements, and security arrangements.

Oslo II is far more complex and politically volatile than the Declaration of Principles, which established only broad and often contradictory guidelines [*New York Times*, 9/25/95]. The main points of Oslo II include redeployment, elections, transfer of powers, and the release of prisoners—leaving a number of issues to be negotiated later [ibid.]. Israel's redeployment from six Arab towns and surrounding villages with the exception of Hebron has proceeded on or ahead of schedule. According to Oslo II, Israel was to redeploy from Hebron by the end of March 1996. The interim phase leaves the Palestinians with more than autonomy but less than a state. Also, Palestinians do not have control over external security, foreign policy, borders, immigration, Jewish settlers living in their midst, or their own currency [*Israel and Palestine Political Report*, 11/95].

The first ever **general election** in the West Bank and Gaza for an 88-seat Legislative Council took place on January 20, marking a genuine milestone in the history of Palestine. The Council has wide-ranging legislative powers, although Israel will be able to exercise a veto on laws that it believes touch directly on its security interests. The outcome of the election was a **clear-cut victory for Yasser Arafat**, confirming him as the undisputed leader of the Palestinians. Despite calls from both the Islamist and PLO opposition to boycott the election, 68 percent in Gaza turned out to vote. Despite the difficulties raised by Israel and the formidable obstacles placed in their way, Palestinians in East Jerusalem participated as both candidates and voters. However, only around 40 percent of eligible Palestinians voted in Jerusalem. Of the 88 elected members of the Council, 50 were from Arafat's Fatah movement. Still, some well-known leaders from the opposition were also elected, and they will certainly make the debates more colorful [*New York Times*, 1/21/96; *The Economist*, 1/29/96; *Middle East International*, 2/2/96].

The **assassination of Israeli Prime Minister Yitzhak Rabin** on November 4, 1995, did not substantively affect the unfolding Israeli-Arab process—the assassin's stated goal. Indeed, in some ways the assassination might have marginally contributed to a hastening of the process. Yigal Amir of Herzilya, a law student at Bar Ilan University, shot Rabin as he was entering his car at the conclusion of a massive peace rally in Tel Aviv. Amir told investigators that he acted alone and had "received instructions from God to kill Prime Minister Rabin." A three-judge court handed down a life sentence after rejecting his lawyer's argument that he only meant to paralyze the Prime Minister. **The Shamgar Commission of Inquiry** into the assassination charged that for years the General Security Service has failed to protect the nation's leaders properly [*Jerusalem Post International*, week ending 11/18/95; week ending 4/6/96].

In the weeks following the assassination of Rabin, his successor, **Shimon Peres**, moved quickly but cautiously to consolidate his leadership. His immediate challenge was to push through a peace agreement that faces opposition from a large segment of Israeli society in an election year, and to prove to his people that he is not soft on security. The first serious security problem to face Peres was a series of **terrorist suicide acts** perpetrated in late February and early March 1996 by the extremist Palestinian group Hamas. Israel's Ambassador to the United Nations, Gad Yaacobi, told the Secretary-General that Israel finds itself engaged in all-out war against Hamas and other terrorist organizations [A/51/74]. In the immediate aftermath of these bombings, **Israel ordered a separation of the Israeli and Palestinian populations**. Israel also demanded that the Palestine Authority crack down on the terrorists, their infrastructure, and their means of support in accordance with the interim agreement.

Peres desperately needed to show the opposition in Israel that the Palestinian leadership remained an effective partner for security. Spelling out the American blueprint for dealing with Hamas, the U.S. Ambassador to Israel, Martyn Indyk, said: "The policy of co-opting Hamas has failed,

Arafat must understand that what he does now will affect the very future of the peace process" [*Al-Ahram Weekly*, 2/29–3/6/96]. Peres said he would keep the West Bank and Gaza sealed indefinitely, barring 2 million Palestinians, including 60,000 workers, from entering Israel. The closure costs the Palestinian economy $4 million a day in lost wages and export [ibid.]. **Arafat's response was swift, positive, and effective.** The steps he took earned him praise from Washington and Tel Aviv. However, the situation caused by the closure was tantamount to a declaration of war, according to **Nasser Al-Kidwa, Permanent Observer of Palestine at the United Nations.** The Security Council met on April 15 to consider Israel's closure, but the United States believed the meeting was unnecessary and counterproductive [U.N. press release SC/6206].

PNC Amends Charter

The Palestinian-Israeli peace process took a historic step forward on April 24 when the Palestine National Council (PNC), meeting in Gaza, voted by 504 to 54 with 14 abstentions **to revise its Charter.** Of the 669 members, 97 were absent, including members of radical movements who refused to attend any discussions on changing the historic document. Among the revisions are clauses denying Israel's right to exist or declaring that Palestine can be liberated through armed struggle alone. The Charter is the founding document of Palestinian nationalism. It was drawn up in 1964 and amended in 1968 after Israel's seizure of the West Bank. Yasser Arafat first committed the PNC to change those articles at the original 1993 Oslo Accords and again in the "interim agreement" signed in September 1995. After the Palestinian Legislative Council elections in January, Peres warned the PLO leader that there would be "no movement" to final status talks unless the Charter was amended. Following a wave of suicide attacks in Israel, the stance of Peres became harder still. Before agreeing to the Israeli army's redeployment in the West Bank city of Hebron, Peres said, "I want to see where we stand on the issue of the Palestine Charter."

The PNC decision was welcomed by Peres, hailing it as "the most important change in the last 100 years." Senator Arlen Specter, a co-chairman of the Peace Accord Monitoring Group in Congress as well as an original sponsor of legislation that linked compliance to receiving U.S. assistance, called the decision a "first step" and said **Congress would continue to watch the PLO closely on other issues,** such as its war against terrorism. Secretary of State Warren Christopher called the decision "a historic milestone on the road to reconciliation and peace between the people of Israel and the Palestinians." One day after the PLO decided to amend its Charter, and four weeks before Israel's national elections on May 29, the central committee of Israel's Labor Party **voted to drop its**

opposition to Palestinian statehood [*Christian Science Monitor*, 4/27/96; *Jewish Telegraphic Agency*, 4/25/96; *Middle East International*, 4/26/96; *New York Times*, 4/25/96].

Meanwhile, the Israeli Cabinet decided in May that the **Israeli army will redeploy in Hebron on June 12.** A contingent of 32 observers from Norway took up their duties on May 15 on the city's streets. The observer group, formed under the provisions of the self-rule accord, has no police powers and can only document incidents, sending reports to an Israeli-Palestinian committee. It has a mandate to operate for three months, but the period can be extended by mutual agreement. Under the Israeli-Palestinian accord, the Israeli army is supposed to hand over most of Hebron to a Palestinian police force, while remaining to guard the Jewish enclaves and the Tomb of the Patriarchs, a shrine holy to both Muslims and Jews [*New York Times*, 5/16/96; *Jerusalem Post International*, week ending 5/25/96].

Palestinian and Israeli negotiators met in Taba on May 5 to inaugurate **final status talks,** which are to cover such issues as Jerusalem, Jewish settlements, refugees, borders, and the political status of any future Palestinian entity [*Al-Ahram Weekly*, 5/9–15/96].

Fighting Terrorism

In response to the bombings in Israel, a hastily summoned meeting took place in Sharm el-Sheikh, Egypt, on March 13 **to launch a coordinated campaign against terrorism and to salvage the threatened peace process.** The summit was hosted by President Hosni Mubarak of Egypt, who co-chaired the conference with President Clinton. The four-hour gathering did not result in any solution to terrorism or concrete steps to save the peace, but it was an impressive show nonetheless. Leaders and officials of 27 nations, including Britain, Canada, France, Germany, Italy, Japan, Russia, Spain, and Turkey, were present. Also participating were representatives of the European Union and U.N. Secretary-General Boutros Boutros-Ghali. In all, 13 Arab nations attended. Yasser Arafat represented the Palestinians, bringing to 14 the number of Arab delegations. Prime Minister Shimon Peres represented Israel.

Iran, Iraq, Libya, and Sudan were not invited because the United States considers them exporters of terrorism. **Lebanon and Syria refused to attend**, maintaining that a better forum would have been the reconvening of the Madrid Conference. On the eve of the summit, Egypt became involved in a **dispute over the order of priorities** of the conference: saving the peace process or fighting terrorism. In the end a compromise was reached. A joint communiqué, read by Clinton, said: "The summit had three fundamental objectives: to enhance the peace process; to promote security; and to combat terror." He said the leaders pledged to pursue those ends by political and economic means, by closer cooperation, and by establishing a working group to seek practical methods for coordination.

In a follow-up to the summit, political and intelligence experts from 29 countries and organizations convened at the State Department on March 29 to draft specific recommendations to fight terrorism. The two-day meeting in Washington became a forum for the Palestinians and some European and Arab countries to criticize Israel's closure policy against Palestinians. However, Secretary of State Christopher helped broker a modest relaxation of the border closing. At the same time, the United States urged donor countries to expedite aid for the Palestinians, who received only small amounts of the $1.8 billion they have been promised over the past two years. The Washington meeting focused on a number of topics to promote cooperation in fighting terrorism. **The conflict in Lebanon in April forced the cancellation of a third meeting**, which was scheduled for Luxembourg [*New York Times*, 3/14, 30/96; *Middle East International*, 3/29/96].

Israel and Syria

On the **Syrian-Israeli track**, problems of security, seen and unforeseen, continue to dominate peace discussions between the two nations whenever they engage in meaningful talks. Syria, meanwhile, has not deviated from its demand that Israel recognize Syrian sovereignty over the whole Golan Heights and that it withdraw to the line of June 4, 1967. Israel's acceptance of this principle is a Syrian precondition before normalization between the two countries can be established. During a number of encounters between the Syrian and Israeli delegations at the **Wye Plantation conference** in Maryland (December 1995 through March 1996) the same issues of security and normalization were discussed over and over without progress.

By early February, senior U.S. officials were gloomy about the prospects of rapid progress in the Syrian-Israeli peace talks [*Washington Post*, 2/9/96]. The decision by Peres to hold early elections was based on his conclusion that Syrian President Hafez al-Assad simply refuses to be hurried. According to Peres, there are four major issues between Israel and Syria: (1) the nature of peace and normalization, (2) security arrangements, (3) the placement of final lines, and (4) the interphasing of the agreement [*Middle East International*, 6/9/95]. In clearer language, **the core issues** that have bedeviled four years of unfruitful Israeli-Syrian talks are **the nature of Syria's offer** and **the time needed to carry out the agreement**. In late May, following his negotiating efforts that led to the understanding reached in southern Lebanon, Secretary of State Christopher and his negotiating team spoke skeptically about the possibility of an early agreement between Israel and Syria. Christopher signaled his growing doubts about the outcome in a *Los Angeles Times* interview on May 3, saying "I am more concerned than ever as to whether [Assad] will be able to execute his intention for peace because of his suspicion and fear." U.S. officials had envisioned a ground-breaking Israeli-Syrian deal in 1996 that would cap what they expected would be Christopher's last year in office. But at midyear it seemed doubtful that Christopher would achieve his goal by the end of President Clinton's first term [*Washington Post*, 5/25/96].

UNIFIL

It was Israel's shelling of a U.N. Interim Force (UNIFIL) camp in southern Lebanon on April 18 that prompted the Western powers to seek U.N. intervention by the Security Council [S/Res/1052]. Prior to that attack, which killed scores of Lebanese refugees who had sought safety in the camp and wounded many more, the United States conducted a vigorous campaign urging Lebanon and its supporters not to bring Israel's invasion of southern Lebanon before the Council. The Arab draft resolution, which condemned the attack on Lebanon, lost by default. It received only four votes (China, Egypt, Guinea-Bissau, and Indonesia), with the rest of the Council members abstaining. The second draft resolution—sponsored by France, Germany, Honduras, Italy, Poland, the Russian Federation, the United Kingdom, and the United States—was adopted unanimously. The resolution deplored the attack on UNIFIL's site and reaffirmed the Council's commitment to Lebanon's territorial integrity, sovereignty, and political independence as well as the security of all states in the region. Meanwhile, the Secretary-General dispatched a senior military officer to conduct an immediate investigation into the shelling of the U.N. base [S/PV/3653/4/15/96].

However, the **General Assembly** met at the request of the Muslim group and **voted to condemn Israel** for attacks on civilians in south Lebanon. The vote was 64 in favor, with 65 abstentions. Only two countries, Israel and the United States, voted against it. The Assembly regarded Israel responsible for compensation, and called for an immediate cessation of hostilities and for strict respect for Lebanon's territorial integrity and sovereignty [U.N. press release GA/9070, 4/25/96]. Even so, because the General Assembly's resolution is toothless, the **role of the United Nations in Lebanon was once more marginalized**. Rather, it was **Secretary of State Christopher** and the cooperation of power brokers that brought about the truce between Israel and Hizbollah and that revived—perhaps even strengthened—the old understanding that had been earlier brokered by Christopher.

On May 7 the U.N. Secretary-General presented to the Security Council the report submitted to him by his military advisor, Major General Franklin van Kappen, following his mission to Lebanon and Israel.

The mission sought to establish the facts regarding the tragic events that took place at Qana, Lebanon, on April 18, in which more than 100 Lebanese civilians were killed in the headquarters of the Fijian battalion of the U.N. Interim Force in Lebanon (UNIFIL). The report said that **the Israeli artillery attack did not appear to be a mistake,** as the Israeli government has insisted.

"While the possibility can not be ruled out completely, it is unlikely that the shelling of the United Nations compound was the result of gross technical and/or procedural errors," said the report [S/1996/337]. The Secretary-General sent the report to the Security Council over the objections of the United States, which argued that recrimination was not useful at a time when a fragile cease-fire was being established on the Israeli-Lebanese border [*New York Times*, 5/8/96].

Israel denied accusations raised in the report and insisted it was unaware civilians were in the compound. The Israeli government charged that the United Nations had contributed to the incident by sheltering Hizbollah. James Rubin, spokesman for the U.S. Mission to the United Nations, said **Ambassador Albright was disturbed** that the report "chose to draw unjustified conclusions about this incident that can only divide and polarize the environment." **Israel's Foreign Minister, Ehud Barak, warned Boutros-Ghali that the report was liable to damage relations between Israel and UNIFIL.** A well-known Israeli commentator wrote that the U.N. report provides an opportunity to assess "the incorrect and superfluous presence of UNIFIL" [*Jerusalem Post International*, week ending 5/18/96].

Israel's Major General David Zur, chief liaison officer with foreign armies, said that UNIFIL has failed in its mission in Lebanon. He said Israeli top commanders are not meeting with UNIFIL's leaders and the Israeli army is reassessing its whole relationship with the peacekeepers [ibid., week ending 5/25/96]. Meanwhile, representatives of the United States, France, Israel, Lebanon, and Syria held several meetings in Washington to reach an operational agreement to monitor the understanding that brought to an end Israel's offensive in Lebanon. **The April 26 cease-fire is based on the 1993 "gentlemen's agreement,"** except that the present understanding is in writing and will be monitored. According to the document, armed groups in Lebanon are not to attack Israel with any type of weapons; Israel is prohibited from attacking Lebanese civilians or civilian targets in Lebanon; attacks on civilian infrastructure are banned, as is the launching of attacks into Israel's occupation zone from areas of civilian habitation; and the parties retain the right of "legitimate defence" within stipulations of the understanding. In addition to the monitoring group, a consultative committee is to provide the means for the reconstruction of Lebanon. The understanding is between Lebanon and Israel, and **Syria is not a guarantor.** Also, the understanding **does not call for disarming**

the militias. It was agreed in Washington that the monitoring group will be headquartered in En Naqura on the border between Lebanon with Israel and will be headed alternately by France and the United States. The monitoring group becomes operational when complete agreement is reached on the details [*Middle East International*, 3/10/96].

Peres and Arafat in Washington

On April 30, President Clinton and Prime Minister Peres **concluded two days of intensive discussions on a broad range of issues relating to the relationship between their two countries.** According to a joint statement, the two leaders agreed that, in view of continuing threats to regional peace and stability, and in particular the dangers posed by proliferation of weapons of mass destruction and advanced military technologies, U.S.-Israeli strategic cooperation will grow in importance [White House Press Office, U.S.-Israel Joint Statement, 4/30/96]. With respect to Israel's security, Clinton reaffirmed America's commitment to maintain Israel's qualitative edge and to preserve and strengthen Israel's capability to deter and defend itself, by itself, against any adversary or likely combination of adversaries. **The two leaders signed the U.S.-Israel Counter-Terrorism Cooperation Accord,** which sets out practical measures to combat terrorism. Clinton and Peres also took note of the **joint statement on theater missile defense cooperation,** signed by Peres and Secretary of Defense William Perry on April 28 [ibid.]. Yasser Arafat was warmly received in the Oval Office by Clinton on May 1. Arafat described his meeting with Clinton as "very successful, warm and fruitful." The following day he met privately with Secretary-General Boutros-Ghali at U.N. Headquarters. He told newsmen that he asked the Secretary-General for more U.N. involvement in the Middle East peace process [*New York Post*, 5/3/96].

The Security Council and Sudan

Sudan has become **the third Arab country under some form of sanctions** imposed by the Security Council following those imposed on Iraq and Libya. The Council agreed on April 27, 1996 to impose mild sanctions on Sudan unless it hands over the three men accused of trying to assassinate President Hosni Mubarak of Egypt last year [S/Res/1054]. **The resolution was adopted 13–0,** with Russia and China abstaining. The resolution also urges Sudan to stop supporting terrorism, and requires it to reduce the staff of its diplomatic missions around the world and to restrict the movements of its diplomats. Furthermore, international organizations would be barred from holding conferences in Sudan. These measures were to become effective May 10 should Sudan not surrender the three men in question. The Council agreed to meet again 60 days after the May 10 deadline to see whether Sudan had complied with the demand and to decide whether to adopt further measures [*New York Times*, 1/27/96]. **Egypt, supported** by other Council members, resisted U.S. pressure for tougher sanctions. The Egyptian Ambassador, Nabil Elaraby, **lobbied for diplomatic sanctions,** saying his country did not want the Council to punish the people of Sudan. He also feared that military sanctions could lead to internal instability [*Al-Ahram*, 4/29/96]. For several weeks in April the United States pressed Council members for stronger measures against Sudan, but without success. Madeleine Albright said for the first time on April 3 that the United States has **evidence directly implicating the Sudanese government in the attempted assassination** [*New York Times*, 4/4/96]. A week later the United States announced the expulsion of Ahmed Yousif Mohamed, the second secretary of Sudan's Mission to the United Nations, on charges of terrorist and espionage activities [ibid., 4/11/96].

The complaint against Sudan was first brought to the attention of the Security Council by Ethiopia, in whose capital, Addis Ababa, the abortive attempt was made on the life of Mubarak as he was being driven to the conference hall of the summit of the Organization of African Unity (OAU). On January 31, 1996, the Council adopted **Resolution 1044** condemning the failed attempt. It called on Sudan to extradite the three suspects to Ethiopia and to desist from engaging in terrorist activities. The resolution requested the Secretary-General to seek the cooperation of the government of Sudan with the consultation of the OAU and to report to the Council within 60 days. In his report, the Secretary-General informed the Council that, with regard to the three suspects, "The Government of the Sudan has not yet complied with the demand of the Council" [S/1996/179]. In February, a U.S. official said continued defiance could pose a **"natural analogy" with Libya** [*Washington Post*, 2/1/96].

Israel's Elections and the Peace Process

With the Arab-Israeli peace process at a critical juncture, Israel's general elections on May 29 showed that Israel is split down the middle about the risks and rewards of continuing the peace effort. Peace, security, and the threat of terrorism emerged as the dominant issues of the election campaign. **Benjamin Netanyahu,** the Likud leader, was confirmed as the winner by the narrowest of margins. Netanyahu won over **Prime Minister Shimon Peres** of the Labor party by 29,457 votes: 1,501,023 to 1,471,566 [*Financial Times*, 5/28/96; *New York Times*, 6/1/96]. At 46, Netanyahu will be Israel's youngest Prime Minister. The introduction of a new voting system, under which Israelis voted separately for Prime Minister and for Parliament, was aimed at strengthening the office of the Prime Minister and at bringing an end to the multiplicity of parties. In fact, it did just the opposite: It has weakened that office and strengthened the small parties.

The election results guaranteed that **the new Prime Minister will have to rely on religious and immigrant parties to form a coalition,** giving them a strong influence in national and international affairs [*New York Times,* 6/1/96].

The **Clinton administration pledged its continued support to the Israeli people.** President Clinton said he hoped the Middle East peace process could be maintained, and he invited Netanyahu to come to Washington soon after forming his government. The administration will let him know what in its view is feasible in the peace process. At the same time, the administration **urged Arab leaders not to prejudge the new government** [*New York Times,* 5/31/96; Federal Press Service, 5/31/96]. Several administration officials conceded that, if Netanyahu remains true to his campaign promises, **he could jeopardize progress** toward the peace arrangements that the White House favors. One official cited Netanyahu's pledge not to withdrew Israeli forces from Hebron and not to cede the Golan Heights to Syria. Netanyahu has also declared his opposition to an independent Palestinian state.

It is difficult to conceive how Netanyahu would negotiate with Syria without making territorial concessions [*New York Times,* 5/31/96]. The Palestinian leadership urged him to respect all previous arrangements, and the **Arab League** voiced concern that the Likud victory will cause serious problems for the peace process [ibid., 6/1/96].

Prior to Netanyahu's first official visit to Washington in July to meet with President Clinton, Secretary of State Christopher met with Israel's newly elected Prime Minister in Jerusalem. Christopher then flew to Cairo for talks with President Mubarak and Yasser Arafat. Christopher's visit did little to assuage Arab apprehension at Netanyahu's refusal to accept the land-for-peace formula underwritten by the international community since the 1967 Six-Day War [*Al-Ahram Weekly,* 6/27–7/3/96; *Financial Times,* 6/26/96].

6. The Former Soviet Union
By Erika H. Burk

Tajikistan

Three years after the end of all-out fighting in Tajikistan's civil war, ongoing military operations and other violations of the cease-fire continue to cast doubt on the two sides' commitment to an effective cease-fire. And even after considerable rounds of negotiations, most under U.N. auspices, they have failed to resolve fundamental political differences.

At the outbreak of the civil war in 1992, the hard-line ex-Communist regime was opposed by a loose coalition of radical, liberal Islamic, and regional clan-based groups. By 1994 the groups had coalesced into an opposition force capable of coordinating armed actions and presenting a united position at talks and consultations with the government. By this time too the Tajik opposition had formed ties with militant Islamic groups in Iran and Afghanistan and was receiving military and political support from them.

A **peacekeeping force under the auspices of the Commonwealth of Independent States (CIS)** has been **stationed along Tajikistan's 1,200-kilometer border with Afghanistan** since October 1992, but by 1994 the war had begun to affect directly the security interests of Pakistan, Iran, Afghanistan, and Russia as well as Tajikistan's Central Asian neighbors. The outflow of refugees into neighboring countries and the destabilizing fighting on the Russian-guarded CIS border served as the catalyst for a meeting in Moscow of all the parties to the dispute in the summer of 1994, with full support from the United Nations.

A second round of talks, in Teheran, yielded the **Agreement on a Temporary Cease-fire and the Cessation of Other Hostile Acts on the Tajik-Afghan Border and Within the Country for the Duration of the Talks (the "Teheran Agreement")** [S/1994/1102, Annex I, 9/27/94], which continues to serve as the basis for talks. Security Council Resolution 968 [12/16/94] established a **U.N. Mission of Observers in Tajikistan (UNMOT)** to assist the Joint Commission (composed of representatives of both parties) in implementing the cease-fire; investigate reports of cease-fire violations and report them to the U.N. and Joint Commission; and keep in close contact with parties to the conflict, the Mission of the Conference on (now the Organization for) Security and Cooperation in Europe, the CIS peacekeepers, and the Russian border forces. The Security Council also "acknowledged positively"—but did not authorize—the CIS peace-keepers.

At the third round of inter-Tajik talks (Islamabad, October 20–November 1, 1994) the parties agreed to extend the Teheran Agreement until February 6, 1995. Despite an escalation in the fighting at the Afghan border between the Tajik Islamic opposition and Russian border guards during the spring of 1995, the cease-fire was extended again, until mid-August 1995.

A fourth round of inter-Tajik talks was held in Almaty, Kazakhstan, May 22–June 1, 1995, but continued tension along the Tajik-Afghan border and inside Tajikistan, and the unwillingness of the negotiating parties to address their basic political differences, brought only stalemate [S/1995/799, 9/16/95].

From August 2 to 17, in an effort to break the deadlock, the U.N. Secretary-General's Special Envoy, Ramiro Piriz-Ballon, shuttled four times between Tajik President Emomali Rakhmonov in Tajikistan's capital of Dushanbe and Tajik opposition leader Abdullo Nuri in Kabul [ibid.].

These indirect talks concluded with the signing of a **Protocol** on the fundamental principles for establishing peace and national accord in Tajikistan [S/1995/720, Annex, 8/17/95].

Parties to the Protocol agreed on the substance of forthcoming negotiations and expressed their willingness to modify the format of the inter-Tajik negotiations so as to conduct a continuous round beginning September 18. Still unresolved was the issue of venue, and they left to the Special Envoy the problem of resolving it. The Tajik government was insisting that the talks be held at Ashkhabad, Turkmenistan, while the opposition was equally adamant about Teheran, Vienna, or Almaty. And there matters stood until late October, when the U.N. Secretary-General broached the subject to President Rakhmonov and other heads of state who were attending the General Assembly. Shortly thereafter the government of Turkmenistan invited the Tajik opposition to visit Ashkhabad for a series of discussions on the venue question, which led to an agreement in principle on Ashkhabad as the meeting place for the inter-Tajik talks [S/1995/1024, 12/8/95].

The delay in resuming negotiations was accompanied by an increase in hostilities on the ground. Each side accused the other of violating the Teheran Agreement—the government citing the deployment of opposition fighters in the Garm, Tavildara, and Gorny Badakhshan regions and the opposition citing the deployment of government troops in Garm and Tavildara—and there were more frequent exchanges of fire between the Russian border forces and the "Self-Defense Forces" (SDF) of the Islamic opposition. SDF threatened to take action against the Russian border forces for alleged harassment of civilians at checkpoints. On October 21 an SDF fighter was killed by Russian border forces at a checkpoint near Buni [ibid.].

UNMOT and the Joint Commission of the Tajik parties continued to investigate complaints by both sides. Most of the government's grievances had to do with cross-border infiltration by opposition fighters and the fighters' movements within Tajikistan. The opposition, for its part, charged that the government was detaining people without charge and maltreating them in detention. From time to time the Russian border forces fired shells or rockets at the Islamic opposition's camps inside Afghanistan—with the intention, they said, of deterring opposition fighters or smugglers from crossing into Tajikistan. On two distinct occasions the Russian border forces in the Moskovskiy district themselves were attacked by rocket fire from Afghan territory, and there were casualties. In an effort to stabilize the situation, UNMOT intervened with authorities at Garm and Dushanbe, and with local leaders and opposition leaders at Taloqan on the Afghan border [S/1995/799, 9/16/95].

The **"continuous" inter-Tajik negotiations** got under way in Ashkhabad on November 30, 1995 [S/1995/1024, 12/8/95] but were immediately overshadowed by an outbreak of fighting in the area of Tavildara, 280 kilometers east of Dushanbe [S/1996/212, 3/22/96]. Although the two delegations adopted a joint declaration on December 13, 1995, deploring the serious violations of the Teheran Agreement and pledging to uphold it in the future, the fighting continued [S/1996/212, Annex I].

In Ashkhabad the two delegations discussed the central political issues for the first time, including possible methods of power-sharing. The Tajikistan government proposed a "consultative forum" and the opposition proposed a council of national reconciliation for a transition period of up to two years. Neither side liked the other's proposal [S/1996/212, 3/22/96].

The second phase of the continuous inter-Tajik talks (January 26–February 18, 1996) was also adversely affected by **widespread violence and instability** in Tajikistan. There were armed insurrections against the government in several places. In the most potentially dangerous of these situations (in Tursunzade), Tajik border guards were taken hostage. In a mutiny (in Kurgan-Tyube), the First Brigade of the Tajik Army took control of the city and subsequently began to deploy troops toward Dushanbe—coming within 15 kilometers of the capital at one point. The tense situation was defused after the government complied with a number of the insurgents' demands, eventually agreeing to replace several senior government officials and grant amnesty to the rebels [ibid.].

As this second phase of continuous talks dragged on, fighting continued between Tajik government forces and opposition fighters near Tavildara [*OMRI Daily Digest*, 2/6/96], where the forces of the two sides had been at a standoff since the opposition's capture of several villages in October 1995. Each side accused the other of initiating the violence. Only days into phase two, Tajik government representatives at the peace talks in Ashkhabad had threatened to withdraw from negotiations, citing a January 30 attack that flagrantly violated the cease-fire agreement [ibid., 2/1/96].

The murder of Mufti Fatkhulla Sharipov, the spiritual leader of Tajik Muslims, on the first day of the Muslim holy month of Ramadan in January 1996, also served to increase tensions between the two parties. Tajik President Emomali Rakhmonov blamed Islamists in Pakistan, Afghanistan, and Iran for the murder, claiming those countries were training guerrillas to "terrorize the people of Tajikistan." Opposition leader Ali Akbar Turajonzoda blamed "those who do not want peace." U.N. Special Envoy Piriz-Ballon attempted to defuse the situation, insisting that neither side's leadership was responsible for the killing [*Transition*, 2/23/96].

On February 24, the Islamic opposition's Zafar Rakhmonov, co-chairman of the Joint Commission, was kidnapped. He had been without bodyguards for some time: The security detail provided by the Tajik government for opposition members of the Joint Commission under the relevant protocol was withdrawn on February 12 and, although UNMOT launched an immediate protest, had not been replaced. Soon the four other members of the Joint Commission representing the opposition in Dushanbe left Tajikistan on security grounds [S/1996/212, 3/22/96].

Observers expected the kidnapping to derail negotiations, but the cease-fire agreement, which expired on February 26, was extended for another three months [*OMRI Daily Digest*, 2/27/96]. Even so, the violence continued. In March, for example, the Afghanistan-based opposition fired ten rockets toward the Russian border guards [ibid., 3/15/96]. U.N. Secretary-General Boutros Boutros-Ghali voiced concern over the fighting and called on both sides to comply strictly with the cease-fire agreement [ibid., 3/27/96].

Although the start of the continuous inter-Tajik negotiations at Ashkhabad back in November had raised hopes for real progress toward a general peace agreement in accordance with the August 1995 Protocol, very little headway was made. The only promising development was an agreement to hold a special session of the Tajik Parliament in which various opposition leaders would participate—a potential turning point in the process of national reconciliation. The session did take place on March 11, 1996, but without members of the opposition, who were concerned about security [S/1996/212, 3/22/96].

Despite the apparent readiness of the Tajik government and the opposition to begin a new round of U.N.-mediated peace talks in mid-April 1996, the Security Council had considerable cause to doubt "the parties' commitment to an effective cease-fire" [S/PRST/1996/14, 3/29/96]. In addition to evidence of ongoing military operations and other violations of the cease-fire, there were reports that UNMOT personnel had been harassed and threatened by both government personnel and opposition fighters and reports that the Afghan government had delayed efforts to establish a UNMOT liaison post at Taloqan in northern Afghanistan that was intended to enhance UNMOT's communication with the opposition [S/1996/212, 3/22/96].

Georgia

In August 1992 fighting broke out in **Abkhazia,** an autonomous republic within Georgia, and over the next year the Abkhazians—a minority in their own republic during the Soviet era—scored a number of military victories, resulting in **the republic's de facto secession.** The Abkhazians' military successes despite small numbers and limited resources were often attributed to the assistance of elements of the Russian military [see *A Global Agenda: Issues/49*, pp. 72–77].

U.N. involvement in Georgia since the outbreak of hostilities in 1992 has included a U.N. and Russian Federation-mediated cease-fire, a series of peace negotiations, and the deployment of U.N. observers and CIS (primarily Russian) peacekeeping forces. Yet two seemingly intractable problems remain: **the status of Abkhazia and Abkhaz resistance to the return of the quarter-million persons who fled Abkhazia for western Georgia** after the capture of the republic's capital, Sukhumi, in September 1993.

The Security Council established a **United Nations Observer Mission in Georgia (UNOMIG)** in August 1993 [S/Res/858, 8/24/93], and in Council resolutions subsequent to the formal signing in Moscow of the **Agreement on a Cease-Fire and Separation of Forces** between Georgia and the Abkhaz authorities (May 14, 1994), the Mission's six-month mandate was revised and expanded to include monitoring the implementation of the Moscow Agreement; observing the operation of the CIS peacekeeping force; and verifying and monitoring the security zone, the restricted weapons zone, and the area in which heavy military equipment withdrawn from the security zone was being stored. UNOMIG was also mandated to monitor the withdrawal of Georgian troops from the strategically important Kodori valley; to patrol the valley regularly; and to investigate and seek to resolve reported violations of the Agreement [S/1994/818, 7/12/94]. While "welcom[ing]" Russia's peacekeepers [S/1994/937, 7/21/94], the Security Council has never formally authorized their dispatch.

UNOMIG has performed the principal talks mandated by the Security Council (operating in the security zone, the restricted weapons zone, and the Kodori valley), but the situation in these areas is unsettled and remains tense. The Abkhaz authorities deployed 309 militiamen in the strategically important Gali region from November 1 to 6, 1995 (this according to a report of the Secretary-General [S/1996/5, 1/2/96], allegedly to enhance security in the period leading up to the Georgian parliamentary and presidential elections, and the local population fled the area.

CIS peacekeepers and UNOMIG began to monitor the Kodori valley closely, meeting several times each day to ensure that tensions did not increase [ibid.]. UNOMIG has been reporting increasing difficulty in carrying out its mandated inspection of the heavy weapons storage sites maintained by the government of Georgia and the Abkhaz authorities. The U.N. group continues to protest the restrictions on its activities, but efforts to carry out the duties assigned to the extent envisioned have been unsuccessful [S/1995/657, 8/7/95].

On occasion, even the freedom of movement of UNOMIG personnel has been restricted, and there have been armed robberies of U.N. military observers in the restricted weapons zone on the Abkhaz side. As the Secretary-General noted to the Security Council: "The **pervasive lawlessness** in the security and restricted weapons zone in Abkhazia, which the authorities allege they are unable to control, has a negative effect on the Mission's ability to meet its mandated tasks" [S/1995/937, 11/8/95].

By November 1995, UNOMIG's on-the-ground operations were revised to allow more military observers to be positioned permanently in the security zone and to redeploy military operations staff from Pitsunda to Sukhumi. The effect was to increase the flexibility of the mission and strengthen its capacity for launching specific operations in response to a particular threat or situation [A/50/731/Add.1].

Although cooperation between UNOMIG and the government of Georgia and the Abkhaz authorities has been satisfactory overall, both parties criticize the United Nations for not doing more for them. The Georgians argue that UNOMIG has failed to protect the returnees in the Gali region; the Abkhazians argue that the mission has failed to prevent armed elements from infiltrating the security zone along the Inguri River. The official response to these criticisms is that UNOMIG has neither the mandate nor the strength to do either job [S/1995/342, 5/1/95].

Under the **Quadripartite Agreement** on the voluntary return of refugees and displaced persons, signed on April 4, 1994 [S/1994/397], the government of Georgia and the Abkhaz authorities agreed to guarantee the safety of displaced persons and to protect repatriated persons, and a commission was created to facilitate this process. The Quadripartite Commission, composed of representatives of the two sides, the Russian Federation, and UNHCR and chaired by the CIS peacekeeping forces, is attended by the Chief Military Observer of UNOMIG, the Chief of Staff of the CIS peacekeeping force, and often representatives of the Gali and Zugdidi regions, local administrations, and militia or police chiefs. Although both sides continue to endorse it at least rhetorically—and the Commission still meets regularly to discuss issues of general security, criminal investigations, hostage exchanges, and humanitarian issues—the estimated 250,000 refugees have not yet been able to return to Abkhazia from Georgia because neither side is able to guarantee their safety.

Indeed, in August 1995 and for some months thereafter, UNHCR discontinued its monitoring of an area of the Gali district outside the security zone after members of the Abkhaz militia fired bullets into a UNHCR vehicle. The agency resumed monitoring in that area in December 1995, in close cooperation with UNOMIG patrols [S/1996/5, 1/2/96].

Expectations of the return of large numbers of refugees to the Gali region increased substantially in May and July 1995 after statements by Georgian politicians in Tbilisi and western Georgia encouraging mass repatriation. The Abkhaz side's policy has been to allow the return of only 200 people per week, and the Abkhazians responded with hostility to the idea of a far larger group. In early July the Commander of the CIS peacekeeping force countered by announcing that a mass return of refugees would be protected by his forces. The Abkhaz side promptly threatened to resume the conflict [S/1995/657, 8/7/95].

In May 1995, in the midst of these verbal sallies, the Quadripartite Commission met again, in Moscow, to explore the possibility of resuming the full-fledged voluntary repatriation program under UNHCR auspices. Soon after that meeting the Abkhaz authorities announced that Abkhazia would begin its own repatriation program—based on the offer of 200 returnees per week—and would register all inhabitants of the Gali district. The Abkhaz authorities said that they expected full participation of UNHCR in the exercise.

UNHCR responded that it was unable to participate in such an exercise because, under the Quadripartite Agreement, the registration of spontaneous returnees was directly linked with, and complementary to, the simultaneous official voluntary repatriation process—which had been stopped. Moreover, the purpose of any such registration, UNHCR argued, should be to extend international protection to those who return spontaneously. Since the existing security situation prohibited UNHCR from providing such protection, it could not become involved. As of spring 1996, UNHCR continued to monitor the situation of returnees and of the local population to the best of its ability, given its limited resources and the difficulties arising from interventions by armed Abkhaz militia [ibid.].

At the request of the Secretary-General, the U.N. High Commissioner for Human Rights sent a senior **human rights** officer to Georgia in the summer of 1995 to explore the possibility of establishing a human rights monitoring mission there. At meetings with the human rights officer during his week-long stay, June 24–July 2, the Georgian government emphasized the human rights problems in the Gali region, including the lack of security for the local population and the snail-like pace of refugee return. The Georgians blamed both problems on the Abkhaz authorities. Abkhaz President Vladislav Ardzinba blamed the human rights violations on bandits and/or Georgian agents. Although Ardzinba offered to cooperate with any future human rights mission and to allow periodic visits by human rights monitors, he strongly objected to a proposed joint mission by the United Nations and the OSCE in Gali.

In a report to the Security Council following the visit of the human rights officer, the Secretary-General argued that the establishment of a joint U.N./OSCE mission would be important for regional stability overall, given its potential for reducing the tensions arising from unsubstantiated accusations of human rights abuses by each side, which have had the practical effect of impeding the return of the refugees [ibid.]. The Security Council "support[ed]" the Secretary-General's efforts to establish a human rights-monitoring mission in the area and "encourag[ed]" him to continue his consultations with the parties to this end [S/PRST/1995/39, 8/18/95].

On October 1, 1995, the Secretary-General appointed Liviu Bota as **Deputy to Special Envoy** Edouard Brunner. Bota, who was asked to live in the area so as to provide a continuous U.N. presence at a senior political level, serves as head of the UNOMIG Mission and is mandated to work with Brunner to find and implement a comprehensive settlement based on three elements defined by the Security Council: the safe and early return of the refugees and displaced persons, maintenance of the territorial integrity of the Republic of Georgia, and the creation of a special status for Abkhazia [ibid.].

During Russian-led negotiations chaired by Deputy Prime Minister A. A. Bolshakov in Moscow, October 20–25, 1995, Russia proposed that discussions resume on the basis of a draft protocol offered by Moscow [S/1995/937, 11/8/95]. This draft built on elements derived from earlier negotiations and sought to identify an acceptable status for Abkhazia within the borders of the former Georgian Soviet Socialist Republic. Its terms included the identification of the competences of the federal authorities, the establishment of a federal legislative body, the treatment by that body of questions directly affecting Abkhaz interests, and issues concerning the return of refugees and displaced persons [S/1995/657, 8/7/95]. The Abkhazians would not agree to the draft protocol as a basis for negotiation and set their own terms for the resumption of talks: Russia's willingness to lift the naval blockade of Sukhumi, the Abkhazian capital. The two sides could agree only on one thing: to meet again under Russian Federation auspices. A new round of Moscow-led talks began in early November 1995 [S/1995/937, 11/8/95].

Throughout the fall of 1995, Georgian President Eduard Shevardnadze had pressed the CIS to give the CIS peacekeepers **"police functions,"** the better to protect the Georgian population against possible reprisals by Abkhaz militia. Although this proposal was on the agenda of the CIS Heads of State at their January 1996 summit, no decision was taken on it. The issue was raised again, and rejected, at the meeting of CIS Defense Ministers in Moscow on March 27. At that time, representatives of the Russian Foreign Ministry argued that only the United Nations was empowered to give peacekeeping forces a mandate for "peace enforcement" [Liz Fuller, "The Vagaries of Russia's Abkhaz Policy," Open Media Research Institute Analytical Brief, 3/29/96].

At the summit of CIS Heads of State, Shevardnadze had also sought to **expand the peacekeepers' territorial mandate,** arguing for their deployment throughout the whole territory of Abkhazia, not just the Gali district. Abkhazian President Ardzinba rejected this proposal out of hand, stating that the only basis for continued talks should be the "declaration on measures for a political settlement of the conflict" and the Quadripartite Agreement signed in 1994. He went on to say that only a union agreement between Georgia and Abkhazia, in which both sides enjoy equal rights, would offer a guarantee against the renewal of hostilities [S/1996/5, 1/2/96].

The Georgian parliament continued to push the issue, angering the

Abkhazians. On April 17, 1996, it adopted a resolution calling for the withdrawal of the Russian peacekeeping forces from the border between Abkhazia and the rest of Georgia unless the mandate of these forces was expanded in such way that they could protect ethnic Georgian refugees wishing to return home [*OMRI Daily Digest*, 4/18/96].

The sole promising development appears to be Abkhazia's willingness to create a federal union of Georgia and Abkhazia, reported in the Russian media in February 1996. According to the personal envoy of Abkhaz leader Ardzinba, the proposed union would contain elements of both a federation and a confederation. Previously, Abkhazia had rejected any Georgian proposals that Abkhazia become a federal unit within Georgia, arguing instead for a confederation [ibid., 2/15/96].

By January 1996 the U.N. Security Council appeared to be losing patience with the Abkhaz authorities. In that month it called upon the parties, "in particular the Abkhaz side," to make progress toward a comprehensive political settlement [S/Res/1036, 1/12/96]. It went on to demand that "the Abkhaz side accelerate significantly the process of voluntary return of refugees and displaced persons by accepting a timetable on the basis of that proposed by the UNHCR." UNOMIG's mandate was extended until July 12, 1996, subject to review if any changes were made in the mandate of the CIS peacekeeping forces [ibid.].

Armenia and Azerbaijan

Tensions between the Azerbaijan government and the populations of the **predominantly ethnic Armenian enclave of Nagorno Karabakh** erupted into war in 1988 when residents of the enclave sought to unite with Armenia, which supported their efforts with money and arms. An upsurge in fighting in April 1994 resulted in intensified peace efforts on the part of the mediators, the **Minsk Group of the Organization for Security and Cooperation in Europe** (Germany, the United States, Belarus, France, Italy, Sweden, the Czech Republic, and the Russian Federation). The **cease-fire brokered by the Minsk Group in May 1994 has largely held** [for more detail, see *A Global Agenda: Issues/50*, pp. 77–79].

But resolution of the **status of the enclave** itself is proving elusive. Nagorno Karabakh remains Azerbaijan territory on paper, and Azerbaijan President Heydar Aliyev has ruled out the possibility of granting Nagorno Karabakh the status of an independent state, most recently during his meetings with the Minsk Co-Chair in April 1996 [*Periscope Daily Defense News Capsules*, 4/11/96]. However, **Armenia controls one-fifth of Azerbaijan territory,** including a strategic highway that crosses the occupied territory and effectively links Nagorno Karabakh with Armenia proper [United Press International, 3/14/96].

In the months since summer 1995 the Russian Federation and the

OSCE Minsk Group have intensified their efforts to bring about a peace agreement, working through regular rounds of talks focused on the disputed region's status and security. Despite the slow pace of negotiations, these talks have brought about two firsts: On December 19, 1995 (in The Hague), Armenia and Azerbaijan held their first bilateral talks on the status of Nagorno Karabakh [BBC Summary of World Broadcasts, 12/21/95]. And at the end of March 1996, the Minsk Group held its own first meeting with Azeri who still live in or have fled the disputed enclave itself.

Some experts say that the Russian involvement in mediation efforts and willingness to send peacekeepers to the enclave is seen by Moscow as a means of exerting pressure on Azerbaijan. Relations between the two countries were damaged in 1994 when Azerbaijan signed with an international consortium the **"contract of the century"**—worth $8 billion—for the extraction of the estimated 40 billion to 200 billion barrels of oil under the Caspian Sea. Oil could also be a major factor in the high-level efforts at shuttle diplomacy by the United States in mid-March 1996: U.S. firms have a strong interest in securing a clear export route for the Caspian Sea oil. The only alternative is the Russian pipeline that crosses war-torn Chechnya and is subject to Moscow's decisions on transit fees [United Press International, 3/14/96].

Clearly, the **OSCE has taken the lead in negotiations** between the parties; U.N. involvement is limited. And, indeed, Secretariat officials have made it clear that this situation remains unchanged, despite the fact that Under-Secretary-General Aldo Ajello has participated in many of the OSCE Minsk Group meetings, and carried out a good-will mission to Nagorno Karabakh in September 1995, meeting with senior-level officials in Azerbaijan's capital, Baku, and in Armenia's, Yerevan. At a press conference in Yerevan at the time, U.N. officials emphasized that Ajello's mission did not signal the opening of a new forum for negotiations but was undertaken simply to indicate the "active interest" of the Secretary-General in a rapid and peaceful settlement and to affirm the "full support" of the world organization for the mediation efforts of the OSCE Minsk Group [*Armenian Reporter*, 9/30/95].

Direct U.N. involvement in Armenia and Azerbaijan has been limited to addressing the **humanitarian needs of refugees and internally displaced persons** affected by or recovering from the conflict. On February 20, 1996, the United Nations issued a supplementary appeal for $37 million to cover the costs of humanitarian operations in Armenia, Azerbaijan, and Georgia over the first five months of 1996. The added funds are intended to support projects undertaken by eight U.N. agencies, the International Organization for Migration, and nongovernmental organizations in the humanitarian field. These and other U.N. agencies have been assisting more than 900,000 people in the Caucasus in communities still affected by or recovering from armed conflict, including 250,000 in Armenia (150,000 displaced); 405,000 in Azerbaijan (346,000 displaced); and 250,000 in Georgia (150,000 displaced and their host families).

It is clear that until there is movement on political fronts, there will be no significant reduction in the number of displaced persons dependent on humanitarian assistance [U.N. press release IHA/588, 2/21/96].

Chechnya

Notable for its absence is any Security Council resolution condemning or taking measures to mediate differences between Russia and the self-declared "independent" Republic of Chechnya in the Caucasus—the newest civil war in the former Soviet Union. As a permanent member of the Security Council, Russia has been able to ensure the Council's silence on this conflict, which has already claimed nearly 30,000 lives and created close to half-a-million refugees—about one-third of the prewar population [*OMRI Daily Digest*, 4/3/96]. The only U.N. discussion of the subject took place at the 52nd session (spring 1996) of the intergovernmental Commission on Human Rights, whose members had in hand a report by the Secretary-General on the human rights situation in the republic [E/CN.4/1996/13]. This report, requested by the Commission on Human Rights during its 51st session [E/1995/23-E/CN.4/1995/176], highlighted the excessive use of force by federal troops in Chechnya. A Russian Foreign Ministry spokesman pronounced the report "incorrect" [*OMRI Daily Digest*, 4/5/96].

7. Cambodia
By Frederick Z. Brown

October 23, 1996, is an auspicious date—the fifth anniversary of the signing in Paris of the **Agreements on a Comprehensive Political Settlement of the Cambodia Conflict** ("Paris Agreements"). And it will have been three years since the stand-down of the **United Nations Transitional Authority in Cambodia (UNTAC),** the peacekeeping organization the international community commissioned to guide that country in the post-settlement period [U.N. Department of Public Information DP/1180-92077, 1/92]. The Paris Agreements called for one of the most complex peacekeeping exercises ever undertaken by the United Nations, and UNTAC was by all odds the most ambitious peacekeeping operation in history. At $1.9 billion, it was also the most expensive. Much has happened in Cambodia over the past half-decade to justify this vast expenditure of money, not to mention the commitment of the U.N.'s prestige. Yet there is also ample reason to be critical of the results to date in terms of the Paris Agreement's mandate regarding political pluralism and respect for human rights.

Optimists will argue that in Phnom Penh and the more secure rural areas, mainly in the southeast of the country, Cambodia's economic rebirth is moving slowly but steadily ahead. There is a fractious press and many indigenous nongovernmental organizations active in community development, education, human rights advocacy, and other activities indicative of a nascent civil society. Pessimists will argue, however, that any gains achieved since 1993 are fragile at best. They cite rampant corruption at the highest levels of the **Royal Cambodian Government (RCG)**, the megadeals in logging and gambling contracts struck by the two Prime Ministers, and the relatively small benefits that have trickled down to rural villages from the comparative glitter of Phnom Penh. They point as well to the personal animosity between **First Prime Minister Norodom Ranariddh** and **Second Prime Minister Hun Sen** and their major disagreements on policy—a situation that could destroy the coalition brokered in 1993, with serious economic consequences. Many critics would claim that it is guns and gold, not laws, that rule Cambodia today.

On the **military** side, Phnom Penh's dry-season offensive against the **Khmer Rouge** failed to capture the areas where the rebels are based—another source of rancor between Ranariddh and Hun Sen. Weakened by defections, the Khmer Rouge are no longer judged to be a direct threat to the central government, but they are biding their time, hoping that rifts within the ruling coalition and rural impoverishment will give them another shot at power. And with a small but disciplined guerrilla force, they continue to hamper reconstruction efforts in the northwestern provinces.

Economic Development

With the Cold War ended, the strategic interests of the five permanent members of the U.N. Security Council are no longer deeply engaged in the country. Today's "interested parties" are the dozens of U.N. agencies, international financial institutions, foreign nongovernmental organizations, and private voluntary organizations that are conducting programs in Cambodia—in effect extending the U.N.'s 1991–93 peacekeeping mission. It is the international donor community, not the RCG, that now provides the essential resources for Cambodia's rebirth.

Cambodia's **macroeconomic situation** has improved. A lively, embryonic private commercial sector is being nurtured by a small middle class. According to the Finance Minister and Senior Minister in charge of Rehabilitation, Keat Chhon, Cambodia's Gross Domestic Product (GDP) rose 7.6 percent in 1995, to $287 per capita. Inflation was held to 3.5 percent, and the Cambodian riel held steady in the range of 2,300–2,600 to the U.S. dollar. Foreign direct investment commitments increased to a total of $2.3 billion, of which $587 million has actually been invested [*Phnom Penh Post*, 5/17–30/96]. The above figures, however, may present a misleading picture. GDP per capita figures include Phnom Penh's relatively high incomes and thus do not adequately reflect the still-depressed conditions in rural areas, which are home to 85 percent of the population. (The World Bank estimates that well over 50 percent of Cambodians live beneath the U.N.'s poverty level.) Moreover, the GDP growth starts from a base of zero or minus growth in the 1991–93 period. Inflation has been kept in check through strong pump-priming by the World Bank and International Monetary Fund.

At the **World Bank-IMF Consultative Group (C.G.)** meeting in Tokyo, July 11–12, 1995, the RCG requested pledges of $1.6 billion for a three-year development plan ($700 million of this amount would consist of pledges made in previous years but not spent). The C.G. replaces the **International Committee on the Reconstruction of Cambodia (ICORC)** format through which donors made their pledges in the 1992–95 period; a final ICORC meeting is planned for 1997, probably in Phnom Penh.

At the heart of the C.G.'s dealing with the RCG will be the manner in which **income from logging exports is to be accounted for and utilized.** Until full transparency and accountability are brought to the handling of receipts from Cambodia's prime natural resource, it is unlikely that international donors will be inclined to continue their financial support for the RCG [ibid.; and *Far Eastern Economic Review*, 3/23/95]. Similarly, donors will be reluctant to continue funding unless doubts are resolved regarding Cambodia's alleged role as a transit corridor for the illegal international narcotics trade and as a locus of large-scale money laundering for narcotics traffickers and Asian criminal syndicates [*Far Eastern Economic Review*, 11/23/95].

Domestic Politics

For the donor community, Cambodia is still a problematic political environment in which to operate. Bitter infighting among the RCG's top leadership threatens to undo whatever modest gains have been made in developing the economy since 1993. Political "stability"—however the term is defined—has come at a high price and could be short-lived. The country's new and fragile democratic institutions, protected in theory by the 1993 Constitution, have been restricted in practice. The National Assembly, which in 1993 was seen as the fundament of civil society, has been rendered all but powerless. The **Cambodian People's Party (CPP)** under Second Prime Minister Hun Sen lost the May 1993 election but continues to dominate the coalition with the party that won it— **FUNCINPEC (the National Unified Front for an Independent, Peaceful, Neutral, and Cooperative Cambodia).** The CPP itself is far from united, and Hun Sen is fearful of plots to unseat him—with some justification, it might be added, given two comic opera "coup attempts" against him already [*Far Eastern Economic Review*, 9/14/95 and 2/22/96].

Meanwhile, FUNCINPEC's membership has been splintered by criticism of First Prime Minister Norodom Ranariddh and the party weakened by the controversial expulsion of former Minister of Finance Sam Rainsy in September 1994. In November 1995, FUNCINPEC Secretary-General (and Foreign Minister) Norodom Sirivudh was accused of plotting to assassinate Hun Sen, jailed, and driven into exile—all this despite the fact that Sirivudh is the half-brother of King Norodom Sihanouk. Sam Rainsy has been allowed to return to Cambodia but remains a vocal critic of the RCG, and his efforts to organize another political party—the **Khmer Nation Party (KNP)**—have been thwarted at every turn. The **Buddhist Liberal Democratic Party (BLDP),** which won ten national assembly seats in the May 1993 elections and was often allied with FUNCINPEC in the parliament, has also suffered leadership splits. Many members have defected to the CPP or FUNCINPEC or gone over to Sam Rainsy. In September 1995 the government banned BLDP's original leader, Son Sann, from holding party rallies and harassed him, often in life-threatening ways: A grenade attack on Son Sann's headquarters and a nearby temple on October 1, 1995 wounded 30 persons [*Bangkok Post*, 10/1/95].

The above are indications of human rights abuses and the continued suppression, and even murder, of public critics of the government—in short, not the kind of political climate envisioned in the 1991 Paris Agreements and the 1993 Cambodian Constitution itself, which states unequivocally that Cambodia is a "multi-party liberal democratic regime guaranteeing human rights, abiding by law" [Preamble to the Constitution; see also *A Global Agenda: Issues/50*].

Refugees

The **U.N. High Commissioner for Refugees (UNHCR)** began emergency relief activities in Cambodia in 1980. Until the 1991 Paris Agreements, UNHCR's work was confined to providing emergency assistance (domestic kits and rice to Cambodians who returned voluntarily from the Thai border camps), supporting village-level integration projects, facilitating family reunification, and protecting asylum seekers. In March 1992, UNHCR became the **Repatriation Component of UNTAC,** and by March 1993 it had managed the move of 362,000 persons from Thai camps to villages mainly in northwestern Cambodia. The Cambodian Red Cross, the World Food Programme, the United Nations Border Relief Organization, the World Health Organization, and the International Federation of Red Cross and Red Crescent Societies all participated in this massive effort under UNTAC supervision.

UNHCR administered the first phase of the Refugee Resettlement/ Rural Development Project under the auspices of the Japan International Cooperation Centre, which handed the project over to the U.N. Development Programme (UNDP) and the Cambodian government's Ministry of Rural Development in March 1994. During 1994 and 1995, UNHCR continued to monitor and provide support to vulnerable returnees in northwestern Cambodia through NGOs and RCG agencies. UNHCR also provided a reception center in Sisaphon for persons internally displaced by fighting or returning from Thailand after taking temporary refuge there when border areas became unstable.

In 1996, with the major task of repatriation completed and an urgent need for UNHCR resources elsewhere in the world, UNHCR has redirected its efforts toward its traditional International Protection mandate although continuing to serve as an advocate for the tens of thousands of vulnerable Cambodian returnees in the northwest who remain in difficult circumstances [UNHCR Cambodia statement, 12/95; and "UNHCR in Cambodia" supplement, *Phnom Penh Post*, 9/22/95].

Human Rights

The presence of the **U.N. Commission for Human Rights (UNCHR)** in Cambodia had its origins in Part III of the 1991 Paris Agreements. Part III underscored the importance of a strong human rights-monitoring capability and resulted in the establishment of the UNTAC Human Rights Component, which operated countrywide during the UNTAC years [Economic and Social Council, E/CN.4/1996/92, 2/2/96]. In early 1993, recognizing the need for continued monitoring after the departure of UNTAC, the Commission mandated a **Centre for Human Rights in Cambodia** and the General Assembly gave its endorsement [A/Res/48/154]. UNCHR's presence in Cambodia is its largest after Rwanda.

The Centre has a variety of responsibilities: assisting in legislative reform and in the administration of justice, human rights teacher training and curriculum development, and lending support to Cambodian NGOs active in the promotion of a civil society. These activities involve not only educating and training the government but also monitoring government activities in such sensitive areas as prison administration, child prostitution, corruption, and military courts and investigating charges of violations of the human rights of specific individuals. UNCHR's dual role— human rights education and technical assistance *and* documentation of human rights abuses—has often placed the Centre in an **adversarial position**. In 1994 the two Prime Ministers announced their intention to phase out the Centre completely in March 1995. Only after strong interventions by the U.N. Secretary-General and concerned foreign governments was this decision reversed, and in March 1996, U.N. High Commissioner for

Human Rights José Ayala Lasso visited Phnom Penh and signed a memorandum of understanding with the government extending the Human Rights Centre's tenure in Cambodia for another two years. Expressing concern over continued human rights abuses, such as arbitrary detention and torture, Ayala Lasso noted that these were "isolated" cases and not government policy. He praised the government's "excellent cooperation" and said the new agreement would strengthen the relationship [*Phnom Penh Post*, 3/8–21/96].

The Commissioner's statements to the contrary notwithstanding, human rights violations—some, as noted, with clear political overtones—were hardly rare occurrences during 1995 and 1996. On May 18, 1996, Thun Bunly, publisher of an antigovernment newspaper, became the latest journalist to be gunned down in Phnom Penh. **The U.S. Department of State human rights report on Cambodia,** written before the political violence against the BLDP and Thun Bunly's murder, stated that "the human rights situation worsened in several respects, including tolerance for opposition views, but it continued to be better than during previous regimes." The Department noted reports of abuses, including political intimidation and instances of extrajudicial killing, and it cited "credible reports" that members of the security forces routinely beat detainees. The Department stated that "the Government lacked the resources or the political will to act aggressively against individuals, particularly members of the military, who were responsible for such abuses" [Department of State Human Rights Report, quoted in *Phnom Penh Post*, 3/22–4/4/96].

Future Elections

Cambodia in 1996 presents the classic example of the glass that is half-full or half-empty, depending on one's perspective. In some important respects, the Royal Cambodian Government created in September 1993 has disappointed both the Cambodian people and their international supporters. Yet the past five years have indeed seen the establishment of a government that, for all its many faults, is growing in its capabilities to administer the country and the emergence of an economy that, though still weak, appears to be staggering in the right direction. And unquestionably Cambodia has come a long way from the barbarity of the Khmer Rouge regime and the civil wars of the pre-1991 era.

The critical events to come are the **1997 elections for leaders at the commune level,** and the **1998 elections for the National Assembly** that will determine which party, or parties, control the government. There are a number of questions that the RCG must address: Will the election law now being drafted (with advice from several quarters in the international community) contain adequate legal and practical measures for fair, free, and open elections? Will the CPP in fact allow FUNCINPEC and the

BLDP to campaign throughout the country? Will Sam Rainsy's party be permitted to organize and run? Will Cambodian NGOs interested in human rights and in election-monitoring activities be permitted to play significant roles in these areas? For the international community, and specifically the United Nations, there are two key questions regarding conditionality: Will the nations that created the Paris Agreements insist upon a strong, countrywide international monitoring presence during the 1997 and 1998 elections? And will the international community put up the substantial funding that is necessary to carry out such a mission?

II
Arms Control and Disarmament
By Kathryn R. Schultz and David Isenberg

In May 1995 the signatories to the nuclear Non-Proliferation Treaty (NPT) agreed to extend the treaty indefinitely. In the year that followed, the U.N. General Assembly and the Conference on Disarmament (C.D.) became the forums for addressing the question of whether the declared nuclear weapons states were complying with the "Principles and Objectives for Nuclear Non-Proliferation and Disarmament" that these states also agreed to at the 1995 NPT Review and Extension Conference. The threats posed by landmines, the flow of small arms, and the proliferation of chemical and biological weapons capabilities were of continuing concern in the United Nations and C.D. as well.

The 50th General Assembly was marked by remembrances of Hiroshima and Nagasaki and by the growing influence of the Non-Aligned Movement (NAM), proponents of the elimination of nuclear weapons, and advocates of a Code of Conduct for arms sales. It was a year in which new nuclear weapon-free zones were created in Africa and Southeast Asia, the nuclear weapons states continued to eliminate nuclear weapons under the START Treaty, North Korea signed a legally binding agreement that will help ensure it will not develop nuclear weapons, and the number of nations submitting data for the U.N. Register of Conventional Arms rose yet again.

It was also a year that saw continued Chinese nuclear testing; resumed French testing; a lack of commitment by weapons states to making deeper reductions in nuclear stockpiles, let alone eliminate such weapons entirely; increasing concern about the spread of weapons of mass destruction; and the continued sales of large numbers of conventional weapons around the world.

The 51st Session will undoubtedly continue to focus on the nuclear weapons states' progress, or lack thereof, toward keeping the three promises they made at the NPT Review Conference: a comprehensive nuclear test-ban treaty (CTBT) by the end of 1996, a ban on the production of fissile materials for weapons purposes, and the "determined pursuit" of the elimination of nuclear weapons. It may well be a year that tests the mettle of the NAM as well as the intentions of the nuclear weapons states.

1. Nuclear Proliferation

Substantial progress has been made in the creation and expansion of nuclear weapon-free zones (NWFZs) in the months since the opening of the 50th General Assembly. On December 15, 1995, after 24 years of work on a blueprint, leaders of the seven ASEAN nations (Brunei, Indonesia, Malaysia, Philippines, Singapore, Thailand, and Vietnam), plus Cambodia, Laos, and Myanmar, officially established the **South East Asia Nuclear Weapon-Free Zone (SEANWFZ).** The Treaty was hailed by Philippines President Fidel Ramos as "ASEAN's and Southeast Asia's contribution to the cause of non-proliferation of nuclear weapons and to the tranquility of our region" [*Disarmament Diplomacy*, 1/96, p. 35].

When the SEANWFZ Treaty was opened for signature in December, none of the world's declared nuclear weapons states signed the relevant Treaty Protocols promising not to test, deploy, or use nuclear weapons in the zone. The United States was concerned over the negative security assurances (NSAs) in the Protocols that would prevent it from using or threatening to use nuclear weapons not only against Treaty signatories but anywhere else in the zone [ibid.]. Concerns of other nuclear weapons states included freedom of navigation of nuclear-armed ships and submarines and "implications for the status of the disputed Spratly Islands, claimed by China and four ASEAN states" [ibid.].

The South Pacific Nuclear-Free Zone got a boost when, on March 25, 1996, the United States, France, and the United Kingdom signed the Protocols to the 1986 **Treaty of Rarotonga.** Russia and China has signed them already. Arguing against the Treaty ten years ago, James Lilley, Deputy Assistant Secretary of State for East Asian and Pacific Affairs under President Reagan, pointed to the fear that signing it would "encourage other areas to adopt similar or more strict nuclear-free zones. It would encourage people to sort of take sections of the Western world and opt out . . ." [quoted by Keith Suter in *Bulletin of the Atomic Scientists*, 3–4/96].

On April 11, 1996, representatives of 43 of Africa's 53 countries signed the **Treaty of Pelindaba** (named for the site, once at the heart of South Africa's nuclear weapons program, where a draft treaty was signed in 1995). This Treaty, initially a response to French nuclear tests in the Sahara in the 1960s, establishes Africa as the world's fifth NWFZ, after the Antarctic Treaty (1959), the Tlatelolco Treaty covering Latin America and the Caribbean (1967), the Rarotonga Treaty covering the South Pacific (1986), and the South East Asia Nuclear-Weapon Free Zone (1995). The effect of the five treaties is to turn most of the Southern Hemisphere into a zone free of nuclear weapons. None of them, however, will affect the travel of naval ships and submarines that may be carrying nuclear weapons [*Washington Post*, 4/12/96].

After much deliberation, the United States, France, China, and Britain did sign the relevant Protocols of the Pelindaba Treaty. Under these, the four nuclear weapons states provide legally binding NSAs to the effect that they will not test, use, or threaten to use a nuclear explosive device against any Treaty party or against any territory in the African zone, provided the party itself is in compliance with the Treaty [Statement by Press Secretary and accompanying White House "Fact Sheet," 4/11/96]. Careful not to "limit options available" too tightly, the United States clarified that this pledge would not apply if any of the parties used any weapon of mass destruction [White House press briefing, 4/11/96].

Unlike the other NWFZs, Africa is home to a former nuclear weapons state—South Africa. (In 1993, South Africa announced that it had built nuclear weapons but destroyed them prior to signing the Non-Proliferation Treaty in 1991.) Unique to the Treaty of Pelindaba is an article requiring the parties to declare all capabilities for manufacturing nuclear explosive devices. Such devices must be dismantled and destroyed and facilities destroyed or converted to civilian use. This article may serve as a useful precedent for the creation of nuclear weapon-free zones in the Middle East and South Asia, since they too are home to (undeclared) nuclear weapons states (Israel, India, and Pakistan).

In December 1995 the General Assembly passed, without a vote, its annual resolution urging states of the **Middle East** to declare their region a NWFZ [A/Res/50/66]. Israel's nuclear facilities, not yet placed under full-scope safeguards of the International Atomic Energy Agency (IAEA), were singled out in a different resolution [50/73; vote 56–2, with 100 abstentions], which urged all states in the Middle East that are not party to the NPT "to renounce possession of nuclear weapons and to accede to the Treaty at the earliest date" [*Disarmament Times*, 12/19/95].

Causing considerable concern in political as well as nonproliferation circles are recent U.S. intelligence reports of a contract between Beijing and Teheran to build a plant in Iran for converting milled uranium ore into gas that could be used for weapons fuel. In 1995, Washington persuaded Russia not to sell Iran gas centrifuges that could be used to enrich uranium gas for weapons, but Russia still plans to sell nuclear reactors to Iran. Both China and Russia have stated that IAEA safeguards would be applied to the output of the plant, but the United States is "convinced that Iran is using its civilian program and its NPT status as cover for nuclear weapons development," says John Holum, Director of the U.S. Arms Control and Disarmament Agency [*Washington Times*, 4/17/96].

Sanctions against Iraq that were designed to bring it into compliance with U.N. resolutions ending the Gulf War in early 1991 remain in place, although oil sanctions are being eased [*Arms Control Reporter,* 1/96, p. 453.A.3]. In a January 1996 report to the U.N. Security Council, the IAEA noted that "Iraq has developed or otherwise acquired many of the technologies required to produce deliverable nuclear weapons" but stated confidently that "adequate provisions are now in place in Iraq to detect the resurgence of a capability to produce significant quantities of nuclear-usable material." The report notes too that the "IAEA has removed from Iraq all existing research reactor fuel, and hence any in-country source of quickly available heavy enriched uranium." It goes on to caution, however, that "vigilance is necessary to prevent the direct acquisition of nuclear weapon-usable material by Iraq in view of the low signature associated with the assembly of a nuclear device." This report was the product of additional inspections in Iraq in October 1995, prompted by information gained from senior Iraqi military commander Lieutenant General Hussein Kamil, who defected in August 1995 [*Disarmament Diplomacy,* 1/96, p. 39]. The U.N. Special Commission (UNSCOM) responsible for scrapping Iraq's weapons of mass destruction notes with concern, however, that "Iraq has yet to provide sufficient evidence that it does not still possess proscribed weapons or materials related to them. . . ." In an April 1996 report to the U.N. Security Council, UNSCOM warned that "relatively minor but highly significant quantities remain unaccounted for" [quoted by Reuters, as printed in the *Baltimore Sun,* 4/12/96]. Without a clean bill from UNSCOM, the lifting of sanctions is unlikely [ibid.].

The General Assembly not only continues to push for the creation of a NWFZ in the Middle East, but also in **South Asia** [A/Res/50/67; vote 154–3–9]. Pakistan joined the majority in urging a NWFZ, while India, insisting that nuclear weapons issues be handled globally, voted against the measure. Although there is little reason to expect a South Asia nuclear weapon-free zone anytime soon, both India and Pakistan held bilateral talks with the United States on the subject of nuclear weapons and regional tensions in 1995 [*Arms Control Reporter,* 1/96, p. 454.A.1].

Talks between the United States and Pakistan eventually resulted in the release of $368 million in **arms to Pakistan,** which Congress had held up because of Islamabad's nuclear weapons program [ibid., 1/96, p. 454.B.215; and 2/96, p. 454.B.220]. A month later, in February 1996, the U.S. Central Intelligence Agency reported that China had exported 5,000 ring magnets for use in gas-enrichment centrifuges to Pakistan in 1995. According to *Nucleonics Week,* these ring magnets would allow Pakistan to double its capacity to enrich uranium, thereby assisting its nuclear weapons program [cited in ibid., 2/96, p. 454.B.220]. The Clinton administration responded by holding up the arms transfer, pending review. In April, President Clinton approved the delivery. As Deputy Secretary of State Strobe Talbott explained the administration's thinking, the delivery of the military equipment, which Pakistan paid for in the 1980s, "provides the best opportunity to engage Islamabad in our [nuclear] nonproliferation strategy and to improve cooperation with Pakistan on such vital issues as counterterrorism and counternarcotics" [*Washington Post*, 4/17/96]. The administration decided not to release the economic aid that had been authorized with the military equipment, however, citing concerns raised by the Chinese exports [ibid.].

In late 1995 the United States, taking a step toward easing relations with its "oldest remaining foe," **removed North Korea from its list of rogue states** [*Journal of Commerce*, 2/2/96]. There was an immediate reason for doing so, noted former U.S. Ambassador to South Korea Donald P. Gregg: "We wouldn't conduct liaison with a pariah" [ibid.]. The "liaison" in question is the Agreed Framework of October 1994 in which North Korea agrees to freeze its nuclear weapons program in exchange for light water reactors (LWRs) and expanded engagement with the international community. Although inspectors are unsure of the fate of any plutonium separated prior to the Agreed Framework (enough for one or two nuclear weapons, by U.S. estimates), a U.S. National Security Council spokesman stated with certainty that "since the Agreed Framework has been in place, [the North Koreans] have not been able to separate one additional nanogram of plutonium" [White House Briefing on U.S.-North Korean Reactor Agreement, 12/15/95, as quoted in *Disarmament Diplomacy*, 1/96, p. 22].

On December 15, 1995, North Korea and the Korean Energy Development Organization (KEDO, formed by Japan, South Korea, and the United States the previous March) codified in a legally binding agreement the nonproliferation commitments made in the Agreed Framework. This agreement details the provision to North Korea of two LWRs and clarifies the financing arrangements. Under the agreement, KEDO will pay for the reactors, a training simulator, and infrastructural support. North Korea will pay for a new power transmission grid and a facility to process fuel rods from the new reactors. Three years after the new reactors are completed, North Korea is to begin repaying KEDO—interest-free and spread out over 17 years. In the words of the KEDO Secretary-General, U.S. chief negotiator Stephen Bosworth: "There are no winners and losers in this negotiation. Both sides have won" [*Disarmament Diplomacy*, 1/96, p. 36].

The United States is prepared to use not only diplomatic and economic means to prevent or curtail the spread of nuclear, chemical, or biological weapons but **military means** as well, said Secretary of Defense William Perry in an April 1996 report, *Proliferation: Threat and Response* [Washington, D.C.: U.S. Government Printing Office], and went on to outline them. Perry, taking up the subject again in a speech on April 18, stated that, were anyone to use a weapon of mass destruction against the United States or one of its allies, the U.S. response "would be both overwhelming and devastating." He would not rule out the use of nuclear weapons [*Washington Times*, 4/19/96].

In fact, as a part of its counterproliferation program, the United States is developing nuclear and non-nuclear earth-penetrating weapons for use against underground military facilities. The U.S. nuclear warhead under development (and expected to be completed by the end of 1996) is a modification of the B-61 nuclear bomb, for which no explosive tests were necessary [ibid.]. It will take at least two more years to field the conventional earth-penetrating warhead [ibid.]. These weapons might be used against such targets as the suspected chemical weapons facility that Libya is constructing in the side of a mountain near Tarhunah in northwestern Libya. "We could not take it out of commission using conventional weapons," explains Assistant Secretary of Defense Harold Smith [Associated Press, 4/23/96]. U.S. policy also does not preclude the use of nuclear weapons in response to an attack by chemical or biological weapons.

2. Nuclear Arms Control

The elimination of nuclear weapons was a popular theme of arms control and disarmament discussions throughout the 50th General Assembly. This was partly due to the fact that the Session coincided with the 50th anniversary of the bombings of Hiroshima and Nagasaki and also to the fact that, at the nuclear Non-Proliferation Treaty Review and Extension Conference the previous May, the nuclear powers had made a formal commitment to "the determined pursuit ... of systematic and progressive efforts to reduce nuclear weapons globally, with the ultimate goal of eliminating those weapons."

In the months following that Conference, at which the parties to the NPT also agreed to extend the Treaty indefinitely, the members of the Non-Aligned Movement (NAM) flexed their muscles at the United Nations and the Conference on Disarmament. For years these non-nuclear states have been seeking to end the five-power monopoly on nuclear weapons under international control, with the aim of eliminating nuclear weapons completely. In 1995 members of the NAM sought to obtain in the General Assembly concrete commitments by the weapons states to reduce and eliminate nuclear weapons—commitments they were unable to get at the NPT Conference. "The time has come for the entire stockpile of these deadly [nuclear weapons] to be destroyed once and for all," declared the NAM at its summit in Cartagena, Colombia, in 1995. The more than 100 heads of state in attendance went on to call for "the adoption of an action plan for the elimination of nuclear weapons within a time-bound framework" [quoted by William Epstein in *Bulletin of the Atomic Scientists*, 3–4/96].

The battle between the weapons states and the leaders of the NAM focuses on the question, **Is the pace of disarmament in keeping with commitments made under the NPT and the "Principles and Objectives**

Statement"? This battle was evidenced by two sets of sharply contrasting resolutions that the General Assembly passed under the heading "General and complete disarmament": three self-gratulatory ones, reaffirming existing commitments [50/70I, 50/70R, and 50/70C], and two calling for the "elimination of nuclear weapons within a time-bound framework" [50/70N and 50/70P].

The most strongly worded of these was Resolution 50/70P [vote 106–39–17]. Introduced by Myanmar on behalf of 34 members of the NAM, it calls for the nuclear weapons states "to stop immediately the qualitative improvement, development, stockpiling, and production of nuclear warheads and their delivery systems, . . . to undertake step-by-step reduction of the nuclear threat and a phased programme of progressive and balanced deep reductions of nuclear weapons, and to carry out effective nuclear disarmament measures with a view to the total elimination of these weapons within a time-bound framework." It also calls upon the Geneva-based Conference on Disarmament—the principal body for negotiating international disarmament agreements—to establish a committee on nuclear disarmament that will "commence negotiations early in 1996 on a phased program of nuclear disarmament and for the eventual elimination of nuclear weapons within a time-bound framework." China voted in favor of the measure; France, the United Kingdom, and the United States voted against it; Russia abstained.

The non-nuclear weapon states also showed their muscle with resolutions aimed at initiating a "convention to prohibit the use or threatened use of nuclear weapons" [50/71E] and at achieving a legally binding "agreement on security assurances to non-nuclear weapon States" [50/68]. Among the weapons states, only China has agreed not to use or threaten to use nuclear weapons against any non-nuclear weapon state or nuclear weapon-free zone at any time and under any circumstances [Jozef Goldblat in *Security Dialogue*, 9/95].

In November 1995 the non-nuclear weapon states had their day in court—the **World Court**. Back in 1993, the World Health Organization had asked the International Court of Justice for an advisory opinion on the legality of the use of nuclear weapons given the health and environmental effects, and the following year the U.N. General Assembly broadened the question to include the *threatened* use of such weapons. Speaking for Egypt at the Court, Professor George Abi-Saab cited a well-known Swahili proverb: "When the elephants fight, it is the grass that suffers." The present request for an advisory opinion, he explained, reflects the desire of the "nuclear grass in the General Assembly" to clarify "the legal limits on the freedom of the elephants" [cited by John Burroughs and Jacqueline Cabasso, *Bulletin of the Atomic Scientists*, 3–4/96].

Of the 45 states that participated in the two weeks of hearings, more than two-thirds contended that nuclear weapons are instruments of mass destruction whose effects are inherently indiscriminate and uncontrollable and therefore illegal. The weapons states countered that the questions posed to the Court are too hypothetical for judicial review and that each situation must be judged separately. Mexico's Under-Secretary of Foreign Relations, Sergio González Gálvez, addressed that point. "To postpone giving a legal opinion on the threat or use of nuclear weapons until an actual case occurs is like substituting medicine with an autopsy," he said [ibid.].

Lending encouragement to those who work toward the elimination of nuclear weapons was the awarding of the **Nobel Prize for Peace** to a staunch antinuclear activist, Joseph Rotblat, and to the Pugwash Conferences on Science and World Affairs that he founded and currently directs. Professor Rotblat, a British citizen, was the only scientist to leave the Manhattan Project before the atomic bomb was finished [*Disarmament Times*, 11/10/95].

Rotblat and Ambassador Jayantha Dhanapala of Sri Lanka, who chaired the NPT Review and Extension Conference, were among the 17 individuals from 12 different nations appointed by Australian Prime Minister Paul Keating to the new **Canberra Commission on the Elimination of Nuclear Weapons.** The Commission is tasked with proposing "practical steps towards a nuclear weapon-free world, including the related problem of maintaining stability and security during the transitional period and after this goal is accomplished" [Commission press release, 1/19/96, reprinted in *Disarmament Diplomacy*, 1/96, pp. 18–19]. The Australian government intends to submit the Commission's report to the 1996 U.N. General Assembly and the Conference on Disarmament.

Although the nuclear states signaled their acceptance of "the ultimate goal of eliminating" nuclear weapons at the NPT Review Conference, a communiqué by the North Atlantic Treaty Organization (NATO) not many months later has been widely interpreted as indicating that the United States, the United Kingdom, and France do not place a high priority on achieving this goal. The November 29, 1995 communiqué, issued after the meetings of NATO's Defense Planning Committee and Nuclear Planning Group, stated that "the supreme guarantee of the security of the Allies is provided by the strategic nuclear forces of the Alliance." The document went on to "reaffirm that Alliance nuclear forces continue to play a unique and essential role in the Alliance's strategy of war prevention, while recognizing that NATO has been able to reduce its reliance on them in the new security environment" [ibid., pp. 29–30].

From all reports, the United States and the inheritors of the Soviet nuclear arsenal have already made considerable progress in implementing the **START I Treaty.** All nuclear warheads based in Kazakhstan and Belarus and more than half of the warheads in Ukraine have been returned to Russia, and the destruction of missile silos in these nations continues

[*Arms Control Today*, 11/95]. Both the United States and Russia have been removing warheads from service and destroying the means of delivering them, in accordance with the terms of the Treaty. Both nations, however, continue to add new delivery systems to their arsenals—among them, the Russian SS-25 ICBM and the U.S. Trident II nuclear submarine, the D-5 SLBM, and the B-2 bomber.

The **START II Treaty** between the United States and Russia, signed in January 1993, was ratified by the U.S. Senate on January 26, 1996. Ratification by the Russian parliament, put off until elections in June, has been complicated by plans to expand the NATO alliance and by U.S. congressional efforts to build and deploy a national missile defense system that would abrogate the 1972 Anti-Ballistic Missile (ABM) Treaty. No follow-on negotiations for deeper cuts in nuclear arsenals have been set.

In addition to "the determined pursuit" of reductions in nuclear weapons "with the ultimate goal of eliminating" them, the nuclear weapons states agreed at the NPT Conference to pursue "a non-discriminatory and universally applicable **convention banning the production of fissile material for nuclear weapons** or other nuclear explosive devices . . ." ["Principles and Objectives for Nuclear Non-Proliferation and Disarmament," 5/95]. A ban on the production of fissile materials, first proposed more than 30 years ago, was originally intended to curb the weapons programs of the nuclear states themselves. It is now widely viewed as a way to curb the *spread* of nuclear weapons.

The Conference on Disarmament began considering a ban on the production of nuclear materials in January 1994 but did not agree to the parameters of the negotiations until March 1995. The nuclear weapons states had insisted that negotiations concentrate on *future* production of fissile materials for military purposes alone, whereas many non-nuclear weapons states and the non-declared weapons states wanted to address the maintenance and management of *all existing* stockpiles of weapons-grade fissile material. Current estimates put those stockpiles at 1,100 tons of plutonium (250 tons of weapons-grade plutonium, 120 tons in separated civil stocks, and 730 tons in spent civilian fuel) and 1,740 tons of highly enriched uranium (HEU) [David Albright et al., *Plutonium and HEU 1995: World Inventory, Capabilities and Policies*, Oxford: SIPRI and Oxford University Press, 1995].

Delegates agreed to accept the mandate favored by the nuclear weapons states without precluding talks on existing stockpiles. This compromise is once again under fire by the NAM and the non-declared nuclear weapons states, many of whom hope to link the formation of an ad hoc committee for negotiating a "Fisban" with the formation of an ad hoc committee to consider the elimination of nuclear weapons themselves. Arguing against this is John Holum, Director of the U.S. Arms Control and

Disarmament Agency, who warns that linkage is "a formula for paralysis" [*Disarmament Times*, 11/10/95].

Speaking for the creation of such a committee, Arundhati Ghose of India stated that the elimination of nuclear weapons was a task "not for an esoteric club of vested interests but for the ad hoc committee on nuclear disarmament in the Conference on Disarmament" [*Disarmament Diplomacy*, 2/96, pp. 9–10]. With committees on a "Fisban" and nuclear disarmament in addition to the ad hoc nuclear test-ban committee, the C.D. would be set to consider each of the commitments made by the nuclear weapons states at the NPT Conference. Should the C.D. fail to establish the two new ad hoc committees, it will have little to do except debate how it should enlarge its membership.

In a related development, the United States and Russia agreed after two years of negotiations on "transparency measures that provide assurances that the sides are fulfilling the obligations undertaken under the HEU Agreement to transform 'megatons into megawatts' " ["U.S.-Russia Joint Statement," The White House, 4/21/96]. Under the agreement the United States is to purchase low-enriched uranium (LEU) that has been blended down from roughly 500 metric tons of HEU from dismantled Soviet warheads. The first shipment of LEU was received at the Portsmouth Gaseous Diffusion Plant (Piketon, Ohio) in June 1995. By the end of April 1996, the White House Press Secretary announced, the total LEU received by the United States "equate[d] to the blend-down of about 8.7 metric tons of HEU"— enough for more than 350 nuclear weapons ["Fact Sheet on the Joint Statement," The White House, 4/21/96].

3. Nuclear Testing

The 50th U.N. General Assembly adopted several resolutions on the subject of nuclear testing. Two of these resolutions called on the **Conference on Disarmament (C.D.)** to give a **comprehensive nuclear test-ban treaty (CTBT)** its "highest priority" [A/Res/50/65 and 50/72A]. The first of these urged the C.D. to "make every effort" to conclude such a treaty "as early as possible in 1996" (pushing up the deadline, "no later than 1996," set in the "Principles and Objectives" adopted at the NPT Review Conference). The intent was to "enable signature by the outset of the fifty-first session of the General Assembly." At the Moscow Nuclear Safety Summit on April 20, 1996, Russia and the Group of Seven industrial countries reaffirmed their commitment to sign a CTBT "by September 1996" [text of the summit statement, reprinted by Reuters, 4/20/96].

Negotiations aimed at achieving a CTBT were clouded by continued Chinese testing and resumed French testing. **China** conducted two tests in 1995—one of them not long after the NPT Review Conference itself—

and another (its 44th) on June 8, 1996. Following this last test, Beijing backed off from its earlier position that "once the treaty enters into force, China will stop its nuclear testing" [*Disarmament Times*, 10/11/95]. Beijing now stated that it would conduct one more test and "after that, China will exercise a moratorium on nuclear testing" [Stephanie Fraser, International Peace Bureau, Report 3/4, 6/15/96].

The French stopped testing in 1991, but resumed underground tests at their South Pacific Mururoa Atoll test site on September 5, 1995. They argued that an additional round of testing would give them the ability to maintain their stockpile using computer simulations and other laboratory experiments and thus (said Foreign Minister Hervé de Charette) the ability "to sign the treaty banning nuclear tests definitively" [ibid.]. The United States has offered to share computer simulation technology to help France maintain the safety and reliability of its nuclear arsenal [*Arms Control Today*, 11/95, p. 29].

Continued nuclear testing by the Chinese and renewed testing by the French sparked protests worldwide and expressions of outrage and cries of betrayal at the United Nations. New Zealand Foreign Minister Don McKinnon, speaking to this point during the General Debate in the opening weeks of the 50th Session, noted that "the cavalier disregard, and the dismissing the views of the many [as expressed at the NPT Review and Extension Conference], has led to considerable disillusionment. It will take a long time to restore that trust" [*Disarmament Times*, 10/11/95].

The Assembly's Resolution 50/70A "strongly deplore[d] all current nuclear testing," urged states to halt nuclear testing, commended the weapons states that were observing a testing moratorium, and asked them to continue until a CTBT enters into force. This resolution, which the First Committee had adopted by a vote of 95–12–45, passed the General Assembly by a vote of 85–18–43 (at the 50th Session only Resolution 50/73, urging Mideast states to declare a nuclear weapon-free zone, passed with fewer affirmative votes). Twenty-three countries changed their Yes to a No between the Committee balloting and the Assembly vote, in part due to intense lobbying by France and its announcement that the tests would end by February rather than May, as previously indicated [ibid., 12/19/95].

The French conducted their sixth and final test in the series on January 27, 1996. The French and Chinese tests bring the number of known nuclear tests worldwide, as of July 1, 1996, to 2,045 (not including the two combat uses of nuclear weapons) [*Disarmament Diplomacy*, 2/96, p. 29; and *Bulletin of the Atomic Scientists*, 5–6/96, p. 62].

It was also early in the new year that U.S. intelligence agencies "picked up some information" indicating a possible **Russian nuclear test** in mid-January. The Norwegian government said there was no evidence of such a test and, indeed, that the Russians could not have conducted one at Novaya Zemlya without Norway detecting it. Scientists at the Norwegian Radiation Safety Institute and Norwegian Seismological Service confirmed the lack of evidence [*Arms Control Reporter,* 3/96, p. 608.B.403–4; *ITAR-TASS,* 3/9/96, excerpted in *OMRI Daily Digest,* 3/9/96].

In late 1995, U.S. spy satellites did record scientific and technical activities at the Pokaran test site in the Rajasthan desert of **India,** leading many to believe that India might be preparing for its second nuclear test. India denied this, asserting that its nuclear program was strictly for peaceful purposes. Pakistan reportedly substantiated U.S. intelligence with its own intelligence reports [*Arms Control Reporter,* 1/96, p. 454.B.216, and 3/96, p. 608.B.398; and Aroosa Alam in *The Muslim* (Islamabad), 2/19/96, as printed in *FBIS-NES,* 2/20/96].

Pakistan's Prime Minister Benazir Bhutto asserted that "India must be restrained if the subcontinent is to be saved" [*London Daily Telegraph,* 1/6/96, as reprinted in *FBIS-NES,* 1/11/96], and there were warnings that the country would take "appropriate measures" if nuclear-capable missiles were deployed along Pakistan's borders [Amb. Munir Akram, quoted by Agence France Presse, 1/23/96]. In the event of an Indian test, the United States would activate the 1994 Glenn Amendment, cutting off all economic and military aid, credits, bank loans, and export licenses [*Disarmament Diplomacy,* 2/96, p. 37].

Continued Chinese testing, resumed French testing, and suspected tests by others were not the only issues preventing the successful conclusion of a complete ban on the testing of nuclear explosives. In order to present a CTBT to the United Nations at the opening of the 51st Session, negotiators determined that the C.D. would have to complete the treaty by the close of the C.D. session on June 28. At the conclusion of the session, Ambassador Jaap Ramaker, the chairman of the CTBT talks, set down a complete treaty text for delegations to take back to their capitals for approval, with the hope that the treaty would be approved promptly when the C.D. reconvened on July 29. Sharp disagreements over matters related to entry into force, the treaty's scope, and linkage of a CTBT with a timetable for nuclear disarmament were responsible for hampering the successful conclusion of a treaty in June.

Central to the debate regarding **entry into force** is how to ensure participation by the five nuclear weapons states and the three de facto nuclear weapons states (Israel, India, and Pakistan) without giving them veto power. While some insist that all of the declared and undeclared nuclear weapons states sign on to a CTBT before it enters into force, others argue that this would give India (which has threatened to boycott the CTBT unless it limits nuclear weapons research and sets a schedule for nuclear disarmament) the ability, in essence, to veto the treaty. To avoid this scenario, many CTBT supporters are pushing for a treaty provision that establishes an as-yet-undetermined number of states to sign on to the treaty in order for it to enter into force. [*Washington Post,* 6/21/96].

Negotiators successfully cleared one of the hurdles regarding the scope of a CTBT when France (August 10, 1995), the United States (August 11), and the United Kingdom (September 14) abandoned their insistence that small hydronuclear tests be allowed under such a treaty. At the Moscow Nuclear Safety Summit in April 1996, Russia reaffirmed its prior commitment (October 23, 1995) to a ban on all nuclear tests, regardless of their yield [*Arms Control Reporter*, 1/96, p. 608.A.3; Alastair Macdonald for *Reuters*, 4/19/96].

No sooner had everyone welcomed the **"zero-yield"** breakthrough than the U.S. Department of Energy announced its intention to conduct six **subcritical nuclear tests** to "ensure the safety and reliability of the U.S. nuclear arsenal." These tests would be conducted at the underground facilities at the Nevada Test Site [*Disarmament Times*, 11/10/95]. The United States claims that subcritical tests are not covered by a future CTBT because there is no nuclear criticality or fission chain reaction; others view such tests as an indication that the weapons states have no intention of following through on their pledge to work at eliminating nuclear weapons. There is also genuine concern that these tests may allow the nuclear weapons states to continue researching and developing new nuclear weapons despite a CTBT. The verification problems that would arise from conducting these tests underground have been noted as well [*Disarmament Diplomacy*, 1/96, p. 9; and Martin Kalinowski in *INESAP Information Bulletin*, 2/96].

Throughout the negotiations the principal obstacle to agreement on the scope of the CTBT was China's insistence that **peaceful nuclear explosions (PNEs)** be allowed. U.S. Arms Control and Disarmament Agency Director John Holum asserts that, to reach an accord, the demand for PNEs will "have to be dropped" [*Arms Control Reporter*, 2/96, p. 608.B.383–84]. It was not until early June 1996 that China backed away from its blanket insistence on PNEs, offering instead a temporary moratorium on PNEs that would be reconsidered at the planned Review Conference ten years after the CTBT entered into force [Stephanie Fraser, International Peace Bureau Report 3/4, 6/15/96].

Concern that a test ban will neither affect the capability of the five declared nuclear weapon states to design and build new nuclear weapons nor prompt them to fulfill their obligations to pursue the elimination of nuclear weapons has prompted India to **link a CTBT with a timetable for nuclear disarmament.** India is cautious about signing away its ability to develop nuclear weapons if the nuclear weapons states plan to maintain their arsenals indefinitely. In the words of Ambassador Arundhati Ghose, it is "important that as we take this step for a CTBT, we ensure that it is a step on the road to nuclear disarmament rather than into a cul-de-sac" [ibid., p. 608.B.387–88].

The United States has decried the Indian demand for linkage. In a speech to the Conference on Disarmament on January 23, 1996, the U.S. Arms Control Agency's Holum warned that "the threat to the test ban wears a benign face. It masquerades as even deeper devotion to arms control. . . . [H]olding one important goal hostage for another is a sure way to fail at both" [ibid., p. 608.B.385].

Given the continuing disputes over a comprehensive test-ban treaty, it will be extremely difficult for the Conference on Disarmament to conclude a CTBT in time for the opening of the 51st Session, let alone before the end of the calendar year. The failure to keep a commitment made at the NPT Review and Extension Conference would deal "a severe blow to the nuclear non-proliferation regime," said U.N. Secretary-General Boutros Boutros-Ghali, "and thereby to peace and security as a whole" [*Greenpeace CTBT Updates*, 3/22/96].

4. Chemical and Biological Weapons

The release in the Tokyo subway of the chemical nerve agent sarin by members of the Aum Shinrikyo sect in March 1995, killing 12 and hospitalizing thousands, was a powerful reminder of the danger of chemical weapons. Another reminder was the uncovering by the U.N. Special Commission (UNSCOM) of the extent of Iraq's chemical and biological weapons programs [S/1995/864, 10/11/95; S/1995/1038, 12/17/95]. According to a March 1996 report of the U.S. Central Intelligence Agency, some 20 countries—nearly half of them in the Middle East and South Asia—already have or may be developing chemical and biological weapons [CIA Nonproliferation Center, *The Chemical and Biological Weapons Threat*, 3/96, p. 1]. A month later, U.S. Defense Secretary William Perry spoke of the government's determination to prevent Libya from completing a new underground factory for producing chemical weapons and did not rule out the use of military force [*Washington Post*, 4/4/96].

The **Chemical Weapons Convention (CWC;** formally the Convention on the Prohibition of the Development, Production, Stockpiling and Use of Chemical Weapons and on Their Destruction, negotiated under C.D. auspices) was opened for signature on January 13, 1993. According to a treaty provision, the CWC will enter into force 180 days after 65 countries have ratified it or two years from the date of signature, whichever is later. As of March 14, 1996, 49 of the 160 signatory nations had ratified the Convention—16 short of need. Some of the missing are already far along in the ratification process. For example, the United Kingdom and India have ratified the treaty but have yet to deposit their instruments of **ratification** with the U.N. Secretary-General. Among the states that are conspicuous for their absence from the list of ratifiers and near-ratifiers, however, are Russia, the United States, and France [*Arms Control Reporter*, 1/96, p. 704.A.2]. The Clinton administration submitted the CWC to the U.S. Senate for its advice and consent back in November 1993, and on April 25, 1996, the Senate Foreign Relations Committee voted to support

U.S. ratification of the CWC—a step closer to ratification but far from the final one. Russia's Duma was not expected to act before the country's June 1996 elections, owing to what one close observer calls "the state of internal debate" on "whether to completely renounce such weapons" as well as to "technological, economic, financial and logistical factors" [Igor Khripunov in *Arms Control Today*, 7–8/95, pp. 15–16]. Still other signatories see little sense in forging ahead with ratification before the two with the largest stockpiles are on board. When all is said and done, the future entry into force of the CWC rests with the United States and its completion of the ratification process.

The dispute over implementation of the **1989 Wyoming Joint Memorandum of Understanding between the United States and Russia** continued in 1995 [see *A Global Agenda: Issues/50*, pp. 98–99]. The Joint Memorandum committed the two nations to a series of data exchanges and on-site verification experiments to demonstrate that the verification provisions they sought in the CWC could be tolerated. Contradictions in Russian data between one exchange and the next and indications of continued Russian research into binary chemical weapons were at the center of the dispute. Although most communication between the sides had taken place via cables, negotiators held one face-to-face session in August 1995, where Russia acknowledged its research into a new binary weapon for the first time. Russia did not, however, complete the CW inspections allowed by the Wyoming Memorandum. In late November 1995 a Russian team conducted challenge inspections at sites in Indiana and Utah, and the following month the U.S. team completed its inspections in Russia (at the Shchuch'ye weapons facility, Maradykovskiy, and in Shikany).

Presidents Bill Clinton and Boris Yeltsin reaffirmed their support of the CWC in a statement at the close of their summit meeting on September 28, 1995. On January 22, 1996, the U.S. Defense Department announced that the country had 3.6 million chemical weapons in its arsenal, representing approximately 31,000 tons of chemical warfare agent [*Washington Post*, 1/23/96]. The Russian chemical weapon stockpile is at least 40,000 tons (a total that does not include CW agents that have been dumped, buried, or sunk but not destroyed) [*Arms Control Today*, 7–8/95, p. 17].

The CWC Preparatory Commission (PrepCom) continues to meet, working out the details of CWC's oversight body—the Organization for the Prohibition of Chemical Weapons (OPCW). The hope is for a fully operational OPCW when the Convention enters into force.

The year saw continued progress on the implementation of yet another treaty, the **Convention on the Prohibition of the Development, Production, and Stockpiling of Bacteriological (Biological) and Toxin Weapons and on Their Destruction (BWC,** in force since 1975, and ratified by 148 states as of May 29, 1996). All five permanent members of the U.N. Security Council are among the ratifiers of this Convention.

Three meetings were held in 1995 by the Ad Hoc Group of the Special Conference, which is "to consider appropriate measures, including possible verification measures, and draft proposals to strengthen the convention." Two more are scheduled for 1996 (July 15–26 and September 16–27) in advance of the fourth BWC Review Conference, to be held in Geneva, November 25–December 13, 1996.

The First Committee lists the BW Convention on its provisional agenda for the 51st General Assembly.

5. Transparency in Armaments and Conventional Arms Control

On October 31, 1995, the U.N. Secretary-General released the third annual report on the **United Nations Register of Conventional Arms**—the only global cooperative security regime dealing with the transfer and accumulation of conventional weapons. Each year the Register collects data on the exports and imports of **seven categories of weapons** during the previous calendar year: battle tanks, armored combat vehicles, large-caliber artillery systems, combat aircraft, attack helicopters, warships, and missiles and missile launchers. Eighty-five nations submitted data on 1994 arms transfers in time for inclusion in the Register's 1995 report [*Arms Control Reporter*, 1/96, p. 707.A.1]—the informal deadline is September 30—and eight more had sent such information along by early February 1996. This brought to 93 the states submitting details of their 1994 weapons exports and imports—up from the 84 states that had supplied 1992 data by November 1993 and the 82 that had reported by November 1992—but still only half of all U.N. member states. (By late November 1995, 67 countries had submitted information for all three years.) When the General Assembly voted on establishing the Register in 1991, 150 members gave their assent.

All of the **top** ten **arms suppliers** have submitted 1994 data to the Register (although Russia's arrived after the 1995 deadline). In fact, of those countries that the world-renowned Stockholm International Peace Research Institute (SIPRI) ranks as the top 25 arms exporters in 1990–94, only one—North Korea— failed to report in 1995 (and, in fact, has *never* reported) [*The UN Register of Conventional Arms: Examining the Third Report*, West Yorkshire, U.K.: Bradford Arms Register Studies, 11/95]. The Register shows that in 1994, for the third consecutive year, the United States and Germany were by far the leading exporters of conventional weapons, and that the top ten exporters accounted for some 94 percent of all exports reported for the year. (The other eight were Belgium, Canada, the United Kingdom, the Netherlands, Russia, Czechoslovakia, Poland, and France.)

The Register also reflects the continuing trade in **second-hand sys-**

tems—a cascading of weapons made surplus by the entry into force of the Conventional Forces in Europe Treaty (CFE, 1991), the unification of Germany, and the end of the Cold War. This surplus accounts for most of the relatively high arms exports of Germany, Belgium, and some East European states in 1994.

The Fiscal Year 1996 Defense Authorization Act signed into law by President Bill Clinton on February 10, 1996, by calling for the disclosure of additional details about U.S. arms transfers, is likely to increase the **transparency of the U.S. submission to the Register.** The 1996 Act reinstates a provision of the Foreign Assistance Act requiring an annual report by the President on military assistance, military imports, and military exports, to include such details as the model and intended role. The exported weapons on which the Executive must supply this information run the gamut from small arms ammunition to fighter planes. The first report is due out February 6, 1997.

The U.N. record shows that some major weapons *importers* did not submit reports, including several that receive U.S. arms (Saudi Arabia, Egypt, Morocco, Kuwait, United Arab Emirates, and Oman)—an important limitation. Yet each year the Register does provide valuable new information. And in 1995, when SIPRI organized its 1994 arms trade data in the same format as the Register's, it became easier to compare the two. Such a comparison reveals that 59 transfers reported to the Register do not appear on the SIPRI list.

The Register continues to be plagued by **inconsistencies,** the majority of which can be attributed to differing national interpretations of the Register's definitions. One Canadian study found that nations are asked to submit data on

> only those transfers considered by the nation to have been effected during the relevant reporting year, in conformity with their respective national criterion used to determine when a transfer becomes effective. . . . Because these statements are vague, and invite the possibility of ambiguities, numerous inconsistencies can appear in the final report.
> [*The United Nations Conventional Arms Register: Canadian Practice in Preparing Its Annual Data Submission*, Ottawa: External Affairs and International Trade, 11/95]

Furthermore, the United Nations has no agreed definition of what constitutes a report; and almost any submission is included in the annual report. Complications also arise from **differing interpretations** of the definitions for reporting categories and lack of shared understanding of when the transfer is considered to be complete—whether at the time of transfer of control, transfer of title, or otherwise.

Owing to inconsistencies, and differences over what should be covered, the Register continues to receive criticism. Absent from the 1995 report, for example, is Egypt, which announced at the 49th General Assembly in the fall of 1994 that it would no longer participate in the Register because that instrument had failed to expand to include inventories, procurement through national production, and weapons of mass destruction [*The Nonproliferation Review*, Winter 1996, p. 77].

The **Conference on Disarmament's (C.D.) Ad Hoc Committee on Transparency in Armaments,** asked to propose additional roles for the Register, not only made little progress in 1994 but also failed to agree on reestablishing the Committee in 1995: Many of the developing states, contending that the Register is skewed because it does not include weaponry produced by the large military-industrial sectors of developed states, said they would refuse to bring the Ad Hoc Committee back to life until the C.D. agrees to expand the Register and include weapons of mass destruction [*Arms Control Reporter*, 1/96, p. 707.A.2].

The issue of **illicit trafficking in small arms, mainly in the black and gray markets but sometimes involving governments,** continues to receive attention by the United Nations. The transfer and accumulation of such arms through such markets is considered to constitute a significant threat not only to local populations but to national and regional security as well. The U.N. Secretary-General called attention to this threat when presenting to the Security Council in January 1995 an addendum to *An Agenda for Peace,* his 1992 report on making the United Nations an effective and efficient tool for promoting international security. Under the addendum's **"peacemaking"** heading, he announced the intention to concentrate on "micro-disarmament," defined as "practical disarmament in the context of the conflicts the United Nations is actually dealing with and of the weapons, most of them light weapons, that are actually killing people in the hundreds of thousands" [*Issues in Science and Technology,* Fall 1995, p. 52].

Just as the memory of the Iran-Contra affair was beginning to fade, another series of covert arms transfers involving the United States, Iran, and (in this case) Croatia became a political issue in the United States. On April 5, 1996, the *Los Angeles Times* reported that back in 1994, despite a **U.N. arms embargo** the United States was pledged to uphold and had publicly insisted on enforcing, President Clinton raised no objections to the creation of an arms pipeline channeling Iranian-supplied weapons into Bosnia-Herzegovina.

The covert arms-transfer issue is also being dealt with by **Working Group II of the U.N.'s Disarmament Commission,** an all-member deliberative body. During its May 15–30, 1995 session, the Commission continued work on "the **Guidelines for international arms transfers** in the context of General Assembly Resolution 46/36H of 6 December 1991," with arms trafficking as the focus [*Disarmament Newsletter,* 8/95, p. 14]. This is described as the "first attempt by the international community to spotlight the problem at the global level, to promote and encourage the development of national strategies for dealing with it, and to foster bilateral and international cooperation and coordination to control it" [ibid.]. The Commission adopted a set of draft guidelines at its 1996 session and will report on them to the 51st General Assembly [A/CN.10/1996/CRP.2].

A significant step toward greater transparency of conventional arms transfers was taken on December 19, 1995, when the 28 nations negotiating a **successor regime to the Cold War-era Coordinating Committee for Multilateral Export Controls (COCOM)** reached agreement on the initial elements of the so-called **"Wassenar Arrangement on Export Controls for Conventional Arms and Dual-Use Goods and Technologies."** This, says the U.S. State Department, will be the first global multilateral regime covering both armaments and sensitive dual-use goods and technology [*Arms Control Today*, 12/95–1/96, p. 24]. Coordination of its members' conventional arms and dual-use item export-control policies are the basis of the regime, to be achieved by establishing formal processes of transparency and consultation and (where appropriate) by attempting to create a multilateral restraint regime.

Transparency is to be achieved by voluntary data exchanges involving four categories of information. First, on a semiannual basis, members will provide information on their transfers of conventional arms to nonparticipating states. These declarations will cover the same seven categories of arms covered by the U.N. Register. Second, on an aggregate and periodic basis, members will indicate the denials of licenses to nonparticipating states for the "basic" items on the group's List of Dual-Use Goods and Technology (Tier 1 items). Third, on an individual basis and "in an early and timely" manner, members will provide information on license denials to nonparticipating states for "sensitive" and "very sensitive" items on the Dual-Use List (Tier 2 items). A final exchange, carried out on an aggregate and periodic basis, covers the transfers of licenses for Tier 2 items to nonparticipating states [ibid.].

Efforts to negotiate controls on the trade in conventional arms continue to have mixed results. One example is the **Review Conference of the Convention on Prohibitions or Restrictions on the Use of Certain Conventional Weapons Which May Be Deemed to Be Excessively Injurious or to Have Indiscriminate Effects (also known as the Conventional Weapons Convention, or CWC),** which met September 25–October 13, 1995, to make changes to the CWC, and especially **Protocol II on landmines.** The latter is judged a failure by virtually all observers, citing its complex rules, discretionary language, and broad exceptions and qualifications. Yet the conference avoided discussing an outright ban on the use of landmines and confined itself to such technical issues as minimum metal content to make mines more detectable and the utility of self-destructing and self-neutralizing mines. The conference did, however, adopt a **fourth protocol,** which **bans the use of lasers specifically designed to cause permanent blindness.**

Owing to the pressure exerted by nongovernmental organizations that work together in the international Campaign to Ban Landmines, the conference was suspended in October and a final session scheduled for April 22–May 3, 1996, in Geneva. That session concluded with agreement on some **new provisions of the Landmine Protocol of the Convention on Certain Conventional Weapons:** All antipersonnel landmines (APL) must be detectable; all non-self-destructing (dumb) APL may be used only in marked and monitored areas; and self-destructing/self-deactivating APL may have a life span of no more than 120 days, with a combined self-destruct/self-deactivate reliability rate of 99.9 percent.

These provisions fail to satisfy those, both in government and out, who held out hope for a total ban on landmines. Among the problems noted in the new articles:

- The amended Protocol lends greater legitimacy to the use of remotely delivered (scatterable) landmines and encourages the use, design, and production of so-called "smart" mines.
- A loophole has been created in the definition of antipersonnel mines through the insertion of the word "primarily." This could well lead to claims that a particular mine made (or said to be made) with a dual purpose falls outside control provisions. For example, a mine that meets all the design elements of a blast antipersonnel mine could have a "primary" role as an airfield denial munition. The amended Protocol does not include such munitions in the category of indiscriminate landmines and would not restrict their use or export.
- Antitank mines fitted with antihandling devices or booby-trapped in such way as to make them de facto antipersonnel mines will not be considered as such under the amended Protocol. This presents a special threat to humanitarian demining teams—and is a direct contradiction of Article 12.5 (ii) of the Protocol, which seeks to protect such demining missions.
- The Protocol does not contain an effective mechanism for ensuring compliance and verification of even the agreed-upon, limited restrictions in the Protocol.
- The scope of the Protocol has not been expanded to include all circumstances of landmine use: The state itself is left to determine when an "internal disturbance" grows into an "internal conflict" and becomes subject to the Protocol.
- The key provisions will not take effect for a decade or more. In the interim, note advocates of a total ban, an additional quarter-of-a-million people will fall victim to landmines.

Canada will host a meeting of pro-landmine-ban states in Ottawa in September 1996.

On May 16 the United States released a "new" landmine policy that was essentially a continuation of the status quo. The President ordered the Pentagon to stop using dumb mines by 1999 but made two important exceptions: They will be allowed along the Korean demilitarized zone and in troop training. This "new" policy conflicts with a bill President Clinton signed into law on February 12, which calls for a one-year moratorium on antipersonnel mine use starting in 1999.

A three-day **International Conference on Mine Clearance** in early June 1995, convened by the U.N. Secretary-General, drew officials from 97 governments and raised some $87 million in direct and indirect pledges of money, services, and equipment. An estimated $33 billion is required to clear the approximately 110 million mines in upwards of 60 countries [documents prepared for International Meeting on Mine Clearance by the Mine Clearance and Policy Unit of the U.N. Department of Humanitarian Affairs, 7/95].

Another effort at controlling conventional arms—this one at the national level—is the **movement to enact domestic codes of conduct governing the transfer of arms between states.** One such attempt by U.S. Senator Mark Hatfield (R-Ore.) and Representative Cynthia McKinney (D-Ga.) came up for a vote in the House of Representatives in 1995. Although it lost by a vote of 262 to 157, it is expected to be brought up in the U.S. Senate in 1996. The European Parliament too has supported the establishment of such a code, and draft codes are being debated in the European Union. Ireland, Germany, Austria, and Romania have presented proposals for developing codes of conduct to the United Nations, and former President of Costa Rica/Nobel Peace Prize winner Dr. Oscar Arias Sanchez is convening a group of fellow-laureates to draft and introduce an international code of conduct at the world body. The hope was to present the draft to the 51st U.N. General Assembly.

III
Economics and Development
By David A. Lynch

1. The Global Economy

The global economy was generally strong in 1995 and remained so at the time of this writing in mid-1996. Despite this, leaders and citizens in many nations find themselves nostalgic for some other economic era. At first glance, this is curious. The global economic downturn of the early 1990s has ended. World economic growth is projected to be 3.7 percent in 1995 and 4.1 percent in 1996 [*World Economic Outlook*, International Monetary Fund (hereafter IMF), 10/95]. Why then are so many people unhappy with the current situation?

Developed nations have the least to complain about in 1996: Growth is strong and inflation is low. Nevertheless, a collective nostalgia has crept into many developed countries for the golden 1950s and 1960s, when high economic growth year after year seemed easy. Stubbornly high unemployment in the face of respectable growth accentuates this nostalgia in many nations.

Developing nations also dream, but not of the past. They look hopefully toward an economically developed future, but do so with some trepidation. Such development requires economic openness, which in turn brings cultural change, increased competition, and greater reliance on foreign capital. This can be a volatile mix, as the Mexican crisis demonstrates. Moreover, development has been uneven. The "emerging" economies of Asia have been the marvel of the world while Latin American success has been more varied, and African success rare.

The economic pain accompanying the transitioning economies' march to capitalism has also led to collective nostalgia. Driven by an uneasiness over the current situation and fear of the future, this nostalgia is often directed at the collectivist past so recently rejected. Communism, to some, looks good, and reforms in some transitioning nations are imperiled. Nevertheless, the transitioning economies *have* furthered their evolution to capitalism; and those that have been at the forefront of reform are significantly outperforming those where reforms have lagged. Better access to Western markets would hasten the rewards and ease the pain of the transition—something that remains a struggle for all of the transitioning nations.

Developed Nations: Nostalgia for the Boom Years

In 1995 developed nations experienced steady although unspectacular economic growth, combined with low inflation. National banks in many large economies, therefore, eased monetary policy during the course of 1995. This resulted in lower interest rates across most of the Organization for Economic Cooperation and Development (OECD), and it set the stage for continued economic growth in 1996. Unemployment in many developed countries, however, remained a significant problem and will remain so in the foreseeable future. Real gross domestic product (GDP) growth in OECD member countries slowed from 2.9 percent in 1994 to 2.4 percent in 1995. Much of this decrease stemmed from North America's slowdown from a robust 4.1 percent GDP growth in 1994 to an unspectacular 2.6 percent in 1995. The Mexican crisis and tight monetary policy in the United States in 1994 and early 1995 account for the weaker North American growth. Japanese growth continued its weak 1994 trajectory in 1995; growth there, dragged down by the highly valued yen, dropped from 0.5 percent to 0.3 percent. European OECD nations' growth was more consistent and positive, increasing from 2.4 percent in 1994 to 2.9 percent in 1995 [*OECD Economic Outlook*, 12/95].

Developed countries' growth in 1996 is predicted to be similar to 1995, with the positive exception of Japan, where a recovering economy is expected to grow 2 percent (and nearly 3 percent in 1997). While this is lower than Japan has been accustomed to during its many boom years, it signals a solid recovery from recession and would be close to the OECD growth average [ibid.].

While OECD growth and inflation were respectable in 1995, unemployment loomed as a significant problem. This was particularly the case in Europe, where 1995 unemployment averaged more than 10 percent across Europe's OECD members. More worrying still was that specific European OECD countries faced dramatically higher unemployment rates than this average. European unemployment is expected to lower slightly during 1996 and 1997 but stubbornly remain over 10 percent [ibid.].

The United States: Strong, with Doubts

A strange dichotomy emerged regarding the U.S. economy during 1995. Although the economy was experiencing steady and sustained growth based on a number of indices—high productivity, solid growth, low inflation, and low unemployment—many in the United States voiced doubt over the future. While hailing U.S. economic progress, President Bill Clinton voiced concern that the country was in a "funk." Observers from both the left and right have denounced the recent downsizing undertaken by many U.S. corporations in the midst of high profits. Many also lamented the growing economic inequality within the nation. Meanwhile, congressional sentiment has turned against extending NAFTA to Chile or Caribbean nations. Nostalgia for the faster and seemingly effortless economic growth of the 1950s and 1960s has become a national pastime. Many observers fear that today's slower growth is not an aberration but the new norm.

How did the U.S. economy fare during 1995, and where is it going in 1996? The answer matters a great deal to the rest of the world. The United States continues to be the world's largest market, exporter and importer, and the dollar the world's most widely used currency. Indeed, the United States is a bellwether economy for the rest of the world. Thus it was worrying that U.S. growth slowed during the first half of 1995 after a strong showing in 1994. Critics charged that the Federal Reserve Bank had overreacted in 1994 and early 1995 to real or imagined signs of increasing inflation. The third quarter brought significantly higher growth, only to have growth slow again in the fourth quarter of 1995. In early 1996, the signs from the United States have been generally strong: solid but unspectacular growth, low inflation, and low unemployment. Fundamental economic indicators in the United States portend similarly solid economic fortunes for 1996. The tight monetary policy of 1994 and early 1995 gave way to a looser policy in July 1995. Interest rates responded, suggesting that growth for 1996 will be similar to that of 1995. U.S. unemployment, at 5.7 percent in April 1996, remains significantly lower than that of most other developed countries, with the notable exception of Japan, at 3.4 percent [*Economist*, 6/8/96]. Another positive indicator was the increase in U.S. exports, spurred in part by a weak dollar. Despite weakness in some markets, especially Japan and Mexico, U.S. exports were strong on the whole for 1995; and exports for 1996 are widely predicted to gain as Mexico, Japan, and other markets rebound. U.S. imports also increased in 1995. Combined with the low dollar, this created a large 1995 current account deficit: $170 billion, or 2.5 percent of GDP [OECD *Economic Outlook*, 12/95].

Budget deficit reduction in 1995 served as a shibboleth for politicians from both parties as they put forth a stream of deficit reduction proposals. History urges caution in assessing such plans, as they are often built on creative and flimsy economic assumptions and more often than not fall apart in the winds of political pressure. The past decade and a half are littered with failed deficit reduction plans. Moreover, the impact of deficit reduction upon the U.S. economy is a matter of debate among economists. How much will deficit reduction lower interest rates, thus spurring long-term growth? How much might lower government spending diminish economic growth in the short term? Will a smaller deficit raise or lower the value of the dollar? While economists debate these points, global financial markets—an increasingly important factor in U.S. economic fortunes—clearly have a preference for smaller deficits. To many, the deficit is taken as an objective measure of U.S. financial credibility. Ironically, as President Clinton and the Republican congressional majority battled over the budget, the yearly federal budget deficit shrank again in 1995 and was much smaller in relative terms than deficits in most industrialized nations. Deficit reduction fever continues in 1996.

Japan: Incipient Recovery

In 1994 Japan's economy began to recover from the recession that had deflated its bubble economy. But in 1994 recovery was ephemeral. The economy faced a setback: the dramatic appreciation of the yen. This appreciation continued into 1995 and dampened economic growth during the year. Moreover, the Japanese banking system, saddled with dangerously high levels of nonperforming loans, was in crisis. These dark clouds finally began to part in mid-1995. The yen appreciation abated during the summer, and prospects for the Japanese economy in 1996 are brighter.

With the high yen, Japanese automakers were forced to raise their prices on some vehicles exported to the United States by more than $1,000. This suddenly made Detroit's autos appear more attractive. Even Japanese cars manufactured in the United States became less competitive, since these use a significant number of parts produced in Japan. The United States is Japan's most important export market, but the yen's appreciation pressured Japan's exports elsewhere as well. In the year ending March 31, 1996, Japanese automobile exports dropped 16.7 percent [*Los Angeles Times*, 4/25/96], and the story was similar in other economic sectors.

The prospects for Japan in 1996 are less gloomy. Consumer confidence has increased, and the yen depreciated significantly relative to its soaring 1995 high. By April 1996 it had lowered to 108 yen per dollar, a 28.7 percent decline in a year [ibid., 4/10/96]. Government policies should help growth in 1996. In September 1995 the Bank of Japan eased its monetary policy and the government introduced a significant fiscal stimulus.

Japan will still face various economic problems. Struggling banks will continue to struggle. Japanese companies must adjust to the still high yen, and Japanese wages are high relative to production elsewhere in Asia. U.S.-Japanese trade rows continue. Japanese unemployment is expected to hit a post-World War II high of 3.5 percent by the end of 1996 [*OECD Economic Outlook*, 12/95]. This is a problem most developed countries envy. Nevertheless, the Japanese unemployment and growth rates will be substantially worse than traditional Japanese levels. To some, this calls into question whether Japan can resume its pre-bubble economic success.

Europe: Jobless Recovery?

Europe's recovery from recession continued in 1995–96. Growth was strong during 1995, but unemployment has emerged as a particularly intractable problem. Europe's OECD members averaged more than 10 percent unemployment, with no significant relief in sight. In some countries that figure is dramatically higher, notably in Spain (over 22 percent), Finland (17 percent), and Ireland (just under 13 percent) [ibid.]. German unemployment was over 11 percent in February 1996, the highest in the postwar period [*Wall Street Journal*, 3/7/96]. To many this is especially disturbing because Germany has long had low unemployment and is the region's largest economy. Many European central banks moved to lower interest rates; 11 loosened monetary policy in December alone [*Christian Science Monitor*, 12/29/95]. This is expected to raise growth rates in 1996 and should therefore also lower unemployment, though only slightly.

The high and intractable unemployment is all the more worrying because European Union (EU) countries wishing to qualify for European Monetary Union (EMU) in 1999 must meet strict economic criteria, known as the Maastricht criteria. Among these are targets for low public debt. High unemployment jeopardizes reaching the debt targets in two ways. First, unemployment strains government budgets—especially in countries with generous unemployment packages, which are common in the EU. Second, unemployment undermines political support for rigorous fiscal and monetary policies required to meet the Maastricht criteria.

Germany: Europe's Engine

As with the United States, Germany's strong growth in 1994 weakened somewhat in 1995 as a highly valued deutsche mark weighed down exports. German economic growth of 2 percent during the first half of 1995 was slower than expected [ibid.], and with the slower growth came lower than expected inflation, thus prompting the Bundesbank to loosen monetary policy in March and again in August. Growth continued to be slow in the second half of 1995 (1.5 percent), and more worrying still was the high unemployment—consistently over 10 percent. The unemployment picture remains gloomy in 1996.

Nevertheless, the overall 1996 outlook is somewhat brighter. The OECD predicts that the Bundesbank's looser monetary policy coupled with a lower deutsche mark will spur growth in 1996 above 1995 levels. Growth was slow in the final quarter of 1995 and early 1996. This prompted the Bundesbank to again loosen monetary policy in April 1996.

In 1996 Germany will continue to undergo fiscal tightening. At 2.6 percent of GDP in 1994, Germany's yearly budget deficit had been within the Maastricht required 3 percent. But that figure rose to 3.6 percent in 1995 [*Economist*, 1/20/96]. Hence, the Helmut Kohl government has moved to lower Germany's budget deficit. In March 1996 the government announced a spending freeze to pay for unemployment-related spending. Analysts expect continued austerity in 1996. The German fiscal house is normally tidier than that of many other European countries, but these have not been normal times. Government spending increased to cope with the record unemployment and the unification of East and West Germany. Budget difficulties and high unemployment have led some to question whether the Maastricht criteria should be met on time, or at all. But the Kohl government remains strongly in favor of the EMU, and 1996 will bring policies that match this goal.

France: The Economic Policy Dilemma

French economic fortunes during 1995 were mixed. Growth was sound, but slower than the previous year, in which France climbed out of recession. In 1995 other problems, such as unemployment and the budget deficit, were more troublesome. French unemployment, 12.5 percent in mid-1994, lowered to 11.5 percent during mid-1995, a rate that held roughly steady in early 1996 [*OECD Economic Outlook*, 12/95; *Economist*, 11/25/95, 1/20/96]. Related to these problems, the franc came under pressure in March 1995. A strong franc is considered essential, if France is to enter into the EMU in 1999. Thus the Bank of France moved to raise interest rates. This dampened demand and in turn lowered the growth rate and exacerbated the unemployment and budget problems. The franc troubles of March subsided and monetary policy was subsequently eased over the summer of 1995, until the franc came under renewed downward pressure in October. Interest rates were again raised until the pressure again subsided. Despite the fluctuations in interest rates and the value of the franc, growth is expected to be stronger in 1996 as French export markets recover and French domestic demand improves.

A question has emerged for 1996 and 1997: Can France simultaneously meet the Maastricht debt and inflation criteria, maintain a strong franc, and reduce unemployment? The French are faced with a dilemma. To keep on target for EMU, the franc must not become too weak relative to the deutsche mark. This requires French interest rates to be higher than they would be otherwise. This in turn slows economic growth, raises unemployment, and makes reducing debt—one of the Maastricht criteria—more difficult. The French government found that cutting budgets is difficult indeed, as underscored by the turbulent strike by public sector workers in late 1995. The more the Maastricht criteria are considered unreachable by markets, the more downward pressure the franc may encounter. The French economic dilemma will not be easy to solve.

Other Developed Countries

During 1995 Italy's GDP growth was a strong 3 percent, but Italy struggled to lower high unemployment and inflation. Over 12 percent as 1995 began, unemployment lowered as the year progressed but remained over 10 percent over the course of 1995. Inflation also lowered as 1995 unfolded, but was approximately 5 percent for the year [unless otherwise noted, material in this section is drawn from *OECD Economic Outlook*, 12/95].

British growth slowed during most of 1995 to approximately 2 percent, but inflation was low and the economy is predicted to grow at a more rapid 2.5 percent in 1996.

The Canadian recession was among the deepest of the developed countries, and the Canadian economy was among the last to recover. In 1994 the Canadian recovery was strong, with growth of 5.5 percent. Growth slowed in 1995, however, as tight monetary policies worked their way through the economy and as the U.S. economy weakened. The uncertainties arising from Quebec's separatist efforts, including the dramatic vote over independence in the summer of 1995, certainly did not help Canadian economic fortunes. In 1996 the outlook for growth is rosier because of lower interest rates and a stronger U.S. economy.

New Zealand, proud of its heritage as the birthplace of the welfare state, went through much soul-searching as it shed some layers of its welfare system during the 1980s. Growth in 1995 was approximately 3.5 percent. This is strong, but less robust than 1993 and 1994, when growth was 5.2 percent and 6.2 percent, respectively. The OECD expects growth to pick up during 1996. The strong growth should ease the difficulties of soul-searching, although that process is likely to continue. New Zealand's growth is expected to be approximately 3 percent in 1996, assuming that New Zealand's Reserve Bank continues its tight monetary policies.

While 1995 brought continued tough times for Turkey, the problems were different from those of the previous year. Whereas 1994 was a recessionary year for the Turkish economy, economic growth was strong in 1995, up 6 percent in the first half compared to a year earlier. But there are numerous, disconcerting problems—inflation, public debt, and currency devaluation among them. Inflation, which hit 120 percent in 1994, lowered to 80 percent in 1995 but was expected to remain troublesome into 1996 [*Wall Street Journal*, 2/12/96]. The Turkish lira has faced downward pressure, which has required Turkey to issue high-interest, short-term Treasury bills. Government debt has risen to levels that alarm many, including the International Monetary Fund (IMF). Moreover, high government spending and a weak currency are likely to continue and stand in the way of inflation reduction [ibid.]. On a brighter note, Turkey reached a trade agreement with the EU in January 1996. This is helpful, but more helpful still would be full EU membership. EU membership, combined with the low lira, would be a boon for exports and would therefore make Turkey an attractive investment site.

The European Union: Currency Unification?

Imagine watching an economic competition—a triathalon of sorts. The events require a great deal of exertion and pain, but in this competition being the fastest is not the goal. Rather, the winners will be those that can demonstrate a level of competency before an impending deadline.

As spectators take seats in the stadium, critics would point out that only a few of the competitors appear lean, while others seem flabby indeed. A few even appear injured and require a heroic performance to successfully complete the course before the deadline. As the starting gun goes off, instead of dashing toward the water for the first event, the competitors commence to lobby one another in an attempt to alter the rules of the race. Perhaps completing two of three events should be sufficient, some argue. Some competitors want to move the finish line. Some hint they can't or won't finish the race and voice doubts about whether the event is worth the pain required. Moreover, some competitors are allowed to miss the race altogether, yet they are not disqualified. Meanwhile the clock ticks.

This, some observers argue, is the situation the European Union faces as it moves toward monetary union. But optimists would argue that this characterization is unfair. There are many positive elements to recommend reaching EMU. Yes, there are difficulties, but some important spectators, namely markets, have lent the effort thus far some credibility. As of this writing, there have been no recent market attacks on EU currencies of the magnitude of those of 1992 and 1993, which forced Great Britain and Italy out of the European exchange rate mechanism (ERM) and then prompted the EU to significantly widen the ERM fluctuation band. Importantly, downward pressure on the French franc during 1995 was pushed back. Moreover, changes in the Maastricht criteria may yet save the day for monetary integration. What is likely to transpire?

As the deadline for the final stage of EMU approaches, what is certain are the existing Maastricht criteria that apply to countries wishing to be among the first to reach monetary union. These include specific thresholds of debt, exchange rate stability, and inflation. For instance, yearly budget deficits are required to be below 3 percent of a nation's GDP and total public debt under 60 percent of GDP. On January 1, 1999, the currency rates of those countries meeting the Maastricht criteria will be fixed, and the currency—the "euro"—will be launched. On July 1,

2002, the national currencies of EMU nations will no longer be legal tender. Countries wishing to qualify under the current criteria must meet them well before January 1999. Statistics for 1996 and 1997 are likely to be used for judging adherence to the Maastricht criteria. It is certain, therefore, that only a handful of the EU's 15 nations—perhaps only Germany and Luxembourg—will be able to meet the criteria in the years before 1999 without making dramatic policy changes. Most EU countries do not meet the debt criteria, let alone other criteria. Even Germany did not meet the yearly budget deficit criterion in 1995, although it has taken steps to meet the target for 1996.

Does this mean that EMU is doomed? No. A combination of three developments would make the system workable. Countries can dramatically change their economic policies; the EU can take advantage of an escape clause in the Maastricht treaty; and the Maastricht criteria can be altered.

The first option for reaching EMU by 1999 is doubtful, if taken alone. EU countries could change policies to meet the Maastricht criteria, but it is questionable whether governments are willing and able to do so. It is not merely a matter of the EU member governments altering policies. For the policies to be sustained, the governments must convince their citizens that monetary union is in their best interest. Against a setting of high unemployment, this argument is politically difficult to make. Polls show that EU member governments have some way to go before their citizens are convinced [see, for instance, *Economist*, 1/27/96]. Moreover, politicians within some countries are divided as to whether monetary union is a worthy goal. This has always been the case in Great Britain, but it is now taking root in other, more solidly pro-EU countries.

Some combination of the other two options, coupled with less dramatic economic policy changes, is more likely. Maastricht has an escape clause allowing changes if the criteria are not met by the end of 1997. As it becomes more obvious that many countries will not be able to meet the stringent Maastricht criteria within the time constraint, pressure increases to weaken those criteria. There has been talk of granting countries more time or moving to a "two track" Europe with some countries entering into monetary union by the deadline and others later or not at all. (In the Maastricht treaty Britain reserved the right to opt out of monetary union altogether.) A likely outcome is that some combination of these proposed changes will be adopted. During 1996, EU member governments will decide what changes, if any, should be made to facilitate EMU.

No matter what final criteria are agreed upon, it is essential that Germany and France, long the driving force behind a more integrated Europe, enter into monetary union. With these two currencies integrated, others would be more likely to follow. Should the two largest competitors successfully complete the triathalon and demonstrate the gains that follow—for instance lower interest rates or lower inflation in France and increased trade between the two nations—there will be a great deal of momentum for other EU nations to take part.

Developing Nations: Colds, Pneumonia, and Mixed Fortunes

It is an old adage that when developed countries catch a cold, developing countries get pneumonia. For much of the post-World War II era, there was some evidence to support this adage. Economic downturns in developed nations led to more severe downturns in developing nations. Now, the IMF maintains, developing countries can grow despite tough times in developed countries. In fact, the growth may be partially explained by recession in developed nations. How so? With lower interest rates and lower returns found in the recessionary developed economies, the capital of developed countries flowed more rapidly to developing countries [*World Economic Outlook*, IMF, 10/95]. During the recession of the early 1990s, many developing countries attracted record levels of investment from developed countries, spurring spectacular growth. This was particularly the case in Asia, where annual economic growth between 5 and 10 percent is now commonplace.

Unfortunately, this phenomenon does not extend to all developing regions. The old adage appears still to hold true for much of Africa and the Middle East, where growth continues to be more closely tied to the economic fortunes of developed regions [ibid.]. During the recent recession, these regions failed to draw significant levels of investment and generally had lower economic growth rates. What accounts for these divergent fortunes? According to the IMF, the difference is explained by the diversification of exports found in successful developing countries as compared to the continued reliance on relatively few commodities in less successful ones. The Middle East's developing nations have had to weather low oil prices, hindering the many economies in the region that are reliant on oil exports. Countries dependent upon only a few commodities are highly vulnerable to downturns in the demand for these products. Often this demand is influenced greatly by economic activity in developed countries. Export diversification, moreover, brings increased possibility for intraregional trade, which has expanded significantly in Asia and Latin America, thus further enabling developing countries in these regions to weather recessions in developed regions.

There is little controversy that export diversification is desirable. What is more controversial is how developing nations successfully establish diversification and increase regional trade. According to the IMF, this is caused by greater economic liberalization. Chile is often cited as a case in point. This proposition, however, remains controversial in many developing countries. Skepticism about the efficacy of the liberal economic development model espoused by the IMF, the World Bank, and many developed countries increased when Mexico, a prime exemplar of this development model, ran into trouble in 1994 and 1995. During much of 1995, many countries were fearful of a Mexican-style economic crisis. These fears eased somewhat as the turbulence in the aftermath of the Mexican crisis subsided, but skepticism remains.

Despite this uneven record, the developing countries' economic growth, taken together, is strong and is predicted to remain so into 1996 and beyond. The IMF estimates that developing economies will grow at a 6.5 percent annual rate into the foreseeable future, a level significantly higher than the 2.5 percent expected growth in the industrialized economies. At these rates, output in developing nations would be greater than that in developed nations by 2004 [ibid.]. Even in this scenario, however, uneven development would remain a substantial problem. Currently, Asian success is common, Latin American success is patchy, and African success remains rare.

2. Development Outlook

Private Capital Development: An Encouraging Trend

Developing economies have greater access to developed economies' capital than ever before, and many developing countries are taking advantage of it. Taken together, private and official capital flows into developing countries were a record $231 billion in 1995 [*New York Times*, 3/13/96]. In fact, according to the World Bank, multinational corporations' foreign direct investment (FDI) in developing countries has more than tripled during the 1990s [*Los Angeles Times*, 3/14/96; *New York Times*, 3/16/96], with a 13 percent increase in 1995 [*New York Times*, 3/13/96]. Much of this can be attributed to the end of the debt crisis, combined with developing countries' policies to liberalize investment. The U.N. Conference on Trade and Development (UNCTAD) has chronicled this liberalization: Between 1991 and 1994 it notes 368 changes in laws and regulations that liberalized investment. During the same period UNCTAD found only five changes that did not promote liberalization [*World Investment Report, 1995 UNCTAD*, as reported in *UNCTAD Bulletin*, 11–12/95].

The nature of capital flows to developing regions is changing. Private actors now account for a higher percentage of investment in developing countries than do official actors. This has been the case since 1991, and in 1995 the trend deepened: 72 percent of capital flowing into developing countries came from private actors [*New York Times*, 3/13/96]. To many, this bodes well. Developing countries are becoming more integrated into global financial markets, thus taking a step toward alleviating their traditional capital dearth. To some in developing countries, however, this has worrying implications. Many nations fear that with foreign investment comes the potential for a crisis similar to Mexico's. During that crisis, both Mexican and foreign capital rapidly fled Mexico, exacerbating the drop in the peso. But this need not happen elsewhere. A significant portion of Mexico's foreign investment was portfolio investment, which can be easily withdrawn. FDI is more stable: It is much harder to move a factory than it is to sell stocks or bonds. Moreover, the domestic Mexican savings rate was low relative to similarly developed countries, thus heightening the impact of foreign capital flows.

It is encouraging that many developing nations are attracting significant amounts of FDI. In fact, despite a drop of more than half in portfolio investment since 1993, capital flowing to developing countries has increased. Much of this can be attributed to FDI. As with so many barometers of development progress, Asia leads the way. Asia's developing economies lead both in the absolute level of FDI and in the ratio of FDI to portfolio investment. China alone accounted for roughly a third of developing countries' FDI, at $38 billion in 1995. The Pacific Rim and East Asia, including China, attracted $53.7 billion in FDI—significantly more than other regions. The Western Hemisphere's developing nations attracted $17.8 billion of FDI. In the Western Hemisphere, portfolio investment is greater than FDI, compared to Asia where the reverse is true. European and Central Asian developing countries attracted $12.5 billion. During the same period significantly lower levels of FDI went to the Middle East and North Africa ($2.1 billion) and sub-Saharan Africa ($2.2 billion) [ibid.]. Most capital flowing into Africa remains official lending. In the words of the OECD's Development Assistance Committee (DAC), "In Sub-Saharan Africa dependence on official development financing remains almost total. . . ." The DAC does offer some hope for private investment, noting that policy changes in some African nations have made them more attractive investment sites [*Development Cooperation, 1995 Report*, DAC].

Privatization has been at the heart of many developing countries' strategies to attract capital. Privatization has indeed brought a great deal of investment, but it has also brought some controversy. The foreign investors often shed workers. Moreover, the original nationalization was sometimes a matter of national pride. Mexico's nationalization of the oil industry during the 1930s has a symbolic significance akin to that of George Washington in the United States; Mexican schoolchildren saved change to donate to the effort. It should not be surprising, therefore, that resistance to petrochemical industry privatization has emerged in Mexico. Within many developing countries there has been resistance to privatization, despite the needed capital that it brings.

While privatization has been an effective method of raising capital, success has been uneven. Latin America has been the leader in privatization, although proceeds peaked there in 1991 and have been declining annually since. Nevertheless, from 1988 to 1994, Latin America accounted for more than half of all developing countries' privatization proceeds. East Asia and the Pacific have been slower to embrace privatization, but since 1992 the process has been speeding up. In 1994 their proceeds were roughly equal to those in Latin America. Across most of Africa, privatization has been far less successful. In 1994 total privatization proceeds in developing countries was $21 billion. Sub-Saharan African privatization accounted for only $800 million of this figure [*Economist*, 3/23/96].

Debt and Development: A Worrying Trend

While the role of private actors has increased markedly, official loans and grants remain important to developing regions. First, international organizations such as the World Bank serve as a direct capital conduit to developing countries. Second, these institutions send signals to private actors about the state of developing economies. A World Bank or IMF stamp of approval, for instance, helps private investors feel more secure about investing in a given country.

The role of the World Bank, IMF, and similar actors is often controversial, with loans contingent upon market reforms. Fiscal austerity and increased economic openness are not welcome in countries accustomed to a large public sector and protection from international economic competition, and not everyone is convinced that liberal economic reforms actually help. For instance, many African countries that have undergone World Bank-led adjustment programs are still mired in poverty, and many saw per capita GDP drop despite reforms. Supporters of such programs rightly contend that the unreformed economies in Africa fared even worse. Nonetheless, the performance of African countries undergoing World Bank-led adjustment has been problematic. During 1995, one reason for this less than stellar performance became more salient: multilateral debt.

Various official lending institutions have been criticized for creating a high level of debt in developing countries. These institutions make loans to developing nations, which then must struggle to service the debt. Scant export earnings are put toward retiring the multilateral debt, but fall short. Developing countries must then turn to the same lending institutions for more loans to cover the debt. Thus, loaned money flows right back to the lending institutions. Critics, such as the private aid organization Oxfam, contend that this revolving debt is a hindrance to development for some countries. In 1980, according to Oxfam, 20 percent of debt servicing in the most indebted nations went to paying back multilateral loans. In 1994 that figure rose to a staggering 50 percent [*Financial Times*, 2/20/96]. During the same time period the amount paid back to multilateral institutions by these countries more than tripled, from approximately $1 billion to $3.3 billion.

Oxfam criticizes both the multilateral lending institutions— primarily the World Bank and the IMF—and the recipient governments. It contends that in 1993 and 1994, for every three dollars flowing into the most indebted developing nations from the World Bank-affiliated International Development Association (IDA), two dollars flowed back to the World Bank through debt servicing. A portion of the remaining one dollar went to service IMF debt [ibid.]. Oxfam notes that between 1991 and 1993, Zambia's debt payments were roughly the size of government spending on health and education [ibid.]. Uganda spends approximately $3 per person on health and $17 per person on creditors, mostly multilateral institutions [*New York Times*, 3/16/96].

Moves are afoot to address this issue. The World Bank and the IMF have named 40 poor countries as officially indebted and have begun discussing ways to alleviate this problem. There has even been talk about debt relief in these debt relief-averse institutions. For the 20 nations with debts above 200–250 percent of their export earnings, the requirements would be three years of IMF-approved economic policies. As a reward, qualifying countries could then write off the majority of their bilateral debt over the next three years. If the debt burden were still significant, multilateral debt relief would then be approved, followed by still greater bilateral debt relief [*New York Times*, 3/16/96; *Economist*, 3/23/96]. The program is not yet fully developed, however, and questions remain. The paramount question is whether funding will be adequate. Moreover, some developed countries are hesitant to grant debt relief for fear that this would encourage other countries to be less responsible in borrowing and debt servicing.

Foreign Aid: Another Worrying Trend

Many observers feared that with the end of the Cold War the developed countries would lose interest in foreign aid for developing regions. These fears were well founded—especially regarding the United States, long the largest aid donor. According to an OECD report, Japan, France, and Germany are now the top three donor nations. The United States has slipped to fourth place, with U.S. contributions dropping by 26 percent in 1995 [*Christian Science Monitor*, 6/19/96]. The mood in Washington has shifted sharply against foreign aid—a trend that accelerated with the 1994 Republican congressional majority. Furthermore, as both parties address the budget deficit, austerity at home means that support for foreign aid is politically less tenable. Much criticism of foreign aid centers upon its effectiveness, on the one hand, and bureaucratic waste, on the other hand.

Not only has bilateral U.S. foreign aid been affected but so too has U.S. support for many multilateral institutions. For example, U.S. funding for the United Nations Development Programme (UNDP) is expected to be cut by more than half for 1996—from $113 million in 1995 to as little as $52 million [UNA-USA, *Washington Weekly Report*, 5/24/96]. In 1994, U.S. contributions to multilateral aid organizations decreased 8 percent [*Development Cooperation, 1995 Report*, DAC].

This trend is not unique to the United States. Many, though not all, developed countries are cutting back. In 1994 multilateral and bilateral foreign aid as a percentage of GNP of the OECD's Development Assistance Committee countries decreased to its lowest level since 1973 [*IMF Survey*, 1/8/96]. Aid by non-DAC nations also fell to a record low [*Development Cooperation, 1995 Report*, DAC]. Multilateral institutions increasingly find themselves seeking money in a less hospitable environment. This often means fighting for money already pledged or finding money from other sources. For instance, in March 1996 developed nations pledged to replenish the International Development Association (IDA) with $22 billion over three years, 1997–99 [*Wall Street Journal*, 3/20/96]. These are funds that go to the poorest of countries on easy terms, such as repayment over 35 years with a 10-year grace period. This was an important victory for the IDA, but it was not an unqualified one. The United States has yet to pay the $934 million it pledged for 1994–96, and it will not make any contribution to the new fund's first year. Further, donor governments decided that half of the $22 billion would have to come from the World Bank's own profits and other resources [ibid.].

As private capital has become increasingly important for development, the role of the International Finance Corporation (IFC) has grown. The IFC is affiliated with the World Bank but works with private actors, not governments, and seeks to direct capital into developing countries through a variety of strategies. Common to these strategies is use of the IFC as a catalyst for private capital. Despite tough times in foreign aid, the IFC has made dramatic increases in its financing for developing regions since 1990—both in direct financing and with the private financing that this attracts. Increasing private capital flows to developing countries combined with growing skepticism about foreign aid in donor nations suggest that the IFC's prominence will continue to grow.

Notable Performances Among Developing Countries

For proponents of liberal economic development models, there have always been certain countries to hold up as strong role models. During the 1980s, Bolivia and Ghana were popular examples; and until its crisis began in December 1994, Mexico was also a case in point. In the 1990s, economic liberalization has broken out and new role models abound. How have these developing countries fared?

Uganda: Back from the Dead

In the aftermath of domestic turmoil, including despotic government and a civil war, the Ugandan economy was devastated in the mid-1980s. Infrastructure was in ruins, debt and inflation were high, and poverty was widespread. Since then the Ugandan economy has made numerous reforms: Prices have been liberalized, the civil service cut, the exchange rate lowered, and capital flows eased. The IMF credits these reforms, coupled with political stability, for nearly a decade of positive economic fortunes. Growth has averaged roughly 6 percent per year since 1987; inflation dropped to approximately 6 percent in 1994; and exports have been diversified [*World Economic Outlook*, IMF, 10/95; much of this section draws upon this source].

Still, significant problems remain, notably a large debt burden and widespread poverty. The IMF calls for continued reforms to alleviate these problems and sustain past advances.

India: Reform Doubts?

During the post-World War II era, the Indian government's development approach was famously interventionist. Therefore, India's steps toward economic liberalization during the 1990s have been remarkable, despite being less extensive than reforms in many other developing countries. The liberalization program began in 1991, when India turned to the IMF for support. The reforms have been credited with attracting foreign investment and helping the Indian economy to grow. But in 1995 and 1996 India has been sending mixed messages to foreign investors. While India continued to liberalize, there were high-profile efforts to resist foreign investment. An American icon, Kentucky Fried Chicken, and Enron, a U.S. energy company, both faced opposition to their FDI projects. A Kentucky Fried Chicken restaurant was closed by government officials for spurious health reasons. Enron had signed a $2.8 billion contract to deliver power, only to have a state government subsequently cancel the contract. Both companies successfully weathered these investment storms, but such events have made some observers question the Indian commitment to liberalization. Other companies seem willing to risk similar turbulence: Government approval of FDI and actual investment levels doubled from 1994 to 1995 [*Economist*, 2/17/96].

Latin America: Searching for Tigers

From Mexico to Tierra del Fuego, countries have moved toward economic liberalization during the late 1980s and first half of the 1990s. The leading reformers have been Mexico and Chile, often called Latin American tigers, but other nations in the region have also taken steps toward liberalization.

1995 began with fears that the Mexican crisis might lead to financial instability in other Latin American countries. The region did go through a so-called "tequila effect," characterized by lower inward capital flows. But as 1995 progressed, capital flows to the region increased, and it became apparent that no Mexican-style crisis would develop.

Economic performance in the region as a whole was strong in 1995. Growth in Central and South America (excluding Mexico) was 3.4 percent [*OECD Economic Outlook*, 12/95; Mexico is excluded from the OECD's statistics for the region as a whole]. This statistic masks the fact that there were varied fortunes within Latin America. Chile, the region's most liberalized economy, had another Asian tiger-like economic performance in 1995, when the economy grew by 8 percent. Since 1990 the Chilean economy has grown by 41 percent [*Economist*, 2/10/96]. Such success has markedly lifted Chilean social indicators, such as those developed by UNDP.

Other extremes of growth in the region were negative. The crisis shrank Mexico's GDP by 6 percent in 1995 [ibid., 3/9/96], and capital flight and an austerity program shrank the Argentine economy by 2.5 percent, requiring an IMF bail-out. By late 1995 Argentina had weathered 20 percent unemployment [ibid., 11/18/95, 2/10/96]. On the brighter side, capital flows into Argentina were stronger at the beginning of 1996, and growth for the year was expected to be slow but positive. Venezuela also had a tough 1995. After shrinking by nearly 3 percent in 1994, the Venezuelan economy grew only slightly in 1995. Here, too, the IMF was needed. In April 1996 the IMF announced a $1.4 billion standby loan for Venezuela [*Los Angeles Times*, 4/23/96].

Latin America traditionally has had problems with inflation, but generally it fared well in 1995: Inflation was 7.5 percent across the region, excluding higher inflation in Brazil and Venezuela. Inflation in Brazil was 25 percent, yet this was hailed as a major accomplishment by President Fernando Henrique Cardoso; 1994 inflation was 930 percent. Venezuelan inflation was 60 percent in 1995. Unlike Brazil, however, Venezuelan inflation shows no signs of slowing down in 1996.

Mexico: Toward Health?

During much of the 1980s the patient was in dire straits; the Mexican economy reached its nadir with the debt crisis of 1982 and the recession of 1986. The recommended course of treatment was a diet of economic liberalization. Thus, the Mexican economy, one of the most protected in the world, underwent an amazing transformation toward openness. The openness was designed to strengthen the Mexican economy: Exercise, in the form of international competition, would invigorate Mexican producers (those that survived) and foreign investment would serve as nutrients, helping the economy grow. The results were impressive. Inflation fell below 10 percent, a major achievement. Foreign investment was high, exports boomed, the economy grew rapidly, and the economic prescription received an important concurring second opinion: The United States voiced its approval of the reforms with the North American Free Trade Agreement (NAFTA).

Before NAFTA was even a year old, however, the patient suffered a stroke. In December 1994 the peso was devalued 15 percent, then allowed to float. It sank, dropping by half during late 1994 and into 1995. Interest rates rose to astronomical levels, economic activity was sharply curtailed, Mexico's middle class (little that there is) found itself poorer, and the poor found themselves even more in need.

Mexico's condition stabilized thanks to emergency funds provided by the international community, notably the United States. By August 1995 Mexico had used $23 billion of these funds, and the crisis had indeed stabilized. How, then, to get the Mexican economy on its feet again? President Ernesto Zedillo decided that the economic liberalization diet should progress. Stabilization was successful, but economic pain continues: As noted above, the economy contracted 6 percent during 1995 and continued to shrink in the first quarter of 1996 [*Wall Street Journal*, 3/14/96], and the unofficial unemployment rate is thought to be between 15 and 20 percent [*Los Angeles Times*, 2/29/96]. Nevertheless, there has been some progress. Foreign capital has returned to Mexico. The dramatically lower peso has made Mexican exports more competitive in foreign markets, thus keeping some industries alive in the face of dampened domestic consumption. The peso has appreciated from its 1995 lows. What is the prognosis for Mexico? The OECD predicts growth, led by exports, to be 3 percent during 1996. This is not enough to revive the Mexican economy to its pre-crisis strength, but it is a start.

The Asian Dragon, Tigers, and Cubs

The Asian economic boom continues. The Asian tigers—Hong Kong, Singapore, South Korea, and Taiwan—again registered high-growth performances. In recent years the Asian "cubs," such as Indonesia, Malaysia, and Thailand, have been moving steadily in the tracks of the tigers, and they did so once again in 1995 with growth of 7.3 percent, 9.6 percent, and 8.5 percent respectively. In the seven most dynamic emerging Asian economies, growth averaged 7.8 percent for the year.

The Asian economic miracle, however, is an uneven one. The region is more diverse than is commonly believed. For instance, to call South Korea and Taiwan "emerging" markets does not do them justice. Many of the region's economies, such as Singapore's, are moving to higher value-added production, leaving labor-intensive production for lower-wage nations. On the other hand, the boom has yet to find its way into some of the region's economies. Generally, development has been most successful in East Asia, and less marked elsewhere. Even within countries, generalizations can distort reality. Overall Chinese growth has been phenomenal, but many rural areas of China remain mired in poverty and seem little affected by the expansion in the coastal regions. Each year, however, the generalization of an "Asian miracle" seems more accurate. The growth continues, and more Asian countries are taking part in the rapid economic expansion. Indeed, the astronomical development across Asia stands ready to surpass the historic post-World War II expansion in Europe, Japan, and North America.

Amid the success, there is also some trepidation. The expansion has raised the wealth of many Asian countries, but numerous problems remain and many new ones have emerged precisely because of the expansion. Environmental problems mount, cultural changes loom, infrastructures strain, competition increases, and urban areas swell with new arrivals from rural regions. China faces rural-to-urban migration of a magnitude and rapidity that is perhaps unprecedented in human history. The prospect of rising consumption spreading across Asia—with more cars, refrigerators, and other energy-consuming products—worries many environmentalists.

China: The Dragon Is Awake

China has been the world's fastest-growing economy during the 1980s and 1990s, but at a cost of high inflation. During 1995, policies to fight inflation worked, but they also lowered growth, which nonetheless remained robust. Inflation fell from over 27 percent in late 1994 to 11.2 percent in November of 1995 [*Economist*, 2/10/96]. Economic growth in 1995 was 9.5 percent, down from 11.8 percent in 1994 and 13.4 percent in 1993 [*OECD Economic Outlook*, 12/95; *Asian Development Outlook 1995–1996*, Asian Development Bank]. Export growth was extremely high in 1995: By mid-year the dollar value of exports had grown by 40 percent. For 1996 growth is expected to be 10.5 percent, although this will depend heavily on the extent to which the government continues its vigilance against inflation.

China is becoming more assertive with other economic actors as its economy grows. Many analysts have noted that China increasingly uses the right to invest or sell in the Chinese market as leverage with which to gain local production commitments or technology transfers from foreign firms. But the conditions that China often places on foreign investment have not dissuaded foreign companies, and in 1995 foreign investment in China was a record $38 billion [*New York Times*, 3/13/96]—second only to the United States.

The United States has been pressing China on a number of economic and noneconomic issues: piracy of software, music, and movies; entry into the World Trade Organization (WTO); relations with Taiwan; and human rights practices. In April 1996, presumably in retaliation for this pressure, China rescinded an order for Boeing jetliners in favor of its European competitor, Airbus Industrie. Europe generally has taken a softer stand than the United States on the conditions for China's entry into the WTO and on human rights violations. While the Chinese economy has been awake for some time, the Chinese government is now also awake—and asserting itself more forcefully in international politics.

Transitioning Economies: Facing Ahead or Behind?

There is a joke that says Boris Yeltsin has done in a few short years what communism couldn't do in 70 years: make communism look good. Many voters in Russia and other transitioning nations agree. They have increasingly voted for Communists, many of whom are unreformed and antireform. This has led to some backsliding on reform, but for the time being reforms have survived.

The economic fortunes of the transitioning countries are varied. The Czech Republic—a recent addition to the OECD—is experiencing solid economic growth (4 percent in 1995) combined with relatively low inflation (9 percent in 1995). In Slovakia and Poland, 1995 growth was 6 percent and 6.5 percent respectively. But other transitioning economies are not faring nearly so well. The Russian economy shrank approximately 4 percent in 1995, with 140 percent inflation. Amazingly, this is an improvement over 1994, when the Russian economy was in a free fall: GDP dropped 15 percent, with 226 percent inflation. It is predicted that 1996 will prove economically brighter for Russia. It will also bring international succor: In February 1996 the IMF agreed to a $10.2 billion loan for Russia, to be disbursed over three years [ibid., 2/23/96].

While these statistics are at once hopeful and discouraging, they should also be viewed with caution, as many statistics in the region are of questionable accuracy. Some transitioning economies are clearly succeeding while others are not. The problems faced across the region are many: privatization, slow growth, high inflation, unemployment, currency weakness, underdeveloped financial systems, and pollution. These problems vary greatly from country to country. For example, Russia has been successful at privatization, and official unemployment has been lower than in many other transitioning economies, but growth and inflation remain troublesome. Elsewhere, growth has been strong. Through these dissimilar fortunes, some trends for the region do emerge. In 1995 unemployment remained worrying; inflation generally slowed; FDI increased but remained low; and growth was somewhat better.

What accounts for the varied fortunes of the transitioning economies? Partially, it is the degree to which countries have embraced reforms.

The Visegrad nations—the Czech Republic, Hungary, Poland, and Slovakia—have been at the forefront of the transition to capitalism and are experiencing economic success to a greater degree than most transitioning countries. By contrast, the Russian judicial system does not offer investors—domestic or foreign—much comfort. Belarus, Moldova, and Ukraine have been slower to embrace reforms and consequently have met with worse economic fortunes. In such countries as Armenia, Azerbaijan, Georgia, and Tajikistan the devastation of war is an additional hurdle to economic success.

FDI remains weak in most of the transitioning economies, although it was somewhat stronger in 1995. The inability of transitioning countries to attract FDI is more notable when compared to developing countries elsewhere. For instance, 1993 and 1994 FDI in *all* transitioning countries was roughly equivalent to that of Argentina alone during the same period [*World Investment Report, 1995*, UNCTAD]. Moreover, the FDI level is all the worse given its uneven distribution. According to UNCTAD, the Visegrad nations have captured over half of FDI going to transitioning economies.

FDI is of course influenced by the state of reforms in transitioning countries. It is also influenced by the degree of trade access these countries have to world markets. It is therefore a positive development that export growth in 1995 averaged 20 percent for Russia and seven other Eastern European transitioning economies. Of particular importance to these economies is access to Western European markets, which, with their geographical proximity and low wages, could make them magnets for investment.

A number of developments have increased access. For instance, the EU has had association agreements with the Visegrad nations since 1991 (extended to both the Czech Republic and Slovakia after the division of Czechoslovakia). These agreements have opened trade and boosted exports to the EU, but some disappointment has since emerged over the fact that the agreements allow protectionism in the EU to continue in various forms. For instance, sensitive economic sectors may be exempted. Typically, these are precisely sectors in which the Visegrad nations could best take advantage of EU markets. Nonetheless, the association agreements are better than no agreement, and other transitioning economies have successfully clamored for them, namely the three Baltic countries, Romania, and Bulgaria.

What many European transitioning countries truly seek, however, is full EU membership. This would be an exceedingly important step in their transition, were it to happen. The Visegrad nations, with the exception of Slovakia, are at the front of the queue by virtue of their more advanced state of transition. Slovakia has been reprimanded by the EU for its dearth of democracy and is likely to be excluded from EU membership. Current EU member nations are divided about the wisdom of widening the union. Adding these or other countries would likely require changes in the EU's voting mechanism. Moreover, most of the EU's budget already goes to two programs: agricultural subsidies and development aid to poorer EU regions. Extending full membership to the Visegrad nations, let alone other transitioning economies, would either add an enormous burden to the EU budget for these categories or would lead to scaled-back commitments. Scaling back is not enticing to countries that receive significant levels of agricultural subsidies, such as France, or to countries that receive significant regional development funding, such as Greece, Portugal, and Ireland. The Inter-Governmental Conference (IGC), which EU member governments began in March 1996, will meet throughout the year and possibly into 1997 to decide precisely these matters.

3. World Trade

Free Trade Marches On, but Slows to Catch Its Breath

Many trends prevalent in the international trading system over the past decade continued in 1995 and into 1996: The level of world trade increased, the trend toward regional trading arrangements continued, and the trading system came under (and survived) the familiar pressure of bilateral trade battles. But the trade environment has undergone an important evolution. The establishment of the World Trade Organization in January 1995 and the increasing resistance to U.S. bilateral pressure have subtly changed the nature of bilateral trade rows.

Trade growth in 1995 was 8 percent, according to the WTO, down from 9.5 percent in 1994 [*Economist*, 4/6/96]. The WTO expects 1996 growth to be slightly slower, at 7 percent. Strong growth in trade is partially explained by the liberalization brought about by the establishment of the WTO. The WTO brings freer trade in agriculture, services, textiles and apparel, and other areas that had been outside the purview of its predecessor, the General Agreement on Tariffs and Trade (GATT). Moreover, trade will continue to grow freer in the coming years as the Uruguay Round's tariff reductions and other liberalization measures are phased in.

The impact of the Uruguay Round, which created the WTO, will be greater still as more countries enter the WTO. As of January 1996 there were 27 countries seeking entry into the 112-member organization—mostly transitioning economies, including Russia [ibid., 1/13/96]. China is still not a WTO member. As noted above, the United States has been resisting China's entry into the WTO until China makes a number of liberal economic reforms. Bringing China, Russia, and other countries into the WTO will extend free trade's growing reach.

The WTO's first anniversary in January 1996 brought its first dispute settlement panel decision. Venezuela and Brazil charged that the United States violated WTO rules by giving domestic producers greater leeway than foreign producers in meeting new gasoline standards. The panel of experts ruled for Venezuela and Brazil. The United States appealed, and the appellate body ruled against it. The decision is final. The WTO's dispute resolution mechanism is more streamlined than was GATT's, where stalling was easier and implementation of decisions was by consensus only, often a difficult achievement. The WTO dispute resolution mechanism—including consultations, the panel decision, and the appeals process—takes place within 18 months and implementation is stopped only by consensus. The successful resolution of this and other disputes will be essential if the WTO is to be significantly more effective than GATT. As 1996 began there were over 20 trade disputes awaiting WTO rulings [*Christian Science Monitor*, 1/17/96]. Thus, we will know more about the WTO's effectiveness by its December 1996 ministerial meeting in Singapore.

Regional Trade Arrangements: To Expand or Not to Expand?

The trend toward growing regionalism continued in 1995 and 1996, although not consistently. For instance, there has been movement toward expanding NAFTA since it went into force in January 1994, most particularly to include Chile. And many Caribbean nations have sought legislation granting them NAFTA "parity." But these efforts stalled in 1995, as the mood in the United States turned markedly against extending NAFTA. The Mexican crisis decreased Mexican demand for U.S. goods and therefore weakened U.S. political support for extending NAFTA. Moreover, the congressional coalition that initially voted for NAFTA in 1993 collapsed with the 1994 election. Democrats that survived the election, especially in the House of Representatives, tended to be opponents of NAFTA. Additionally, many Republican freshman are hostile to free trade, which also took a beating from presidential candidate Pat Buchanan. Combined, these factors ended the prospects of Clinton winning "fast track" authority that would allow the administration to negotiate an agreement with fewer congressional hurdles than normal legislation. In the fall of 1995 Congress dropped a bill that would have extended NAFTA parity to 24 Caribbean nations. Chile had been formally invited to join NAFTA at the December 1994 Summit of the Americas and had subsequently negotiated with the United States about the terms of inclusion. But talks were hampered by the lack of fast track authority, and it eventually became obvious that none would be forthcoming. Concomitantly, Chile decided to change its tack: It has negotiated with Canada to establish a bilateral pact and it has put greater emphasis on joining

Mercosur—the Southern Cone group dominated by Brazil and including Argentina, Paraguay, and Uruguay.

For its part, Mexico has been unhappy with U.S. roadblocks to the implementation of NAFTA. For example, the United States used safety concerns to delay implementing liberalization of U.S.-Mexican trucking, and it took steps to protect Florida tomato growers from Mexican competition.

Still, the political climate in the United States has not stopped all momentum toward free trade. In the fall of 1995 the United States extended trade benefits to Andean Group countries that previously had been reserved for Caribbean nations. The Clinton administration has also continued to press for hemispheric free trade through the Summit of the Americas. Here, other countries, notably Brazil, have been more hesitant, preferring to first concentrate on Mercosur.

Movement toward hemispheric free trade continues on a number of other fronts. Mexico has reached bilateral agreements with numerous Latin American countries, and more are in the works. Chile and other countries in the region have likewise concluded various bilateral agreements. Other regional groups abound, ranging from the small Central American Common Market to the larger Andean Group (Bolivia, Colombia, Ecuador, Peru, and Venezuela) and Mercosur. Groupings in the Americas vary in the depth of their integration. NAFTA, for instance, calls only for free trade, while the Andean Group and Mercosur are customs unions with both internal free trade and a common external tariff.

Mercosur began as a free trade agreement in the mid-1980s between Argentina and Brazil, widened to include its other members, and then deepened in 1994 into its present status as a customs union. Mercosur has been considering an agreement with Chile and Venezuela but is moving cautiously. In December 1995, Mercosur signed a free trade agreement with Bolivia and a framework agreement with the EU. The latter agreement calls for economic and political cooperation that may lead to lowered trade barriers between the two regions.

The Asia Pacific Economic Cooperation forum (APEC), consisting of 18 Pacific Rim countries, has been of growing importance and has also recently met with mixed success. The grouping was established in 1989 and was not initially considered to be of particular significance. This changed in 1993 when President Clinton made APEC a cornerstone of his trade policy with the Pacific Rim. Under U.S. pressure, APEC has begun to give some structure and commitment to the platitudes of freer trade, which such international arrangements always bring. Not all of the APEC countries are fond of these efforts. Many Asian nations in the forum prefer a less formal arrangement than the United States has been seeking. Some analysts note that this may be a difference in style. It is argued that Asian nations seek greater consensus and less formality, whereas the legalistic United States and other non-Asian APEC countries call for detailed formal standards that necessarily involve haggling. But to call the differences stylistic ignores the fact that there are genuine policy disputes. Some Asian countries, Malaysia especially, prefer closer trade ties to other Asian countries and would like to exclude the United States. Some fear closer integration because it would expose inefficient industries to greater international competition. For example, South Korea, China, Japan, and Taiwan have all resisted freer agricultural trade in APEC. Nevertheless, under U.S. insistence, APEC has moved toward formality, and concrete measures leading to freer trade have been approved. In 1994, APEC members meeting in Indonesia agreed to remove all trade barriers by 2010 for industrialized members and by 2020 for developing members.

In the November 1995 APEC summit in Osaka, Japan, member nations developed steps to achieve this broader goal. To critics, the steps are less stringent than found in many other trade agreements. For instance, those not complying are merely held up to criticism by other members. Nevertheless, as proponents note, APEC continues its evolution toward being a regional grouping with significant world implications.

Bilateral Trade Rows: The United States and Japan

The familiar thrust and parry pattern in U.S.-Japanese trade relations continued in 1995 and into 1996. The United States accuses, Japan denies, the United States threatens, Japan resists, both sides talk, Japan makes concessions (often cosmetic), and the argument is set aside until disagreements emerge regarding the concessions. The United States then reaccuses and the pattern repeats itself.

In January 1996, Ryutaro Hashimoto became Japan's new Prime Minister, and many analysts expect a more assertive Japan under his leadership. Why? Just prior to his tenure as Prime Minister, Hashimoto—then Minister of International Trade and Industry—led Japan in the U.S.-Japanese automotive talks that went from acrimony to sanctions and were a notable example of increasing Japanese resistance to U.S. trade demands. Hashimoto has been a proponent of the "Japan that can say no" school of thought.

Does it follow that Japanese resistance to U.S. bilateral trade demands is likely to increase? Yes, for two reasons. First, as of this writing, the Japanese are refusing to discuss renewing the landmark semiconductor agreement, first signed in 1986, establishing targets for Japanese imports of foreign (U.S.-dominated) semiconductors. The United States has hailed this as a precedent-setting agreement because Japan assented to a measurable indicator of its economy's openness. Japan, however, regrets agreeing to such a measurable indicator; it is managed trade, not free trade. Japan insists that meeting the target means the government must encroach upon decisions that should be left to private economic actors. Many trade disagreements since the semiconductor pact have involved the United States trying to pin Japan to a specific and quantifiable goal post, with Japan resisting exactly this. The semiconductor pact expired during the summer of 1996 and so far Japan has refused to even discuss its renewal.

The second reason that Japan is increasingly resisting U.S. bilateral trade pressure is the existence of the WTO, which contains a highly effective dispute resolution mechanism (described above). U.S. threats of bilateral sanctions would likely be declared in violation of the WTO. If this were to happen, the United States would be placed in an unenviable position: adhere to the WTO ruling, which would strengthen the organization's power and legitimacy, or ignore the ruling at the cost of dealing the WTO a crippling blow.

Some assert that these two developments have led to a change in Japanese behavior. But there has also been a change in U.S. behavior. The United States is becoming more exasperated and therefore more willing to use sanctions unless numerical targets are set and subsequently reached—witness the auto trade row during the summer of 1995.

The U.S.-Japan trade front is not totally bleak. The strong yen relative to the dollar may alleviate some of the tension as U.S. goods become more competitive in Japanese markets. The United States has made significant inroads in Japanese markets in many economic sectors, including automotive trade, which accounts for most of the U.S. trade deficit with Japan. Moreover, bilateral agreements have been successfully concluded in a number of areas. Some successes, however, will not hide the fact that more tension is likely in 1996 and 1997.

Bilateral Trade Rows: The United States and China

U.S.-Japanese conflicts are not new to the global trading system, but other bilateral disputes have increased in rancor, and none more so than those between the United States and China. The U.S.-Chinese trade relationship is of growing importance, with trade flows at record levels. Chinese exports to the United States have been significantly larger than U.S. exports to China. In fact, the U.S. trade deficit with China is second only to its deficit with Japan. It is telling that the two countries do not even agree on the size of that deficit. The statistical issue of contention is whether goods transshipped through Hong Kong, with some level of value added, should be categorized as coming from China or Hong Kong. Whether transshipments through Hong Kong are included in the calculus or not, clearly U.S.-Chinese trade is of greater economic and political significance than in the past. Also increasing the saliency of U.S.-Chinese trade is the fact that China is asserting itself politically as it becomes economically more powerful. Putting aside U.S.-Chinese acrimony over a host of other issues, such as Taiwan and human rights, the trade relationship itself has become increasingly tense.

High on the Chinese agenda is entry into the WTO. To be more precise, it is the conditions for entry into the WTO that are contentious. China wants easy entry terms that developing countries are afforded, while the United States has been the leading proponent of requiring China to meet more stringent developed-nation criteria. The U.S. priority in the bilateral relationship has been China's weak enforcement of U.S. intellectual property rights. Companies operating in China produce U.S. company-copyrighted software, movies, and music but pay no royalties. Worse still, some of the pirated goods are then exported. The two countries reached an agreement in February 1995 in which China would enforce copyright laws at 29 specific pirate production sites, but the United States has since charged that China's enforcement has been inadequate and is threatening sanctions anew. At the time of this writing, a new agreement appeared imminent, and sanctions were likely to be averted.

The United States has leverage that goes beyond China's entry into the WTO, notably the yearly extension of China's most favored nation status (MFN). Denying MFN would raise tariffs on Chinese goods entering the United States and could, therefore, be a potent bargaining chip. But wielding that chip risks Chinese retribution. As noted above, in April 1996 Boeing lost a large Chinese contract to rival Airbus specifically because of U.S.-Chinese political tension. As with overall U.S.-Chinese ties, the trade relations face an acrimonious future.

Foreign Exchange Relations: Turbulent Normalcy

1995 was another year of turbulence in currency markets. This is becoming the norm. In 1992 and 1993 many European Union countries' currencies came under heavy pressure. The markets bet that the British and Italian governments could not keep the pound and lira high enough to keep them within the exchange rate mechanism (ERM), a band that keeps member currencies close to the German deutsche mark. Despite government bluster and open coffers, the markets bet right, and these two important currencies dropped out of the ERM. The ERM band was subsequently widened substantially. In 1994 there was more turbulence in foreign exchange markets. The primary developments were the collapse of the Mexican peso, which had reverberations for capital flows to other developing countries, and the fall of the U.S. dollar relative to the yen and deutsche mark. The latter three currencies are the world's largest, and therefore their value holds global implications.

The first half of 1995 witnessed a continuation of many of these trends. The peso remained weak, losing more than 20 percent of its value relative to the dollar from May to November 1995 [*OECD Economic Outlook,* 12/

95]; the yen continued its ascent. Then came a reversal. The peso strengthened; by the end of 1995 the yen had fallen by roughly a quarter from its 1995 high. The deutsche mark also weakened compared to the dollar. To many analysts, the turbulence in the second half of 1995 was welcome. The "overvalued" yen in 1994 and the first half of 1995 had economists scratching their heads. Based on the fundamentals, such as the size of the budget deficit, inflation, and growth, many economists argued that the dollar should have been much stronger against the yen and the deutsche mark. Nevertheless, the dollar kept falling. In a concerted effort that began to show results in August 1995, monetary officials in Germany, Japan, the United States, and elsewhere acted to correct this perceived imbalance, and were widely credited with an effective intervention in the currency markets. Importantly, they moved with the markets, buying dollars even as their price was increasing, thus strengthening a market trend toward the stronger dollar.

While the dollar was weak relative to the yen and deutsche mark, it was still strong relative to many other currencies—notably those of Mexico and Canada, two of the most important U.S. trading partners. This offset some of the inflationary pressures that a weaker currency might bring.

For many European countries, the strong deutsche mark was a significant problem in 1995. Those European Union nations still hoping for EMU in 1999 need to keep their currencies close to the EMU's anchor. In France—Germany's primary EMU partner—the franc weathered episodic downward pressure in 1995. Other European currencies, such as the Italian lira, the Spanish peseta, and the Swedish krona, came under greater pressure during 1995. This raises an important question: Will markets view the EU's steps toward EMU in 1996 and 1997 as credible? Only time will tell.

Other currencies came under pressure in 1995 and early 1996 as well. The Turkish lira and the South African rand weakened. In February 1996 the South African rand took a rapid fall. Inevitably, comparisons with Mexico emerged. But fears of a Mexico-like crisis in South Africa are misplaced: The underlying South African economy is much stronger. South African growth is predicted to be 4 percent in 1996, with 8.7 percent inflation. Importantly, its current account deficit is small. Moreover, the rand's drop was far less dramatic than was the peso's [*Economist*, 2/24/96].

Currencies in many developing Asian counties also came under pressure in 1995, but for these nations the foreign exchange pressure was different from what is usually associated with developing countries—or at least different from the problems that make headlines. Many developing Asian countries have experienced rapid growth combined with high inward investment. This puts upward pressure on their currencies. Countries such as Thailand and Malaysia are loathe to see their currencies appreciate, fearful that this would harm their products' competitiveness in foreign markets and, therefore, discourage foreign investment. On the other hand, if the undervalued currencies do not appreciate, the result may be inflation. Relative to the currency exchange rate problems faced by Mexico and other developing countries, however, this is a good problem to have.

IV
Global Resource Management

1. Environment and Sustainable Development
By Gail V. Karlsson

Human Effects on Climate Change

The most significant event in the environmental arena this past year was the release of a report by the **Intergovernmental Panel on Climate Change (IPCC)** stating that "the balance of evidence suggests a discernible human influence on global climate" [IPCC Second Assessment Report, *Summary for Policymakers: The Science of Climate Change*, IPCC Working Group I, 12/95]. The IPCC report, adopted in Rome in 1995, represents the consensus of over 2,000 scientists from around the world. The group was first assembled by the U.N. Environment Programme (UNEP) and the World Meteorological Organization (WMO) in 1988, prior to the negotiations on the climate change treaty, to provide objective assessments of scientific research on climate change.

The first IPCC report, issued in 1990, was not able to identify with certainty a human-induced effect on climate distinct from natural climate variability. Considerable scientific process has been made since 1990, however, as new data and analyses have become available. Despite pressures from some oil-producing states and fossil fuel-related companies to emphasize continuing uncertainties, the 1995 IPCC report concluded that "the observed warming trend is unlikely to be entirely natural in origin" [ibid., p. 4]. Atmospheric concentrations of greenhouse gases, including carbon dioxide, methane, and nitrous oxide, have grown significantly as a result of human activities, according to the report, mostly due to fossil fuel combustion, land-use changes, and agricultural practices [ibid., p. 1]. Since carbon dioxide and nitrous oxide can remain in the atmosphere for long periods of time, even centuries, their concentrations would continue to increase even if emissions remained at present levels.

The IPCC's "best estimate" is that **global mean surface air temperatures will show an increase of 2 degrees from 1990 to 2100.** The projected range is 1 degree to 3.5 degrees, reflecting differing assumptions about future population and economic growth, land use, technology, energy availability, and fuels. The average sea level is expected to rise about 50 centimeters during the same period, due to melting glaciers and ice sheets, and to continue to rise in future centuries [ibid., p. 5].

The projected changes sound small, but the impact could be catastrophic. Even slightly higher average temperatures could result in a variety of regional effects: a greater number of extremely hot days and severe droughts in some areas, and heavier rainfall and flooding in others [ibid., p. 6]. With about half the world's population living along coastlines, a small rise in sea level would present a serious threat to large numbers of communities—especially in conjunction with more intense rainfall or serious storms. The report also warns that "sustained rapid climate change could shift the competitive balance among species and even lead to forest dieback, altering the terrestrial uptake and release of carbon" [ibid., p. 7].

While the report is far from cheerful, the very existence of the IPCC highlights the essential role of the United Nations in identifying and investigating critical environmental issues requiring international attention. More important, the United Nations has established the legal framework for addressing many of these issues through international treaties on climate change, biological diversity, and desertification as well as through treaties to protect the oceans and the ozone layer.

Climate Change Treaty

The **second Conference of the Parties to the U.N. Framework Convention on Climate Change (FCCC)** met in July 1996 to review the policy implications of the IPCC report, progress made by parties toward meeting existing commitments to reduce greenhouse gas emissions, and measures for strengthening future commitments. The first Conference of the Parties, held in Berlin in April 1995, had concluded that the current commitment of industrialized countries—to reduce greenhouse gas emissions to 1990 levels by the year 2000—is not adequate. Consequently, the Conference adopted the "Berlin Mandate," which established a process for strengthening the commitments of the industrialized countries. An ad hoc group is negotiating a protocol or other appropriate legal instrument to be adopted at the third meeting of the Conference of the Parties, scheduled for 1997.

The 1995 IPCC report added greater impetus to the negotiations on emission reduction targets. It also highlighted the need for further scientific assessment. At the February meeting of the FCCC subsidiary committees, some countries asked the IPCC to prepare regionally oriented analyses of climate change, to help identify predicted impacts in specific areas of the world [*Earth Negotiations Bulletin*, Vol. 12, No. 26; hereafter *ENB*]. Others have asked for an analysis of the projected social and economic effects of specific proposals for new emission reduction commitments.

At the March 1996 meeting of the Ad Hoc Group on the Berlin Mandate, the IPCC Chair, Bert Bolin, pointed out that various options are available to achieve 10 percent to 30 percent reductions of greenhouse gas emissions at little or no cost [*ENB*, Vol. 12, No. 27]. He also concluded that the economies of all countries could benefit from the implementation of policies and measures to mitigate climate change [ibid.]. Available options include increased use of such renewable energy sources as wind and solar power, reduced consumption of energy through efficiency and conservation, and use of non-fossil fuels. Many feasible measures have not been instituted because of political and economic barriers. The representative of the Marshall Islands argued that it is inappropriate for some countries to focus on the economic costs of reducing oil revenues when other countries are threatened with complete inundation from rising sea levels [ibid.].

U.N. Climate Agenda

In light of the potential consequences of global warming, the United Nations has moved to integrate the climate-related activities of UNEP, WMO, and other specialized agencies into a U.N. "Climate Agenda." The goal is to promote and support national climate research and response efforts. One thrust of the program will be to help countries reduce their social and economic vulnerability to climate variations, whether naturally occurring or man-made [*Climate Agenda*, p. 16]. The agenda also emphasizes public outreach to communicate new advances in climate-related issues and to encourage responsible behavior [ibid., p. 24].

In a related effort, the U.N. Development Programme (UNDP) has proposed a new **Initiative for Sustainable Energy,** seeking to make energy policies serve the goals of sustainable human development. Since more than 85 percent of the world's primary energy supply comes from fossil fuels, climate change mitigation will require a major overhaul of the current world energy system. Moreover, approximately 2.5 billion people in developing countries currently lack access to commercial energy supplies. UNDP would promote a leapfrogging strategy by which developing countries can bypass energy systems currently used by industrialized countries and move directly to more efficient technologies and renewable sources of energy.

The interconnections between atmospheric conditions, energy use, and sustainable development were also on the agenda of the February 1996 meeting of the **U.N. Committee on New and Renewable Energy and on Energy for Development.** One report presented at the meeting noted that measures to protect the atmosphere face a number of competing social and economic policy concerns [E/C.13/1996/CRP.2, 2/8/96]. Some of the concerns, such as poverty relief, health care, housing, and employment, are understandably given higher priority in many countries than the mitigation of uncertain climate threats. Although substantial energy increases are needed to satisfy basic human needs in developing countries, the report warns that "it would be virtually impossible for the majority of the world's population to enjoy similar resource intensive energy-use patterns as those prevailing in the industrialized countries" [ibid.]. To provide energy services while avoiding harmful environmental side effects, policy-makers should focus on energy-efficiency improvements and on "decarbonization"—that is, a shift to low-carbon and carbon-free energy sources [ibid.].

Furthering the goal of decarbonization, the **U.N. Educational, Scientific and Cultural Organization (UNESCO)** has initiated its own program to promote the use of renewable and nonpolluting energy, and is organizing a **World Solar Summit,** to be held in Zimbabwe in September 1996. The purpose of the Summit is to launch a world solar program demonstrating the economic and environmental advantages of renewable energy sources—including wind, solar electricity, hydro, geothermal, ocean thermal, and biomass [U.N. press release EN/230, 2/13/96].

Commission on Sustainable Development

The U.N. Commission on Sustainable Development (CSD) reviewed many climate-related issues at its fourth meeting, held in New York in April 1996. Each year the CSD's program of work concentrates on specific chapters of **Agenda 21**—the grand plan for sustainable development adopted at the 1992 U.N. Conference on Environment and Development. In 1996 the CSD program covered Chapter 9 on the protection of the atmosphere and Chapter 17 on the protection of the oceans and coastal areas. The Commission also reviewed progress on implementing the program of action for sustainable development of small island states and progress on reaching international agreement on the protection of forests.

The report on the atmosphere prepared for the CSD noted that although industrialized countries had made improvements in energy efficiency, their overall demand for energy was increasing. Despite the FCCC commitments, very few countries have adopted policies that will stabilize emissions at the 1990 target level [E/CN.17/1996/22/Add.1]. The highly developed economies of the industrialized countries, dependent as they are on intensive energy use and consumption of fossil fuels, offer the greatest potential for near-term emissions reductions. They are also the least vulnerable to an adverse environmental impact from global warming, and they have the greatest financial and technological resources for mitigating or adapting to climate variations [ibid.]. Currently, the economies of developing countries do not make a substantial contribution to greenhouse gas emissions. Yet their greater reliance on agriculture makes them more vulnerable to weather patterns, and their low national incomes limit their ability to adapt to climate variations [ibid.].

Small Islands

Small island developing states feel particularly vulnerable to the effects of climate change. At the 1995 Conference of the Parties to the Framework Convention on Climate Change, the **Alliance of Small Island States** presented a draft protocol for strengthening emissions reduction commitments by industrialized countries. The Alliance was disappointed that the Conference failed to adopt the protocol, opting instead for the "Berlin Mandate" process, which delayed any new legal agreement until at least 1997.

The coral reefs surrounding many small islands are extremely vulnerable to changes in water temperature and sea level. They are also among the world's most biologically productive and diverse ecosystems. A special program—the International Coral Reef Initiative—has been organized by a group of concerned governments and U.N. agencies to highlight the value of reef ecosystems and the threats they face from human activity.

Within the **U.N. Department of Policy Coordination and Sustainable Development (DPCSD),** a new unit has been established to oversee general implementation of the program of action on sustainable development in small island developing states adopted at the 1994 Barbados Conference. One of the items specifically requested in Barbados was construction of a vulnerability index to assess the social and economic implications of sea level rise. In November 1995 the Second Committee (Economic and Financial) of the General Assembly asked the DPCSD to compile such a vulnerability index, to be prepared in conjunction with the U.N. Conference on Trade and Development (UNCTAD) [A/C.2/50/L.47]. UNEP and the U.N. Centre for Human Settlements are also working with small island states on adaptive strategies and disaster-related issues [A/50/422].

A number of Caribbean islands were severely battered by hurricanes in 1995. Their economies, heavily dependent on agriculture and/or tourism, were badly damaged, and their resources for rebuilding are limited. The 1995 IPCC report concluded that there is not enough evidence yet to determine whether global warming will cause more frequent tropical storms or changes in the directional patterns of such storms. But recent occurrences of intense storms and erratic weather have raised suspicions that global warming is already affecting the frequency and severity of natural disasters [*Scientific American*, 2/96].

In addition to the perils of climate change, Pacific islands have had to face fears about the environmental risks of nuclear weapons tests. At the November 1995 meeting of the Second Committee of the General Assembly, Papua New Guinea, speaking on behalf of the South Pacific Forum, called for a comprehensive environmental impact assessment of the nuclear weapons tests conducted by France. The Australian representative described nuclear testing by France and China as "backward steps in the progress made towards sustainable development" [U.N. press release GA/EF/2693, 11/1/95].

Oceans

The CSD's discussion on protection of the oceans emphasized the need for better protection of coastal and marine resources. Chapter 17 of Agenda 21 calls for action on integrated coastal zone management plans, prevention of land-based sources of marine pollution, and conservation of marine life, in addition to sustainable development of small islands and protection of the atmosphere. Recently, significant progress has been made in the form of agreements to address marine pollution and the conservation of marine species.

In November 1995 more than 100 governments attended a UNEP conference in Washington, D.C., where they adopted a **Global Plan of Action for the Protection of the Marine Environment from Land-Based Activities.** Most marine pollution is caused by the 3.5 billion people living in coastal regions and consists primarily of municipal sewage, industrial wastes, agricultural runoff, and soil erosion. Contamination from land-based activities threatens food security, public health, commercial fishing, tourism, and the viability of coastal communities as well as critical marine habitats [UNEP(OCA)/LBA/IG.2/7].

The Washington Declaration, also adopted at the November 1995 meeting, focused special attention on two areas: inadequate sewage management and "persistent organic pollutants"—that is, man-made toxic compounds, such as dioxin, that tend to accumulate in animals and people and can cause adverse health effects in places far from their original source [UNEP(OCA)/LBA/IG.2/6]. It specifically sought the development of a new legally binding global agreement addressing the manufacture and sale of persistent organic compounds that get released from industrial production processes, waste disposal, and chemical leaks and spills and as a by-product of incineration. Once dispersed into the environment, they are almost impossible to clean up [UNEP(OCA)/LBA/IG.2/7].

Another marine conservation agreement called for in Chapter 17 of Agenda 21 and adopted in August 1995 was a treaty on high seas fisheries management, formally called the **U.N. Agreement for the Implementation of the Provisions of the U.N. Convention on the Law of the Sea Relating to the Conservation and Management of Straddling Fish Stocks and Highly Migratory Fish Stocks.** The Law of the Sea gave coastal states jurisdiction over adjacent waters up to 200 miles offshore and charged them with conserving and managing marine life in those areas, but the high seas were traditionally viewed as global commons and were largely unregulated. Some species migrate over large areas of the open seas and do not fall within the jurisdiction of any of the coastal states. Other species straddle the boundaries of the 200-mile regulated zones and are therefore subject to the jurisdiction of more than one coastal state. Years of unregulated commercial fishing, the growth of fishing fleets, and wasteful fishing methods that involve catching and discarding nontargeted species have resulted in substantial depletion of important fish stocks. And some territorial disputes over fishing waters have led to serious international conflicts. The objective of the new agreement is to ensure long-term conservation and sustainable use of straddling and highly migratory fish stocks as well as to resolve disputes peacefully [A/ CONF164/37, 9/8/95]. Regional fishing organizations will be responsible for regulating and enforcing sustainable fishing practices in their areas [ibid.].

In a similar effort to promote sustainable fishing practices, in December 1995 a group of 95 governments adopted the **Kyoto Declaration and Plan of Action on the Sustainable Contribution of Fisheries to Food Security** [E/CN.17/1996/29]. In view of the importance of marine fisheries to world food supplies, and projected shortfalls by 2010, signatories agreed to follow the U.N. Food and Agriculture Organization's Code of Conduct for Responsible Fisheries and to apply a precautionary approach to management of fisheries and ecological habitats.

Forests

There has been no international agreement as yet on what constitutes sustainable use and management of forests. There is, however, a generally greater appreciation of the multiple benefits provided by forest ecosystems—and not just tropical rain forests. In addition to timber products, forests provide food and fuel for human needs, habitats for animals, watershed protection, and absorption of carbon dioxide emissions.

At its April 1995 meeting, the CSD established an Intergovernmental Panel on Forests to review existing forest management institutions and instruments to determine whether a treaty or other legal agreement was warranted. A report presented at the second session of the Intergovernmental Panel on Forests, held the following month in Geneva, identified two key barriers to effective implementation of national forestry programs: the slow pace of policy reforms and the lack of coordination in land-use planning [E/CN.17/IPF/1996/8]. Political conflicts of interest about land-use priorities, together with increasing agricultural demands, tend to thwart forest protection efforts. According to the report, "the most effective policy measures related to deforestation usually fall outside the forestry sector and concern population and human development policies, land distribution and tenure, industrial development, trade, etc." [ibid.]. It would seem that forestry programs, therefore, must be integrated into national land-use policies and economic development plans, not devised separately.

At the international level, deeply divisive issues remain, particularly concerning trade-related initiatives, such as tropical timber certification and eco-labeling. Many countries are reluctant to accept market restrictions on their exploitation of national forest resources in order to further international environmental objectives [*ENB*, Vol. 13, No. 3]. The final report of the International Forest Panel is to be presented at the 1997 meeting of the CSD.

Consumption Patterns

A report to the 1996 CSD meeting concluded that current consumption patterns in industrialized countries are unsustainable not so much because they exhaust nonrenewable resources but because they degrade renewable resources such as agricultural land, accelerate species loss, and discharge dangerous wastes into the environment [E/CN.17/1996/5]. Global sustainable development will require industrialized countries to show that resource-efficient, low-pollution life styles are possible and desirable, since "the Western consumer life-style currently serves as a model and inspiration to millions of people in poorer countries" [ibid.]. To date, little progress has been made in this area. Western consumers generally want more, not less. And developing countries, intent on increasing their own consumption levels—in part by exporting goods or raw materials to markets in industrialized countries—are quite suspicious of any initiatives that might limit their economic growth or create new trade barriers. More progress has been made in the area of improving energy efficiency and reducing production waste. This strategy maximizes both economic competitiveness and environmental quality. Yet low world energy prices and widespread energy subsidies have undermined energy conservation programs [ibid.].

The U.N.'s **High-Level Advisory Board on Sustainable Development,** meeting in January 1996 for its fifth session, considered the potential of new communications and information systems to promote sustainable development. Benefits include increased availability of remote education opportunities, networking to strengthen civil society, reduced "brain drain," since professionals in remote areas can collaborate with distant colleagues, and reduced dependence on energy-consuming transportation systems. However, use of these new technologies does run the risk of promoting even greater globalization of consumerism and increased dominance of multinational companies [E/CN.17/1996/31]. "The communications revolution represents an enormous challenge, because it will change family life and people's relationships with their spiritual traditions, social customs, and social hierarchies" [ibid.].

With regard to energy issues, the High-Level Advisory Board agreed that a move toward sustainable energy and transportation policies will require removal of energy subsidies and reorientation of energy research programs. "The main obstacle to the wide utilization of both energy efficient measures and renewable sources of energy, including solar, wind and tidal energy technologies, is the competitive advantage of fossil fuels, which is likely to prevail as long as their environmental costs are not internalized" [ibid.].

General Assembly Review of Agenda 21

In December 1992 the General Assembly adopted Resolution 47/190 in which it decided to review the implementation of Agenda 21 after five years. Accordingly, the 50th Session of the General Assembly adopted Resolution 50/113 calling for a one-week Special Session in June 1997 to conduct an overall appraisal of progress on Agenda 21 as well as the environmental treaties and agreements that have been adopted since the Earth Summit and the other U.N. global conferences since 1992.

The principal objective of the Special Session is to maintain political momentum for sustainable development by convening heads of state to set priorities for the future of the CSD in a negotiated political document. The Special Session is also intended to identify remaining gaps in existing legal instruments and institutions. Particular attention will be given to ways of implementing existing agreements and to coordinating environment and development efforts in a holistic manner rather than attempting to pursue piecemeal programs.

According to Nitin Desai, Under-Secretary-General for Policy Coordination and Sustainable Development, the Special Session should be given a status almost equal to that of a global conference [*ENB*, Vol. 5, No. 43]. Moreover, the role of nongovernmental organizations at the U.N. preparatory conferences and in the CSD must be properly recognized. For example, many cities and towns have produced their own Agenda 21 programs, and these important sustainable development efforts by community organizations and local municipalities were highlighted at the Habitat II Conference held in Istanbul in June 1996. Although Resolution 50/113 specifically recognized the need for contributions from major groups during the Special Session, there was some controversy at the 1996 CSD session about whether nongovernmental groups should be allowed to address the General Assembly directly.

Biodiversity

Humans are causing the extinction of other species at an alarming rate. In an urgent effort to conserve remaining life-forms and ecosystems, governments signed the **Convention on Biological Diversity** in 1992 at the Earth Summit. The Convention entered into force in December 1993 but has been slow to take effect because, unlike the climate change treaty, it was not preceded by extensive scientific studies. In order to remedy that problem, UNEP commissioned a **Global Biodiversity Assessment**—a comprehensive scientific research project involving 1,500 experts worldwide [UNEP press release, 11/14/95]. The project was funded by the Global Environment Facility, a financing mechanism jointly administered by the World Bank, UNDP, and UNEP (see "Financing Sustainable Development," below).

The Global Biodiversity Assessment, presented in November 1995 to the second Conference of the Parties to the Convention on Biological Diversity, warns that the adverse effects of human activity are threatening the very foundation of sustainable development: "Loss of biological resources and their diversity threatens our food supplies, sources of wood, medicines and energy, opportunities for recreation and tourism, and interferes with essential functions such as the regulation of water runoff, the control of soil erosion, the assimilation of wastes and purification of water, and the cycling of carbon and nutrients" [*Global Biodiversity Assessment: Summary for Policymakers*, Cambridge University Press, 1995]. Increasing human demands, the failure of economic markets to recognize the true value of biodiversity, and inadequate government management policies are all key factors in the loss of habitats and species.

Fundamental evolutionary processes are at risk. Since genetic variation within species is the ultimate basis for evolution, loss of gene diversity threatens the ability of ecological communities to resist or recover from environmental disturbances—including long-term climate change [ibid.]. Many species will not be able to relocate fast enough to respond to projected changes in temperature, rainfall, and sea levels. The Global Biodiversity Assessment discusses a variety of possible management measures, including protected ecological areas and gene banks. It also emphasizes, however, that conservation must be integrated into overall national decision-making and economic development: "Most effects on biodiversity result from the secondary consequences of activities such as agriculture, forestry, fisheries, water supply, transportation, urban development, energy and so forth" [ibid.]. For effective change, local communities need to be educated about the importance of conservation and, perhaps more important in poorer countries, to be given an opportunity to share in the economic benefits derived from habitat-protection initiatives [ibid.].

The importance of local benefit sharing was one of the primary messages delivered at the meeting of the Conference of the Parties to the Convention on Biological Diversity held in Jakarta in November 1995. The theme of the session was "Biodiversity for Equitable Welfare of All People" [*ENB*, Vol. 9, No. 39]. The parties agreed to provide input into the CSD's Intergovernmental Panel on Forests, particularly on the protection of forest dwellers and indigenous peoples and the fair sharing of the benefits from use of their traditional knowledge. They also adopted a decision urging conservation of marine and coastal biodiversity [UNEP/CBD/COP/2/19]. Other decisions covered the establishment of a permanent secretariat in Montreal, continuation of the Global Environment Facility as the interim financing mechanism, and preparation of a protocol on safety in the biotechnology industry [ibid.].

The decision on biosafety calls for negotiation of a protocol covering the safe transfer, handling, and use of living organisms modified by modern biotechnology. In December 1995 a group of government-designated experts organized by UNEP met in Cairo for a "global consultation" on this topic and adopted technical guidelines for biosafety relating to research, development, and marketing of living products. Anticipating finalization of these guidelines, the Conference of the Parties noted that they could be used as an interim mechanism during development of the biosafety protocol, and as a complement to it after adoption of the protocol [UNEP press release, 12/1/95].

Patenting of living organisms remains a contentious issue, especially the extent to which such patenting would grant rights to multinational drug and chemical companies at the expense of local communities and indigenous groups. A decision on intellectual property rights adopted by the Conference of the Parties calls for a preliminary study of their effect on protection of traditional knowledge and transfer of biotechnology [*ENB*, Vol. 9, No. 39]. There was also discussion of the need for collaboration with the World Trade Organization on the issue of trade-related intellectual property rights.

The Conference of the Parties to the biodiversity treaty was scheduled to meet again in November 1996 in Buenos Aires.

Desertification

With close to a billion people suffering from losses of cropland and rangeland, desertification is closely linked to hunger and poverty as well as to the loss of wildlife habitats. The need for concerted international action was discussed in Chapter 12 of Agenda 21 and led to the adoption in 1994 of the **Convention to Combat Desertification.**

The desertification convention is likely to come into effect in 1996 or early 1997. Meanwhile, the International Negotiating Committee on Desertification continues in existence, preparing for the first session of the Conference of the Parties and promoting urgent action on drylands in Africa. The Negotiating Committee met in Geneva in February 1996, primarily to discuss institutional arrangements for implementation of the treaty. It was to meet again in September 1996 in New York.

Ambassador Bo Kjellen of Sweden, who chairs the Negotiating Committee, expressed concern that the desertification treaty is not sufficiently well known or integrated into development strategies [*ENB*, Vol. 4, No. 86]. The representative from Burundi noted that decision-makers have difficulty distinguishing between the desertification treaty and the biodiversity and climate change conventions [ibid.]. Since the adoption of the desertification treaty, a number of countries have held "awareness days" and national forums, and the General Assembly proclaimed June 17 as World Day to Combat Desertification and Drought [A/Res/49/115]. Public awareness among the people directly involved with the land is particularly important given the treaty's "bottom-up" approach to conservation, emphasizing initiatives that are compatible with the skills, customs, and traditions of dryland inhabitants.

Besides lack of recognition, the desertification treaty suffers from limited funding. During the October 1995 meetings of the Second Committee of the General Assembly, the representative of Benin complained that the desertification treaty had received fewer financial contributions than had the climate change and biodiversity conventions, and that its secretariat was smaller. He called for equal treatment for all the conventions [U.N. press release GA/EF/2692, 10/31/95].

UNDP and UNEP have been proceeding with programs to build awareness and to mobilize resources for desertification control, particularly in Africa. The two agencies signed a new agreement in 1995 reorganizing a prior joint venture into a **Partnership to Combat Desertification and Drought.** Moreover, the UNDP Executive Board agreed to rename the U.N. Sudano-Sahelian Office (UNSO) in view of its role in helping affected countries to develop national action plans on desertification. It is now called the Office to Combat Desertification and Drought.

At the February 1996 meeting of the International Negotiating Committee on Desertification, UNDP was considered as a possible choice to host the "global mechanism" for the desertification treaty intended to promote mobilization of financial resources. UNDP Administrator Gus Speth suggested a possible co-hosting arrangement with the International Fund for Agricultural Development (IFAD) [*ENB*, Vol. 4, No. 86]. IFAD's mandate is to address the needs of the rural poor, many of whom live in fragile ecosystems. The Fund expects to provide $150 million to $200 million annually for poverty relief in marginal areas and is currently working to mobilize additional resources, especially for countries in sub-Saharan Africa.

Financing Sustainable Development

Within the operations of the World Bank, the International Development Association (IDA) provides preferential loans to the poorest countries, raising its funds from donor countries rather than from the capital markets. Despite threats to cut IDA contributions, most notably by the United States, donors have committed to putting in another $11 billion over the next three years [*The Economist*, 3/26/96]. The World Bank has attempted to respond to vociferous criticism of its environmental policies by incorporating environmental concerns into the loan decision-making process from the beginning rather than as an add-on. The "new environmentalism" touted by the Bank portrays economic development and environmental sustainability as partners, not enemies [*Mainstreaming the Environment* (Summary), World Bank, 9/95]. It also recognizes that the commitment of affected communities is often critical to the success of a project, together with the engagement of local businesses and farmers [ibid.].

In March 1996, World Bank President James Wolfensohn and Secretary-General Boutros Boutros-Ghali launched a new ten-year joint project for poverty relief in Africa entitled the **U.N. Systemwide Special Initiative on Africa,** itself part of the U.N.'s larger New Agenda on the Development of Africa in the 1990s. Twenty-two of the 25 poorest countries are in Africa [*New York Times*, 3/17/96]. Fifty-four percent of all Africans live below the U.N. level for absolute poverty, and it is the only area where poverty is expected to increase over the next ten years [ibid.]. The U.N. Special Initiative will require up to $25 billion, mostly from reallocation of existing national and international budget priorities. The World Bank will take the lead in raising these funds, which will be used for basic education and health, water and food security, good governance, and peace building [U.N. press release ORG/1207, 10/17/95].

In an attempt to incorporate environmental concerns into its assessment of a nation's economic health—and into national decision-making—the World Bank has adopted a new accounting approach that measures natural resources as wealth [*The Economist*, 9/23/95]. The new program measures the value of a country's natural resources not only on the basis of their ability to generate income but also on their overall contribution to society. Consequently, economic growth that depends primarily on the consumption of irreplaceable natural resources would be viewed as *depleting* wealth rather than creating it.

The World Bank will be playing a key role in the U.N.'s action plan to help countries achieve the sustainable development goals set out in the most recent series of global conferences on population, social development, and women's rights. The Bank has agreed to chair an interagency task force on "the enabling environment for people-centred sustainable development" [U.N. press release ORG/1207, 10/17/95]. The task force, one of three organized by the U.N.'s Administrative Committee on Coordination, will focus on macroeconomic policies, poverty eradication, external debt relief, and international trade issues. The IMF, UNDP, UNCTAD, and UNICEF will also participate.

The Global Environment Facility (GEF), jointly administered by the World Bank, UNDP, and UNEP, funds projects addressing global warming, biodiversity conservation, ozone depletion, and protection of international waters. Specifically, it functions as the interim financing mechanism for the climate change and biodiversity conventions and supports the Montreal Protocol on protecting the ozone layer. Following a three-year pilot phase, the GEF received a $2 billion replenishment in 1994 to be used over a three-to-five-year period. By July 1995 only 11 projects, totaling $103 million, had been financed from the replenishment [*Mainstreaming the Environment,* p. 8]. At the October 1995 meeting of the General Assembly's Second Committee, the delegate from India complained that procedures for GEF project approval are too complex, taking almost two years to complete. Noting that the replenishment was at only a minimum acceptable level, he declared that "the time has come to deliver results on the ground on a large scale if the GEF is to make any impact and retain any credibility as a source of funding" [Statement, 10/31/95].

The 1996 meeting of the CSD again considered innovative mechanisms for funding sustainable development, such as global taxes and user charges, but these have been strongly resisted by many governments—including the United States. Official development assistance to developing countries has remained relatively low in recent years and is not likely to increase. The average percentage of GNP contributed by donor countries is 0.3 percent, the lowest since 1973 and substantially below the 0.7 percent set as a target in Agenda 21 [E/CN.17/1996/4, 2/22/96]. The CSD also considered measures that governments could take to support sustainable development policies within their own borders, including such economic instruments as carbon taxes, the elimination of damaging subsidies (e.g., for use of fuel, water, pesticides, and fertilizer), conservation trust funds, user fees, and tradable pollution permits. "Green" investment funds are yet another way to encourage the channeling of private investment into environmentally sound activities.

Although some developing countries are attracting private capital from abroad, many have not been able to replace dwindling foreign aid with direct financial investments. The World Bank reported that in 1995 capital flows from industrialized countries and international agencies to developing countries totaled $230 billion, 70 percent of which was private [*New York Times,* 3/21/96]. Much of that investment went to China and newly industrializing economies in East Asia and Latin America; "sub-Saharan Africa is being left in the dust" [ibid.].

Trade

The **U.N. Conference on Trade and Development (UNCTAD)** was established over 30 years ago, primarily to promote international trade and market access for poorer countries. Some countries, intent on streamlining U.N. operations, argue that recent economic successes in East Asia, together with the creation of the World Trade Organization (WTO), have made UNCTAD obsolete. WTO was formed in 1994 at the end of the most recent Uruguay Round of negotiations under the General Agreement on Tariffs and Trade (GATT). The purpose of GATT agreements has been to remove trade barriers in order to increase market access and fuel global economic growth.

UNCTAD's new leader, Rubens Ricupero, a former Brazilian finance and environment minister, defends its role as a forum where international trade policy can be discussed in the context of sustainable development. Many poorer countries, particularly in Africa, are badly positioned to gain financially from increased globalization of world trade. A mere 15 countries—the major industrialized nations and the emerging East Asian economies—account for 70 percent of all trade in goods and services, according to a 1995 WTO report [U.N. Development Update, No. 12, 11–12/ 95]. Loss of export preferences and higher food import bills resulting from the Uruguay Round will adversely affect the trade balance of a number of African nations [UNCTAD Bulletin, No. 33]. UNCTAD is currently working on provisions in the trade agreement to provide more favorable treatment for the least-developed countries.

The ninth meeting of UNCTAD, held in Johannesburg, South Africa, in April 1996, attracted representatives of 188 countries for discussions on the theme of "promoting growth and sustainable development in a globalizing and liberalizing world economy." The Conference is UNCTAD's highest policy-making body and normally meets every four years to adopt major policy guidelines. South African President Nelson Mandela called for more dialogue on world trade to ensure that poor countries are not discriminated against [ibid.]. Secretary-General Boutros-Ghali affirmed the importance of UNCTAD both as an advocate for the most disadvantaged countries and as an irreplaceable forum for democratizing international economic relations [U.N. press release SG/SM/5971, 4/26/96].

Many environmentalists fear that overemphasis on trade liberalization and market growth will result in the degradation of natural resources and a lowering of environmental protection standards. But developing countries fear that environmental protection requirements will further limit their access to international markets. For example, in April 1996 a WTO panel ruled that U.S. regulations on environmental standards for imported gasoline, issued by the Environmental Protection Agency under the Clean Air Act, discriminated against foreign oil refiners [New York Times,

4/30/96]. A new Committee on Trade and Environment has been organized by the WTO and will give a report to the WTO's first ministerial meeting, scheduled to be held in Singapore in December 1996. One of the topics under discussion is whether WTO rules should exempt the trade provisions of existing international environmental treaties. The Montreal Protocol, for example, restricts trade in ozone-depleting chemicals, and the Basel Convention limits exports of hazardous wastes.

Even without specific trade provisions, however, environmental treaties have effects on economic competitiveness and may impose higher costs on developing countries. In 1995 the CSD invited UNCTAD to analyze the relationship of environmental protection to international competitiveness, job creation, and development. The study will be presented to the CSD at its 1997 meeting [E/CN.17/1996/8/Add.1, 4/10/96].

2. Food and Agriculture
By Martin M. McLaughlin

A revival of interest in the problems of hunger and malnutrition, which surfaced toward the end of 1993, was reflected in a General Assembly resolution welcoming the decision of the **Food and Agriculture Organization (FAO) to convene a "World Food Summit" in Rome, November 13–17, 1996,** "at the level of heads of State or Government" [A/C.2/50/L.51, 12/4/95; A/Res/50/109]. The Director-General of FAO was invited to report on its results to the General Assembly via the Economic and Social Council (ECOSOC).

The world food problem—now generally referred to as "the question of food security"—is dealt with regularly and directly by several U.N. agencies: the FAO, the International Fund for Agricultural Development (IFAD), the World Food Programme (WFP), and the Consultative Group on International Agricultural Research (CGIAR—a consortium of 16 international agricultural research centers, which celebrates its first quarter-century in 1996).

Indirectly, the food security problem is also a focus of the World Health Organization (WHO), the United Nations Environment Programme (UNEP), the United Nations Development Programme (UNDP), the United Nations Children's Fund (UNICEF), the U.N. High Commissioner for Refugees (UNHCR), and, of course, the World Bank Group—the regional banks, the International Monetary Fund (IMF), and the World Trade Organization. This last, created at the end of the Uruguay Round of GATT, could end up having greater impact on global food security than any (or even all) of the others.

Moreover, although the topic of food and agriculture is not often addressed directly by the General Assembly or by ECOSOC, it has regularly appeared as a subtheme of or counterpoint to their consideration of many other topics—and especially those having to do with the civil conflicts and disasters that lead to refugee situations, and hunger, in many parts of the world. Food and agriculture has also been a significant element of many of the U.N.'s series of international conferences, e.g., on Environment and Development (Rio, June 1992), Human Rights (Vienna, June 1993), Population and Development (Cairo, September 1994), Social Development (Copenhagen, March 1995), Women (Beijing, September 1995), and Human Settlements (Habitat II; Istanbul, June 1996).

Growing Concern about World Hunger

The November 1996 World Food Summit was announced at FAO's 50th anniversary conference in Quebec in October 1995. Its agenda is expected to emerge from the draft policy statement and program of action that were considered, along with 16 technical papers, at five regional conferences held between March and July 1996. When the world leaders gather at the Summit, combining "a global perspective with recognition of the national and regional realities that affect food security," they "are expected to adopt a policy statement and plan of action on universal food security, for implementation by all parties concerned: governments, international institutions, and all sectors of civil society," says one publicity handout [WFS/NGO/Info.1, 12/95].

The Summit is the culmination of a series of events calling attention, inter alia, to the problem of world hunger. The World Bank held a conference on the subject in November 1993 at which the Earth Summit's sustainable agriculture goals were reaffirmed and it was agreed that helping the poor farmers of food-deficit countries to grow more food is both an urgent task and a viable goal [ESD Series No. 3, 12/94]. A year later the U.N. Secretary-General published the first comprehensive U.N. report on the food situation in many years [A/49/438, 9/27/94]. It concluded that, given the prospect of recurrent shortfalls in food production in several food-deficit regions, and continued population growth, the needs of **800 million to 1 billion chronically hungry people** (more than a seventh of the world's population) were bound to occupy a top spot on the international agenda for the foreseeable future.

Other reports on the world food situation, from those of FAO to those issued by the U.S.-based Worldwatch Institute and Bread for the World, confirm the assessment that, despite continuing production increases, **there is no certainty of world food security.** This was also the conclusion of a Conference on Hunger and Poverty convened by the International Fund for Agricultural Development (IFAD) in Brussels at the end of November 1995 [IFAD, 2/96], whose documents are especially pertinent to the preparations for the upcoming Summit. And the decline in the food supply noted in the Secretary-General's report has continued, despite some gains in the food-exporting industrialized countries. None of this augurs well for global food security.

The World Food Summit will mark the second time the U.N. system has attempted to deal with "the problem of food security." The first was the World Food Conference of November 1974, also held in Rome, which created the International Fund for Agricultural Development, FAO's Committee on World Food Security, FAO's Global Information and Early Warning System on Food and Agriculture (GIEWS), and the now moribund World Food Council.

On a parallel track, and following up its November 1993 Conference on alleviating hunger, the World Bank created in June 1995 a Consultative Group to Assist the Poorest (CGAP), with $200 million for microfinance programs; and in February 1996 it convened in Mali the first of four planned regional workshops. In addition to making its own preparations for the Summit, the Bank is making a bid for leadership in the food security/sustainable agriculture arena. One earnest effort was the assignment of a team from the rural development and agriculture department to prepare a report, "From Vision to Action in the Rural Sector," and the invitation to nongovernmental organizations and other interested parties to discuss it on April 23, 1996. Noting that "World food needs could double over the next 30 years," the report concludes that "rural poverty must be reduced" and that "environmental degradation must be reversed" [Executive Summary, 2/23/96].

The 1974 World Food Conference concluded that the best way to relieve world hunger was to increase food production in the food-deficit countries. Twenty-two years later, it appears that the reverse has happened: Grain production increased in the industrialized, exporting countries, while production for local consumption decreased (or at best stagnated) in countries marked by continuing food insecurity. As a result, these nations have more hunger than ever.

There are several reasons for this. One is that many of these countries must export much of the food they grow in order to earn foreign exchange to service a foreign debt that has more than quadrupled since the 1974 Conference, reaching a total of $2.068 trillion in 1996 [*World Debt Tables, 1996*, vol. 1] and that is owed mainly to creditors, commercial and governmental, in the industrialized world. Another is the organization and operation of the global food system—a segment of the increasingly integrated global economy—which tends to reward the rich and punish the poor. A third is the combination of supply- and demand-side constraints that characterize the world food and agriculture economic equation.

Organization and Operation of the Food System

In 1995, as usual, the world produced enough food to provide every human being a diet that would sustain normal human activity. But the 800

million people the FAO says are chronically hungry do not have access to
that food; they can neither grow it nor buy it. This "hidden crisis" has
worsened since the U.N. World Food Conference in Rome brought it to
world attention nearly 22 years ago. Since then this problem of chronic
hunger—different from the recurrent famines that shock us on the nightly
news—has remained on the list of U.N. and world community concerns.

Ironically, attention to the problem lessened during the 1980s, even
as the power of transnational food corporations increased their domination of a global food market that has been steadily liberalized and deregu-
lated through the GATT Uruguay Round process. Meanwhile, poor people have been further marginalized by structural adjustment—the central
development policy of the World Bank and most bilateral aid donors.

Gains in food production have taken place, but mainly in the industrialized food-exporting countries, where capital-intensive agriculture is
the norm. In the food-short countries, production for domestic consumption has declined, and poor people have no greater access to food than
they had before. World population continues to grow at between 90 million and 95 million people per year, and rising affluence in the industrial-
izing developing countries—notably China—allows many people to consume greater amounts of more expensive foods, adding to the qualitative
pressure on the food supply already exerted by overconsumption in the
industrialized world, which more than matches the quantitative pressure
of population growth.

Now, however, FAO reports that global food production—
especially of cereal grains, the world's basic staple food—declined more
than 3 percent in 1995, bringing world grain stocks substantially below
the level of reserves deemed necessary to ensure against a significant crop
failure [*Food Outlook*, 11–12/95]. Adverse weather reduced output in most regions; and countries afflicted by civil conflict—notably Afghanistan, Iraq,
and several African countries—were especially hard pressed. At the same
time, 90 million to 95 million people were once again added to the world's
population, nine-tenths of them in the poorest food-short countries.

As crop yields stagnated or declined almost everywhere, prices rose
for all major grains, and none more so than wheat—a fact that translates
directly into higher prices for cereals and bread, and indirectly for meat
and dairy products. Whether this price escalation results from smaller
supplies or greater demand, it will have the greatest impact on those
whose poverty already leaves them least able to cushion it.

Trade arrangements in the global food system add to this pessimistic
picture. The world produces annually about 1.9 billion tons of the basic
staple, cereal grains. Nearly half is produced in the industrialized countries, which exchange a third of it among themselves. In fact, most food
is consumed in the country or region where it is grown. Only 10 percent
of total production, less than 200 million tons, is traded, but nine-tenths

of those exports begin in the industrialized countries. The poor countries' tenth is mainly low-priced primary commodities, of which they try to export more in order to service their debts. But their efforts to compete succeed in driving the commodity prices down, and their food imports include expensive processed foods, which actually increase their debts.

People's access to food depends on how fairly the growers, suppliers, processors, marketers, and regulators manage the international food system. But when 40 percent of the grain is fed to animals, most of whose products (meat, milk, and eggs) find their way to the tables of prosperous people, and another large percentage of the grain is processed into high-priced packaged cereal products, sweeteners, and motor fuel while hundreds of millions of people face starvation daily, this system clearly is not working. Moreover, the poor are thus doubly penalized: They get less food and, by and large, they get poorer quality food.

Whether corporate agribusiness drives poor peasants from fertile valleys to eroding hillsides to make way for cattle destined for export or farmers in industrialized countries pour chemicals on their land to increase export-based profit, the losers are the land, the people, and the environment. Added to the organizational problems and the current decline in overall production are the resource constraints in the system. Most obvious **on the supply side** are increasingly limited land, water, energy, and technology. Add to this environmental stress, often unfavorable weather conditions, and the lack of research directed toward sustainable and subsistence agriculture.

Roughly one acre of land is under cultivation for every person on the planet, and it will be at least as costly and difficult to bring more land under the plow as it will be to maintain the productivity of what we now have. Water is even more scarce and is being used up far faster than it can be replenished. Energy, mainly petroleum, is used for fertilizer, pesticides, irrigation, drying of grain, transportation of food to market, and refrigeration, among other things. Although petroleum energy seems for the moment to be in adequate supply, it faces a steadily increasing demand and is an inexorably declining asset that produces toxic wastes affecting both consumers and agricultural workers. Technology and the research accompanying it are devoted more to the capital-intensive temperate zone agriculture of industrialized country consumers and exporters than to the needs of subsistence farmers and other poor people in the developing world. Fewer than half the 200-plus board members of CGIAR's 16 centers are from the developing countries, and 14 of the 16 board chairs and directors-general are from the industrialized world.

On the demand side, overconsumption by the majority of people in the industrialized countries of the North and their elite counterparts in the South, coupled with their dominance of the international economic system, intensifies pressure on the food supply.

Prospects for the World Food Summit

Pressure for convening the 1996 World Food Summit (WFS) came not only from the official organs of the United Nations but also from two events, already mentioned, in which nongovernmental organizations (NGOs) were active participants.

The first was the Quebec Global Assembly on Food Security, convened in October 1995, roughly the same time as the FAO's 50th anniversary conference. The Assembly called on the FAO "to facilitate and cooperate to enable nongovernmental organizations, people's organizations, and social movements to host a major NGO forum before the World Food Summit in November 1996."

The second event was the Conference on Hunger and Poverty, organized by IFAD in Brussels, November 20–21, 1995, whose action program, passed unanimously, "emphasized that in a world of plenty it is morally and ethically unacceptable that nearly one billion people live in conditions of endemic hunger and poverty" [Programme of Action, I]. In its description of the Food Summit, FAO acknowledges the leadership role of NGOs: "NGOs have a very important role to play . . . in analyzing problems of food insecurity and proposing remedial action at various levels . . ." [WFS/NGO/Info.1]. NGOs in both industrialized and developing countries are often closer to the grass-roots and household food security situation than are governments, multilateral institutions, and the private sector.

As for the Summit itself, the draft program goes on to outline several commitments that it hopes the heads of state will adopt and NGOs will push, among them:

- We shall ensure the political, social and economic environment, based on the equal participation of women and men, that is most conducive to food for all;
- We shall ensure that policies and institutions contribute to improving access by all to nutritionally adequate and safe food at all times;
- We shall ensure that food, agriculture and rural development policies encourage adequate and reliable food supplies at the household, national and global levels, and promote sustainable agricultural and rural development;
- We shall ensure that food and agricultural trade policies are conducive to improved food security.

Other commitments deal with emergency situations, research, and various support activities [WFS 96/3].

NGO coalitions in several countries are not only actively engaged in preparations for the Summit but have participated in preparations for some of the regional preparatory meetings and their own preliminary and possibly parallel forums on these issues. Many NGOs are also lobbying their own governments, especially in the industrialized world, to send qualified delegations and adopt forthcoming positions on the basic issues.

Sustainable Agriculture: The Solution Generally Sought

The central focus of the Summit is world food security, by which is meant, in the words of one draft document, "that food is available at all times, that all persons have means of access to it, that it is nutritionally adequate in terms of quantity, quality, and variety, and that it is acceptable within the given culture. Only when all these conditions are in place can a population be considered 'food secure' " [CFS 96/3].

In international development terms, food security implies the ability of people to grow or to buy enough food to maintain an adequate diet. The FAO says that about 800 million people lack that security and will continue to fall short for the next 15 years or more unless there is a dramatic change in the international food system.

In the thinking of the organizers of the Summit and of the NGOs, the way to achieve food security is through sustainable agriculture. But what *is* sustainable agriculture? A series of 1994 issue papers on the subject by Patricia Allen and colleagues at the University of California, Santa Cruz, sheds some useful light on the issue. The most fundamental question, Allen says in an undated paper, is "who and what do we want to sustain?" Her problematic answer: "The general vision of scientists and activists for sustainable agriculture is one that reduces environmental degradation, preserves or restores the family farm, and removes contaminants from human consumption. . . . This vision is usually considered achievable within our current socioeconomic systems." Beyond these considerations, however, Allen wonders whether there might not be some deeper questions: "What role, for example, does the current mode of agricultural production, based on maximizing short-term profits and foreign exchange, play in causing agricultural problems?" Despite manifest social problems, she observes that "dominant sustainability discourses tend to rely on technology as the solution" [paper dated 12/94]. Her alternative:

> We need to conceptualize agriculture in a way that includes not only the production process itself, but all of the related backward and forward linkages, i.e., the whole of the food and agricultural system. . . . Thus, sustainable agriculture would maintain the resource base and provide the means for everyone to secure adequate amounts of nutritious, safe food and fiber. This in turn is predicated on the development of nonexploitative relations in terms of race, class, gender, species, and nation. . . . Ending social inequality and poverty—at a global level—is therefore a precondition for solving environmental and social problems in agri-

culture. Without the resolution of social equity issues, the structures of domination that led to environmental degradation in the first place will be reproduced. [ibid.]

Sustainability, of course, applies not only to the food and agriculture system but also to the global economy as a whole. The term was accepted and emphasized at the Social Summit in March 1995 in Copenhagen. But as in the case of the draft document for the World Food Summit, the international community's readiness to accept the concept of sustainability without resolving its ambiguities reflects, in part, its unwillingness to deal with the abject failure that an honest and thorough analysis of the present global economic system might reveal. **It is, in fact, not sustainable agriculture or sustainable development but sustainable communities and societies that should be the goal.**

Winners, Losers, and Power Brokers in the Global Food System

Two countries promise to have the strongest impact on the global food situation for the foreseeable future. The first is **China,** whose increasing industrialization and urbanization have already accelerated the deterioration of its land and water and rendered it less able to feed itself. China has a fifth of the world's population and a fifteenth of its arable land. Grain is a land-intensive crop, and China has a scarcity of arable land. Moreover, soil erosion, increasing urbanization, the conversion of crop land to industrial uses, the deterioration of water supplies, and steady population growth will further test the country's ability to feed itself [*IFPRI Report*, 10/95].

Even under the grain self-sufficiency policy of the past 40 years, China has increased grain imports to meet domestic demand, shifting from a net exporter of 12 million tons in 1993 to a net importer of 23 million tons in 1995—more than a tenth of all grain available in the world market [*Food Outlook*, 11–12/95]. It is worth recalling that when the Soviet Union bought up the U.S. grain crop in 1972, prices skyrocketed, hunger increased dramatically in some areas of the world, and the crisis that followed prompted the convening of the 1974 World Food Conference. In 1993–94 grain prices increased sharply in China because of farmers' reactions to inflation expectations and the reduction of grain cultivation in the coastal provinces, where grain production was no longer to farmers' comparative advantage. Any further growth of Chinese agriculture will depend on increases in inputs, technological change, and government policies to encourage their use [*IFPRI Report*, 10/95].

China is likely to need even more imports in future years; and it will be able to afford them—which many other food-deficit countries will not—especially as prices are bid up in view of the increased demand.

The second major nation is the **United States,** still the world's economic giant, with an enormous impact on the international food system. U.S. trading companies and agribusinesses have immense economic power and little regulation. Nearly half the grain that crosses borders is grown in the United States. The global price of grain—and therefore the basis of farmers' livelihoods everywhere—is set in bidding on the floor of the Chicago Board of Trade. U.S. agricultural exports reached $54.1 billion in fiscal year 1995; they are expected to reach $60 billion in 1996 and to increase by 7 percent annually for the remainder of this century. What happens in the U.S. food system and what the United States does about food policy have profound effects on the global food system and the lives of those millions of hungry people in food-deficit countries, as well as on the roughly 35 million people in the United States who live below the poverty line and are having a hard time making ends meet.

Finally, to illustrate the contrast among regions and countries, there is **sub-Saharan Africa,** where the most appropriate word is "vulnerability." In March 1996 the United Nations launched a new Systemwide Special Initiative on Africa, with World Bank participation. One of its major focuses is on food security, and the Special Initiative's Programme for Action summarizes the relevant facts this way:

> Per capita food production has declined because the population has been growing faster at an average rate of 3.0 percent per annum than food production, which has been increasing at an average rate of 2.0 percent per annum. . . . During the 1980s, average daily caloric intake was 87 percent of requirements. Forty percent of the population does not have enough food. Hunger and undernutrition are widespread, particularly among children and women.

Conclusion

Widespread hunger and malnutrition have been almost commonplace in the history of humankind, but today the conviction deepens that famine and starvation are not inevitable. It is increasingly clear that the technical ability to feed a growing human family exists and will continue to be developed. What is lacking, as President John F. Kennedy observed three decades ago, is the *will* to ensure the access of everyone to the food that is available. To create that political will is the central ethical issue in moving from the indicative (technology) to the imperative (morality). But even today, when the Cold War that claimed the world's attention and resources for so long has faded, the will to adopt the policies and practices that will move toward food security continues to elude us.

The economic structures, moreover, seem inappropriate for so high a purpose. Today competition has to take place in an ever-more-aggressive global market dominated by powerful forces that judge progress, success, and victory by constantly rising levels of consumption rather than by pursuit of the common good. Corporate control of food production and distribution is growing, and the requirements of sustainability are largely ignored. Conferences, reports, and draft documents strongly resist an analysis that would reveal the structure of the global economy, the relative power of the actors in it, and the impact of these factors on the possibility of food security.

The food system is a subset of the international (economic) system. Improvement of the food system is part of making the economic system work better, i.e., part of development. Development requires economic growth, but that growth is neither sufficient nor primary. The overriding goal—in fact, the definition—of development is improvement of the quality of life. Meeting food needs, therefore, involves a development strategy, not just a feeding program (though that effort, which has been cut in half over the past three years, may be essential and urgent at the start). The strategy is determined by the political process; therefore, poor people need to participate in that process so that they can choose something other than poverty and hunger as their lot.

3. Population
By Craig Lasher

With all five of the U.N.'s major international conferences of the 1990s concluded, the international community should now turn its attention to implementing the ambitious agreements that have been negotiated on environment, population, social development, women, and urbanization. Since the **International Conference on Population and Development (ICPD),** held in Cairo in September 1994, most if not all U.N. member states have a better understanding of the gravity of global population problems and how they bear upon the agendas of the four other conferences. But the question remains whether the international community will find the necessary political will and financial resources to stabilize world population.

Actions taken during the remainder of this decade will determine the size and pace of population growth into the next century. World population currently stands at 5.7 billion, and is increasing at nearly 95 million people annually. The most recent projections of population in the year 2050 range from a low of 7.9 billion to a high of 11.9 billion. Effective implementation of the Conference's goals and objectives and meeting the expanded financial commitments contained in the ICPD's 20-year **Programme of Action** would result in world population growth at levels below the U.N. medium projection of 9.8 billion people [*Population Newsletter,* 12/95]. Under any of these scenarios, demographic factors pose serious environmental, security, and development challenges to the international community. (For a thorough review of the Cairo Population Conference as well as its relationship to the March 1995 World Summit for Social Development see *A Global Agenda: Issues Before the 50th General Assembly of the United Nations.*)

Family Planning and Reproductive Health at the Women's Conference

About the time the 50th Session of the U.N. General Assembly started in New York, the Fourth World Conference on Women was concluding in Beijing (September 4–15, 1995). At that Conference, advocates for improvements in the status of women were successful in building upon the agreements adopted at Cairo and in other international forums [*Washington Post,* 9/15/95]. After the final preparatory committee meeting, women's health advocates were concerned that the Vatican and some predominantly Catholic and Muslim countries would attempt to undermine the progress made at the ICPD. In the end, the two principal documents emerging from Beijing—**the Platform for Action and the Beijing Declaration**—not only reiterated ICPD language but, in some instances, went further on reproductive health and rights [A/CONF. 177/20].

Delegates to the women's conference adopted, word for word, the definition of reproductive and sexual health from the Cairo Programme of Action. The Beijing documents also cite verbatim the ICPD's carefully crafted compromise on the need to address the problem of unsafe abortion. But the agreements go even further in calling on governments to "consider reviewing laws containing punitive measures against women who have undergone illegal abortions."

The most important advance in the area of reproductive health in the Beijing platform is language recognizing that "the human rights of women include their right to have control over and decide freely and responsibly on matters related to their sexuality, including sexual and reproductive health, free of coercion, discrimination, and violence" [*New York Times,* 9/11/95]. The document includes language balancing needs of young people for confidential reproductive and sexual health services and the responsibilities of parents for their children's health care. It also calls upon governments to eliminate female genital mutilation, and recognizes the importance of sex education in preventing both unwanted pregnancy and HIV/AIDS.

Delegates agreed on the need to seek "new and additional" financial resources to carry out the Conference's ambitious platform for action; but unlike the ICPD, the Beijing Conference did not set specific funding targets for mobilizing resources. A number of donor countries facing government budget cuts, such as the United States, emphasized the importance of more effectively utilizing existing funds. Both the ICPD and the Beijing Conference succeeded in establishing new norms for the international community, but the commitment to provide the financial resources to transform conference rhetoric into meaningful improvements in women's lives remains to be seen.

Population at Habitat II

The last of the decade's major U.N. conferences was Habitat II (formally known as the U.N. Conference on Human Settlements), which convened in Istanbul in June 1996. (For a full report on the conference, see Chapter V, "Habitat II," in this volume.) It would be difficult to think of a more urgent, and largely forgotten, issue on the global agenda as urbanization—or one so closely tied to population factors. Almost half of the world population—2.6 billion people—live in cities, and projections suggest that the figure will climb to two-thirds by the year 2025. Cities are currently growing by a million people each week, exacerbating a long list of urban problems in both the developed and developing world, such as shortages of adequate housing, lack of basic services, deteriorating infrastructure, pollution, and congestion [UNFPA, *State of World Population 1996*].

Rapid urbanization and the appearance of "megacities" in the late 20th century is without historical precedence. In 1950 only one city in the world, New York, had a population of more than 10 million people. In 1990, 12 cities topped that level. It is now projected that in 20 years, 27 cities will exceed 10 million people—23 of which will be in the developing world [ibid.]. The investments in housing, water and sanitation, transportation, public health, and education needed to support rapidly growing urban populations continue to strain economies and governance. The high number of young people in developing-country cities puts additional pressure on housing and social services and necessitates the creation of new jobs in situations where unemployment and underemployment are frequently widespread.

The growth in urban populations is primarily a result of the increase in total world population—about a billion people every 11 years. Over 95 percent of future population growth will occur in developing countries, and almost three-quarters of that increase will be in cities and towns [*ICPD News*, 2/96]. Future population increases are unavoidable, but the large difference between the U.N.'s high and low projections—a difference of 720 million people over the next 20 years—has important implications for the goal of sustainable urban settlements [UNFPA, *State of World Population 1996*].

The preparatory meetings for Habitat II, however, produced a draft document that—by the standards of population experts—gave inadequate attention to the role of demographic factors in problems associated with rapid urbanization [*The Habitat Agenda* (unedited draft), 3/4/96]. Among the important issues related to the dynamics of urban growth not addressed by the document were the potential impact on cities of alternative scenarios for future population growth; the role of high fertility rates in cities as well as migration fueled by even higher fertility rates among rural populations; the young age structure of urban populations in developing countries; the emergence of megacities; and the social and economic implications of rural to urban migration. During the Habitat II preparatory process, UNFPA had sponsored two scientific symposiums (one in cooperation with Habitat) to bring the issues of population, internal migration, and urbanization into better focus [*ICPD News*, 2/96].

Implementation of the Cairo Programme of Action

Like the agreements negotiated at the other major international conferences, the ICPD Programme of Action is not binding on member states. If implemented, however, it is likely to have a profound influence on population policies and programs around the world. Follow-up mechanisms need to hold governments accountable for such implementation and to measure progress toward the Programme's goals.

Commitment of a whole new magnitude of financial resources remains the key to achieving the ICPD's ambitious objectives. Both donor and developing countries need to increase funding for family planning and reproductive health, and for the social sector generally. As Dr. Nafis Sadik, UNFPA Executive Director and Secretary-General of the Conference, stated, "Without resources . . . the Programme of Action will remain a paper promise" [*ICPD 94*, 9/94]. However, the prospects for major increases in donor assistance for population do not appear promising [*Earth Times*, 3/15/96]. Japan, the United Kingdom, and the Nordic countries—with the exception of Sweden—continue to increase their support for population programs. But overall contributions remain far below the trajectory required to achieve ICPD funding goals. Total donor assistance stands at less than a third of the $5.7 billion donor target level for the year 2000 adopted in Cairo. Population assistance has been negatively affected by pressure on foreign aid budgets in many industrialized countries; and in other countries a lack of priority for population programs remains a constraint on increasing contributions. A major disappointment has been the continuing lack of interest on the part of France, Italy, and Spain, all of which have large development assistance budgets.

Nevertheless, several donor countries have significantly increased funding for population programs since the Cairo Conference [E/CN.9/1996/ 6]. For example, the German government has honored its pledge during the ICPD process to increase its financial contributions. German aid for population programs doubled from 1990 to 1994, and it increased again by more than a third in 1995. Likewise, in the Netherlands the parliament has called for 4 percent of bilateral and multilateral foreign aid to be allocated for reproductive health programs by 1998. If implemented, Dutch population assistance could triple from about $50 million currently to over $150 million a year by 1998.

At the same time, allocations to population programs in a number of other countries, most notably the United States, are moving in the other direction. U.S. population assistance, which in recent years has accounted for roughly half of all donor assistance, will decline by at least 35 percent because of funding restrictions imposed by family planning opponents in Congress. The funding cut does not bode well for further increases from other donors. Under the Cairo Programme of Action, developing countries are expected to provide two-thirds of the $17 billion total target figure for the year 2000. The poorest of the developing countries are likely to continue to fall short of their share of the funding target, although information on specific country implementation of the agenda is still fragmentary. A survey of UNFPA field representatives in 78 nations revealed that many were earnestly attempting to incorporate the Conference's recommendations into national population programs and strategies and to commit additional, scarce financial resources [*Earth Times*, 3/15/96].

One concrete initiative emerging from the developing world is an expanded effort to encourage South-to-South cooperation. Ten developing countries (Bangladesh, Colombia, Egypt, Indonesia, Kenya, Mexico, Morocco, Thailand, Tunisia, and Zimbabwe), calling themselves the **Partners in Population and Development,** announced in Cairo their intention to cooperate in training, research, and information exchanges and to share their expertise in reproductive health and family planning with other developing countries. UNFPA, the World Bank, and the Rockefeller Foundation are supporting this potentially important development [*ICPD News*, 2/96].

Despite what now appears to be discouraging news on prospects for finding all of the necessary financial resources, the United Nations moved quickly on ICPD implementation and has sought to reorganize itself to implement the Cairo agenda more effectively. The 49th General Assembly devoted three plenary meetings to consideration of the Conference report [A/CONF.171/13]. All of the speakers who addressed the two-day plenary session endorsed the achievements of the Conference and applauded the document's emphasis on the need to empower women and on a comprehensive approach to family planning and reproductive health. Most of the statements concentrated on implementation, particularly resource allocation and institutional arrangements for supporting and monitoring follow-up [*ICPD 94*, 11/94]. The General Assembly unanimously adopted a resolution in December 1994 on ICPD implementation, negotiated by its Second Committee and sponsored by Algeria for the Group of 77 and by China and Indonesia for the Non-Aligned Movement [A/Res/49/128]. The resolution emphasized the importance of enhanced cooperation and coordination by all relevant agencies, organizations, and programs of the U.N. system and outlined a three-tier intergovernmental mechanism, consisting of the General Assembly, ECOSOC, and a revitalized Population Commission, to play the central role in the implementation.

In recognition of the broader approach endorsed in Cairo, the Population Commission was renamed the **Commission on Population and Development** and now meets annually instead of every two years. The membership of the Commission was increased from 27 to 47 countries [A/Res/50/124], and countries were encouraged to expand the composition of their delegations beyond demographers, who have traditionally dominated, to individuals with broader population policy experience. The newly reconstituted Commission on Population and Development has a dual role: continued oversight of the U.N.'s demographic research activities and monitoring of the progress toward the programmatic and funding goals of the Cairo Conference. The Commission's 1996 session was devoted to the theme of reproductive health and rights, and it considered a comprehensive review of the subject prepared by the U.N. Population Division [ESA/P/WP.133]. It also approved the text of a resolution to be considered by ECOSOC stressing the need for an accelerated international response to the commitments made in the ICPD Programme of Action and requesting improved reporting on annual financial assistance provided to population activities [U.N. press release POP/615, 3/1/96].

At the request of the Secretary-General, Sadik convened and chaired the Inter-Agency Task Force on ICPD Implementation, composed of high-level officials from various key parts of the system, to ensure a common and integrated strategy. Through the Administrative Committee on Coordination, all U.N. agencies and organizations have reviewed how they might promote implementation of the Programme of Action [*ICPD 94*, No. 21, 11/94]. The Task Force issued guidelines for U.N. resident coordinators to strengthen the in-country programming process, and it successfully prompted U.N. agencies to adjust their programs and priorities to reflect the ICPD goals. Given the success of the Task Force, the Administrative Committee on Coordination went on to expand the concept to a total of three task forces charged with the unified follow-up of the recommendations of all the recent international conferences.

In announcing the creation of this new system of task forces, Secretary-General Boutros Boutros-Ghali stated that "it is important to reach international agreement as we have at these conferences, but it is even more important to implement those agreements. We have secured the commitment of all the agencies of the United Nations to put the full weight of the UN system behind helping countries achieve the goals agreed to in these conferences" [*ICPD News*, 2/96]. The original ICPD Task Force has now become the **Inter-Agency Task Force on Basic Social Services,** charged with addressing the issues of population, basic education, primary health care, water and sanitation, shelter, and social services. Although UNFPA became the initial chair, the broadened mandate ensures that the focus on the ICPD agenda will inevitably be diluted. The two other task forces are on employment and sustainable livelihoods, chaired by the International Labour Organisation, and on the enabling environment for people-centered sustainable development, chaired by the World Bank.

The closer cooperation within the U.N. system on implementation of international conference recommendations is exemplified by the launch of a Special Initiative on Africa—a $25 billion effort to improve basic education and health on that impoverished continent. All of the global conferences of the 1990s have stressed the value of increasing access to health care and education, especially for girls, and many of the specialized agencies have a role to play. UNFPA, for example, will be helping to strengthen the infrastructure and staffing of health services provided by African governments and others and to incorporate appropriate information about reproductive and sexual health and family life into school curricula. The initiative also mandates new measures to improve donor coordination and increase aid effectiveness [UNFPA press release, 3/15/96].

Not surprisingly, UNFPA has been the most active agency within the U.N. system on ICPD implementation. In addition to its leading role in interagency coordination mechanisms, UNFPA convened four regional consultations on ICPD follow-up immediately after the conference with representatives from Central and Latin America, Arab states and Europe, Asian and Pacific countries, and Africa [UNFPA press release, 12/15/94]. UNFPA's technical and geographic divisions have been charged with reviewing all country programs for conformity with the principles of the Programme of Action.

UNFPA also established an internal task force on ICPD implementation under the direction of Sadik, which took over many of the functions of the ICPD secretariat. The duties of the task force include coordination within UNFPA; communication of developments in the General Assembly, ECOSOC, and other U.N. bodies; and integration of the Programme of Action into country programs in cooperation with personnel working in the field. The task force has a two-year mandate [ibid., 12/21/94].

Contributions to UNFPA

Following its success in organizing the ICPD, UNFPA has seen a steady upward trend in contributions from member states at a time when support for many U.N. agencies has been falling. As the only multilateral organization with a mandate focused exclusively on population, UNFPA remains a central player in ICPD implementation. In 1995, UNFPA's total income was a record high $306 million, up significantly from $262 million in 1994. Agency officials estimate that 1996 income will reach about $325 million [E/CN.9/1996/6].

At the annual meeting of the joint executive board of the U.N. Development Programme and UNFPA in June 1995, new programmatic and policy directions for UNFPA were endorsed [*ICPD News*, 7/95]. In response to the series of technical reviews and regional consultations, UNFPA will concentrate its core funding in three program areas: reproductive health, including family planning and sexual health; population and development strategies; and advocacy. In addition, it was reaffirmed that all activities in UNFPA-supported programs will be undertaken in accordance with the ICPD Programme of Action, in particular with Chapter II, "Principles." UNFPA also plans to expand its role in global contraceptive procurement.

While a number of donor countries have increased their assistance to UNFPA, leaders of the new Republican majority in the U.S. Congress have vowed to reduce U.S. involvement in the United Nations, and anti-abortion activists continue to press for the United States to again withdraw its contribution from UNFPA because of the agency work in China where, it is contended by some, the government practices forced abortions. After nearly a decade of nonfunding under two Republican presidents, the Clinton administration resumed funding of UNFPA with a 1993 contribution of $14.5 million. The United States furnished $40 million in 1994 and $35 million in 1995. The contribution will fall to just over $20 million in 1996 as a result of the funding restrictions on population assistance enacted by Congress in January 1996.

U.N. Population Awards

The winners of the U.N. Population Award for 1995 are Letitia Ramos-Shahani, a parliamentary leader on population both in her own country of the Philippines and internationally, and Pathfinder International, a leading U.S. family planning organization [U.N. press release POP/606, 2/23/96].

As a member of the Philippine Senate, Ms. Shahani has been a leading advocate for population policies and programs for more than 30 years. She was instrumental in the founding of the Philippine Legislators Committee on Population and Development and has been widely credited with shaping the positive policies of Philippine President Fidel Ramos, her brother. Internationally, Shahani has been active in the parliamentarians' movement as a member of the Global Committee of Parliamentarians on Population and Development. She headed her country's delegation to the Beijing women's conference and served as secretary-general of the 1985 international women's conference in Nairobi.

Since its founding in 1957, Pathfinder International has provided funding, contraceptive supplies, and technical assistance to more than

2,000 programs in 30 countries. The organization began supporting family planning services even before the involvement of the U.S. government, and has pioneered many advances in the field—often in challenging and sometimes hostile circumstances. To date, 29 indigenous family planning organizations have been established with grants from Pathfinder. In several instances, Pathfinder has sustained national programs with private funds when foreign assistance was unavailable.

4. Law of the Sea, Ocean Affairs, and Antarctica
By Lee A. Kimball

The entry into force of the 1982 U.N. Law of the Sea (LOS) Convention in November 1994 reaffirms the important functions performed by the Division for Ocean Affairs and the Law of the Sea (DOALOS) in the U.N. Legal Office in New York. The action set in motion two further institutional developments: (1) the meeting of states parties to the LOS (SPLOS) and (2) the establishment of the International Seabed Authority (ISA) on a provisional basis, in accordance with the 1994 Agreement modifying the previously controversial deep-seabed mining provisions of the Convention [see *A Global Agenda: Issues/49*, pp. 197–98]. Several industrialized nations have ratified the LOS Convention together with the Agreement. The latter will enter into force once ratified by 40 countries, including five developed nations qualifying as pioneer investors in deep-seabed mining. By May 1996 the LOS Convention had received a total of 88 ratifications and the Agreement 48. One more industrialized pioneer investor must ratify the Agreement before it enters into force.

Other major developments in ocean affairs during the past year include the adoption in August 1995 of the Agreement for the Implementation of the Provisions of the U.N. Convention on the LOS of December 10, 1982, relating to the Conservation and Management of Straddling Stocks and Highly Migratory Fish Stocks [A/50/550, 10/12/95]; the adoption by the Food and Agriculture Organization's General Conference in November 1995 of the complementary, nonbinding Code of Conduct for Responsible Fishing; the adoption in November 1995 of the Global Programme of Action on Protection of the Marine Environment from Land-Based Activities (GPA) [A/51/116; see *Issues/50*, pp. 167–68]; the adoption by the conference of parties to the Convention on Biological Diversity of an action program on marine and coastal biodiversity [UNEP/CBD/COP/2/19, 11/30/95]; the adoption in October 1995 of the operational strategy for international waters (marine and freshwater) by the Council of the Global Environment Facility (established jointly by the U.N. Development Programme, U.N. Environment Programme, and World Bank); and the review by the U.N. Commission on Sustainable Development (CSD) in

April 1996 of the oceans chapter of Agenda 21, the action program adopted by the 1992 U.N. Conference on Environment and Development (UNCED).

The International Seabed Authority

Two meetings of the Authority's plenary Assembly took place in 1995 (March 11–22 and August 5–16), but it was February 1996 before a formula was agreed upon for allocating seats on its 36-member Executive Council. This cleared the way for elections, including the election by consensus of Satya N. Nandan of Fiji as Secretary-General of the Authority. The Council's five chambers are constituted initially as follows: (1) consumers/importers: Japan, Russia, United Kingdom, United States; (2) seabed mining investors: China, France, Germany, India; (3) producers/exporters: Australia, Chile, Indonesia, Zambia; (4) developing nations: Bangladesh, Brazil, Cameroon, Nigeria, Oman, Trinidad and Tobago; and (5) regional representation/balance: Argentina, Austria, Cuba, Egypt, Italy, Kenya, Republic of Korea, Malaysia, Namibia, the Netherlands, Paraguay, the Philippines, Poland, Senegal, South Africa, Sudan, Tunisia, Ukraine [ISBA/A/L.9, 3/22/96]. Once the Secretary-General takes up his position, he will inherit from the U.N. Secretary-General responsibility for administering the Authority's secretariat, which is headquartered in Kingston, Jamaica [A/Res/50/23]. The ISA will continue to be funded out of the U.N. regular budget until the end of the year after entry into force of the 1994 Agreement, after which the Convention's contracting parties are fully responsible [A/C.5/50/28, 11/17/95].

The August 1996 meeting of the ISA will elect members of its Finance Committee, the next president of the ISA Assembly, and the first chairman of the Council; review the ISA's proposed budget; and adopt the Council's rules of procedure [ISBA/A/L.9, 3/22/96]. Its substantive efforts will be devoted to monitoring trends in minerals markets and technology development, as well as any activities carried out by pioneer mining entities, until such time as further interest develops in mining the seabed beyond national jurisdiction.

Meetings of States Parties to the LOS Convention

The SPLOS meetings have also concentrated to date on administrative matters. The election of 21 judges to the International Tribunal for the LOS, located in Hamburg, Germany, took place August 1, 1996, while the election of the 21 members of the Commission on the Limits of the Continental Shelf has been postponed until March 1997 [SPLOS/5, 2/22/96; SEA/1507, 12/1/95; see also *Issues/50*, p. 165]. The budget for the Tribunal's start-up phase through the end of 1997 was finally agreed to in March 1996 [SPLOS/

8, 4/10/96]. These expenses will be borne by states parties to the Convention. Following the election of the judges, they will have a four-week organizational and swearing-in session commencing October 1, 1996. The Tribunal is expected to begin functioning in January 1998 [SEA/1511, 3/4/96, and SEA/1512, 3/8/96]. SPLOS met twice in 1995 (May 15–19 and November 27–December 1) and again March 4–8, 1996; it was to meet next for the elections July 24–August 2, 1996. The July meeting was also to complete work on draft protocols on privileges and immunities and review the Tribunal's financial rules [SPLOS/8; SEA/1513, 3/8/96]. Further arrangements will have to be made for the Continental Shelf Commission elections in 1997.

Institutional Arrangements for Reviewing Ocean Affairs

Every year the U.N. General Assembly considers the full range of developments in international ocean law and policy covered by the Convention, based on a report prepared by DOALOS [A/50/713, 11/1/95, and Corr. 1]. The annual review covers peace and security, navigation and maritime safety, maritime boundaries, fishing, marine environmental protection, marine and coastal biodiversity, marine science, illegal drug trafficking and other crimes at sea, maritime terrorism, dispute settlement, and other matters. Since numerous global and regional organizations and legal instruments are concerned with ocean affairs, including development and financial agencies, DOALOS plays an essential role in monitoring developments to ensure uniform interpretation of LOS Convention provisions and to encourage coordinated actions. The developments considered below in land-based pollution and fisheries, including Antarctic fisheries, are indicative of these legal and institutional relationships. As agreed in 1994, a special report is to be prepared for the 51st Session of the General Assembly on the impacts of entry into force of the LOS Convention for U.N. system instruments and programs [A/Res/49/28].

The annual General Assembly LOS resolution [A/Res/50/23] was adopted on December 5, 1995, by a vote of 132 in favor with one against and three abstentions. It calls for uniform and consistent application of the Convention and technical and financial cooperation so that all states may implement it effectively. During the debate, numerous governments expressed appreciation for the annual report and the assistance provided to states by DOALOS [A/50/PV.80 and 81].

The 51st General Assembly will also have before it the results of the CSD review of the oceans chapter of Agenda 21. While the CSD reports to ECOSOC, there will be a Special Session of the General Assembly in June 1997 to consider progress in implementing Agenda 21 five years after the Rio Summit, in particular the follow-up institutional arrangements. Sustainable ocean development poses particular challenges, in view of the broad substantive scope of the LOS Convention and the many institutions involved. Strong links between the CSD review and the annual General Assembly review are critical, as is coordination between their respective secretariats. The interagency mechanism established after UNCED—the Inter-Agency Committee on Sustainable Development (IACSD)—helps coordinate U.N. system reporting and may begin to play a greater role in systemwide program coordination. Its subcommittee on oceans and coastal areas is another important component of U.N. institutional arrangements on oceans. The 1995 GPA reinforces links with UNEP's oceans activities and regional seas agreements. It calls for periodic intergovernmental review of implementation, convened by UNEP, and identifies UNEP as secretariat.

The decisions adopted by the CSD for approval by ECOSOC recommend that, subject to the outcome of the 1997 Special Session, the CSD periodically review Agenda 21 oceans issues, drawing on reports coordinated by the interagency subcommittee. (The CSD may decide on other modalities for reviewing these issues.) Recognizing that the LOS Convention provides the overall legal framework, the results of the CSD review are to be considered by the General Assembly under a consolidated agenda item, "oceans and the law of the sea." The U.N. Secretary-General is invited to consider how to improve the status and effectiveness of the interagency subcommittee. In order to guarantee the availability of independent scientific advice, the U.N. Secretary-General and the heads of other sponsoring agencies are to review arrangements for the Joint Group of Experts on the Scientific Aspects of Marine Environmental Protection (GESAMP), an advisory body established in 1969 by several U.N. organizations [E/C.17/1996/L.20, 5/1/96]. The CSD decisions further specify institutional follow-up to the GPA, with special reference to interagency arrangements for an information clearinghouse. The 1997 Special Session will determine how to integrate the outcome of the UNEP-convened intergovernmental review of the GPA with the work of the CSD [E/CN.17/1996/L.19, 5/1/96]. Further CSD decisions give impetus to several oceans-related initiatives endorsed by other global and regional bodies [E/CN.17/1996/L.23, 5/2/96].

The institutional follow-up to the 1995 Fisheries Agreement was settled more simply, with the decision that it will be reviewed by the General Assembly under the LOS agenda item, together with the other important fisheries issues noted below [A/Res/50/24]. The Agreement was opened for signature on December 4, 1995, and will enter into force with 30 ratifications. The 50th General Assembly adopted a second fisheries resolution, addressing large-scale pelagic driftnet fishing, unauthorized fishing in zones of national jurisdiction, and fisheries by-catch-and-discards [A/Res/50/25]. It reiterates last year's themes [see *Issues/50*, pp. 166–67], stressing that states must comply with the global moratorium on high seas driftnet fishing and prevent their flag vessels from undertaking unauthorized fishing. (The United Nations cites continuing failures to do so.) The resolution urges all states and relevant international organizations to take measures to avoid wasteful fishing practices consistent with international legal instruments, including the FAO Code of Conduct, and calls on development assistance organizations to give priority to helping developing nations improve monitoring and control of fishing operations [see also background documents A/50/549, 552, and 553]. A further report on these matters is to be presented to the 51st General Assembly. Thereafter, the Secretary-General is to report biennially on the Agreement, and to ensure that reporting on all major fisheries-related activities is well coordinated. The CSD decision on fisheries elaborates on the General Assembly resolution, highlighting aspects related to sustainable fisheries, such as excess fishing capacity, habitat protection, nondestructive fishing practices and technologies, and the precautionary approach specified in the 1995 Agreement and the FAO Code. It recommends that FAO prepare a report on these matters for its Committee on Fisheries and for submission to the U.N. Secretary-General for the review of oceans issues [E/CN.17/1996/L.22, 5/2/96].

With respect to funding for sustainable ocean development, the Global Environment Facility (GEF) operational strategy emphasizes land-based activities—the source of more than three-quarters of marine pollution—and the protection of marine and coastal biodiversity, in keeping with its mandate for tackling global issues. GEF activities must be consistent with a country's international legal obligations.

Antarctica

Antarctica did not appear on the 50th General Assembly's agenda, but the 51st Assembly will have before it reports of the XIX and XX Antarctic Treaty Consultative Meetings. The prospects in 1996 for entry into force of the Antarctic Treaty's 1991 Protocol on Environmental Protection are much better than in 1995, with 22 of the 26 necessary ratifications received by May 1996. Those yet to ratify are Finland, Japan, Russia, and the United States. There are currently 26 consultative parties to the Treaty (decision-making) and 17 nonconsultative parties (may not take part in decisions). The only recent accession is that of Turkey, in January 1996.

The XX Consultative Meeting convened in Utrecht, the Netherlands, April 29–May 10, 1996. Its main agenda items were further discussions of a liability annex to the Protocol and organizational matters related to the establishment of a secretariat, including its status, functions, and privileges and immunities. Intersessional work on these items will precede the XXI Consultative Meeting in Christchurch, New Zealand, May 19–30, 1997. Additional discussions took place on efforts to determine the potential environmental impact of tourism in Antarctica and the need for self-regulation by the tourist industry, in particular by tour operators and flag vessels from countries that are not party to the Antarctic Treaty.

Standard forms for advance notification and postseason reporting will be tested during the coming year. An Antarctic Data Directory System is expected to be operational by 1997, and the next Consultative Meeting will consider how to use the Internet for exchanging advance information on Antarctic operations, including available hydrographic charts and suitable technologies. A report on best available techniques produced by the managers of national Antarctic programs will be updated periodically in light of changing technologies.

The Commission established by the 1982 Convention on the Conservation of Antarctic Marine Living Resources (CCAMLR) continues to meet annually at its headquarters in Hobart, Australia. There are now 22 Commission members and seven acceding states, the latter invited to attend as observers. The XIV Meeting (October 4–November 3, 1995) made progress in elaborating the first detailed strategy for ecosystem management, and noted that "CCAMLR has become a pioneer in the development of precautionary approaches to management . . . and should continue to work at the forefront" [*Report of the XIV Meeting of the Commission*]. (CCAMLR approaches were influential in developing the 1995 U.N. Fisheries Agreement.) Reports on incidental mortality of seabirds in the Convention area led to the adoption of stronger measures to avoid mortality due to longline fishing and further efforts to collaborate with fishery management bodies responsible for regions adjacent to the Convention area.

With respect to LOS issues, the Commission deliberated whether fish stocks occurring both within and outside the area should be considered "straddling stocks" within the definition of the LOS Convention (and the 1995 Agreement), and whether mandatory vessel notification or an automated vessel monitoring system to control illegal fishing were consistent with flag states' rights on the high seas under international law. Illegal fishing in the CCAMLR area by member states was a major concern, and there were reports of an increase in fishing by nonparty states. Differing views were expressed about coastal state enforcement initiatives off islands within the Convention area where sovereignty is not in dispute, and about the operation of CCAMLR's international system for observation and inspection in these areas [ibid.]. There was no agreement on a mandatory vessel notification system or the introduction of an automated vessel monitoring system, although some countries are initiating a satellite-linked system for their vessels on a voluntary basis.

A final legal issue relates to the development of the liability annex by the Antarctic Treaty Consultative Meeting. Most Commission members took the view that it should not apply to harvesting activities regulated by CCAMLR but could apply to activities or events associated with harvesting, such as an oil spill [ibid., Annex 6].

V

Social and Humanitarian Issues

1. Human Rights
By Stephen P. Marks

Human rights in the United Nations has been, to a large extent, the story of the tension between the principle that the United Nations cannot intervene in the domestic affairs of states and the principle that states must act with the United Nations to realize fully all human rights. What was inconceivable in the early years because of the first principle—launching independent investigations of country situations and thematic issues, for example, or denouncing specific practices in specific countries—is commonplace today because of the second principle. Of course, the target countries still invoke "nonintervention" in an attempt to avoid scrutiny or censure, despite the consensus reached at the **World Conference on Human Rights in Vienna** in June 1993 that "the promotion and protection of all human rights is a legitimate concern of the international community" [Vienna Declaration and Programme of Action, Part I, par. 4].

The human rights agenda of the 51st Session of the General Assembly is as rich as in previous years, both in the quantity of issues and situations considered and in the political tensions behind the diplomatic language. The previous Session considered and adopted over 200 resolutions, of which 54 dealt with human rights, advancement of women, and related matters. This was also the 50th Anniversary of the United Nations, during which the reaffirmation of faith in the Organization and its human rights purposes could not mask the inevitable divergences in political agenda. Even the celebratory rhetoric did not always meet the aspirations of governments and NGOs that take seriously the pledge of all member states to "take joint and separate action in co-operation with the Organization for the achievement of . . . universal respect for and observance of human rights and fundamental freedoms" [U.N. Charter, Articles 55 and 56]. For example, for the commemorative ceremony on October 24, 1995, the assembled heads of state and government adopted a **"Declaration on the Occasion of the Fiftieth Anniversary of the United Nations"** [A/50/48] that barely touches on human rights: In the section called "Equality," containing

173

three of the Declaration's 14 paragraphs, the Assembly pledged itself to "promote and protect all human rights," with special reference to "the full and equal participation of women, children, vulnerable groups, indigenous peoples, refugees and displaced persons and minorities"; and respect for humanitarian law and international human rights law is mentioned briefly in the section on "Justice." In the opening address at another commemorative event—the forum at U.N. Headquarters on October 25 on **"Human Rights: Agenda for the Next Fifty Years"**—U.N. Secretary-General Boutros Boutros-Ghali said that "no theme is of greater importance than the rights of the human person. . . . [It is] the founding principle and ultimate goal of the United Nations." On the program too was the High Commissioner for Human Rights, José Ayala Lasso, who stated that to promote democracy, peace, and security, states must ensure that respect for human rights is at the top of their national agendas and must support implementation of human rights standards in preventive diplomacy and peace operations. Moving beyond moral admonition to more practical and institutional changes, Ambassador Ayala Lasso called for a Human Rights Council—an intergovernmental body for policy-making and coordination that would include NGOs, an idea that is not yet officially on the agenda.

Another politically significant occasion was the first-ever opening by the Secretary-General of the annual session of the Commission on Human Rights in Geneva (March 18–April 26, 1996), a functional commission of the Economic and Social Council (ECOSOC), established in 1946 in accordance with Article 68 of the Charter. While recognizing that "violations must be denounced on a case-by-case basis wherever they occur," he also called for a "true human rights diplomacy," referring to the penetration of human rights concerns into all the U.N.'s activities, whether through specialized components of peace operations, linkages with development and environment programs, or the substantive issues dealt with at the Rio, Cairo, Copenhagen, and Istanbul conferences [U.N. press release SG/SM/5924/Rev.1, 3/15/96]. As on numerous other occasions, the Secretary-General placed human rights in the political context of the promotion of democracy within states and in the international community.

One can consider human rights issues before the United Nations in a broad sense as all human rights-related activity throughout the system, whether the protection of refugees and internally displaced persons by the U.N. High Commissioner for Refugees (UNHCR); the implementation of labor standards by the International Labour Organisation (ILO); the development of standards and training by the Crime Prevention and Criminal Justice Division in Vienna; the supervision of human rights during peace operations; the creation of machinery for trial and punishment of individuals responsible for war crimes, crimes against humanity, and other gross and systematic violations of human rights; or efforts by the

Commission on the Status of Women and numerous agencies and programs to ensure gender equality and improve the status of women.

Taking a narrower approach to the U.N.'s work in human rights, one can explore the activities of the Commission on Human Rights and its Sub-Commission on Prevention of Discrimination and Protection of Minorities, the treaty-monitoring bodies, the High Commissioner for Human Rights, the Centre for Human Rights, and the Third (Social, Humanitarian and Cultural) Committee of the General Assembly, which considers the human rights items brought before that body. Since many dimensions of the U.N.'s human rights work are taken up elsewhere in this volume, the present chapter takes the narrower approach, with an occasional look at the work of the Security Council, the Fifth (Administrative and Budgetary) Committee, and the Sixth (Legal) Committee. After a review of the politics of human rights decision-making and of the human rights bureaucracy, the chapter will look at current thematic issues of human rights, country situations, and human rights procedures.

The Politics and Bureaucracy of Human Rights

High Commissioner for Human Rights and the Centre for Human Rights

Long desired by activists and visionaries, the post of High Commissioner for Human Rights was created by the General Assembly in 1994 at its 48th Session following lukewarm endorsement by the Vienna Conference [Vienna Declaration and Programme of Action, Part II, par. 18]. The highest U.N. official responsible for human rights at that time was the Assistant Secretary-General (ASG) for Human Rights and Director of the Centre for Human Rights, the Geneva-based unit of the Secretariat in charge of human rights. The ASG—law professor and former Foreign Minister of Senegal Ibrahima Fall—was an obvious candidate for the post. In order to negotiate the creation of the post, the Third Committee created an open-ended working group to consider the two paragraphs of the Vienna document on "adaptation and strengthening of the United Nations machinery for human rights," starting with the question of the High Commissioner [A/48/632/Add.5]. The Ambassador of Ecuador, José Ayala Lasso, was elected chair and succeeded in producing a compromise on the mandate of the post that made possible its adoption on December 20, 1993 [A/Res/48/141]. The High Commissioner, according to this mandate, has "principal responsibility for the United Nations human rights activities" and a vague commission "to promote and protect" human rights, including the right to development, to provide advisory services and technical assistance, to coordinate education and information activities, to "engage in dialogue with governments," and to "enhance international cooperation"—this in addition to coordinating, rationalizing, and streamlining human rights throughout the U.N. system and supervising the Centre for Human Rights. The resolution, borrowing the Vienna language, also spoke of the need for "a continuing adaptation of the United Nations human rights machinery to current and future needs in the promotion and protection of human rights" and for U.N. human rights organs to "improve their coordination, efficiency and effectiveness" [Vienna Declaration and Programme of Action, Part II, par. 17].

This preoccupation with "coordination, efficiency and effectiveness" has been perceived by many Western countries and NGOs as code language for limiting investigations of violations in specific countries, although these same countries certainly favor the sort of streamlining that would bring a stronger and more cost-effective human rights program. Since the creation of the High Commissioner post, debates have focused on strengthening the human rights bureaucracy (High Commissioner and Centre for Human Rights), on "streamlining" human rights procedures, and on linking human rights to development problems. Activists tend to perceive the "streamlining" as an attempt to weaken the U.N. human rights machinery and the concern with development issues as an effort to dilute the agenda.

Once the question of the High Commissioner was settled, the open-ended working group of the Third Committee elected a new chair, Ambassador Danilo Türk of Slovenia, to guide it through the remaining issues on "adaptation and strengthening of the United Nations machinery for human rights." Secretary-General Boutros-Ghali appointed Ambassador Ayala Lasso to the High Commissioner post, with the rank of Under-Secretary-General (USG). Mr. Fall continued as ASG—an uneasy cohabitation.

On the matter of **strengthening the Office of the High Commissioner for Human Rights/Centre for Human Rights,** the Assembly and the Commission on Human Rights have addressed the problem of resources and of division of labor.

Regarding **resources,** the political organs have requested the Secretary-General to make additional human and financial resources available in order to carry out mandated activities entrusted to the Centre and the High Commissioner [Commission res. 1995/64 and A/Res/50/187]. The Commission found that the response to the Assembly's request for resources had been inadequate and expressed concern that there was "a serious and increasing imbalance" between mandate and resources and that "the difficult financial situation of the United Nations human rights programme has created considerable obstacles in implementing in full and on time the various procedures and mechanisms" [res. 1996/82]. The Commission again requested the Secretary-General to make available additional resources "within the overall regular budget."

With respect to the **division of labor,** the Secretariat is plagued by the continuation of a bureaucratically and humanly untenable situation in the coexistence of the post of High Commissioner and of the Assistant Secretary-General for Human Rights. Occupying offices of similar size on the fifth floor of the wing of the Palais des Nations that houses the Centre, they continue to receive delegations, plan for the future, and prepare and deliver speeches to the same bodies but rarely embody the "unity of action" called for by the Secretary-General [see E/CN.4/1996/50/Add.1, containing the speeches of each to the "meeting of special rapporteurs/representatives/experts and chairpersons of working groups of the special procedures . . . and advisory services"]. The tension is taking its toll on the individuals concerned and on their staff members.

Restructuring the Bureaucracy

It was this situation, as well as the pressures on the United Nations to downsize and streamline and the new mandates from the General Assembly, that led the High Commissioner to commission a **management study by Price Waterhouse,** setting as his goal a Centre that is a "model of excellence in management and a positive example for other part[s] of the system" [statement by the High Commissioner, 4/9/96].

The Assembly and the Commission, despite reservations by some Western states, articulated a division of labor in which the High Commissioner "sets the policy directions and the priority of action and the Centre implements those policies under the direction of the head of the Centre, the Assistant Secretary-General for Human Rights" [A/Res/50/187 and Commission res. 1996/82]. The restructuring of the Centre did not conform strictly to this division of labor.

In its consensus resolution on the 1996–97 program budget, the General Assembly added a requirement—that the High Commissioner establish "a new Branch, the primary responsibilities of which would include the promotion and protection of the right to development" [A/Res/50/214, par. 37]. The Commission (by a vote of 34–16–1) called for another addition: the establishment of a "program unit in the Centre for Human Rights for the promotion of economic, social and cultural rights, in particular those related to the debt burden of developing countries and the implementation of the right to development" [res. 1996/12].

The High Commissioner announced his **restructuring** plan to the delegates in Geneva on May 30, 1996. Based on a "new philosophical approach to the organization of work," the new structure will break with the previous principle of servicing particular bodies and use instead a "functional approach" such that "with no additional coordination layer, the various activities will be coordinated within the normal work process and thus produce comprehensive outputs so that we 'can speak with one voice' " [statement on restructuring by José Ayala Lasso, 5/29/96].

The substantive responsibilities of the management units are to be as follows:

1. Research and analysis, including promotion and protection of the right to development, as well as research "on the whole range of human rights issues of interest to United Nations bodies" and publications and information.

2. Support for meetings of treaty bodies, the Commission, and the Sub-Commission as well as for processing country reports and for complaints procedures.

3. Support for field activities and missions, international decades, lectures and training courses, special rapporteurs and working groups, and advisory services.

The restructuring is expected to be approved and put in place over the summer of 1996. The top management is expected to maintain the current cohabitation arrangement, with the ASG in a subordinate position to the Under-Secretary-General. Administrative and "Management Planning, Monitoring, Evaluation and Co-ordination" units are at the intermediate level. The heads of the three management units, who were designated ad interim in May 1996, are supposed to report to the ASG but also to have direct access to the High Commissioner. The Fifth Committee will consider the budget reflecting this restructuring and review the freezing of post and personnel moves. In 1995 only **4 of 21 posts** scheduled for the Office of High Commissioner were established; the 17 temporary posts will be considered by the Fifth Committee. Some 30 percent of the staff are on two-month contracts, which is hardly conducive to attracting quality staff and keeping up morale.

The High Commissioner will submit another report to the Assembly highlighting his efforts to implement his mandate, including restructuring the human rights program, and his views of "adaptation . . . to the current and future needs." The report is likely to be similar to 1995's [A/50/36], covering the range of matters listed in the High Commissioner's mandate (promotion, protection, thematic issues, human rights machinery, and implementation of the Vienna Declaration and Programme of Action). The High Commissioner will name countries when significant developments affecting certain countries fall under the rubrics of the report—in 1995, for example, Burundi, Rwanda, and the former Yugoslavia were mentioned under "preventive and responsive activities"; and Malawi, Cambodia, and Haiti under "assistance to countries in transition to democracy."

Consensus and Containment

Governments that feel threatened by U.N. scrutiny of country situations pursue several strategies. One, drawing on the Vienna language regarding the "need to avoid duplication" [Vienna Declaration and Programme of Action, Part II, par. 1], is to propose that different reports be merged into a single document with a page limitation, thus diminishing or eliminating references to specific countries. Another is to seek decision-making by consensus. The Commission deferred a **proposal to make consensus the rule,** introduced by the "hard-line" states (China, Cuba, and Iran, sometimes supported by India, Indonesia, Algeria, and others) [E/CN.4/1996/L.2], deciding to consider the matter in 1997 [Commission decision 1996/114]. The Chairman stated that "[p]reference for consensus does not mean a change of the rule of procedure . . . nor the elimination of voting . . . when there clearly is no possibility of reaching consensus" [Report of the Commission, E/CN.4/1996/L.10/Add.3, par. 21]. Consensus would presumably discourage resolutions creating special procedures or denouncing a particular country when a minority of countries opposes them.

In the end, 90 percent of the Commission's 99 resolutions and decisions were adopted by consensus. Votes were taken on such controversial issues as the "occupied Arab territories," Lebanon, "unilateral coercive measures," dumping of toxic and dangerous products, structural adjustment programs, foreign debt, and forced evictions, all of which generated a substantial number of negative votes or abstentions from developed countries. There were negative votes and abstentions on resolutions dealing with Cuba and Iran as well.

Taking up the problem of **annual repetition of virtually identical resolutions,** the Assistant Secretary-General for Human Rights suggested to the Commission that it consider dropping repetitive language from resolutions as an economy measure, considering the $1,300 per page cost of producing resolutions [speech by Ibrahima Fall at the closing session of the 52nd session of the Commission on Human Rights, 4/26/96]. It is unlikely, however, that the biannualization or triannualization of resolutions will become as common in the Third Committee or at the Commission as it is in the Second Committee, at least when it comes to country resolutions.

After streamlining and consensus, the third politicized aspect of the human rights agenda is the **focus on international economic issues,** such as structural adjustment, foreign debt, and development—issues prominent in the current debates of the **Working Group of the Third Committee.** Among the subjects of drafts now circulating are strengthening U.N. action for economic, social, and cultural rights; the right to development and role of international financial institutions; human rights in peace operations; and human rights education. Since some of these ideas are not particularly popular among certain Western countries, particularly the United States, a resolution covering such matters will require considerable diplomacy and give-and-take. This politically charged counterpart to the issue of strengthening the High Commissioner and the Centre is likely to be reflected in the resolution on **follow-up to the Vienna Declaration**

and Programme of Action. In 1995 the General Assembly, while "recognizing the urgency of eliminating denials and violations of human rights, as expressed in the Vienna Declaration and Programme of Action," also recognized "the importance of dialogue and cooperation between Governments and non-governmental organizations in the field of human rights" and stressed the need to cover all mandates from Vienna and other bodies, which would expand the scope of the Secretariat's work on economic and development issues [A/Res/50/201]. Also prominent in the resolution on follow-up to Vienna is U.N. systemwide action, which gains its significance from the fact that among the task forces of the Administrative Committee on Coordination dealing with systemwide follow-up to world conferences there is none so far for the Vienna Conference. The Commission welcomed the High Commissioner's consultations on this topic, encouraged the General Assembly to continue examining revisions to the medium-term plan of the human rights program, and requested the Secretary-General to continue holding meetings of governments in Geneva twice a year on activities affecting the Centre and its restructuring [Commission res. 1996/83]. The High Commissioner will probably make proposals in his report on the "adaptation to current and future needs" dimension of Vienna.

Thematic Issues

The Assembly and the Commission consider an array of themes that reflect human rights realities in much of the world and the political priorities of influential U.N. member states. Many thematic issues deal with group rights and problems, while others concern particular forms of discrimination, the rights of women, security of the individual, the development process, and activities that promote human rights.

Group Rights and Problems: Self-Determination, Indigenous People, and Minorities

The human rights agenda of the United Nations devotes considerable space to group rights, especially self-determination of peoples, indigenous issues, and the rights of minorities. During the 1960s and 1970s the item on self-determination reflected the decolonization priority of developing countries and their opposition to apartheid and to "Israeli occupation of Arab territories." Remaining decolonization issues are the responsibility of the Fourth (Special Political and Decolonization) Committee. Resolutions continue to be adopted on the Middle East and the Western Sahara. In 1995 the Assembly adopted (without reference to a committee) resolutions on the Middle East peace process [A/Res/50/21] and the situation in the Middle East [A/Res/50/22]. It also adopted a resolution, following Third

Committee consideration, on Palestinian self-determination [A/Res/50/140] and, following Fourth Committee consideration, on the report of the Special Committee to Investigate Israeli Practices Affecting the Human Rights of the Palestinian People and Other Arabs of the Occupied Territories [A/Res/50/29]. The Commission recently reaffirmed its position on occupied Syrian Golan [res. 1996/2], violation of human rights in the occupied territories [1996/3], Israeli settlements [1996/4], and "occupied Palestine" [1996/5]. While these Commission resolutions had at least one negative vote (that of the United States) and several abstentions, a resolution welcoming the Middle East peace process, the Palestinian elections of January 1996, and the establishment of the Palestinian Authority and calling on members to provide technical assistance for the authority was adopted by consensus [1996/7].

The hope of self-determination was also behind the Commission's expression of support for the referendum on Western Sahara [res. 1996/6], which remains bogged down in the seemingly interminable process of identifying eligible voters.

The **"use of mercenaries as a means to violate human rights"** is on the General Assembly's agenda because it is also a means "to impede the exercise of the right of peoples to self-determination." Under this item the 50th Assembly reaffirmed that this practice is contrary to the U.N. Charter and called on states to ratify a convention on the issue and cooperate with the Special Rapporteur [A/Res/50/138]. The resolution was adopted by a vote of 106 to 18 (mainly Western countries), with 31 abstentions (mainly Eastern European countries). The European Union maintained that the **Special Rapporteur on Mercenaries** had exceeded his mandate and that mercenary activities consume valuable resources of the Centre for Human Rights and are best dealt with as a criminal problem. The Assembly also adopted by consensus a general resolution on **universal realization of the right of peoples to self-determination,** in which it opposed "acts of foreign military intervention, aggression and occupation" and requested a report from the Secretary-General on the subject at the 51st Session [A/Res/50/139]. The politicized language developed by the Commission over the years is unlikely to be of much assistance in resolving the self-determination crises of the post-Cold War world. As one observer points out: "The Commission's failure to have developed any more sophisticated notions of self-determination will inevitably return to haunt it" [Philip Alston, *The United Nations and Human Rights. A Critical Appraisal,* Oxford: Clarendon Press, 1992, p. 189].

Self-determination as a process of popular determination of the political status of a territory is bound up in the issue of elections and democratization, although this issue is not part of the General Assembly's item on self-determination. It is a highly politicized issue due to the need of many developing countries for technical assistance in carrying out elections and for political legitimation through international approval of the results, on the one hand, and the suspicion of Third World countries that the West intends to impose a particular style of democracy, regardless of local customs and needs, on the other. The Assembly ritually adopts two resolutions. One is on **strengthening the role of the United Nations in enhancing the effectiveness of the principle of periodic and genuine elections and the promotion of democratization.** In that text, adopted without a negative vote, the Assembly considered that the High Commissioner and the Centre for Human Rights should "support democratization activities related to human rights concerns"—including education, training, legislative and judicial reform, assistance to national institutions, and reporting on international obligations—and requested the Secretary-General to provide the Electoral Assistance Division with adequate human and financial resources to carry out its mandate, "within existing resources" [A/Res/50/185]. The second resolution, on **respect for the principles of national sovereignty and noninterference in the internal affairs of States in their electoral processes,** was adopted by a vote of 91–57–21. Its co-sponsors (Burma, China, Cuba, Gambia, Iraq, Laos, Libya, Namibia, North Korea, Sudan, Tanzania, Uganda, Vietnam, and Zimbabwe) sought support for a strong noninterventionist position, according to which states would "refrain from financing or providing, directly or indirectly, any other form of overt or covert support for political parties or groups and from taking actions to undermine the electoral process in any country" [A/Res/50/172]. The text also reaffirmed that the United Nations would provide electoral assistance only "at the request and with the consent of specific sovereign States . . . in strict conformity with the principles of sovereignty and non-interference in the internal affairs of States," although this would not exclude assistance "in the context of regional or international peace processes." Some delegations, including the European Union, suggested that the resolution was not in conformity with Articles 55 and 56 of the Charter, by which member states pledge to take joint and separate action to promote universal human rights.

Another group rights issue high on the human rights agenda is that of **indigenous peoples** (or "people," as they are now called, in response to concern that the plural would enhance their claims to self-determination and independence). The United Nations proclaimed in 1993 the **International Decade of the World's Indigenous People** [A/Res/48/163]; a United Nations Voluntary Fund for Indigenous Populations had already been established [A/Res/40/131]. The 50th General Assembly adopted the program of activities for the Decade [A/Res/50/157], and the Commission invited the High Commissioner and the Coordinator of the Decade to implement "as a matter of priority and within existing resources" a series of specific measures requested by the General Assembly and designed to involve indigenous people in the Decade and in national and international activities [res. 1996/39].

One of the goals of the Decade is the adoption of the **draft Declaration on the Rights of Indigenous Peoples** [E/CN.4/Sub.2/1994/2/Add.1], elaborated over many years by the Sub-Commission's Working Group on Indigenous Populations. The draft declaration is now in the hands of an open-ended intersessional working group of the Commission, in which organizations of indigenous people are expected to participate, with assistance from the Voluntary Fund [Commission res. 1995/32 and A/Res/50/156].

Since the Vienna Conference, the Assembly and the Commission have been exploring the idea of establishing a **permanent forum for indigenous people in the U.N. system.** A workshop on this matter was held in Copenhagen in June 1995 [E/CN.4/Sub.2/AC.4/1995/7], and the Sub Commission adopted a resolution on it [Sub-Commission res. 1995/39]. The Commission adopted a resolution too [res. 1996/41] and decided to add an item to its agenda entitled **"Indigenous issues"** [decision 1996/102]. It also requested the Secretary-General to give the **Special Rapporteur conducting a study on treaties,** agreements, and other constructive arrangements between states and indigenous populations the assistance necessary to conclude his study [decision 1996/109]. (This language may reflect impatience with the delays of the Special Rapporteur—a Cuban—in completing his report.) The continued importance given to indigenous issues, the prospects for eventual adoption of the draft declaration, and the active participation of indigenous representatives in these actions make this one of the most dynamic aspects of the U.N.'s human rights work. Nongovernmental organizations are particularly in evidence here; and unlike the case with self-determination issues, only a handful of states drive indigenous issues.

The normative work of the United Nations has gone a step further with respect to minorities, the subject of a General Assembly declaration in 1992 [A/Res/47/135]. The **Declaration on the rights of persons belonging to national or ethnic, religious and linguistic minorities,** amplifying Article 27 of the International Covenant on Civil and Political Rights, seeks to protect the individual rights of persons belonging to such minorities. The General Assembly has urged states to give effect to the Declaration, invited the Secretary-General to make available to governments "qualified expertise on minority issues, including the prevention and resolution of disputes to assist in existing or potential situations involving minorities," and requested that the Centre make available ("within existing resources") financial and human resources adequate to this purpose [A/Res/50/180]. This resolution suggests a linkage between the U.N.'s human rights agenda and the preventive diplomacy strategy of *An Agenda for Peace.* In 1995 the Commission authorized the Sub-Commission to create an **intersessional working group** to promote these rights [res. 1995/24], which has met twice and, in 1996, requested the Secretary-General to make experts available to government to help in the prevention and resolution of disputes concerning minorities [res. 1996/20]. The item will be taken up at the 51st General Assembly.

Discrimination and Exclusion: Racial and Religious Intolerance, Internally Displaced Persons, and Mass Exodus

The issue of racism has been a constant concern of U.N. bodies, as witness the launching of **three Decades to Combat Racism and Racial Discrimination and two world conferences on the subject** (in 1978 and 1983). The first two Decades are acknowledged by member states as having failed to attain their objectives, since "millions of human beings continue to this day to be the victims of various forms of racism and racial discrimination" [Commission res. 1996/8]. These Decades generally offer programs of meetings and publications and otherwise attempt to disseminate information that, owing to lack of resources and often of interest, have little impact on behavior. The U.N. Secretary-General has been asked to transmit the results of consultations with governments, intergovernmental organizations, and NGOs regarding **"the possibility of holding a world conference to combat racism, racial discrimination, xenophobia and related contemporary forms of intolerance"** [res. 1996/8]. The 50th General Assembly dropped references to the timetable for the conference (originally 1997, later 1998) [A/Res/50/136], and requested member states to follow up on previous world conferences, making use of all available mechanisms to combat racism. The Secretary-General was asked to prepare an annual report for ECOSOC about all the activities of U.N. bodies and the Specialized Agencies to combat racism and racial discrimination, analyzing the information received about them. It was also noted that, unless there is some sort of supplemental financial contribution, very few of the activities planned for 1994–97 will be carried out.

The idea of the world conference will be revisited at the 51st Session of the General Assembly. Many governments are reluctant to approve such an event for reasons related to cost, the potential for political impasse, and "conference fatigue." Cuba and Morocco are strong supporters of such a conference, as is the Philippines, which suggests including the issue of migration.

Member states are currently focusing on racist acts perpetrated against migrant workers, refugees, and racial, ethnic, and religious minorities; and on "ethnic cleansing." In 1995 the Assembly considered the interim report of Maurice Glèlè-Ahanhanzo, the Commission's **Special Rapporteur on contemporary forms of racism** [A/50/390]. The resolution [A/Res/50/135], adopted by a vote of 106–18–31 in the Third Committee but by consensus in the Plenary, expressed full support for the work of the Special Rapporteur in language similar to that of Commission resolution

1995/12. The Rapporteur had, in fact, undertaken a mission to the United States, from which emerged the conclusion that "social dysfunctions existed in that country stemming from residual racism and racial discrimination" [E/CN.4/1996/72 and Add.1]. The U.S. representative welcomed the efforts of the Special Rapporteur but said that, given the tradition of freedom of the press, her government was unable to support his recommendation for monitoring the media. Promoting censorship of the press was one means of polarizing society, she added. The Commission went on to express "its full support and appreciation" to the Special Rapporteur, extended his mandate for three years, condemned "categorically" the role of the media "in inciting acts of violence motivated by racial hatred," and cited discrimination against "Blacks, Arabs and Muslims, xenophobia, negrophobia, anti-Semitism and related intolerance" as subjects for study by the Rapporteur [res. 1996/21].

On the subject of **elimination of all forms of religious intolerance,** the human rights bodies are primarily dealing with the implementation of the 1981 Declaration on the Elimination of All Forms of Intolerance and of Discrimination Based on Religion or Belief [A/Res/36/55] and the work of the **Special Rapporteur on religious intolerance** [E/CN.4/1996/95 and Add.1 and 3]. In 1995 the Assembly urged states to ensure that public officials do not discriminate on the grounds of religion and that people have a right to freedom of religion or belief [A/Res/50/183]. The resolution also expressed support for the work of the Special Rapporteur ("appointed to examine incidents and governmental actions in all parts of the world that are incompatible with the provisions of the Declaration and recommend remedial measures" [ibid.]), and emphasized the important role of NGOs. In 1996 the Commission called on states to take a series of legislative, judicial, administrative, and educational steps to prevent acts of intolerance and discrimination; and it called on the Special Rapporteur, inter alia, to "apply a gender perspective in the reporting process" and to be able to respond effectively to information, by contacting governments on cases and situations drawn to his attention [res. 1996/23]. The Commission and the General Assembly will continue consideration of this item at their next sessions.

Regarding **internally displaced persons (IDPs),** concerning whom the Vienna Conference called for "lasting solutions" [Vienna Declaration and Programme of Action, Part I, par. 23], the General Assembly called for a "more concerted response by the international community" [A/Res/50/195]. Extensive work had been done by Special Representative of the Secretary-General Francis Deng, assisted by a program at the Brookings Institution and the Refugee Policy Group, including a compilation and analysis of legal norms [E/CN.4/1996/52 and Add.1 and 2]. The 50th General Assembly noted the efforts of the **Special Representative on IDPs,** called upon the Commission to consider establishing a framework based on the Representative's report, and welcomed the extension of his mandate for another three years [A/Res/50/195]. The Commission resolution commended the Special Representative "for the catalytic role he continues to play to raise the level of consciousness about the plight of internally displaced persons," called on him to continue to develop an appropriate framework, and called on the High Commissioner for Human Rights to promote the human rights of IDPs as part of the program of advisory services [res. 1996/52].

In a related resolution on the **importance of human rights in the early warning and prevention of mass exoduses in the emergency operations of the United Nations,** the General Assembly deplored ethnic intolerance as a cause of forced migrations and invited the cooperation of Special Rapporteurs and Representatives to seek information on mass exoduses and population transfers, to be forwarded to the High Commissioner for Refugees. The Secretary-General is also invited to make available "the necessary resources within the regular budget" for consolidating and strengthening the emergency preparedness and response mechanisms to prevent all human rights abuses that contribute to mass exoduses [A/Res/50/182]. The Commission commended him and his efforts to promote a comprehensive strategy [res. 1996/52].

The issue of mass exoduses is being addressed by the Secretary-General and the High Commissioner for Human Rights as well. An ad hoc Working Group on this topic was initiated by the Administrative Committee on Coordination with a view to providing consultations on early-warning mechanisms.

Women's Rights as Human Rights

The U.N. Charter and numerous human rights texts, especially the Convention on the Elimination of All Forms of Discrimination against Women (1979), reaffirm equality between men and women. The Commission on the Status of Women (created in 1946 as a functional commission of ECOSOC) has primary responsibility for women's issues, although in recent years these issues have gained prominence in human rights bodies and at the U.N.-sponsored world conferences, which stressed the empowerment of women and girls and the need to view women's rights as human rights. The 50th Assembly adopted resolutions on the **girl child** [A/Res/50/154], **women in rural areas** [A/Res/50/165], **traffic in women and girls** [A/Res/50/167], and **violence against women migrant workers** [A.Res/50/168]. It also endorsed the Declaration and Platform of Action of the **Fourth World Conference on Women** [A/Res/50/42] and adopted a detailed resolution on follow-up to the conference [A/Res/50/203; see also "The Status of Women" section of Chapter V]. Turning inward, the Assembly expressed its support for the International Research and Training Institute for the Advancement of Women (INSTRAW) [A/Res/50/163], voted to postpone a merger of INS-

TRAW and the United Nations Development Fund for Women (UNI-FEM) [A/Res/50/162], called on the Secretary-General to implement the strategic plan for the **improvement of the status of women in the Secretariat** [A/Res/50/164], and requested UNIFEM to direct greater attention to the issue of **violence against women** and to consider establishing, in conjunction with other agencies, **a trust fund to support efforts to eliminate such violence** [A/Res/50/166].

The United Nations has enhanced the human rights agenda in a crucial way by elaborating the **Declaration on the Elimination of Violence against Women,** which the General Assembly adopted in 1993 [A/Res/48/104], and by appointing Radhika Coomeraswamy of Sri Lanka **Special Rapporteur on violence against women** [Commission res. 1994/45]. Her reports [E/CN.4/1995/42, E/CN.4/1996/53 and Add.1 and 2] have been well received by the Commission and NGOs, one of which described the first report as "a landmark in the history of the United Nations" [International Service for Human Rights, *Human Rights Monitor*, 5/95, p. 26]. At its 1996 session, the Commission endorsed the Special Rapporteur's detailed recommendations and called for intensified efforts at the international level to integrate the equal status and human rights of women into the mainstream of U.N. systemwide activity. The Commission also emphasized the duty of governments to refrain from engaging in violence against women, to take appropriate and effective action concerning acts of violence against women, whether those acts are perpetrated by the state or by private persons, and to give victims access to appropriate remedies as well as to specialized assistance [res. 1996/49]. The 1996 Commission went on to endorse a decision of the Sub-Commission to appoint Linda Chavez of the United States as **Special Rapporteur on systematic rape and sexual slavery during periods of armed conflict** [Commission decision 1996/107].

Individual Security and Administration of Justice

The administration of justice and the treatment of detained persons are the core of the **U.N.'s civil and political rights agenda** and a major concern of Western countries and of the many developing countries that believe that government's dark practices are not beyond scrutiny. Among the mechanisms here are international conventions, convention-monitoring bodies to review the progress of states parties in fulfilling treaty provisions, special procedures that allow rapporteurs and working groups to deal with specific cases of abuse, and technical assistance for states that need assistance in meeting treaty standards.

Prevention of torture is a regular on the agenda of the Assembly and the Commission. It is the raison d'être of the **Committee against Torture,** which monitors implementation of the **Convention against Torture and Other Cruel, Inhuman or Degrading Treatment or Pun-**

ishment [see note of the Secretary-General on the status of the Convention, E/CN.4/1996/34, and the report of the Committee, A/50/44]; the **Voluntary Fund for Victims of Torture,** to assist with rehabilitation; and a **Special Rapporteur,** in the person of the noted scholar and former Amnesty International legal advisor Nigel Rodley. Rodley's latest annual report and recommendations [E/CN.4/1996/35 and Add.1 and 2] were endorsed by the Commission [res. 1996/33], which described itself as "appalled at the widespread occurrence of torture and other cruel, inhuman or degrading treatment or punishment" and invited the Special Rapporteur to examine torture directed primarily against women and children. The Commission also considered the report of a working group on a **draft optional protocol** to the convention that would establish a **preventive system of regular visits to places of detention** [E/CN.4/1996/28] and asked the group to meet for two weeks prior to the Commission's next session "with a view to the expeditious completion of a final and substantive text" [res. 1996/37].

There are other working groups, on **arbitrary detention** [Report, E/CN.4/1996/40; Commission res. 1996/28] and on **enforced disappearances** [Report, E/CN.4/1996/38; res. 1996/30]; and other Special Rapporteurs, who report regularly on the **independence and impartiality of the judiciary, jurors and assessors, and the independence of lawyers** [Report, E/CN.4/1996/37; res. 1996/34], on **states of emergency** [res. 1996/36, requesting ECOSOC approval for the updating of the report by the Special Rapporteur of the Sub-Commission], and on the **right to restitution, compensation, and rehabilitation for victims of grave violations of human rights** [Report by the Sub-Commission's Rapporteur, E/CN.4/Sub.2/1993/8, and by the Secretary-General, E/CN.4/1996/29; Commission res. 1996/35]. The Commission also invited governments to provide training in human rights and **administration of justice,** including **juvenile justice,** to all judges, lawyers, prosecutors, social workers, and others concerned with juvenile-justice matters [res. 1996/32] and, in a resolution on **human rights and forensic science,** based on a report by the Secretary-General [E/CN.4/1996/41], invited states to apply the Principles on the Effective Prevention and Investigation of Extralegal, Arbitrary and Summary Execution and invited the Secretary-General to draw up a list of experts to help international mechanisms, governments, and the Centre for Human Rights monitor violations and train local teams [res. 1996/31].

In a resolution on **hostage-taking,** the Commission demanded that all hostages be released immediately and without any preconditions; called upon states to prevent, combat, and punish the taking of hostages; and urged all special rapporteurs and working groups to address (as appropriate) the consequences of hostage-taking in their forthcoming reports [res. 1996/62]. In their resolutions on **human rights and terrorism,** the General Assembly and the Commission reaffirmed "that all measures to counter terrorism must be in strict conformity with international human rights standards" and urged states to prevent, combat, and eliminate terrorism [A/Res/50/186; Commission res. 1996/47]. The Assembly went on to request the Secretary-General to consider the possibility of a **voluntary fund for victims of terrorism.** The issue will be discussed again in 1997, at the 52nd Session of the Assembly, and the European Union has suggested that the Sixth Committee is more appropriate than the Third Committee for discussion of this item.

In a Cuban-sponsored resolution dealing with **respect for the right to universal freedom of travel and vital importance of family reunification,** the Assembly called upon all states "to allow the free flow of financial remittances by foreign nationals residing in their territory to their relatives in the country of origin" and called upon states to refrain from enacting this type of "coercive" legislation that could have an adverse effect on family reunification. The resolution was adopted by a vote of 86 to 4 (Canada, Israel, Japan, and the United States) with 80 abstentions [A/Res/50/175].

The Development Process

The concern of the majority of the member states with issues of economic development naturally finds its way onto the human rights agenda of the United Nations, sometimes resisted by one or more Western countries. A case in point is the **"right to development."** The General Assembly adopted a Declaration on this right in 1986 [A/Res/41/128, the United States casting the only negative vote], and the Vienna Human Rights Conference called it "a universal and inalienable right and an integral part of fundamental human rights" [Vienna Declaration and Programme of Action, Part I, par. 10]. Regularly reaffirmed in the General Assembly and the Commission (with Washington regularly abstaining or opposing), the right to development has been under study by a Working Group for many years. At the 1996 Commission, the resolution on the right to development was passed by consensus for the first time. This resolution established an **intergovernmental group of ten experts** with a two-year lease to elaborate a strategy for implementing the Declaration on the Right to Development [res. 1996/15].

Poor countries have often used the right to development to amplify their demand on the industrialized world for a transfer of resources, in the form of foreign aid or debt forgiveness. Several Western countries and NGOs find such rhetoric a time- and resource-consuming diversion from more pressing human rights concerns. In between are many donor countries, development agencies, and NGOs that recognize the potential for good of the right to development, if taken seriously. These groups note that

1. The right, as defined in the 1986 Declaration, supports the position that all human rights, including the civil and political, must be re-

spected in development planning and implementation and that, consequently, **underdevelopment and lack of resources cannot be a pretext for violation of human rights** [Declaration on the Right to Development (hereafter DRD), Article 6(3)].

2. The right to development means that development policies should be revised to meet **human-centered and participatory** elements of the definition in the Declaration, in accordance with the duty of states "to formulate appropriate national development policies" [DRD, Article 8(1)].

3. The right implies that **human rights violations are an obstacle to development** and that the removal of such violations is a necessary part of development.

4. Reference to **"fair distribution" of the benefits of development and nondiscrimination in development** could be used to block or reduce support for projects that fail on either of these grounds.

5. The states' duty to ensure "active, free, and meaningful participation" [DRD, Article 2(3)] and "encourage popular participation in all spheres as an important factor in development" [DRD, Article 8(2)] could have a profound effect on **democratization and the empowerment of civil society.**

If national policy and development agencies took seriously these principles, the result would not be the reinforcement of prerogatives of authoritarian states or of the claims of poor countries against rich ones, as some seem to fear. In short, say those who recognize the potential of the right to development, the Declaration is a more balanced text than the politicized debate would suggest.

The High Commissioner for Human Rights is responsible for promoting the right to development among other rights and is expected to establish a dialogue on the subject with Specialized Agencies and international financial institutions, perhaps using his New York office as the focal point for these efforts. As mentioned in the context of the restructuring, the Assembly requested the Commissioner to create a branch whose primary responsibilities include this right, which he has sought to do in Management Unit 1. He appears to favor dialogue with development agencies (such as UNDP and UNICEF) and the international financial institutions, especially the World Bank. He is also considering the execution of one or more pilot projects in this area.

Numerous other development-related issues are part of the human rights agenda of the United Nations, including human rights and **extreme poverty** [Commission res. 1996/10], under study by a Special Rapporteur of the Sub-Commission [E/CN.4/Sub.2/1995/15]; **special problems that the developing countries face in their efforts to achieve economic, social, and cultural rights,** also under study [Commission res. 1996/11]; the effects on human rights of **economic adjustment policies** [res. 1996/12], in regard to which an open-ended working group was established to elaborate a set of basic policy guidelines [Commission decision 1996/103]; human rights and the **environment** [res. 1996/13], which has its own Special Rapporteur [E/CN.4/Sub.2/1994/9 and Corr.1]; effects of **dumping of toxic and dangerous products and wastes** [Commission res. 1996/14], also rating a Special Rapporteur [E/CN.4/1996/17]; **migrant workers** [Commission res. 1996/18]; basic **workers' rights** [res. 1996/60]; and **forced evictions** (broadly, "development-based displacement"), in respect to which an expert seminar will be developing guidelines [decision 1996/104].

Promotional Activities

The U.N.'s human rights work is sometimes broken down into two categories: **"protection"** (responding to human rights abuses after the fact) and **"promotion"** (taking preventive measures to enhance the prospects for human rights observance in the future). The latter efforts are reflected in the agenda items on national institutions, human rights education, and the 50th anniversary of the Universal Declaration of Human Rights, as well as those on Advisory Services and Technical Assistance.

The resolution on **national institutions for the promotion and protection of human rights** essentially calls upon the Secretary-General to give a high priority to requests from member states for assistance in establishing and strengthening national human rights institutions, to be funded by the voluntary contributions of member states [A/Res/50/176]. To assist in this process, the Centre for Human Rights has published a handbook, *National Human Rights Institutions* [HP/P/PT/4], and set up a Coordinating Committee. The committee was created at the Second International Workshop on National Institutions for the Promotion and Protection of Human Rights (Tunis, December 1993). The Third Workshop (Manila, April 1995) [E/CN.4/1996/8] recommended that national institutions participate in U.N. human rights bodies, and the Commission went on to endorse this idea for itself and its subsidiary bodies [Commission res. 1996/50]. A Fourth Workshop is scheduled for Latin America in 1996 or 1997, as funds permit.

Over the past year both the Assembly and the Commission have recognized "the important and constructive role" that NGOs may play with national institutions [A/Res/50/176 and Commission res. 1995/50 and 1996/50]. The U.N. Secretary-General will report to the Commission at its 53rd session and to the Assembly at its 52nd on the progress made in **strengthening and promoting the role of national institutions and NGOs in the protection of human rights.**

Because human rights bodies have been established connections by regional organizations in Europe, Africa, and the Americas, the Commission's **institution-building efforts** are focused on the Asia and Pacific region. Four workshops have been held in the region since 1990, the last of which recognized the importance of a step-by-step process, beginning with national institutions, as has been the case in Mongolia, Nepal, Pakistan, Papua New Guinea, Sri Lanka, and Thailand. The Commission requested the Secretary-General to establish an open-ended team made up of representatives of regional governments and of the Centre for Human Rights, "which could consult with" NGOs and will prepare the next workshop [res. 1996/64]. Since the governments of the region often claim that human rights are an import from the West, the resolution repeatedly alludes to the declaration of the Bangkok preparatory meeting for Vienna and the Vienna Conference language on "national and regional particularities and various historical, cultural, and religious backgrounds."

The **United Nations Decade for Human Rights Education 1995–2004** was proclaimed by the General Assembly in 1994, in response to a suggestion of the Vienna Conference [Vienna Declaration and Programme of Action, Part II, par. 82]. A **Plan of Action for the Decade,** prepared by the High Commissioner with input from governments and NGOs, defines actors and types of activities, stressing mobilization at the grass-roots [A/49/261/Add.1-E/1994/110/Add.1]. The General Assembly and the Commission repeat in their resolutions on this item the definition of human rights education as "a comprehensive life-long process by which people at all levels in development and in all strata of society learn respect for the dignity of others and the means and methods of ensuring that respect in all societies" [A/Res/50/177 and Commission res. 1996/50].

The High Commissioner is mandated to coordinate the Decade. He reported in 1995 on the implementation of the first year of the Decade, and appealed to governments, "in accordance with national conditions, to establish a national focal point for human rights education" or strengthen existing mechanisms [A/50/698]. At the Commission, he reported on the implementation of the Plan of Action of the Decade [E/CN.4/1996/51]. The Commission requested the High Commissioner "to accelerate, within existing resources, the implementation of the Plan of Action" and to get views of governments on ways of increasing support for the Decade, especially regarding NGO activities" [res. 1996/44]. The Commission also repeated the invitation to governments to establish national focal points and plans of action. The Centre for Human Rights, Commission on Human Rights, treaty-monitoring bodies, U.N. Specialized Agencies and programs, and other "competent intergovernmental and non-governmental organizations" are requested to support the implementation of the Plan of Action. Specifically, international, regional, and national NGOs—particularly those concerned with women, labor, development and the environment, and social justice—human rights advocates, educators, religious organizations, and the media are called upon to increase their involvement in human rights education and to cooperate with the High Commissioner's implementation of the Plan of Action. Finally, the Commission requested the High Commissioner to study the advisability of establishing a voluntary fund for human rights education activities, including the activities of NGOs. In the meantime, governments and NGOs have been implementing projects as part of the Decade, such as the July 1996 conference of educators on the pedagogical foundations of human rights education, organized by the government of Costa Rica and the People's Decade of Human Rights Education-International, an NGO, with the support of the High Commissioner.

The General Assembly adopted in 1995 a separate resolution on the **United Nations Decade for Human Rights Education: culture of peace,** in which it encouraged member states, regional organizations, NGOs, and UNESCO to take action to ensure "education for peace, human rights, democracy, international understanding and tolerance" and requested the Secretary-General, along with the UNESCO Director-General, to report at the 51st General Assembly on UNESCO's "Towards a culture for peace" project [A/Res/50/173]. UNESCO already has responsibility for implementing its 1974 Recommendation on Education for International Understanding, Co-operation and Peace, and Education Relating to Human Rights and Fundamental Freedoms and figures prominently in the Plan of Action for the Decade. It is investing in the "culture of peace" program in several postconflict situations (El Salvador, Angola, Mozambique, and Burundi), but it is not clear why these efforts are not noted in a single resolution on the Decade.

The Commission adopted a resolution on the preparation for the **50th anniversary of the Universal Declaration of Human Rights,** which is to be coordinated by the High Commissioner for Human Rights. The resolution calls for governments, treaty-monitoring bodies, U.N. organs and agencies, and NGOs to become involved in preparing for this 1998 event [res. 1996/42].

Field Operations and Support to Governments

One of the most significant developments of the post-Cold War human rights agenda is the expansion of promotional work into field operations and major technical assistance projects, under the heading of **Advisory Services, technical cooperation and the Voluntary Fund for Technical Cooperation in the Field of Human Rights.** The Centre is currently responsible for field missions in Burundi [res. 1996/1], Cambodia [res. 1996/54], Somalia [res. 1996/57], Haiti [res. 1996/58], and Guatemala [res. 1996/59], sometimes at the modest level of an independent expert, as in Somalia, where one such individual is developing a program of Advisory Services [E/CN.4/1996/14; Commission res. 1996/57], and sometimes at the higher level of commitment, involving a Special Representative or Rapporteur and a field office, as in Cambodia [report on the role of the Centre for Human Rights, E/CN.4/1996/92; report of the

Special Representative, E/CN.4/1996/93] and in Burundi [report of the Secretary General, S/1996/116, and of the Special Rapporteur, E/CN.4/1996/16 and Add.1].

These field operations are **a departure from the more traditional provision of experts to help governments adapt national legislation or develop national institutions,** for which the Centre operates a **Voluntary Fund for Technical Cooperation in the Field of Human Rights.** The Commission would like to see "more efficient management rules, periodical evaluations of the programme and projects and the dissemination of evaluation results, including programme implementation and financial accounting reports," suggesting some dissatisfaction with the operation of the Fund and the Programme.

The Commission emphasized the importance of human rights field officers in "countries in transition or reconstruction after situations of armed conflict or internal disturbance, with the consent of the Government concerned," and invited the High Commissioner to explore cooperation with other U.N. bodies and NGOs in carrying out projects [res. 1996/55]. The operational capacity of the Geneva office is seriously strained by both the increase in demands for traditional sorts of expert assistance and the more recent attempts at larger-scale peace-building. The restructuring alone will not solve the problem, although it has the advantage of merging into Management Unit 3 the special procedures, under which the special rapporteurs and working groups function, and Advisory Services, under which recommendations from the special procedures are implemented on the ground. The deeper question relates to the ability of the Geneva bureaucracy, which is oriented toward research and meeting-servicing, to adapt to the political and logistical needs of operational programs. To be effective, the Geneva office would have to become the hub of a network of efficient field operations, capable of both rapid deployment in emergencies and of sustained efforts to carry out the human rights components of postconflict peace-building.

For many years governments have sought to use **Advisory Services** as an alternative to direct scrutiny by the Commission under the category of gross violations of human rights—an earnest of their intention to cooperate. Advisory Services are also used by the High Commissioner and the Secretariat to establish a foothold for human rights improvements in places where the government is more likely to accept a funded project than an independent investigator. For example, Togo was removed from the list of gross violators in exchange for an agreement on technical assistance, signed on March 23, 1996 [Commission res. 1996/67]. The Human Rights Centre is slowly adjusting to the politics and logistics of Advisory Services. These political and logistical complexities are compounded by the new demands to deploy in "countries in transition or reconstruction," as illustrated by the postconflict cases discussed next.

Country Situations

Human rights problems in specific countries come under U.N. scrutiny either because they are essential elements of attempts by the United Nations to end an internal or international armed conflict or because sufficient political momentum has accumulated to bring them under the "1503" or "1235" procedures described at the end of this section.

Human Rights in Armed Conflicts or Postconflict Situations

One of the most noticeable changes in U.N. activities relating to human rights in the post-Cold War world is explicit concern for human rights in the context of maintenance of international peace and security. Acting under Chapter VII of the U.N. Charter (breaches of the peace), the Security Council has imposed sanctions and deployed troops or authorized multinational forces in response (at least in part) to human rights concerns in such places as Somalia, Rwanda, Burundi, Haiti, and Bosnia. With respect to other conflicts, such as those in El Salvador and Cambodia, the Security Council acted under Chapter VI (pacific settlement of disputes) and deployed peacekeeping operations, including human rights components, to oversee the implementation of U.N.-negotiated comprehensive political settlements and to embark on the exceedingly complex work of **postconflict peace-building (PCPB)** [*Supplement to An Agenda for Peace, A/50/60 S/1995/1, par. 47–56, An Agenda for Development, A/48/935, par. 21–25*]. Several working groups of the General Assembly and interagency gatherings are studying the coordination of PCPB and the importance of human rights elements in it. The countries most zealous in guarding the principle of national sovereignty tend to disparage the importance of these elements, while people with field experience firmly believe that strengthening the judiciary, professionalizing and demilitarizing the police, empowering human rights NGOs, dealing with the past through trials, establishing truth commissions or compensation procedures, and conducting human rights education on the broadest possible scale will help to prevent a recurrence of the conflict.

Current U.N. efforts in Rwanda, Burundi, the former Yugoslavia, Cambodia, Haiti, Angola, and Guatemala are part of a PCPB strategy, although Burundi is more properly viewed as an effort at preventive action. The human rights field operations and resolutions concerning these countries will be reviewed below, followed by brief mention of the General Assembly and the Commission's continuing concerns about human rights in conflict situations not yet ready for PCPB, such as Iraq, Liberia, Sudan, and Afghanistan.

The **human rights field operation in Rwanda (HRFOR)** developed out of the High Commissioner for Human Rights' early involvement in the Rwandan crisis, which broke the day after he took office in April 1994. In May 1994 the Commission on Human Rights held an emergency session, at which it appointed a **Special Rapporteur to monitor human rights in Rwanda** [res. S-3/1]. His report [E/CN.4/1995/7], based on a visit in June 1994, concluded that it was appropriate to use the term "genocide" to describe what had occurred and that a tribunal should be established to try those responsible for this violation of international humanitarian law.

The Rapporteur made a second visit, in July 1994, with a focus on the flight of Hutu refugees, and afterwards gave his support to the High Commissioner's plan for a human rights-monitoring mission. In August the High Commissioner concluded an agreement with the Rwandan government and launched an appeal for voluntary contributions to support such a field operation. Although governments pledged almost $18 million, the High Commissioner had to hold an emergency meeting in Geneva to discuss the financial difficulties of HRFOR, which operated on an advance from the Central Emergency Revolving Fund that is being repaid under threat of terminating the operation [U.N. press release DH/2057, 1/11/96]. Plagued by lack of funds and problems with recruitment and supply, the operation also suffered from an overly ambitious mission: to investigate violations of human rights and humanitarian law; to monitor ongoing human rights violations and prevent violations through the presence of human rights field officers; to cooperate with other agencies in confidence-building, repatriation, and rebuilding civil society; and to carry out technical assistance projects in administration of justice and human rights education [Report of the United Nations High Commissioner for Human Rights, "Human Rights Field Operation in Rwanda," A/50/743, par. 9].

A small operation with a budget of a few million dollars is unlikely to make much progress toward PCPB goals. Further, by attempting to collect evidence of human rights violations for the Special Rapporteur and the International Tribunal for Rwanda [ibid., par. 26–37] and, at the same time, visiting places of detention to "urge . . . review . . . [of] cases where arrests appear not to be based on strong indications of criminal responsibility" [par. 21], the mission becomes both prosecutor and defender—an impossible situation. The mandate undoubtedly reflected a good-faith effort to cover the essential human rights concerns, but the credibility of the operation was compromised in practice. In October 1995, hoping to overcome some of these difficulties, the High Commissioner appointed as head of HRFOR Ian Martin, a former Secretary-General of Amnesty International and former head of the human rights division of the Civilian Mission in Haiti. Martin immediately carried out a thorough revision of procedures and established a more constructive working relationship with the Rwandan government [Report of the United Nations High Commissioner for Human Rights, "Making Human Rights a Reality," E/CN.4/1996/103, 3/18/96, par. 126].

HRFOR—while small, still the largest of the field operations for which the High Commissioner is responsible—continues to suffer from serious financial and logistical problems. As the High Commissioner has acknowledged, the "unforeseeability and inadequacy of [financial contributions] have greatly hindered retention of staff . . . and have been enormous impediments to coherent and stable planning at all levels" [ibid., par. 134]. At the 1996 session of the Commission on Human Rights, Lloyd Axworthy, Minister of Foreign Affairs of Canada, observed that "If Rwanda had taught the international community anything, it was the need for more effective coordination among the different parts of the United Nations and for early warning, rapid reaction, and prevention systems that would respond in time to impending large-scale human rights abuses," and he announced that Canada would contribute a further $500,000 to HRFOR [U.N. press release HR/CN/728, 4/4/96].

Anticipating the likely renewal of **genocidal violence in Burundi**, the High Commissioner signed an agreement with the government on September 22, 1994, for a major program of **technical assistance and Advisory Services.** He opened an office in Bujumbura in 1994, with a mandate to deploy human rights observers, bring cases of alleged violation to the attention of the authorities, and recommend remedial action. In April 1996, with a contribution of $434,293 from the European Union and an additional $200,000 pledged by Spain, the High Commissioner deployed five observers to Bujumbura and hoped to increase the force to 35 [U.N. press release HR/1295, 1/16/96, and E/CN.4/1996/103, par. 122].

The High Commissioner and the Special Rapporteur have expressed alarm at the situation in Burundi, describing it as one that "could degenerate and explode at any moment" [E/CN.4/1996/103, par. 121]. Echoing these concerns, the Secretary-General brought the issue before the Security Council, which called for negotiations and an end to violence, and invited governments, intergovernmental organizations, and NGOs to be ready to cooperate with the government "in initiatives for comprehensive rehabilitation . . . , including military and police reform, judicial assistance, development programmes and support at international financial institutions" [S/Res/1049, 3/5/96]. The Commission devoted a special day to Burundi, at the conclusion of which it condemned all threats to the democratic process in Burundi and demanded an immediate end to violations of human rights and acts of violence and intimidation. It also called upon the Secretary-General to strengthen the Bujumbura office and urged the High Commissioner to increase the number of human rights observers deployed throughout the country [res. 1996/1].

The High Commissioner also deploys a **human rights field operation in the former Yugoslavia,** essentially to support the Special Rapporteur on the human rights situation in that territory [E/CN.4/1996/103, par. 108]. From 1992 until 1995, former Prime Minister of Poland Tadeusz Mazowiecki served as Special Rapporteur, resigning in disgust in July 1995 after the fall of Srebrenica and Zepa because the United Nations could not protect these "safe havens." "I wondered if the train I was on was that of the United Nations or the League of Nations," Mazowiecki is reported to have said. "I want to make the leaders of the United Nations think" [cited by Fouad Ajami in *U.S. News and World Report,* 10/23/95]. He has been replaced by Elisabeth Rehn, former Defense Minister of Finland. Her reports, like those of Mazowiecki, have been commended by the Commission, which noted with concern that past recommendations have not been fully implemented and extended the Special Rapporteur's mandate. This came with a request that Rehn submit periodic reports on her visits to Bosnia, Croatia, and the Federal Republic of Yugoslavia, which will be made available to the Security Council and the Organization for Security and Cooperation in Europe (OSCE) [Commission res. 1996/71].

Operationally, the High Commissioner set up **a mission separate from other deployments of civilian personnel** in Bosnia: The U.N. Mission in Bosnia and Herzegovina (UNMIBH) is to deploy 49 civilian affairs officers; the OSCE mission (250–300 monitors); the European Union Monitoring Mission; and the International Police Task Force (IPTF, 1,700 strong). While it is important for the High Commissioner to be able to deploy human rights monitors to hot spots anywhere, it is perhaps not the best use of scarce resources to do so where the United Nations has already deployed civilian officers under the peacekeeping budget. The High Commissioner has proposed to participate in the implementation of the General Framework Agreement for Peace in Bosnia and Herzegovina (**the Dayton accord**) by training international human rights monitors, providing human rights experts to the High Representative responsible for implementing civilian aspects of the peace agreement, and continuing support to the Special Rapporteur and the special process on missing persons [E/CN.4/1996/103, par. 111]. If funding and staffing can be assured and if the proposed training is successful, this experience might suggest a valuable new direction for U.N. system collaboration in PCPB. Otherwise, the High Commissioner's tendency to deploy small, underfunded missions to all hot spots may lead member states and outside observers to question the usefulness and viability of such missions even more than they do at present.

The 1996 Commission adopted an exhaustive resolution with 47 operative paragraphs on the situation of **human rights in Bosnia and Herzegovina, Croatia and Serbia, and Montenegro,** expressing outrage at the numerous violations and at the failure of the parties to arrest and transfer to the Ad Hoc War Crimes Tribunal in The Hague the indicted persons, as required by the Dayton agreement [res. 1996/71]. It also commended the High Commissioner for the training of monitors and for his support to the Special Rapporteur. The resolution's section on PCPB insists that the parties to the agreement comply with their commitments to promote and protect democratic institutions, and it goes on to appeal for contributions to "the Commission on Human Rights for Bosnia and Herzegovina." In this omnibus resolution were two issues that the General Assembly had dealt with in separate resolutions: **rape and abuse of women in the areas of armed conflict in the former Yugoslavia** [A/Res/ 50/192; by consensus] and the **situation of human rights in Kosovo** [A/Res/50/ 190; vote 115-2-43]. These issues will be on the agenda of the 51st Session of the General Assembly.

As the **U.N. Transitional Authority in Cambodia (UNTAC)** prepared to wind down in 1993, two important steps were taken by the Commission on Human Rights at the initiative of UNTAC's **Human Rights Component:** It appointed a **Special Representative on the situation of human rights in Cambodia** [res. 1993/6] and it set up an **office of the Centre for Human Rights in Phnom Penh** to continue much of the work of the Component. The field office got off to a slow start and has been threatened with closure by the government. In 1995 the General Assembly requested the Special Representative on the situation of human rights in Cambodia, Australian judge Michael Kirby, in coordination with the office of the Centre for Human Rights in Cambodia, to continue to evaluate the extent to which his recommendations have been implemented [A/ Res/50/178]. The Assembly encouraged the government to request support from the Centre for the establishment of an "independent national institution for the promotion and protection of human rights." In discussions in the General Assembly's Third Committee, the delegate of Cambodia expressed his government's wish that the Centre continue its efforts.

Most of the work of the Centre's Phnom Penh office is funded through voluntary contributions to the **Trust Fund for a Human Rights Education Programme in Cambodia,** set up by the Human Rights Component during UNTAC's mandate. Reports to the General Assembly and the Commission cover the activities of this Trust Fund [A/50/681/Add.1] and of the Centre [E/CN.4/1996/92]. The country's monarch, King Norodom Sihanouk, has intervened to avoid a rupture of relations between the Centre and the government. Tensions were also reduced by the agreement on "five points" to enhance cooperation between government and Centre that was negotiated by the U.N. Secretary-General's Special Envoy, Marrack Goulding, in May 1995.

The human rights situation continues to deteriorate, however, noted Justice Kirby [E/CN.4/1996/93], whose recommendations and conclusions regarding such matters as independence of the judiciary, establishment of the rule of law, good governance, freedom of expression, and the promotion of a multiparty democracy were endorsed by the Commission [res. 1996/54]. Justice Kirby has since resigned and was replaced by the equally impressive and competent former Secretary-General of Amnesty International Thomas Hammarberg. The Commission strongly urged the government of Cambodia to promote and uphold the effective functioning of multiparty democracy, expressed grave concern over continuing atrocities by the Khmer Rouge, and expressed "particularly grave concern" about "the reluctance of the courts to charge members of the Cambodian military and other security forces for serious criminal offences, . . . which in effect places persons in authority above the principle of equality before the law."

Haiti, Angola, and Guatemala are still other countries in which field operations are deployed under a human rights mandate. In **Haiti,** an independent expert—Adama Dieng of Senegal, Secretary-General of the International Commission of Jurists—has been verifying the country's compliance with its human rights obligations, recommending improvements [E/CN.4/1996/94], and an International Civilian Mission and a Commission for Truth and Justice have been operating with international assistance. The Centre for Human Rights itself has prepared a program of legislative reform, training of judicial personnel, and human rights education. Another PCPB effort is being made in **Angola,** where the **United Nations Angola Verification Mission (UNAVEM III)** was established in February 1995 to help the government of Angola and UNITA achieve national reconciliation and restore peace in the country. In spring 1996 the mission was extended for only two months [S/Res/1055, 5/8/96], expiring on July 8, 1996. The Security Council expressed its "profound regret at the overall slow pace" of the implementation of the Angolan peace process, stressed "the need for respect for human rights, and urged the Angolan parties to give greater attention to preventing and investigating incidents of human rights abuse." In **Guatemala** the United Nations is providing Advisory Services through an independent expert and the **U.N. Mission for the Verification of Human Rights and of Compliance with the Commitments of the Comprehensive Agreement on Human Rights in Guatemala (MINUGUA).** Despite continued violations of human rights (indigenous peoples have suffered most), there have been positive developments in human rights verification, as noted in the reports of the independent expert [E/CN.4/1996/15] and of MINUGUA. The Commission exhorted the government to take a series of measures to apply the independent expert's recommendations [res. 1996/59]. This PCPB operation—a joint effort of the U.N. Secretariat's Department of Political Affairs and the U.N. Development Programme—is proving a successful form of collaboration that combines monitoring and institution-building.

On the **situation of human rights in Afghanistan,** the 50th General Assembly welcomed the cooperation between the Afghan government and the **Special Rapporteur** and urged cooperation with the U.N. Special Mission to Afghanistan [A/Res/50/189]. The Afghan authorities are called upon to investigate the fate of those who have disappeared in the conflict, apply the amnesty decree in a nondiscriminatory manner, and bring the perpetrators of human rights abuses to trial. The 1996 Human Rights Commission extended the Special Rapporteur's mandate, called on the Afghan parties and authorities to respect human rights, including investigating thoroughly cases of disappeared persons, and invited the United Nations to offer Advisory Services and technical assistance "once national reconciliation is achieved and upon request of the governmental authorities," with the hope of enshrining human rights in the future constitution [res. 1996/75]. The issue will be discussed at the 51st General Assembly.

The deterioration of the **situation in Liberia** led to the Security Council's resolution of January 29, 1996, in which it stressed "the importance of respect for human rights in Liberia as well as the need to rehabilitate promptly" the country's penitentiary system [S/Res/1041]. Echoing the Security Council, the Commission on Human Rights, through a Chairman's statement, called upon all the parties to implement the Abuja Agreements and called upon member states, intergovernmental organizations, and NGOs "to provide Liberia with technical and financial assistance to cope with the humanitarian situation and to provide ECOMOG [the seven-nation Military Observer Group set up by the Economic Community of West African States] the necessary logistical and financial support to enable it to carry out its mandate" [E/CN.4/1996/L.10/Add.3, par. 25].

The **situation of human rights in the Sudan** is scrutinized by a **Special Rapporteur**, Gáspár Bíró of Hungary, who has reported to the Commission and the Assembly such gross human rights violations as the practice of slavery, forced displacement, and government collusion in the sale and trafficking in children [A/49/539, A/50/569, E/CN.4/1995/58, and E/CN.4/1996/62]. The General Assembly expressed deep concern about the grave human rights violations in this country, urged the government "to cease immediately all aerial attacks on civilian targets and other attacks that are in violation of international humanitarian law," and deplored the consequences for innocent civilians of the use of landmines by government and rebel forces. So controversial did the topic turn out to be in the Third Committee that votes had to be taken on three operative paragraphs. One, urging the government of Sudan "to investigate without delay" the cases of slavery and similar practices, was adopted on a vote of 85–17–49. The representative of Sudan protested that the voting constituted gross interference in the internal affairs of her country. Another paragraph, which welcomed the recommendation of the Special Rapporteur that human rights monitors to be placed at various locations in Sudan as soon as possible, was approved by a vote of 85–14–50. The third contentious paragraph, which deplored Sudan's refusal to cooperate with the Special Rapporteur, was approved by a vote of 87–15–40. The resolution as a whole was adopted by a vote of 94–15–54 [A/Res/50/197]. At the 1996 Commission on Human Rights, in response to pressures from the Security Council, Sudan reversed its position and said the Special Rapporteur would be welcome in Khartoum and that it would cooperate with his mission. Explaining the reversal, Abdel Aziz Shiddo—Minister of Justice, Attorney General, and Chairman of the Advisory Council for Human Rights of the Sudan— said that the Special Rapporteur has shown disrespect for Islam but had since confirmed his respect for this major world religion and expressed regret if his writings were misunderstood [U.N. press release HR/CN/741, 4/18/96]. The Commission, in a detailed resolution drawing on the most recent report of the Special Rapporteur [E/CN.4/1996/62], expressed outrage at attacks on civilian relief efforts and called for prosecution of those responsible [res. 1996/73]. It also "deeply regret[ted]" Sudan's refusal, since 1993, to allow the Special Rapporteur to visit the country and the "unacceptable threats against his person." Welcoming the government decision to extend cooperation to the Special Rapporteur, the Commission called on Sudan to allow him "free and unlimited access to any person and any area in the Sudan" and to allow the placement of human rights monitors, among other recommendations of the Special Rapporteur. The General Assembly will have this item on the agenda of its 51st Session.

The General Assembly has regularly adopted resolutions on the **situation of human rights in Iraq,** strongly condemning human rights violations of the gravest nature [A/Res/49/203]. The 1995 Commission had asked the **Special Rapporteur,** Max van der Stoel, a former Foreign Minister of the Netherlands and current OSCE High Commissioner on National Minorities, to submit an interim report to the Assembly [res. 1995/76]. That report found no improvements whatsoever in the human rights situation within the country, and at its 50th Session, the Assembly condemned "the massive and extremely grave violations of human rights for which the Government of Iraq is responsible," singling out summary and arbitrary executions, torture, decrees prescribing cruel and unusual punishment, including mutilation, enforced and involuntary disappearances, and arbitrary arrests and detention. The Assembly called upon Iraq to uphold its obligations under the two human rights covenants and to nullify Revolution Command Council Decree No. 840 penalizing the expression of competing views [A/Res/50/191; vote 111–3–53].

The 1996 Commission's detailed resolution on Iraq [res. 1996/72] found "persisting massive and grave violations of human rights" with "no signs of improvement," endorsed the Special Rapporteur's proposal for the deployment of human rights monitors, and, naming five categories of rights, strongly condemned massive and grave violations under each. The Commission also made numerous specific demands on the Iraqi government and extended the Special Rapporteur's mandate for another year. The situation will be discussed at the 51st Session of the General Assembly.

Other Country Situations Under U.N. Scrutiny

Of the country situations brought up at the 52nd Commission on Human Rights in 1996, the one that may have received the most attention in the West, particularly in the United States, was that of **China**. At the Commission the European Union introduced a draft resolution, co-sponsored by 26 developed countries, that would have recognized China's accomplishments in development and progress in the legal sphere but would express concern about the country's record with regard to assembly, association, expression, religion, due process, fair trial, and administration of justice and invite the government to cooperate with all thematic and special rapporteurs and working groups [E/CN.4/1996/L.90]. China, which had launched a massive diplomatic effort virtually at the moment the previous Commission came to a close, managed to obtain a vote of 27–20–6 on a motion to take no action on the draft resolution. (At the 51st Commission in 1995, this procedural motion had been defeated for the first time in four years, although the resolution itself was one vote short of carrying.) Human Rights Watch commented at the 52nd Commission that "[t]his dismal performance . . . raised serious questions about whether the U.N.'s most prestigious human rights body can function effectively when a large and economically powerful country like China can successfully escape scrutiny" [Human Rights Watch press release, 4/23/96].

In November 1995, following the hanging in Nigeria of nine Ogoni activists, Ken Saro-Wiwa among them, the United States attempted—unsuccessfully—to raise the issue in the Security Council, where compulsory sanctions could have been taken. The matter was also brought to the General Assembly, which, after an intense debate, adopted a resolution on the **situation of human rights in Nigeria** [A/Res/50/199; vote 101–14–47], condemning the arbitrary executions, expressing deep concern about the human rights situation in the country, and welcoming the decision to suspend Nigeria from membership in the British Commonwealth. The Assembly requested the Commission on Human Rights and its **Special Rapporteur on summary and arbitrary executions** to report on the situation in Nigeria at the 1996 Commission session but, in the absence of the political will to do more, did not go on to urge member states to take voluntary economic measures against Nigeria's military regime.

In both the General Assembly and the Commission, African delegations managed to tone down the operative sections of the resolution on Nigeria. Perceiving a trend of resolutions critical of African states, they have tended to resist procedures targeting African countries. The 1996 Commission called upon the government of Nigeria to ensure observance of human rights, specifically by restoring habeas corpus; by releasing all political prisoners, trade union leaders, human rights advocates, and journalists in detention; by guaranteeing freedom of the press; and by ensuring respect for the rights of all individuals, including members of minorities. The same resolution of the 52nd Commission asked the two thematic special rapporteurs who had requested an investigative visit to the country to submit to the 53rd session a joint report on their findings [res. 1996/79]. Of the 32 sponsors, the only African state was South Africa.

In 1995 the General Assembly resolution on the **situation on human rights in Iran** expressed concern at the high number of executions; the considerable cases of torture and cruel, inhuman, or degrading punishment; the lack of guarantees of due process of law; the *fatwa* issued against Salman Rushdie; and the discriminatory practices against minority religions, including the Baha'is and Christians [A/Res/50/188; vote 78–27–58]. The Assembly went on to request the government to allow the Special Representative to visit Iran without imposing conditions and called for the implementation of agreements with humanitarian organizations.

Subsequently, the **Special Representative of the Commission on the situation of human rights in the Islamic Republic of Iran** and the **Special Rapporteurs on religious intolerance and on freedom of opinion and expression** were able to visit the country [E/CN.4/1996/95/Add.2 and E/CN.4/1996/39/Add.2]. The Commission welcomed these developments but expressed its concern at the failure of the government to meet international standards for the administration of justice, notably with respect to pretrial detention, lack of access to defense lawyers, and executions in the absence of guarantees of due process of law; and with respect to the use of torture and cruel, inhuman, and degrading treatment or punishment [res. 1996/84; vote 24–7–20]. The Commission was also concerned at the discriminatory treatment of minorities by reason of their religious beliefs, notably the Baha'is, and decided to extend the mandate of the Special Representative for an additional year.

The 50th General Assembly adopted a resolution on the **situation of human rights in Myanmar (Burma),** welcoming the release of Nobel Peace Prize winner Daw Aung San Suu Kyi but deploring continued violations of human rights that have resulted in flows of refugees to neighboring countries [A/Res/50/194]. The resolution urged the government "to take all necessary steps toward the restoration of democracy in accordance with the will of the people as expressed in the democratic elections held in 1990." The winners of those elections are still excluded from participating in the meetings of the National Convention that was created to prepare the drafting of a new constitution. The General Assembly resolution also strongly urged Burma to ensure the protection of the rights of ethnic and religious minorities, and to end the violations of the right to life, acts of torture, abuse of women, forced labor, forced relocations, disappearances, and summary executions, among others [A/Res/50/194]. The 1996 Commission, for its part, strongly urged Burma to release immediately and unconditionally all detained political prisoners, to ensure their physical integrity, and to permit them to participate in the process of national reconciliation. Welcoming the release of Aung San Suu Kyi, the Commission urged the government to allow her freedom of movement and "to open immediately a substantial political dialogue with her and with other political leaders" [E/CN.4/1996/65; Commission res. 1996/80]. The Commission decided to extend for one year the mandate of the **Special Rapporteur.** (The Rapporteur, Professor Yozo Yokota of Japan, resigned the post and has been replaced by Rajsoomer Lallah of Mauritius.)

In its resolution on the **situation of human rights in Cuba,** the General Assembly welcomed the government's authorization of a visit to Cuba by a delegation of international human rights organizations and welcomed as well the release of a number of political prisoners. It continued to deplore the human rights situation on the island, however, and called upon the government to cooperate fully with the **Special Rapporteur** and to adopt measures to bring the observance of human rights and fundamental freedoms into conformity with international human rights instruments [A/Res/50/198; vote 62–23–72]. The representative of Cuba had asserted that the voting on the resolution was being imposed by the United States, that the government of Cuba had nothing to be ashamed of, and that Cuba would never accept "this gross draft no matter how well disguised, nor will it accept a Special Rapporteur no matter how neutral and independent he may look." A similar resolution was adopted by the Commission [res. 1996/69, vote 20–5–28], extending the mandate of the Special Rapporteur, Carl-Johan Groth, for a year [for report of the Special Rapporteur, see E/CN.4/1996/60].

NGO human rights activists had been frustrated over the failure of the Commission to appoint a Special Rapporteur on **the situation of human rights in Colombia.** Once again diplomacy by the government, including a visit by the High Commissioner and an expressed willingness to cooperate with the thematic rapporteurs and the International Committee of the Red Cross, forestalled the appointment of a Special Rapporteur. Through a statement by the Chairman of the Human Rights Commission, the 1996 Commission did express its deep concern about summary executions, disappearances, and torture in Colombia and called on the government to prevent such acts. It also requested "the High Commissioner on Human Rights to proceed, upon the initiative of the Government of Colombia and the identification of adequate sources of financing, to establish at the earliest possible date a **permanent office in Colombia** with the mandate to assist the Colombian authorities in developing policies and programs for the promotion and protection of human rights and to observe violations of human rights in the country" [Report of the Commission, E/CN.4/1996/L.10/Add.3, par. 24]. Although a Special Rapporteur was not established, this "permanent office" with a double mandate—

assistance and monitoring—could prove to be an innovative and effective means of achieving the same results.

The Commission has been criticized by NGOs for its failure to address adequately **human rights violations by Indonesia, especially in East Timor.** The Commission made a series of specific demands on the Indonesian government through a resolution in 1993 [res. 1993/97] and statements by the Commission chairman in subsequent years. Few of these demands have been implemented [Amnesty International, *Indonesia & East Timor: When Will the Commission Take Action . . . ?* (AI Index: ASA 21/10/96), 2/96, p. 14]. The High Commissioner visited Indonesia in December 1995 and succeeded in obtaining agreement by the government to pursue investigations, ratify the Torture Convention, and allow the Centre to open a human rights office in the country [ibid., pp. 19–20; Report of the High Commissioner, E/CN.4/1996/103, par. 95; and Report of the High Commissioner for Human Rights on his visit to Indonesia and East Timor, 12/3–7/95, E/CN.4/1996/112, par. 23–29]. The Commission welcomed the visit of the High Commissioner to the country and noted with satisfaction the understanding reached with the Indonesian authorities concerning the **upgrading of technical cooperation in the field of human rights.** It also welcomed the continued cooperation of the government with the Commission and its mechanisms, including **Jakarta's statement of intent to invite a thematic rapporteur for a visit in 1997** [Chairman's statement of 4/23/96, E/CN.4/1996/L.10/Add.10, par. 86]. Amnesty International has recommended that the human rights office in Jakarta supervise the implementation of recommendations by U.N. bodies, receive petitions and gather information, issue public reports, and advise the government—and that it be able to hire independent experts, with unimpeded access to all areas of Indonesia and East Timor [AI, *Indonesia & East Timor*, pp. 19–20].

Human Rights Procedures

The U.N. human rights machinery is a complex web of working groups, rapporteurs, and monitoring bodies that operate either on the basis of treaties binding only the states parties or on the basis of a mandate from the Commission on Human Rights, ECOSOC, or the General Assembly.

Implementation of Human Rights Treaties

The **International Covenants on Human Rights** (1966, entering into force in 1976)—one on civil and political rights, the other on economic, social, and cultural rights—are supervised by the Human Rights Committee [A/50/40] and the Committee on Economic, Social and Cultural Rights [E/1995/22], respectively. Both committees review reports from states parties on steps taken to implement the text; the Human Rights Committee examines individual complaints against countries that have ratified the Optional Protocol to the Covenant, and the Committee on Economic, Social and Cultural Rights is drafting an optional protocol that will permit it to do the same.

In their annual resolutions on the subject, the Assembly and the Commission usually express concern about overdue reports, derogations from Covenant rights during states of emergency, and the broad reservations by which states limit the obligations they undertake when ratifying these covenants [A/Res/50/171; Commission res. 1996/16]. The issue of reservations is of special interest to the United States, whose first report on civil and political rights (having ratified the covenant only in 1992) was considered by the Human Rights Committee in March 1995 [CCPR/C/81/Add.4]. The Committee regretted the extent of the U.S. reservations and found two of them incompatible with the very "object and purpose" of the Covenant [CCPR/C/79/Add.50, par. 14].

The General Assembly and the Commission also consider other treaties that are of particular significance to particular states, among them the **International Convention on the Protection of the Rights of All Migrant Workers and Members of Their Families** [A/Res/50/169] and the **Convention on the Rights of the Child.** With respect to the latter, the 1996 Commission adopted a detailed resolution, with 50 operative paragraphs, referring not only to the Convention and the **Committee on the Rights of the Child** but also to the Declaration and Plan of Action of the 1990 World Summit for Children, the Copenhagen and Beijing conferences, and the Programs of Action for the Prevention of the Sale of Children, Child Prostitution, and Child Pornography and on the Elimination of Exploitation of Child Labor [res. 1996/85]. Regarding the Children's Rights Convention, the Commission called on states parties to withdraw reservations incompatible with the object and purpose of this instrument; requested the working group on an optional protocol dealing with children in armed conflicts to finalize its draft; and noted with appreciation UNICEF's support to the Committee on the Rights of the Child. (Thanks to UNICEF, that Committee has more opportunities for site visits and research than any other treaty body.) The Commission resolution deals too with the protection of children affected by armed conflicts [for report by the Secretary-General, see E/CN.4/1996/110 and Add.1], and the sale of children, child prostitution, and pornography [for report of the Special Rapporteur, see E/CN.4/1996/100].

The 50th Assembly and the 1996 Commission also addressed the matter of effective implementation of international instruments rights, including reporting obligations under such instruments [A/Res/50/170; Commission res. 1996/22]. Both resolutions are notable for drawing on the meeting of the expert group on the integration of gender perspectives into U.N. human rights activities and programs [A/50/505] and on the meetings of the chairs of treaty-monitoring bodies. Here, the Commission appeals for additional resources for treaty bodies and notes the potential benefits of **computerized information-retrieval systems**—one of the recommendations of a recent UNA-USA study on the international protection and promotion of human rights [*Inalienable Rights, Fundamental Freedoms: A U.N. Agenda for Advancing Human Rights in the World Community*, New York: UNA-USA, 1996, p. 43]. Encouraging states parties to enlist the help of Advisory Services and technical assistance in complying with their treaty obligations is another interest of the Commission, as is the dissemination of information on the treaties and follow-up to the recommendations of treaty bodies. The Secretary-General will report to the General Assembly on measures taken and obstacles encountered in the implementation of the resolution and on the conclusions and recommendations of the meetings of the heads of the treaty bodies.

Special Procedures Under Mandates of Rapporteurs and Working Groups

Most agenda items dealing with specific countries and thematic issues are based on reports by the special rapporteurs or working groups that are mandated to investigate and analyze the situation, cooperate with the governments concerned, and report back to the Commission or the Assembly. These special procedures grew out of procedures, both confidential and public, that were developed slowly during the Cold War.

The **confidential procedure:** In 1970 the Sub-Commission and the Commission were authorized to examine summaries of the hundreds of thousands of petitions that reach the United Nations annually to determine whether they contain evidence of **"a consistent pattern of gross violations of human rights"** in a particular state [ECOSOC resolution 1503 (XL-VIII)]—and somewhat later began to make public the list of situations revealing such a pattern. (Members of the Commission, however, are still prohibited from referring in public debate to the confidential decision or the materials on which the decision was based.) No country wants to appear on the list of situations identified by the Commission and Sub-Commission as revealing such a pattern, and many feel under particular pressure to avoid appearing on that list. In 1996 the situations on the "black list" were Armenia, Azerbaijan, Chad, Mali, Nepal, Saudi Arabia, Sierra Leone, Slovenia, Thailand, and Uzbekistan. (Azerbaijan, Mali, Nepal, Slovenia, and Thailand were subsequently dropped.) This **"1503 procedure"** is secretive, laborious, and subject to political manipulation. Nevertheless numerous observers agree that although this procedure requires a considerable investment of time and energy, it does bring effective pressure to bear on many governments that abuse human rights [see, for example, Philip Alston, "The Commission on Human Rights," in Alston, ed., *The United Nations and Human Rights*, New York: Oxford University Press, 1992, pp. 152–53].

The **public procedure:** In 1967 the Commission and Sub-Commission were given the job of "examin[ing] information relevant to gross violations of human rights" and "in appropriate cases . . . mak[ing] a thorough study of **situations which reveal a consistent pattern of violations of human rights**" [ECOSOC resolution 1235 (XLII)]. Under the ground rules of this "**1235 procedure,**" the Commission holds an annual public debate on such situations, during which governments and NGOs draw attention to country-specific information. When there is sufficient political support, the Commission may mandate special rapporteurs or working groups to investigate the situation in specific countries, and it regularly adopts resolutions based on the reports of investigations and studies. In 1996, for example, it reviewed situations and reports and adopted resolutions on Burundi, Equatorial Guinea, Southern Lebanon and Western Bekaa, Cuba, China (no-action decision on a draft resolution), former Yugoslavia, Iraq, Sudan, Afghanistan, Rwanda, Zaire, Nigeria, Myanmar (Burma), East Timor (statement by the Chairman), Chechnya (statement by the Chairman), Iran, and Cyprus.

Since 1980 the Commission has developed a variety of "**thematic mechanisms**" through which significant human rights problems become the object of study, without reference to a specific country. Currently reporting to the Commission are working groups on (1) forced or involuntary disappearances, (2) arbitrary detention, and (3) the right to development (this last will be replaced by an intergovernmental expert group); working groups that are drafting texts on (1) an optional protocol on the sale of children, (2) an optional protocol on children in armed conflicts, (3) a declaration on human rights defenders, (4) a declaration on rights of indigenous peoples, and (5) an optional protocol to the Torture Convention; and a working group on communications under the 1503 procedure. Also reporting to the Commission are 11 special rapporteurs—on extrajudicial, summary, or arbitrary executions; freedom of opinion and expression; racial discrimination and xenophobia; torture; religious intolerance; mercenaries; sale of children, child pornography, and child prostitution; internally displaced persons; independence of the judiciary; violence against women; and the effects of toxic and dangerous products—and there is also a special process for dealing with missing persons in the former Yugoslavia. These matters are usually listed separately on the Commission agenda, and a more limited number appear on the agenda of the Third Committee. These procedures broke new ground by allowing for direct requests to governments to provide information or take immediate action, and for on-site fact-finding (subject, of course, to consent of the state concerned).

The granting or holding back of consent to visits by thematic or country rapporteurs has been suggested as a **criterion for election to membership on the Commission,** the idea being that states that do not honor their obligation under the Charter to cooperate with the United

Nations on human rights matters should not have the honor of sitting on the Commission. The exclusion would not be based on level of respect for human rights, only on the refusal to cooperate [UNA-USA, *Inalienable Rights, Fundamental Freedoms*, pp. 27, 42].

In a resolution on the subject of thematic procedures, the 1996 Commission commended governments that have invited the thematic rapporteurs and groups to visit their countries and encouraged other governments to cooperate more closely with these procedures. It also encouraged the rapporteurs and working groups to monitor progress by governments and report on follow-up actions [res. 1996/46]. The Commission invited NGOs to continue cooperating with the procedures and asked the rapporteurs and working groups to include "gender-disaggregated data" on the problems covered and to focus on women's issues. Many of these recommendations have emerged from meetings of the High Commissioner with special rapporteurs and chairs of working groups and Advisory Services [E/CN.4/1995/5, Annex; and E/CN.4/1996/50, Annex]—meetings that the Commission encourages. One perennial resolution, on the other hand, is clearly motivated by a desire to weaken these procedures. Introduced by Cuba at the 50th Session, this resolution—on "strengthening of U.N. action in the human rights field through the promotion of international cooperation and the importance of **non-selectivity, impartiality and objectivity**" [A/Res/50/174; by consensus]—stresses the principle of nonintervention.

The development of action-oriented mechanisms to promote and protect human rights worldwide and the desire of member states to preserve national sovereignty create a tension that is inherent in the intergovernmental nature of the United Nations and will continue to inform the Organization's human rights agenda. Governments, acting through the United Nations, have found it in their interest to agree on international human rights standards and monitoring mechanisms, and then vote on the basis on narrower political interests when it comes to the application of those standards and mechanisms. As one of the most insightful observers has noted, "United Nations votes are not the only way, or even the most effective way, to express that interest in the observance of rights. The critical question is not whether politics has primacy over law, but whether political interests, in both short and long terms, are served by régimes that respect basic human rights" [Oscar Schachter, *International Law in Theory and Practice*, Dordrecht/Boston/London, Martinus Nijhoff Publishers, 1991, p. 347].

2. Refugees and Internally Displaced Persons
By J. Lee Byrd and Kanya D. Tampoe Sanders

In 1951 the General Assembly created the Office of the **United Nations High Commissioner for Refugees (UNHCR)** to address the needs of (in the official definition) "persons fleeing their country of origin because of a well-founded fear of persecution based on race, religion, nationality, membership in a particular social group, or political opinion." UNHCR's work is guided by the **1951 U.N. Convention Relating to the Status of Refugees** and its **1967 Protocol,** and for most of these years the emphasis has been on achieving a "permanent solution" to the refugees' problems, mainly through local settlement or third-country resettlement.

UNHCR remains the lead agency within the U.N. system when it comes to assisting or protecting refugees. But changes in the nature and scale of "involuntary migration"—among them, the dramatic increase in the number of internally displaced persons—have compelled UNHCR and others in the international community to reexamine traditional approaches to "the refugee problem." Also contributing to the need for a more comprehensive approach to displacement is the post-Cold War period's multiplicity of complex humanitarian emergencies that are being unleashed by internal conflict in countries with already fragile economic, social, and political institutions [U.S. Mission to the United Nations, *Global Humanitarian Emergencies, 1995,* p. 1]. At the same time, many nations around the world are more reluctant to grant protection to asylum seekers. Given this combination of factors, the new approach to population displacement also addresses problems within the country of origin that have given rise to refugee crises and that keep displaced people from their homes. Until recent years, any U.N. effort to address such internal conditions would have been unthinkable, based on an international consensus that the Organization had no authority to "intervene in matters which are essentially within the domestic jurisdiction of any state" [John Harris, ed., *The Politics of Humanitarian Intervention,* Save the Children, 1995, p. 3].

High Commissioner for Refugees Sadako Ogata notes that a stronger U.N. commitment to preventive diplomacy and conflict mediation, the encouragement of greater respect for human rights—along with monitoring to ensure such respect—and the forging of better linkages between relief and development would contribute considerably to the solution (and prevention) of refugee problems.

Institutional Collaboration

In the early 1990s the increasing number and complexity of emergencies worldwide challenged the ability of the international community to respond to humanitarian needs and forced the United Nations to increase its institutional capacity and improve interagency coordination. In 1992, Secretary-General Boutros Boutros-Ghali created the **Department of Humanitarian Affairs (DHA)** to coordinate emergency relief activities among U.N. agencies and nongovernmental organizations (NGOs), establishing a new model of international emergency response.

DHA is the focal point of the U.N.'s humanitarian system. At the onset of a complex emergency, the **Emergency Relief Coordinator of DHA,** an Under-Secretary-General, seeks to facilitate a comprehensive international response, assigning responsibilities to U.N. operational agencies and working closely with governments of both donor and recipient countries. The fact that the Emergency Relief Coordinator chairs the **Inter-Agency Standing Committee (IASC)**—consisting of the executive heads of those operational agencies as well as the International Committee of the Red Cross (ICRC) and other intergovernmental and nongovernmental organizations—serves to strengthen the coordination of emergency humanitarian assistance.

To meet the far-reaching needs of displaced persons caught up in humanitarian emergencies, UNHCR collaborates with other U.N. agencies that are expert at filling particular needs. To ensure the delivery of emergency relief early in a crisis, UNHCR coordinates its efforts with the U.N. Disaster Relief Organization (UNDRO). To ensure that the needs of children are fulfilled it cooperates with the U.N. Children's Fund (UNICEF); to deliver and distribute food, with the World Food Programme (WFP); to supply medical assistance and essential drugs, the World Health Organization (WHO); and to link up humanitarian relief and long-term development, the U.N. Development Programme (UNDP). Because mandates frequently overlap during complex emergencies, UNHCR often makes cross-mandate arrangements with other U.N. agencies. Despite such efforts, effective coordination and prevention of duplication continue to elude the U.N.'s humanitarian response system.

As UNHCR carries out its ever-more-frequent **operations in countries of origin and in zones of active conflict,** it may also **work with peacekeeping forces** to ensure the successful return, resettlement, and reintegration of refugees and internally displaced persons. This it has already done in the former Yugoslavia, Cambodia, and Angola. "Refugees are most likely to exercise their right to repatriate voluntarily when they feel that their security can be assured," notes *State of the World's Refugees 1995,* and UNHCR's Executive Committee has insisted that repatriation programs be carried out under conditions of absolute safety. Since human rights violations are often the cause of these mass population displacements, UNHCR works with human rights bodies too, including the office of the U.N. High Commissioner on Human Rights, to monitor conflict and postconflict situations. In some instances, specially created civilian structures, such as ONUSAL in El Salvador, take on the monitoring and protection functions.

UNHCR also collaborates with hundreds of NGOs to provide relief and legal assistance to displaced persons. To facilitate this collaboration, UNHCR and the **International Council on Voluntary Agencies (ICVA)** initiated Partners in Action (PARINAC), which opened with a year-long series of consultations, culminating in a conference in Oslo in June 1994. The more than 450 NGOs participating in these consultations discussed such matters as internally displaced persons, emergency preparedness and response, the relief-to-development continuum, and the NGO-UNHCR partnership. Here they examined operational relationships and criteria for building better, more constructive partnerships and, in the Oslo Plan of Action, made a commitment to create new mechanisms for responding to humanitarian emergencies. The kind of cooperation and collaboration envisioned at Oslo has yet to be realized, however.

International Refugee Protection

The **failure of many countries to ratify the 1951 Convention Relating to the Status of Refugees and its 1967 Protocol** continues to impede international efforts on behalf of refugees. When UNHCR attempts to fulfill its mandate to protect displaced persons in refugee-receiving countries that have not yet ratified the Convention or the Protocol, for example, the government can effectively bar access of UNHCR to refugee populations within that territory. And those states that have ratified the Convention and the Protocol but either fail to comply with the provisions or interpret them narrowly are another impediment to international efforts on behalf of refugees. Encouraging U.N. member states to ratify and implement these international instruments and comply with their provisions continues to be a priority.

The legal definition of a refugee remains the one provided in the 1951 Convention. This definition was shaped during the Cold War, when the causes and characteristics of population displacement were different from what they have been in recent years. First, the majority of refugee situations today involve large numbers of people rather than one or a few individuals. Second, most current refugees are not fleeing persecution directed at themselves as individuals but, rather, are fleeing life-threatening conditions of general violence and repression. Some states have granted safe haven to persons fleeing such circumstances, despite the fact that the international legal regime relating to refugees does not extend to them, and this practice is noted in the 1994 General Conclusion on International Protection [A/AC.96/839, par. 19(n)]. At the same time, informal mechanisms are being developed to extend UNHCR's mandate to refugees fleeing internal violence and civil wars. In 1994 the Executive Committee of UNHCR encouraged UNHCR to assist all persons whose life and liberty would be in danger if they were to return to their countries of origin because of armed conflicts [A/AC.96/839, par. 19].

Then there is the phenomenon of the massive humanitarian emergency, such as what we have witnessed in Bosnia, Burundi, and Rwanda, in which refugees flood into neighboring countries, often countries with struggling economies and without the infrastructure or the financial capability to absorb the hordes of newcomers. As a result, the neighboring governments attempt to close the border and force the refugees back, sometimes through violent means. UNHCR has highlighted the need for legal protection of refugees in such mass influx situations [EC/1995/SCP/CRP.3]. It has also called upon the more affluent countries to share the burden borne by the refugee-receiving countries [ibid.]. The need for burden-sharing, however, does not end with financial and technical assistance but extends to liberal resettlement and asylum policies.

Gross human rights violations by state and nonstate actors pursuing "ethnic cleansing" policies not only have caused some of the massive refugee movements of recent years but have presented to UNHCR the special problem of protecting the people targeted for ethnic cleansing in their own country. Here, UNHCR has faced a moral dilemma: whether to evacuate the vulnerable populations, thus indirectly assisting the perpetrators of ethnic cleansing, or take on the near-impossible task of protecting those at risk in their places of origin. The Ad Hoc International War Crimes Tribunals for the former Yugoslavia and Rwanda are attempting to hold accountable those responsible for such crimes against humanity, although these efforts are frustrated by the difficulty of arresting and extraditing high-ranking officials charged with masterminding the atrocities.

In certain other cases it is the **militarization of refugee camps,** especially those close to the borders of the country of origin, that make particularly difficult the exercise of UNHCR's protection mandate. UNHCR's mandate to protect refugee camps is based on the premise that these camps house civilian populations, but when the camps are transformed into rebel bases-in-exile, they become targets for military action. Preserving the humanitarian character of these camps to ensure the safety of their civilian refugee population requires the cooperation of the very parties whose activities are undermining the international community's ability to protect that population in the first place [A/AC.96/850].

Voluntary Repatriation and Return

In the past decade, UNHCR has recognized **voluntary repatriation** as the preferred solution to many refugee problems, and has facilitated repatriation whenever possible. In 1985 the Executive Committee adopted Conclusion 40, which outlined practical means of promoting repatriation and ensuring durable solutions through rehabilitation and reintegration assistance. Thanks largely to UNHCR's repatriation initiatives, approximately 10 million refugees have returned to their homes since 1990. Today, the agency's primary concern is to address the problems that continue to plague countries of origin and to "promote the creation of condi-

tions that are conducive to voluntary return in safety and with dignity"
[UNHCR Handbook, *Voluntary Repatriation: International Protection, 1996*, p. 5].

Although repatriation is usually viewed as desirable by both displaced populations and the international community, it presents important challenges to the humanitarian system. *First,* spontaneous or premature repatriation often endangers returnees as well as national reconciliation efforts. As noted, UNHCR is directed to promote repatriation only when conditions are favorable for the refugees' return, but it remains the case that refugees are sometimes repatriated to countries that have not seen the end of armed conflict and/or massive human rights violations. The estimated 100,000 Angolans repatriated in 1991 and 1992, after the government and the National Union for the Total Independence of Angola (UNITA) reached a peace agreement, found themselves in this situation when UNITA rejected the results of the scheduled elections and the fighting resumed. Then there is the case of the Burmese refugees in Bangladesh who were subjected to abuses and coerced into returning to Myanmar after the governments of both countries signed a bilateral repatriation agreement in 1992. These examples demonstrate that (in the words of the UNHCR Executive Committee) "for repatriation to be a sustainable and thus truly durable solution to refugee problems, it is essential that the need for rehabilitation, reconstruction, and national reconciliation be addressed in a comprehensive and effective manner" [A/ AC.96/839, sec. iii, par. 19aa].

Second, reintegration of refugees in the country of origin strains the capacities of UNHCR and the international system, especially when that country has suffered from years of warfare and has neither the resources nor the infrastructure for absorbing returnees. Although refugees who have returned home do not officially fall within the mandate of UNHCR, the agency has increasingly assumed responsibility for reintegrating them in their local communities.

Given the many demands on UNHCR, noted the Executive Committee during its 46th session, "other organizations, within and outside the United Nations, must gradually take over lead agency responsibilities from UNHCR in the reintegration and reconstruction phases" [A/AC.96/ SR.499, par. 26]. Recognizing too the limited role that UNHCR can play in monitoring and protecting the safety of returnees, High Commissioner Ogata has appealed to human rights agencies to complement UNHCR's efforts to promote the safety of returnees.

Asylum

States parties to the International Refugee Convention Relating to the Status of Refugees incorporate its provisions in domestic asylum laws and policies. Today, the trend among the world's most affluent countries—

including those with traditions of providing asylum to refugees—is toward increasingly **restrictive asylum laws and procedures** and increasingly **narrower interpretations of the 1951 Convention's definition of a refugee.** Organizations and individuals concerned about such trends point out that even the traditional definition fails to take into account the raison d'être of the Refugee Convention: to provide protection for those fleeing life-threatening circumstances. And many groups concerned with the protection of refugees have urged a broader interpretation of "refugee," one that recognizes the refugee-creating circumstances described in the 1969 OAU Convention Governing the Specific Refugee Problems in Africa, the 1984 Cartagena Declaration on Refugees, and still other human rights standards, both regional and universal.

Lethargic economies, rising racism, and xenophobia, compounded by illegal immigration and abuse of asylum procedures, have contributed to this restrictive trend. Tightening of borders and forcible mass returns, violation of obligations under the refugee convention, and limitation of access to asylum procedures and to review of asylum claims are some of the measures states have taken to prevent refugees from entering their territory and making a bid for asylum [A/AC.96/850, par. 6]. Other laws and policy responses to asylum seekers and refugees, such as "safe third country" and "first country of asylum," and admission agreements between countries, also keep refugees in limbo and subject to chain deportations and other forcible relocations, all without effective protection mechanisms. Purportedly designed to restrict illegal immigration and abuse of asylum, such laws and practices have served to thwart genuine asylum seekers and refugees.

At the same time, a few countries (prominently, Canada and the United States) have begun to broaden domestic asylum laws to allow a claim of **"gender-based persecution"** (not included under the 1951 Convention and 1967 Protocol), recognizing that women and girls may be harassed, abused, and otherwise subjected to violence in their countries of origin simply by reason of being women. In June 1996 the highest administrative tribunal in the U.S. immigration system awarded "its first recognition of genital mutilation as a form of persecution and a basis for asylum" to a young woman from Togo [*New York Times*, 6/14/96].

Complex Emergencies

The post-Cold War world has witnessed the **proliferation of complex humanitarian emergencies**—situations whose causes and effects are a tangle of such elements as internal conflict, mass population displacements, famine, and the breakdown of already fragile economic, political, and social institutions. Between 1978 and 1985 there were on average five new complex emergencies a year. In 1995 there were 20 going on all at once, threatening more than 40 million people [U.S. Mission to the United Nations, *Global Humanitarian Emergencies, 1995*, p. 1].

The creation of DHA in 1992 demonstrated the U.N.'s desire to address complex humanitarian emergencies more effectively. Through its Emergency Relief Coordinator, DHA coordinates the U.N. response to complex emergencies and proposes **consolidated appeals for funds** on behalf of all U.N. agencies, the International Organization for Migration (IOM), and some NGOs. Both DHA and UNHCR have established revolving funds to cover start-up costs for early response at the onset of a crisis, DHA's Complex Emergency Division (CED) has its own Rapid Response Unit, and UNHCR routinely deploys emergency response teams to address needs in the initial phase of emergencies.

Despite such efforts at improving the U.N.'s ability to supply food, sanitation, shelter, and medical care for large numbers of people under emergency conditions, complex emergencies have exposed some enduring problems. One is the problem of overlapping mandates, which continue to inhibit coordination in several areas. Both UNHCR and UNICEF, for example, provide assistance to refugee children, and both UNHCR and WFP deliver food to refugee populations. Another problem is that of ensuring the safety of the humanitarian workers who are attempting to assist civilians in a conflict situation. The General Assembly has expressed a "deep concern at conditions in a number of countries and regions that seriously endanger the delivery of humanitarian assistance and the security of the staff of the High Commissioner and other relief workers" [A/Res/48/116].

It is these problems and limitations of delivering aid under crisis conditions, notes a senior DHA consultant, that have led the United Nations to seek durable solutions to humanitarian emergencies through "national prevention and preparedness policies, preventive diplomacy, conflict resolution, peace-keeping and human rights initiatives, use of military assets, dove-tailing relief and development funding, programmes for the rehabilitation of war- torn societies, national food security policies, and capacity building programmes" [report by Michael Priestley, senior DHA consultant to Peter Hansen, Under-Secretary-General, DHA, 9/21/94, p. ii]. These efforts link the U.N.'s response mechanisms to conflict resolution and socioeconomic rehabilitation.

Internally Displaced Persons

More and more attention is being focused on the issue of internally displaced persons (IDPs), not only because of sheer numbers (30 million at a conservative estimate) but also because of the magnitude of the humanitarian crises with which IDPs are associated. The United Nations and other organizations have struggled with defining an IDP for the purpose of research and study, with the aim of developing appropriate policy, and institutional and operational mechanisms, to respond coherently and effectively to their needs. According to a widely used definition of IDPs, these are "persons who have been forced to flee their homes suddenly or unexpectedly in large numbers, as a result of armed conflict, internal strife, systematic violations of human rights or natural or man-made disasters; and who are within the territory of their own country" [E/CN.4/ 1995/50, par. 116]. Still, debate over an appropriate definition goes on. The Brookings Institution and the Refugee Policy Group, both based in Washington, D.C., are engaged in a collaborative effort to examine the global phenomenon of internal displacement and develop a global strategy for responding to the protection and assistance needs of IDPs. One aspect of this project was a study prepared under the joint auspices of the American Society of International Law and the International Human Rights Law Group that examined international legal standards applicable and most relevant to IDPs. The study concluded that "while existing law covers many aspects of particular relevance to the displaced, there remain areas in which the law fails to provide sufficient protection for internally displaced persons," identifying these areas as personal safety, personal liberty, subsistence needs, movement-related needs, need for personal identification, documentation and registration, property-related needs, need to maintain community and cultural values, need to build self-reliance, and need for international provision of protection and assistance. It also notes that existing law fails to cover the needs of the relief workers and organizations who aid the IDPs [*Internally Displaced Persons and International Law, A Legal Analysis Based on the Needs of Internally Displaced Persons*, 10/95, pp. 182, 183–95].

The circumstances that create IDPs are often the same circumstances that create refugees: persecution, armed conflict, civil war. The main point of difference between them is the fact that, for one reason or another, the IDP did not cross an international border.

Current U.N. policy aims to assist the displaced within their countries before they cross an international border. This approach was intended to lessen the impact of mass influxes on neighboring countries and may also make resettlement, reintegration, and rehabilitation easier when conditions improve, but UNHCR encounters a number of problems when the displaced persons it is attempting to protect are the country's own nationals. Since no international law obliges a government to give an international agency access to nationals of the country for the purpose of protecting them, governments can effectively deny U.N. agencies access to some or all displaced and vulnerable populations in need of assistance. Sri Lanka's government, for example, began in late 1995 to restrict access to certain areas where the displaced are located. In point of fact, IDPs may be fleeing actions of the very government that is responsible for protecting them—and may even be prevented from seeking refuge in places where the government cannot exercise authority over them. The Bosnian,

Afghan, and Sri Lankan cases illustrate how very difficult it is to protect IDPs within conflict zones.

With no organization dedicated to the internally displaced, there has been no one to articulate their needs, raise awareness of potential crisis situations, mobilize and coordinate a prompt humanitarian response in such situations, and negotiate access with governments.

The creation by the Secretary-General of a **Special Representative on Internally Displaced Persons** in 1992 was a considerable step in this direction. Named to the post was Dr. Francis Deng, whose visits to countries with significant IDP populations, such as Rwanda, Burundi, Sri Lanka, Peru, and Colombia, have raised the awareness level of the international community to the complexities of the situation of IDPs. Restricting his ability to do more is a lack of funding for follow-up visits and a mandate limited to reporting his findings. With the alarming increase in IDPs, the Inter-Agency Standing Committee has created an Inter-Agency Task Force on Internally Displaced Persons to develop a more effective response to the needs of the internally displaced for aid and protection. In December 1994 the Standing Committee approved the Task Force's recommendation that the Emergency Relief Coordinator/Under-Secretary-General for Humanitarian Affairs serve as the reference point to receive requests for assistance and protection in actual or developing situations of internal displacement [E/CN.4/1995/50, par. 176]. Additional suggestions for administrative mechanisms to assist the displaced include creating an institution similar to UNHCR, enlarging UNHCR's mandate to respond to the displaced, and consolidating the emergency functions of UNHCR, WFP, UNICEF, and DHA.

3. The Status of Women
By Shareen Hertel

The themes of gender equality and recognition of women's multiple roles in the integration of women into social and economic life ran through discussions on a variety of issues during the historic 50th Session of the U.N. General Assembly. The main point of reference was frequently the **Fourth World Conference on Women,** held in Beijing, September 4–15, 1995.

The Beijing Conference was the capstone of a two-decade-long process that began in 1975 with the World Conference of the U.N. International Women's Year and continued through the U.N. Decade for Women (1975–85) and the World Conference to Review and Appraise the Achievements of the U.N. Decade—the now-famous **Nairobi Conference of 1985** that adopted the **"Forward-Looking Strategies for the Ad-**

vancement of Women" to guide national and international efforts to the year 2000.

The **U.N. Commission on the Status of Women (CSW,** the body created under the U.N. Charter to oversee the preparation of studies, reports, and recommendations on issues affecting the world's women) was asked to serve as the Beijing Conference's preparatory committee, and in this role requested the U.N. Secretary-General to take the first stab at drafting a "Platform for Action" to be refined during successive preparatory committee meetings and finally endorsed by the governmental delegates at the Conference [res. 37/7]. During its next two sessions the CSW steered the member states' (often-contentious) negotiations over the evolving draft. (Once the delegates left China for home, the CSW took on new responsibilities as the lead agency in monitoring the implementation of the Beijing Conference's Platform for Action.)

The delegates and nongovernmental organizations assembled at Beijing received the Draft Platform of Action with its bracketed words and passages, signaling disagreement and indicating the work yet to be done; the Report of the Informal Consultations [A/Conf.177/L.3]; the Report of the Informal Contact Group on Gender [A/Conf.177/L.2]; and reports produced in connection with the regional preparatory process. In the delegates' packets too were the Report of the Secretary-General on the Second Review and Appraisal of the Nairobi Strategies [E/CN.6/1995/3 and Add.1-10], an update of *The World's Women: Trends and Statistics* [ST/ESA/STAT/Ser.K/12], and the *1994 World Survey on the Role of Women in Development* [ST/ESA/241]. The Commission on Human Rights and its Sub-Commission on Prevention of Discrimination and Protection of Minorities supplied a report by the Special Rapporteur on violence against women [E/CN.4/1995/42] and a Plan of Action for the Elimination of Harmful Traditional Practices affecting the Health of Women and Children [E/CN.4/Sub.2/1994/10/Add.1 and Corr. 1]. Country delegations, and still other U.N. agencies and programs, had reports to offer too.

Despite heated debates in preparatory forums and China's 11th hour attempt to isolate the NGO forum that would parallel the main event, the Beijing Conference was one of the largest gatherings of governmental and nongovernmental representatives in U.N. history: More than 30,000 women attended the NGO forum and some 17,000 representatives of government, the media, and NGOs were accredited to the official Conference. The **Provisional Agenda** [A/Conf.177.1] and **Organization of Work** [A/Conf.177.3] were adopted in relatively short order in two days of pre-Conference consultations. Negotiation of the principal policy documents—the Beijing Declaration and Platform for Action—continued almost around the clock for two weeks.

When government delegates arrived at Beijing, the **Platform for Action** still had brackets around a considerable number of words and phrases, fully two-thirds of these stemming from differing interpretations of basic human rights [for background see *A Global Agenda: Issues/50*]. There were brackets too around language accepted at previous conferences (i.e., on women's reproductive health and rights as enshrined in the Declaration and Programme of Action approved at the Cairo Conference on Population and Development), and brackets even around the term "gender" (already a staple of U.N. documents but now inciting fears among some member states that this word—the term "sex" was preferred—would accommodate the perspectives of communities other than the heterosexual).

What was significant about the Beijing document was the acceptance and affirmation of women's "empowerment and their full participation on the basis of equality in all spheres of society." In the end, policy gains from the Cairo Conference were safeguarded too, although some 30 governments entered reservations on key paragraphs concerning reproductive health and rights. And even references to "gender" shed their brackets at the last minute—this owing to the negotiation of a footnote that recognizes a role for religious and cultural values when it comes to implementing the Beijing Declaration and Platform for Action [for an analysis of conference negotiations see International Institute for Sustainable Development (Winnipeg, Canada), *Earth Negotiations Bulletin,* Vol. 14, No. 22; and Women's Environment and Development Organization (New York), *A Brief Analysis of the UN Fourth World Conference on Women,* 1995].

Ultimately, these two documents received the official endorsement of 189 countries and territories (the Platform for Action is annexed to the Report of the Conference [A/Conf.177/20]). Following an Australian-led initiative, some 90 governments committed themselves on the spot to taking specific actions, ranging from a commitment by Austria to grant asylum to women victims of sexual violence, to a pledge by Lebanon to increase the representation of women in decision-making positions (to a minimum of 30 percent by the year 2000), to the announcement by the United States of a $1.6 billion initiative to end domestic violence [for an assessment of the progress in implementing these and other Platform for Action-related commitments, country-by-country, see Women's Environment and Development Organization, New York, *First Steps: What Has Happened Since Beijing?,* a monograph released 3/8/96].

Among the earliest **official analyses of the Beijing process** was the Secretary-General's "Implementation of the Outcome of the Fourth World Conference on Women" [A/50/744], in which he described his plans for institutional reform—notably his decision to "integrate the functions [of an **advisor on gender issues,** called for in the Platform for Action] into the portfolio of" a senior advisor in the Executive Office of the Secretary-General. The Secretary-General ultimately named **Rosario Green** of Mexico. She was expected not only to assist the Executive Office "in facilitating coordination to ensure that a gender perspective is integrated into overall policy-making and programming" but also to chair a proposed "goal-oriented inter-agency task force on the empowerment and advancement of women"—falling under the Administrative Committee on Coordination (ACC)—"to promote sustained and coordinated follow-up to the Platform of Action" [p. 22].

This task force is to function, in turn, in cooperation with three existing high-level task forces under the ACC. Together, the four are charged with coordinating the monitoring and follow-up to the International Conference on Population and Development, the World Summit for Social Development, and now the Beijing Conference. Representatives of the Bretton Woods institutions and the World Trade Organization, already active on the other task forces, have been invited to participate in the newest one.

The Secretary-General's report on implementation also calls attention to his creation of a **high-level board on the advancement of women** to advise him on the follow-up to the conference"—15 to 20 "eminent persons" who will work closely with the Secretary-General and his senior advisor, and with key institutions involved in the implementation process. For expertise and assistance in carrying out this work, the Secretary-General noted in his subsequent **"Follow-up to the Fourth World Conference on Women"** [E/CN.6/1996/3, 3/8/96], the advisor can draw upon the Secretariat's **Division for the Advancement of Women (DAW)** in the Department for Policy Coordination and Sustainable Development, the U.N. Development Fund for Women (UNIFEM), the International Training and Research Institute for the Advancement of Women (INSTRAW), and the new **Focal Point on Women in the Department of Administration and Management (DAM).** This Focal Point—the first appointee is Zuzu Tabatabai—chairs the working group on the status of women in the United Nations, one of three new interagency working groups. The other two working groups focus on policy and research (convened by DAW, assisted by INSTRAW) and operational activities (convened by UNIFEM), respectively.

The future of **UNIFEM** and **INSTRAW** had been debated throughout the Beijing preparatory process, at the Conference itself, and in the General Assembly. A number of industrial countries advocated a merger of the two, under the umbrella of UNIFEM [see *A Global Agenda,* Issues/49, pp. 239–42], while developing countries generally resisted such a move [see the resolutions submitted to the Third Committee on behalf of the Group of 77 by the Philippines, A/C.3/50/L.21 and Rev.1]. The 50th General Assembly, putting an end to the debate for the moment at least, "reaffirm[ed] the original mandate and distinct capacity of [INSTRAW] to carry out research and training for the advancement of women" [A/Res/50/163]. The Secretary-General was requested to report to the 52nd Session on INSTRAW's follow-up to all recent U.N. conferences.

UNIFEM, for its part, will continue "to support innovative activities that directly benefit and empower women" and help to increase "opportunities and options for women in developing countries to participate more effectively in the development of their countries" [A/Res/50/166]. With the help of the U.N. Development Programme (UNDP), UNIFEM is also taking steps to establish a **trust fund to encourage initiatives aimed at the elimination of violence against women.** The General Assembly requested UNIFEM to report on its activities in this field to the Commission on the Status of Women and the Commission on Human Rights [ibid.] and to coordinate efforts with "competent United Nations organs and bodies, in particular the Division for the Advancement of Women, the Special Rapporteur of the Commission on Human Rights on violence against women, the Centre for Human Rights, the Crime Prevention and Criminal Justice Branch, and the United Nations Children's Fund" [ibid.]. UNIFEM has prepared the requested report [E/CN.6/1996/11], and the Administrator of UNDP is holding consultations about the creation of a trust fund.

Asserting its central role in follow-up efforts, the General Assembly decided that an **intergovernmental mechanism made up of the Assembly, the Economic and Social Council, and the Commission on the Status of Women** "should play the primary role in the overall policy-making and follow-up of the [Beijing] Platform for Action" [A/Res/50/203]. Echoing the Platform for Action, members of the Assembly requested ECOSOC to "consider dedicating at least one high-level segment before the year 2000 to the advancement of women, with active participation of the specialized agencies, including the World Bank and the International Monetary Fund." The same resolution invites the World Trade Organization to consider how it might contribute to implementing the Platform for Action.

Within weeks of the Assembly's resolution, the CSW met to refine its role as part of the three-tiered mechanism for Beijing follow-up. High on the agenda of its 40th session, March 11–22, 1996, was a discussion of how the CSW could continue giving proper attention to its standing mandate (activities related to the protection and promotion of women's rights) while following up on Beijing by bringing trends, emerging issues, and new approaches to the attention of ECOSOC and the General Assembly. The Secretary-General suggested a possible multiyear work plan and procedures for relaying information between the Commission and the Council and Assembly [E/CN.6/1996/2]. The CSW also convened three expert panels to consider other reports prepared for it by the Secretary-General that build on the recommendations for action at Beijing—on elimination of stereotyping of women in the mass media [E/CN.6/1996/4], on child and dependent care [E/CN.6/1996/5], and on poverty [E/CN.6/1996/CRP.3]. Corresponding draft resolutions were passed by the Commission [E/CN.6/1996/L.16, L.17, and L.14]. The last two of these explicitly recommended that ECOSOC take into account a gender perspective on child care and on poverty (poverty is the theme of ECOSOC's 1996 substantive "coordinating session").

Reflecting the trend toward wider **involvement of NGOs** in the U.N. process, the Commission had accredited for participation in its 40th session all nongovernmental organizations that received credentials for the Fourth World Conference. Though many NGOs encouraged the Commission to recommend that groups accredited to the Beijing Conference be permitted to apply for consultative status with ECOSOC (and thus be eligible to attend future CSW sessions), the suggestion remained bracketed in the draft resolution the Commission submitted to ECOSOC concerning follow-up to the Conference [E/CN.6/1996/L.13].

The Secretary-General's follow-up [E/CN.6/1996/3] to his report on the implementation of the Beijing Platform was equally noncommittal on NGO access, noting simply that the "future relationship of these NGOs and those accredited to the World Summit for Social Development . . . will be further discussed by the Committee on Non-Governmental Organizations when it meets in 1996" [for discussion of NGO-access issues, see American Council for Voluntary International Action (Washington, D.C.), *Monday Developments*, 4/8/96].

Brackets within the Commission's own final decision concerning "methods of work for dealing with the implementation of the Platform for Action" [E/CN.6/1996/L.12] reflect the challenge of carrying out the work of follow-up without infringing on the mandates of other parts of the system or the independence of member states. The CSW notes that panels of experts should be integral to future sessions of the CSW, but there is no such incisiveness about integrating NGOs into the work of the CSW.

References to the Commission's role in monitoring the systemwide medium-term plan for the advancement of women are bracketed too, and ditto any reference to the Commission's possible use of reports that states parties to the Convention on the Elimination of All Forms of Discrimination against Women have prepared for the Committee that monitors their compliance with the Convention. These reports, some member states argued, could be "of direct relevance to the Commission's task of reviewing and appraising the implementation of the Platform for Action and its task of identifying emerging trends and approaches" [ibid.]. Not a few member governments, however, wished to keep their progress on implementing the promises of Beijing separate from explicit assessments of their progress to sign, ratify, and/or uphold the Convention.

In its draft resolution to ECOSOC, the Commission established the thematic divisions for its multiyear work program (1997–2000). These correspond to the "critical areas of concern" outlined in the Platform for Action itself [see A/Conf.177/20, chap. III, par. 44]. In 1997 the Commission will focus on education and training of women, women and the economy, women in power and decision-making, and women and the environment. Both the Secretary-General's report on the mandate of the CSW and the

Commission's own draft resolution to ECOSOC on follow-up to Beijing recommend that a report on global implementation of the Platform for Action cap the multiyear thematic review scheduled for the year 2000.

Donning its more traditional **human rights** hat, the Commission passed draft resolutions on the release of women and children taken hostage in armed conflicts and imprisoned [E/CN.6/1996/L.1] and on traffic in women and girls [E/CN.6/1996/L.5]. The latter "encourages the Special Rapporteur of the Commission on Human Rights on violence against women and the Special Rapporteur of the Commission on Human Rights on the sale of children, child prostitution and child pornography, as well as the Working Group on Contemporary Forms of Slavery of the Sub-Commission on Prevention of Discrimination and Protection of Minorities, to continue to pay special attention to the problem" and report back to the 51st General Assembly.

The "trafficking" resolution also "encourages the holding of an international conference" on the subject, and notes the decision of the CSW to "remain seized of this matter," to examine the above reports at the CSW's 41st session, and to make "appropriate recommendations to the General Assembly 51st Session."

The CSW also considered a Report of the Secretary-General on **the question of elaborating an optional protocol to the Convention on the Elimination of Discrimination against Women (CEDAW)** [E/CN.6/1996/10 and Add.2], prepared in response to a request by ECOSOC [res. 1995/29]. Under discussion since 1991, the proposed measure aims to strengthen the Convention by introducing the right of petition (a complaints procedure similar to those available under the Covenant on Civil and Political Rights, the Convention on the Elimination of All Forms of Racial Discrimination, and the Convention against Torture). The Secretary-General's report incorporated the views of 15 governments and 19 NGOs, indicating an "overwhelming majority of . . . support for the process" initiated by the Commission and ECOSOC to explore the desirability of adopting such a protocol. The report also referenced the Beijing Platform's support for such "a draft optional protocol . . . that could enter into force as soon as possible" [see A/Conf.177/20, chap. I, Annex II, par. 230, k].

Ultimately, the CSW determined not to endorse the drafting of a protocol on the right of petition, owing to lack of consensus about such matters as confidentiality of complainants and reports, timing and scope of investigations and reports, possible overlap with existing human rights mechanisms, costs of implementation, justiciability of the rights included in the Convention itself, and related issues of remedy and compensation [see the draft report of the Open-ended Working Group created on the subject for the 40th session of the CSW, part II, E/CN.6/1996/WG/L.1/Add.1]. The Commission did, however, request the Secretary-General to prepare a report for its 41st session summarizing "additional views" of governments, along with a "comparative summary of existing communications and inquiry procedures and practices under international human rights instruments and under the Charter of the United Nations" [E/CN.6/1996/L.11].

The 23-member **Committee on the Elimination of Discrimination against Women,** the expert body that monitors the 1979 Convention on the Elimination of All Forms of Discrimination against Women (CEDAW), met for its 15th session January 15–February 2, 1996. Each of the countries that has ratified, or acceded to, the Convention—151 had done so by the time of the 1996 meeting—is required to submit a report within one year of accession and periodic reports at least every four years thereafter.

The Committee considered the reports of eight states parties under its regular procedures (Belgium, Cuba, Cyprus, Ethiopia, Hungary, Iceland, Paraguay, and Ukraine), and (on an exceptional basis) heard an oral presentation on the human rights situation of women in Rwanda by a representative of that government. In response, members of the Committee suggested policy reforms to be undertaken by states parties. One suggestion had to do with creating a witness protection unit within the war crimes prosecutor's office of the International Criminal Tribunal for Rwanda, to protect those who testify about rape and other crimes. Other suggestions encouraged Paraguay to revise its penal code with regard to violence against women, Cyprus to enact special legislation on sexual harassment in the workplace, Ukraine to increase access to family planning services and affordable contraception (and curtail the number of abortions used as a means of birth control in that country), and Ethiopia to address the prevalence of female genital mutilation.

Meeting for just two weeks per year, the Committee's session is the shortest of all the human rights treaty bodies—and far too short to allow it to consider at any single session all the reports it receives from states parties in that year. The 50th General Assembly urged states parties to amend CEDAW's Article 20 so as **to allow for two sessions per year,** each of three weeks' duration and preceded by a one-week working group [A/Res/50/202].

The Committee endorsed the proposed schedule change [CEDAW/SP/1996/4] and recommended to the 51st General Assembly that member states indicate their support for an interim measure allowing the revised schedule to become effective in 1997, pending ratification of such an amendment to the Convention itself by all states parties. The hitch is funding: In a proposed draft amendment to Article 20, states parties to the Convention request that the interim measure be executed "within the overall existing budget framework" [CEDAW/SP/1996/L.1]. It is unlikely that additional funds will be available to make an extra meeting of the Committee possible in 1997 [for detail, see International Women's Rights Action Watch (Minneapolis), *The Women's Watch,* 4/96].

The **U.N. Division for the Advancement of Women (DAW)** is the secretariat for the Committee on the Elimination of Discrimination against Women. It is also the body that the Beijing Platform for Action assigns a "coordinating role in preparing the revision of the system-wide medium-term plan for inter-agency coordination for the advancement of women" for the period 1996–2001. In an attempt to streamline and coordinate the activities of UNIFEM and INSTRAW with those of the Division, all three bodies will "exchange their proposed programs of work for comments before submitting them to their respective governing bodies for approval" [E/CN.6/1996/3].

The Division is likewise asked to "provide enhanced support to the **Special Rapporteur on violence against women** and to assist in monitoring the implementation of the **Declaration on the Elimination of Violence against Women**"—this in light of the Beijing Platform's stress on action to eliminate such violence [A/Res/48/104, as referenced in A/50/744—the Secretary-General's report on implementation of the Fourth World Conference on Women]. To this end, DAW is to develop a database on the subject of violence against women. A joint work plan for DAW and the **Centre for Human Rights** [E/CN.6/1996/13], presented by the Secretary-General for consideration at the 40th session of the CSW, outlines a number of other human rights-related functions of the Division, among them: briefing the High Commissioner for Human Rights in advance of his visits to individual countries; providing a gender analysis of the reports submitted by states parties to the Human Rights Committee, the Committee on Economic, Social and Cultural Rights, and the Committee on the Rights of the Child; providing statistics and related information drawn from reports of states parties to CEDAW as well as from national reports prepared for the Beijing Conference; and briefing the Committee on Economic, Social and Cultural Rights (at its May 1996 session) on the CSW's findings about the elaboration of an optional protocol under CEDAW.

The 50th **General Assembly** itself explored the subject of violence against women in a variety of contexts. One resolution—on violence against women migrant workers [A/Res/50/168]—affirms related commitments that member states already made in the declarations and action programs of the global conferences held at Vienna, Cairo, Copenhagen, and Beijing; and it calls on states to sign and ratify such relevant treaties as the **International Convention on the Protection of the Rights of All Migrant Workers and Their Families.** The same resolution also requests the Secretary-General to convene a meeting of an "expert group" on the subject, with the participation of the Human Rights Commission's Special Rapporteur on violence against women, to "submit recommendations . . . for improving coordination [systemwide] on . . . violence against women migrant workers," and to "develop concrete indicators" on this phenomenon, reporting on his progress to the 51st General Assembly.

In a note to the Commission on the Status of Women [E/CN.6/1996/12], the Secretary-General announced his intention to convene such an expert meeting in the Philippines in late May 1996.

Another Assembly resolution—on **the girl child** [A/Res/50/154]—urges member states to "eliminate all forms of violence against children, in particular the girl child"; and all bodies of the U.N. system are urged to "make commitments to goals and actions relating to the girl child in the revision and implementation of the system-wide medium-term plan for the advancement of women for the period 1996–2001 [E/1993/43] as well as the medium-term plan for the period 1998–2002."

U.N. Personnel Issues

The **status of women employed by the U.N. system** itself—from their disproportionately low numbers in the upper ranks of management (not to mention the ranks of U.N. ambassadors) to the incidence of sexual harassment—has also been the subject of discussion at the General Assembly [A/Res/50/164]. Mainstreaming gender in all discussions of equality, development, and peace was the very purpose of the Fourth World Conference on Women. Mainstreaming gender in the U.N. system's own plans for reform and restructuring has proven an elusive goal, and gender equity a daunting task: Women hold a mere 34.6 percent of all posts subject to geographical distribution systemwide and a small percentage of Director-level posts and above. Women's representation at the Under-Secretary-General and Assistant Secretary-General levels fell from two each in 1995 to one each in 1996. By the same token, there are only seven women among the 187 permanent representatives to the United Nations (185 member states and two permanent observer missions).

To fill the various goals set by the General Assembly on gender parity [A/Res/45/125; A/Res/45/239C; A/Res/46/100; and A/Res/47/93]—notably, 25 percent women in posts at the Director level and above by 1995 and 50 percent women systemwide by the year 2000—two of every three vacancies over the next four years will have to be filled by women [see "Women in the United Nations: Approaching a Critical Mass," DPI 1785, 3/96; see also, *Women and the United Nations,* a monograph by the Franklin and Eleanor Roosevelt Institute, New York, 1995].

A **"Strategic Plan of Action for the Improvement of the Status of Women in the Secretariat (1995–2000)"** [A/49/587 and Corr.1], prepared by the Secretary-General and endorsed by the 49th General Assembly [A/Res/49/167], is being integrated within the overall human resources strategy of the Organization. The 50th General Assembly requested [A/Res/50/164] a status report on women in the Secretariat, and the Secretary-General duly produced one [A/50/691] in which he restated his intention to reach the 45th General Assembly's target of 50 percent women by the year 2000. This report was reissued for the member states participating in the 40th session of the Commission on the Status of Women [as E/CN.6/1996/7] and was accompanied by a revised systemwide medium-term plan for the advancement of women for the period 1996–2001 [E/CN.6/1996/CRP.2].

Although there has been a small increase in the number of women appointed to lower and middle professional-level posts, the number of **women in higher-level posts** has declined markedly (i.e., from 42.9 percent to 30.7 percent at the highest professional level beneath Director, and from 40 percent to 22.2 percent at Director level and above). Even the small increases at the lower and mid-professional level are candidates for extinction, noted the Secretary-General in his report to the CSW, citing the "increase in vacancy rates and cost reductions mandated by the General Assembly" [A/Res/50/215].

Setting an example for others are the seven major development agencies now headed by women—UNICEF, WFP, UNEP, INSTRAW, UNIFEM, UNHCR, UNFPA—with combined budgets in excess of $7.8 billion (nearly a third the size of the U.N.'s entire regular budget for the 1994–95 biennium). A woman was appointed Chief Prosecutor of the International War Crimes Tribunals for Yugoslavia and Rwanda too, replacing Judge Richard J. Goldstone [DPI handout for International Women's Day, 3/8/96]. And in early 1996 the Secretariat received a $30,000 grant from The Ford Foundation to finance **the development of a questionnaire for use in assessing the prevalence of sexual harassment throughout the U.N. system**—and for strengthening policies and procedures to deal with such harassment. Preparation of the survey is estimated to take up to a year (through early 1997) [E/CN.6/1996/7].

The Beijing Platform for Action calls upon all agencies and programs of the U.N. system to appoint a focal point on gender to redress the gender gap in-house. And it calls upon governments to reinforce this effort not only at home but at the United Nations by "tak[ing] action to promote equal participation of women and equal opportunities for women to participate in all forums . . . particularly at the decision-making level, including in the U.N. Secretariat . . ." [Platform for Action, par. 142 (a), A/Conf.177/20]. Improving gender balance is quite literally the challenge of this century if targets are to be met on schedule at a time of fiscal austerity.

4. Drug Abuse, Production, and Trafficking
By Elizabeth K. Madigan

Midway through the **Decade against Drug Abuse (1991–2000)**, the U.N.'s three-front **Global Programme of Action**—international, regional, and national [S-17/2, Annex]—continues to fight an uphill battle against an elusive opponent. The "enemy," in fact, has demonstrated a unique capacity to exploit new technologies, diversify its methods and channels, and take advantage of weaknesses created by changing economic and political circumstances. Today, for example, the old "nature"-based substances like cocaine are facing stiff competition from some ever-more-potent and ever-more-available psychotropic substances, such as the methamphetamines whose manufacture often involves licit precursor chemicals. At the same time, strong anti-money-laundering and confiscation laws offer an effective means of identifying drug traffickers, but efforts to remove the profit motive will be at their most effective only after all states have taken anti-laundering measures, in compliance with the 1988 U.N. Convention against Illicit Traffic in Narcotic Drugs and Psychotropic Substances. Facing an increasing gap between its mandates in the drug-control area and the resources available for implementing them, the U.N. Drug Control Programme is hoping that member states can agree on new funding strategies.

The Global Programme of Action calls on the U.N. Secretary-General to prepare an annual **"International Drug Control Report"** charting the progress of efforts on all three fronts—drug production, trafficking, and demand. In the report prepared for the 50th Session of the General Assembly, he marshaled evidence to support the conclusion that "efforts to reduce demand, to monitor precursors, and to prevent money laundering [are] in need of improvement" [A/50/460]. He reiterated the Economic and Social Council's call for "a global strategy for demand reduction and a draft declaration on the guiding principles of demand reduction." And, addressing the bottom line, the Secretary-General urged member states not only to confiscate the proceeds of illicit trafficking, as called for by the 1988 Convention (Articles 3 and 5), but also to consider using forfeited money for U.N. drug-related projects.

The 50th **General Assembly**'s resolution on "International action to combat drug abuse and illicit trafficking" cites international cooperation as the backbone of anti-drug policy without picking up on the Secretary-General's call for forfeited funds [A/Res/50/148]. The resolution "reaffirms that the fight against drug abuse and illicit trafficking should not" compromise such principles as "respect for sovereignty" and "non-use of force in international affairs"; "reaffirms the importance" of the global action program as "a comprehensive framework" for combating drug production, demand, and trafficking; "reaffirms the role of the Executive Director of the U.N. International Drug Control Programme (UNDCP) in coordinating and providing effective leadership for all U.N. drug-control activities" and gives its support to the **U.N. System-wide Action Plan on Drug Abuse Control** (with a request that SWAP be updated and reviewed on a biennial basis); and "notes with concern the decline of available resources for the [voluntary] Fund of the United Nations International Drug Control Programme." Renewing the Assembly's commitment to combating the drug problem, the resolution goes on to urge all states to ratify and adhere to the several drug treaties: the **1961 Single Convention on Narcotic Drugs,** as amended by the **1972 Protocol;** the **1971 Convention on Psychotropic Substances;** and the **1988 U.N. Convention against Illicit Traffic in Narcotic Drugs and Psychotropic Substances.** And, turning to recent ECOSOC resolutions calling for a second international conference on illicit drugs (the first, in 1988, gave birth to the last-named Convention), it called attention to "the financial and other implications of holding such a conference," without voting yea or nay. It suggested the matter be taken up at the 1996 session of the Commission on Narcotic Drugs (see below).

At the semiannual session of the **International Narcotics Control Board (INCB)** in late fall of 1995—this is the body of experts that monitors legal drug production to trace illegal diversions and monitors states' compliance with drug control treaties—came the announcement of an unusual increase in the medical consumption of **ritalin.** This amphetamine-type stimulant, which is controlled under the 1971 Convention, is judged to be overprescribed by doctors (for attention-deficit disorders)—and able to slip easily between the licit and illicit markets. (UNDCP consulted the INCB in the course of preparing "Amphetamine-Type Stimulants: A Global Review" for the 39th Commission on Narcotic Drugs.)

The INCB annual report for 1995 pointed out two major trends, noted INCB President Oskar Schroeder: Traffickers have targeted new countries and established new routes to obtain or ship precursors, and these people are quick to exploit any vulnerable point in the international control system [press release SOC/NAR/731, 4/22/96].

The **Commission on Narcotic Drugs (CND),** the U.N. system's central policy-making body on drug-related issues, met in Vienna for its 39th annual session, April 16–25, 1996. It was to be a particularly important session, noted UNDCP Executive Director Giorgio Giacomelli at the time, since the subject of drugs had been chosen for the **high-level segment of ECOSOC's annual meeting,** in June 1996, and the member states would be looking to CND recommendations for guidance. What must be conveyed to the U.N. system, Giacomelli added, is that "drug control is a fundamental component of sustainable human development, necessitating a concerted and coordinated approach" [press release SOC/NAR/729, 4/19/96].

Among the key items on the CND spring agenda were the spread of amphetamine-type stimulants, money-laundering regulation, the control of precursors, budgetary concerns, and the prospects of a second international conference [press release SOC/NAR/722, 4/16/96]. At ECOSOC's request and citing the intractability of the problem—the fact, for example, that there is no direct relation between the seizure rate and the amount of consumption—CND has considered demand reduction separately for two years now.

The Commission considered a score of **resolutions** and agreed on 17 to recommend to ECOSOC. One would encourage all member states to require banks and other institutions to establish customer-identification policies (Austria, for one, still permits anonymous bank accounts) and to broaden anti-money-laundering measures [E/CN.7/1996/L.7/Rev.3]. Still other drafts urge governments to take specific action to control precursors and penalize chemical suppliers who fail to cooperate with authorities [E/CN.7/1996/L.2/Rev.2]; urges closer monitoring of psychotropic substances in the licit market [E/CN.7/1996/L.13]; and requests the Executive Director of UNDCP "to develop standard protocols and methods for the profiling/signature of key narcotic drugs and psychotropic substances" [E/CN.7/1996/L.3/Rev.1, as summarized in press release SOC/NAR/737, 4/26/96].

Turning to demand reduction, the CND invited member states to draw up national plans on the subject and promote greater understanding of the consequences of drug abuse [E/CN.7/1996/L.5/Rev.2], requested the UNDCP to continue to render assistance in developing and carrying out those "master plans" [E/CN.7/1996/L.6/Rev.1], and asks the UNDCP Executive Director to continue developing **demand reduction "guiding principles,"** "with due regard for the linkages between demand and supply reduction activities" [E/CN.7/1996/L.14, as summarized in SOC/NAR/737, 4/26/96]. There was "consensus" at the CND that it was time for the United Nations to make a declaration on demand reduction and that a working group should be established to draft guiding principles (though to date no one has acted on the suggestion) [press release SOC/NAR/734, 4/23/96].

Turning to the issue of celebrating the tenth anniversary of the 1988 Convention by holding a **second U.N. conference on illicit drugs,** CND recommended holding a special three-day session of the General Assembly in 1998 to generate new strategies, methods, practical activities, and specific measures to strengthen international cooperation in drug control [E/CN.7/1996/L.16/Rev.1, as summarized in SOC/NAR/737]. This scaled-back version of a drug-control conference reflects the opinion of many developed-country delegates that since money is so tight, it would be better to spend it on fighting drugs than on discussing them [SOC/NAR/727, 4/19/96].

In discussing the **budget for the UNDCP drug program,** Executive Director Giacomelli has pointed out that there can be no sense of "ownership" of the program so long as most states position themselves as *recipients* of UNDCP services. (Ten percent of the UNDCP's budget is supplied by the United Nations, the remainder from voluntary contributions, many of which are earmarked for specific projects and relatively few for the "general purpose fund"—a situation that keeps the UNDCP squeezed for the sort of funds that simply keep the lights on.) Seven countries and the European Union are the main contributors to the UNDCP Fund; and Italy, the United States, and the United Kingdom contribute half of the general-purpose fund. Giacomelli's draft budget for the

1996–97 biennium allots $152.4 million to the general-purpose fund—a "real term decrease" of 25.8 percent since the last biennium [E/CN.7/1995/ 21].

At the December 1995 CND meeting, newly elected CND Chairman Helmut Burke introduced a resolution on a **new system of financing** the program activities proposed by Giacomelli. This system was based on contributions from at least 50 countries, each supplying approximately $300,000 in general-purpose funds each year. Members were also invited to consider contributing a portion of the value of confiscated proceeds to the UNDCP Fund. In its resolution on the subject at its April 1996 meeting, the Commission welcomed the initiative and left it at that [E/CN.7/1996/ L.10].

5. Health
By Carin Abrahamsohn

"Health for All by the Year 2000" continues to drive the work of the **World Health Organization (WHO),** the Specialized Agency that spearheads and coordinates international activities for global health. The World Health Report prepared for the 1995 **World Health Assembly**—WHO's policy-making body—called attention to **the agency's enduring priorities:** to "allocate resources" to "countries and population groups" where minimum levels of health care are not yet established; to enhance the health of the work force and women and children; to help establish basic health care systems and ensure equal access to them; and to strengthen national capabilities in disease surveillance and control. The report's subtitle, "Bridging the Gaps," also called attention to a new reality: The **growing inequity in health between rich and poor and a similarly growing inequity in access to health care.** Among the statistics cited: More than a fifth of the global population of 5.6 billion live in extreme poverty, and half of these people do not have access to essential drugs for treatment of common diseases. Over 12 million children under the age of five die every year in the developing world. In some developing nations, 32 percent of children die before the age of five; the figure is 0.6 percent in most developed countries. Exhorting the world community to greater efforts, the WHO report asserts that "expenditure on health is not a drain on national resources but a prerequisite for economic and social progress." In this work it is joined by the U.N. system's other humanitarian and development programs, departments, and funding sources, prominently the United Nations Development Fund for Women (UNIFEM), United Nations Children's Fund (UNICEF), United Nations Development Programme (UNDP), United Nations Population Fund (UNFPA), and the World Bank.

These joint efforts have borne fruit. **Infant mortality** dropped from 8.2 percent in 1980 to 6.2 percent in 1995, and the life expectancy of all these infants has increased as well [World Health Report 1995]. The percentage of children immunized against six child-killer diseases reached 80 percent in 1990—exactly on target, as set by WHO and UNICEF. WHO now expects to see the eradication of poliomyelitis and dracunculiasis, and the elimination of leprosy, neonatal tetanus, and measles, by the end of this century [*World Health*, 3–4/95, p. 4]. Smallpox was eradicated years ago; the last case was recorded in 1977 (but a decision has been made to put off the destruction of remaining stocks of the virus, stored at U.S. and Russian disease-control centers, until June 30, 1999 [press release WHO/5, 1/26/96].

AIDS

January 1, 1996 is the official birthdate of the **Joint U.N. Programme on AIDS (UNAIDS).** This is a "U.N. family-wide response to AIDS," coordinating the work of five bodies—UNICEF, UNDP, UNFPA, WHO, UNESCO—and the World Bank (a relative newcomer to public health planning but already the largest source of funding for AIDS prevention programs) [*U.N. Chronicle*, 6/94]. The anticipated effect is an integration of ideas and approaches to preventing the spread of AIDS, a reduction in overlap among the efforts of the U.N. family, and the promotion and coordination of fund-raising [*Global Child Health News & Review*, No. 1, 1995]. "Shared Rights, Shared Responsibilities," the slogan of World AIDS Day 1995 (the Day is observed annually on December 1), did double duty—as a herald of this cooperative venture and a way of recognizing the U.N. International Year for Tolerance. UNAIDS, which replaces WHO's Global Programme on AIDS established in 1987, is headed by Dr. Peter Piot, who was in charge of AIDS research at WHO. He reports to the Programme Coordinating Board (PCB) at WHO headquarters in Geneva.

The UNAIDS budget for the 1996–97 biennium is $120 million, consisting of the monies the five bodies have set aside for AIDS-related efforts in this period. At the country level, UNAIDS works to build up the national capability to respond to the epidemic. As a joint program, it will integrate the agencies' various ideas and approaches to preventing the spread of AIDS. At the global level the new program works to focus attention on AIDS and serves as a primary source of policy and technical and strategic guidance. (UNAIDS executive Piot notes that some governments continue to deny that their population is at threat from AIDS [Piot interview with "World Chronicle," 12/1/95]. China's Ministry of Public Health, for example, which reports 2,428 cases of HIV/AIDS but privately estimates 50 times that number, began routine screening of blood and educating against the disease only in October of 1995 [*New York Times*, 11/28/95].) In fact,

AIDS is growing fastest in **Asia:** 3.5 million local citizens are already infected with HIV, the virus that causes AIDS, and unless something is done to halt the spread of the disease, the total will have risen to 12 million by the year 2000 [ibid., 1/21/96]. India alone has 3 million HIV-infected people—more than any country in the world [ibid., 7/8/96]. The disease is also spreading significantly among **women** everywhere on the globe; in the United States it is the No. 3 killer among women 25 to 44, and the leading cause of death among **men** in the same age group [ibid., 2/16/96].

Piot calls attention to the fact that UNAIDS, unlike previous programs, is promoting the creation of support systems and **health care for people who already have the disease.** With such care, many afflicted individuals can live longer and productive lives. WHO efforts to improve health care over many years are helping to make this possible ["World Chronicle" interview, 12/1/95]. The cooperation of governments and nongovernmental organizations (NGOs) are important to the success of all such endeavors.

Education and public awareness campaigns have proven their ability to slow the spread of AIDS in such seriously affected areas as **Thailand** and **Uganda.** In Uganda over the past five years, the number of men 20 to 24 infected with HIV/AIDS fell 80 percent, women 62 percent. Still, the number of Ugandans who die from AIDS remains high: 150,000–200,000 per year [*New York Times*, 4/7/96]. In Thailand, where the government provides funding for explicit AIDS radio ads that are aired at least once an hour and the use of condoms in brothels and massage parlors is now written into law, condom use has doubled since 1990. In that year there were 215,000 cases of HIV/AIDS; the Thai government expects the number to drop to 90,000 by the century's end [ibid., 4/21/96].

Infectious Diseases

The prevalence of AIDS is partly to blame for the rise of yet another disease—**tuberculosis,** from which more people died in 1995 (3 million) than at the turn of the last century. HIV/AIDS patients are 30 times more likely to develop the disease than are people with healthy immune systems [*World Health*, 3–4/95, p. 22]. Multi-drug-resistant strands of the bacteria have been reported in New York City, London, Milan, Paris, Atlanta, Chicago, and hundreds of other cities, thanks to the speed and ease of international travel, and TB is now the leading infectious killer of youth and adults. These are among the findings of "Groups at Risk" [3/21/96], a WHO report issued in response to a situation officially labeled the "global TB emergency." In publications and through other channels WHO is advocating "directly observed treatment" of tuberculosis patients [*World Health*, 11–12/95, p. 30].

Part of the blame for the reemergence of TB and other infectious diseases, says the Director-General of WHO, Dr. Hiroshi Nakajima, is "a fatal complacency among the international community." The **reemerging diseases,** as well as some **30 emerging diseases** that are responsible for the death of 50,000 people a day, were the focus of the World Health Report prepared for the 1996 World Health Assembly.

One "young" disease posing increasing problems is **Ebola** hemorrhagic fever. Outbreaks in Zaire in 1995 (245 dead) and in a small village in Gabon in 1996 (20 infected, 13 dead) have scientific and medical communities struggling to understand it better. WHO sent an international team of researchers (from La Coopération Française, the Gabonese Ministry of Health, and the Pasteur Institute as well as from its own staff) to Gabon in February 1996 to investigate the outbreak and its victims. Ebola appears to be passed through direct contact with blood or bodily fluids of an infected person or animal, and there is as yet no specific vaccine to prevent it or treatment for it [U.N. press releases H/2899, 2/20/96, and H/2900, 2/26/96].

A much older battle, against **poliomyelitis**—an infectious viral disease that attacks the central nervous system, causing permanent paralysis and sometimes death—is being waged in 67 nations. Major outbreaks of the disease were reported in Zaire (400 cases in Mbuji-Mae) and in Russia (140 cases in Chechnya and Ingushetia) in 1995, largely blamed on disintegration of health facilities. During 1996, WHO plans to reach some 80 million children with the agency's **"Six Steps to a Polio-Free Africa"** program [ibid.] that takes advantage of an oral polio vaccine which is easily administered by non-medical personnel and is an especially easy "pill" to swallow [press release WHO/15, 2/21/96].

WHO has good reason to be optimistic about achieving its goal of a **polio-free world by the year 2000,** however, having undertaken on behalf of that goal the largest vaccination campaign since its successful campaign to conquer smallpox. The actual cost of success, WHO estimates, will be $500 million in government and other spending [U.N. press release H/2892, 1/9/96]. Cases of polio have declined 80 percent since 1988, and some 145 countries are already polio-free. The disease has been pronounced eradicated in the Americas, the last case recorded in Peru in 1991 (WHO declares the disease eradicated three years after the last reported case) [ibid.]. In 1995, through the concerted efforts of WHO, UNICEF, UNDP, Rotary International, and various national health agencies, among others, nearly 300 million children under five years of age in 51 countries were immunized against polio.

WHO has also been working steadily to eradicate infectious diseases spawned by the environment—**water-related diseases** in particular—that remain a serious health threat in the developing world. Two of the major scourges have been **African river blindness** (formally onchocerciasis) and **Guinea-worm disease.** A program to fight onchocerciasis was inaugurated in 1974 and has already been successful in 11 West African countries. An expanded, 12-year program reaches out to 16 more. Onchocerciasis is easily controlled by spraying for the flies that spread it and by administering an annual dose of ivermectin to affected populations (the manufacturer is providing the medication free of charge). Guinea-worm disease, spread through contaminated water, has been controlled on the Indian subcontinent and in much of Africa (Nigeria, Niger, and Sudan are major exceptions). WHO is distributing to problem areas the chemical that makes water potable [*New York Times*, 12/6/95].

Another successful campaign—the vaccination of a million people against **yellow fever,** a disease for which there is no specific antidote—involved close cooperation between WHO and the Ministry of Health of Liberia, a country in the throes of a violent civil war. The disease hit its peak in December 1995, when 356 cases were reported and nine deaths confirmed. In the following two months only 20 new cases and a single death were reported [press release WHO/9, 2/9/96].

In the case of malaria—a killer of 1.5 million to 2.7 million people annually [WHO Fact Sheet No. 94, 11/95]—WHO is pursuing a **"Global Malaria Control Strategy"** that includes testing of potential vaccines to prevent the disease. A **vaccine** (designated SPf66) developed and donated to WHO by Colombian researcher Dr. Manuel Patarroyo is not proving to be as effective as hoped—this after more than a year of testing. Although one study in Tanzania showed that SPf66 could reduce the risk of clinical malaria in children by one-third, another study, in Gambia, indicated that the drug did not reduce the number of clinical cases in the group tested [*New York Times*, 8/20/95].

The WHO program has a hand in the **spraying** of the still waters in which malarial mosquitoes breed, and in the development and field-testing of **antimalarial drugs** as well. Since the mosquito-transmitted parasites mutate quickly, becoming resistant to the standard drugs, the search for a cure is ongoing. The Centers for Disease Control in Atlanta, for example, are currently testing pyronaridine, a product of Chinese antimalarial research [ibid., 1/16/96], to unlock the secret of how it works and whether it may have toxic side effects.

The 50th General Assembly called on member states to support antimalarial research and the developing countries' efforts to prevent the disease [A/Res/50/128]. And it asked the Secretary-General to report to the 51st Session on the progress of WHO's Global Malaria Control Strategy.

6. Crime
By Cristian B. Winder

The U.N. holds a **Congress on the Prevention of Crime and the Treatment of Offenders** every five years—the most recent in Cairo in May 1995. The resolutions adopted by this Ninth Congress establish the "crime agenda" for subsequent sessions of the intergovernmental **Commission on Crime Prevention and Criminal Justice (the Crime Commission,** which holds an annual, spring meeting) and, in turn, for the U.N.'s Economic and Social Council and the General Assembly. Day-to-day work in this area has been the responsibility of the **Crime Prevention and Criminal Justice** Branch of the Secretariat, upgraded to a **Division** by the 50th General Assembly in late 1995 [A/Res/50/214].

The Congress's major concerns were "international cooperation and practical assistance for strengthening the rule of law"; "action against transnational and organized crime and the role of criminal law in the protection of the environment"; "management and improvement of police and other law-enforcement agencies"; and "strategies for preventing urban crime, violent criminality, and juvenile crime" [A/Conf.169/16]. Under these headings it considered such matters as drafting a convention against organized transnational crime; the links between terrorist crimes and transnational organized crime; implementation of standard minimum rules for the treatment of prisoners; criminal justice management with relation to accountability of public administration and sustainable development; children as victims—and perpetrators—of crime; eliminating violence against women; and regulating firearms. ECOSOC [E/1995/27] and the 50th General Assembly [A/Res/50/145] endorsed the Crime Commission's recommendations for implementing the resolutions and recommendations adopted in Cairo and asked the U.N. Secretary-General to monitor the nations' progress in translating these recommendations into legislation and policy directives. The Department for Development Support and Management Services of the Secretariat and the United Nations Development Programme (UNDP), the World Bank, and other funding agencies are urged to continue to provide financial support and assistance within the framework of their particular programs. The Assembly asked the Secretary-General to report to the 51st Assembly on the progress to date.

The Congress also provided the impetus for other, related agenda items at ECOSOC, whose 1995 substantive session came just two months after the close of the Cairo meeting, and at the 50th General Assembly, which opened in September 1995.

Working to improve the very foundations of criminal justice management, ECOSOC requested the U.N. Secretary-General to consider establishing (with extrabudgetary funds) a **regional database** in Europe offering governments and others information on international training and technical assistance projects in this area. The U.N.-affiliated European Institute for Crime Prevention and Control has offered to manage the database—a pilot project "aimed at demonstrating the utility" of such a regional database [E/1995/12]. It was during 1995 that the **U.N. Crime and Justice Information Network (UNCJIN)** was formally transferred to

U.N. hands (it had been managed by the School of Criminal Justice at the State University of New York at Albany) and now resides in the U.N. Crime Prevention and Criminal Justice Division in Vienna. UNCJIN, available on the Internet, offers (1) an "interactive electronic discussion list for exchanging information on curriculum development" (and for locating teaching and other opportunities for academics) in the criminal justice field; (2) "a massive data base" (listed on the UNCJIN Gopher) on crime trends, recent court decisions, and the like; and (3) gateways (via the UNCJIN World Wide Web) to related information from other U.N. bodies [*Trends*, No. 4, 1995]. The database is one example of the sort of multinational technical cooperation in the struggle against organized crime that was envisaged by the **Naples Political Declaration and Global Plan of Action** approved by the 49th General Assembly [A/Res/49/159].

At the Ninth Congress the United Nations gained a new and important partner in the work of improving its **technical services** in crime prevention and criminal justice matters. That new partner is the **National Institute of Justice (NIJ) of the United States,** whose Director formalized the arrangement by signing a **Memorandum of Understanding with the UNCPCJ Division**—the first partnership of this kind [*Trends*, No. 4, 1995]. The NIJ is offering to collaborate in seminars and training courses; collect, maintain, and share information; provide comments and advice on the preparation of substantive reports for the Crime Commission and for future U.N. crime congresses; and cooperate with the network of U.N.-affiliated regional institutes.

Cooperation alone will not sustain the UNCPCJ program, whose **administrative budget** for the 1996–97 biennium totals only $5 million, notes Eduardo Vetere, Chief of the CPCJ Division. Indeed, the 50th General Assembly's resolution on strengthening the program [A/Res/50/146] calls attention to "the continued increase in the workload of the Crime Prevention and Criminal Justice Branch of the Secretariat" and "the considerable obstacles to the full and effective implementation of its programme activities" resulting from the "lack of appropriate institutional capacity." It goes on to request the Secretary-General to provide the UNCPCJ program with "the resources necessary for the full implementation of its mandates"—including an increase in its share of the budget—and enlists "significant financial contributions" from member states and the international funding organizations. A report to the 51st Session is requested of the Secretary-General.

Indeed such financial contributions are even more needed today, when the UNCPCJ is asked to become more involved in **peacekeeping missions**—for example, by assisting in the reestablishment of justice systems, as it has already done in El Salvador, Cambodia, Somalia, the former Yugoslavia, Haiti, and Rwanda. The rebuilding of criminal justice systems in war-torn societies is explored in a recent Division study, "Crime Prevention and Criminal Justice Issues in Post-Conflict Reconstruction" (January 1996). It notes that "Almost always in post-conflict situations, success in building democratic institutions, but also in reviving a country's economy, depends largely on the existence of law and order," and it suggests a framework for action in post-conflict reconstruction. In-depth research into local conditions—and advisory services, training, and material assistance in the form of equipment and/or direct grants—are fundamentals.

Urban crime was another area singled out for attention by the Ninth Congress and the 1995 session of the Crime Commission, in anticipation of the United Nations Conference on Human Settlements (Habitat II, held in Istanbul, June 3–14, 1996). As the number of urban dwellers has increased—from 30 percent of the world's population in 1950 to 45 percent in 1995 [*United Nations Chronicle,* Spring 1996]—the services supplied by cities, not least the crime prevention and criminal justice systems, are being stretched as well, often beyond capacity. One result, observes CPCJ chief Vetere, is that "In industrialized and developing countries alike, cities have become breeding grounds for crime and insecurity" [*Trends,* No. 3, 1994/95]. In the United States alone, the costs of urban crime are estimated at $425 billion a year, or about $4,000 per household [UNDP, *Human Development Report 1994,* cited in ibid.].

ECOSOC adopted the recommended guidelines for cooperation and technical assistance in the field of urban crime prevention [E/1995/9] suggested by the Crime Commission, and requested the U.N. Secretary-General to transmit these guidelines to **Habitat II.** The guidelines include an action plan that would enlist a wide range of collaborators (including social workers, parents, the private sector, and the media) at various levels of crime prevention—namely, primary prevention, prevention of recidivism, post-sentence support, and protection of victims.

Cooperation—among states and among international bodies—is also a prominent ingredient of the General Assembly's prescription for combating **international terrorism,** and the 50th Session's "Measures to eliminate international terrorism" [A/Res/50/53] speaks of the need to reinforce that cooperation. The resolution also requests the Secretary-General "to follow up closely" the implementation of the Declaration on Measures to Eliminate International Terrorism of 1994 [A/49/60, Annex]. A similar item appears on the provisional agenda for the 51st Session.

A separate Assembly resolution expresses concern over "the growing **connection between the terrorist groups and other criminal organizations** engaged in illegal arms and drugs trafficking at the national and international levels, as well as the consequent commission of serious crimes such as murder, extortion, kidnapping, assault, taking of hostages and robbery" [A/Res/50/186]. Again, the prescription for confronting the phenomenon is concerted action.

Turning to a domestic brand of terrorism—that of **violence against women**—the 50th General Assembly "recalls" resolution 8 of the Crime Congress and requests the U.N. Development Fund for Women (UNIFEM) to include the Crime Prevention and Criminal Justice Division as a partner in its effort to eliminate such violence. The Assembly went on to ask the Administrator of the U.N. Development Programme to consult with the Secretary-General, the CPCJ, and the bodies traditionally concerned with the status of women on "the possibility of establishing a trust fund," administered by UNIFEM, to support efforts at eliminating violence against women [A/Res/50/166].

On a related topic, **"Traffic in women and girls"** [A/Res/50/167], the Assembly noted with concern "the increasing number of women and girl children [as well as young boys] from developing countries and from some countries with economies in transition who are being victimized by traffickers." The Ninth Crime Congress had "invited" the Crime Commission to "initiate the process of requesting states' views" regarding the value of elaborating a convention on "this form of transnational organized crime." The Assembly, in turn, "invited" the Crime Commission to "consider appropriate follow-up" at its spring 1996 session and report to the Secretary-General, who will inform the 51st General Assembly about developments in this area, under the item "Advancement of women" [ibid.].

The 51st General Assembly may also consider a **Draft International Code of Conduct for Public Office Holders** after a review by the Crime Commission at its spring 1996 session. The seven-part draft Code outlines some general principles before turning to such specifics as the disclosure of assets, the acceptance of gifts or favors, and disciplinary actions against offenders [ibid., Annex]. The Code recognizes the transnational dimensions and reach of corruption, and its potential for "endanger[ing] the stability and security of societies, undermin[ing] the values of democracy and morality and jeopardiz[ing] social, economic and political development" [E/1995/13].

A new and revised edition of *U.N. and Crime Prevention,* offering a history of international collaboration on crime prevention as well as details of current U.N. system crime prevention programs, was scheduled for release in June 1996 [DPI/1143/Rev.2].

7. Children and Youth
By Jenny M. Engström

In 1996 the **United Nations Children's Fund** celebrates its 50th anniversary. Founded in the aftermath of World War II, the then United Nations International Children's Emergency Fund (its acronym, UNICEF, is retained to this day) focused on the needs of children of war. Later years saw a shift in emphasis from providing emergency relief and assistance to promoting the long-term development of children through a wide variety of programs—in education, nutrition, and child and maternal health. These enlist the cooperation of national governments, and almost invariably the technical expertise and other resources of specialized U.N. agencies and nongovernmental organizations. With the proliferation of civil conflicts in the post-Cold War period, UNICEF is devoting many of its resources to emergencies once again. The hope, says **Carol Bellamy, Executive Director of UNICEF,** is to provide "some consistent normality for children so that development can continue even after the conflict goes away" [*World Chronicle*, 11/21/95].

At its January 1996 session, the UNICEF Executive Board adopted a **"Mission Statement"**—the first in the organization's history. Requested by the Board as part of the agency's management review and reform process, the statement declares that UNICEF "is guided by the Convention on the Rights of the Child and strives to establish children's rights as enduring ethical principles and international standards of behaviour towards children." The statement goes on to affirm UNICEF's commitment to ensuring "special protection for the most disadvantaged children—victims of war, disasters, extreme poverty, all forms of violence and exploitation and those with disabilities" [UNICEF, *First Call for Children*/1996/No. 1].

The administrative and program-support **budget** proposed for the 1996–97 biennium—$346 million—has the same bottom line as the last, but is UNICEF's first to integrate the budgets of headquarters and the regional offices [E/ICEF/1996/AB/L.5]. (Changes arising from the management review under way since 1995 could prompt additional revisions later in 1996.) UNICEF program costs bring the projected total budget to $2.07 billion.

As 1995 drew to a close, Executive Director Bellamy was able to boast that the **Convention on the Rights of the Child,** approved in 1989 and entering into effect by 1990, was about to become the first "truly universal law of humankind" [*World Chronicle*, 11/21/95]. And in fact, by February 1996, the Convention was only six states shy of universal ratification (the United States has signed the Convention but not yet ratified it) [UNICEF, *First Call for Children*/1996/No. 1]. In 1995, in a demonstration of the document's widespread acceptance, the Sudan People's Liberation Movement agreed to comply with the Children's Rights Convention—the first time an insurgent has formally pledged to uphold an international treaty [E/ICEF/1996/7].

The Convention on the Rights of the Child is also the first international treaty to link social and economic rights (including, in this case, the rights to survival, early development, education, and health care) with civil and political rights (here including not only such rights as freedom of expression but also the right to a name and nationality, to participation in decisions affecting his or her well-being, and to protection from sexual exploitation and abuse).

Also groundbreaking was the assertion that the child has a right to an identity distinct from that of parents or nurturers and that the community not only has a duty to protect such an identity but also to give the child a voice in matters such as guardianship or custody. (In some U.S. circles such provisions are branded antifamily and said to undermine "family values" [UNA-USA, *The InterDependent,* Spring 1995; and *New York Times,* 5/2/96].) Parties to the Convention are required to begin reporting on their compliance with treaty provisions within two years of ratification. Overseeing their progress and receiving these reports is the international body of experts established by the Convention—the Committee on the Rights of the Child.

For UNICEF, the most urgent business of the 1990s is the business of preventing conflict, with its devastating impact on the very young. In 1996, UNICEF's annual *State of the World's Children* asserts that "poverty and lack of development fuel hatred and escalate hostility"—and that improvements in the areas of nutrition, health, education, water, sanitation, and family planning would help to prevent it. The report goes on to offer a ten-point **anti-war agenda** that suggests both long-term and short-term means to address the causes of violence and to combat the victimization and exploitation of children in war itself.

The agenda's specific suggestions include a mandatory **"child-impact assessment"** to monitor the effect of sanctions, some special protection for girls and women against the threat of rape, the establishment in international law of "children as zones of peace," and an optional protocol to the Children's Rights Convention to raise the minimum recruitment age from 15 to 18. (UNICEF, currently assisting in the rehabilitation and reintegration in society of former **child soldiers** in Liberia and Rwanda, also ministers to imprisoned Rwandan children accused of participation in the 1994 genocide [*First Call for Children*/1996/No. 1].)

In these and other war-torn countries UNICEF is also providing various forms of assistance to **"unaccompanied children"**—the estimated million separated from their families as a consequence of conflict. The hope is a reunion, and a reintegration into the home community. Aiding the process is the partnership of UNICEF and Kodak in photographing unaccompanied Rwandan children in the refugee camps of Zaire [UNICEF, *Every Child Is Our Child,* 6/95].

Among those enlisted as partners in a General Assembly-ordered **study on the impact of armed conflict on children** and an assessment of their needs [A/Res/48/157], initiated in 1993 and scheduled for presentation to the 51st Session, are the Organization of African Unity; the U.N.'s regional commissions; such specialist bodies as the World Health Organization, the U.N. High Commissioner for Refugees, and the Food and Agriculture Organization; and UNICEF, the Committee on the Rights of the Child, and the U.N.'s Centre for Human Rights. An interim report by the Secretary-General's appointee as leader of the study, Graça Machel, former first lady of Mozambique, holds out the hope of giving "new coherence and fresh impetus to the efforts of the international community" and speaks of her plan to prepare "specific and wide-ranging recommendations for action at the national, regional, and international levels" [E/CN.4/1996/110].

UNICEF itself, which issued $399 million in purchase orders in 1995 [UNICEF, *Supply Division Annual Report 1995*], has sought to **exercise some economic leverage over suppliers** in advancing its anti-war and children's rights agenda [*How to Do Business with the United Nations: The 1996 Update to The Complete Guide to U.N. Procurement*, by Sandrine Tesner, New York: UNA-USA, 1996]. In May 1995, UNICEF pledged to purchase supplies only from companies that do not hire child laborers—a prohibition set forth in the Children's Rights Convention [*First Call for Children*/1995/No. 3]. In December it announced that it would no longer do business with companies that manufacture or sell the anti-personnel mines that have claimed a million victims since 1975, many of them children. Would-be suppliers must sign a pledge to the effect that they have no role in the business of landmines [*How to Do Business with the United Nations*].

Helping to advance the longer-term health and developmental aspects of UNICEF's anti-war agenda are the Fund's traditional **country programs.** In 1995, UNICEF field offices conducted a midterm review of the programs in their bailiwick. The summary report submitted to ECOSOC [E/ICEF/1996/P.L.42] notes the local context, looks at successes and failures, and assesses the mix of objectives and of strategies for meeting them.

Pledged to advance the cause of children's rights by attaining certain goals by the year 2000 are the leaders of member state governments, who met in New York in 1990 for the first **World Summit for Children.** The goals are, in brief: a one-third reduction in the deaths of children under five and a similar reduction in child deaths from acute respiratory infections; a 50 percent decrease in maternal mortality rates, in the rate of malnutrition among children under five, and in child deaths caused by diarrheal diseases; immunization of 90 percent of infants against the childhood killer diseases; eradication of polio and neonatal tetanus; a 90 percent drop in measles cases and a 95 percent drop in measles deaths; completion of primary education by 80 percent of both boys and girls; clean water and sanitation for all; and universal access to high-quality family planning information and services [*The State of the World's Children 1996*]. The cost of achieving these goals is placed by UNICEF at $30 billion to $40 billion more per year than the world community currently spends on such matters [ibid.]. Advances toward the Summit's goals are measured in UNI-CEF's *Progress of Nations,* the fourth edition of which appeared in mid-1996.

In 1996, U.N. member states are due to supply a **formal progress report,** and *The State of the World's Children 1996* anticipates quite a few success stories. Many of these will be in Asia and Latin America, fewer in sub-Saharan Africa, where armed conflict and economic crisis have caused "the vision of the Summit goals [to sink] below the horizon" [ibid.].

An ally in the cause of children's rights is the **Special Rapporteur on the sale of children, child prostitution, and child pornography** appointed by the U.N. Commission on Human Rights—since January 1995, Otelia Calcetas-Santos. Ms. Calcetas-Santos's first (provisional) report labels sexual exploitation, particularly prostitution, one of the most serious and hideous forms of violence against children, akin to torture when it comes to the trauma caused [A/50/456]. Sexual exploitation of children is increasing worldwide and is a profitable industry, netting approximately $5 billion per year [ibid.]. The General Assembly's omnibus resolution on "The rights of the child" [A/Res/50/153] pronounces its support for the Rapporteur's efforts (and requests an interim report in time for the 51st Assembly), "notes the establishment by the Economic and Social Council . . . of an open-ended working group responsible for elaborating . . . guidelines for a possible draft optional protocol to the Convention on the Rights of the Child" vis-à-vis the sale of children, and calls attention to the **First World Congress on the Commercial Sexual Exploitation of Children,** to take place in Stockholm, August 27–31. UNICEF and the NGO Group for the Convention on the Rights of the Child are co-sponsors [*First Call for Children*/1996/No. 1]. The U.N. Secretary-General has been asked to report to the 51st General Assembly on the status of the Children's Rights Convention, the findings of Ms. Machel on the effect of armed conflicts on children, and the exploitation of child labor [A/Res/50/153]. An additional resolution on **"the girl child"** [A/Res/50/154] urges member states, all bodies of the U.N. system, and nongovernmental organizations "to help mobilize the necessary financial resources and political support to . . . achieve goals . . . relating to the survival, development and protection of the girl child in all programmes for children," and urges the Secretary-General to ensure that the girl child is given full attention in U.N. programs to implement the Platform for Action of the Fourth World Conference on Women.

Youth

In 1995, on the **tenth anniversary of International Youth Year (IYY),** the General Assembly adopted the **World Programme of Action for Youth to the Year 2000 and Beyond** [A/50/728]—a policy framework and practical guidelines for national and international efforts to improve the situation of the 1.01 billion people around the globe who are making the transition to adulthood (the United Nations puts this group in the 15–24 age bracket). Covered here are education, employment, hunger and poverty, health, environment, drug abuse, juvenile delinquency, leisure-time activities, girls and young women, and participation of youth in society and in decision-making. These are the issues the General Assembly had identified for the IYY in 1985, and the Programme of Action is intended to build on the foundation laid during that year.

The Programme of Action emphasizes the role of international and regional organizations, governments, nongovernmental organizations (NGOs), the private sector, and young people themselves in implementing policies and projects; partnership is the key. Facilitating these partnerships by helping to ensure effective cooperation with youth and youth-related NGOs and open up the channels of communication between the U.N. system and youth organizations is the U.N.'s tiny—two-member— **Youth Unit.** (Budget constraints brought a 50 percent reduction in staff for this subdivision of the **Division for Social Policy and Development** in 1995. The Unit's regular budget for 1996–97 is $1.4 million—20 percent of the total budget of the Division.) The focal point on youth in the U.N. system, the Unit is also responsible for promoting the implementation of the action program and appropriate follow-up, administers the **U.N. Youth Fund** (established during the 1985 IYY), and offers governments advisory services on youth policies.

The Youth Unit wears still another hat—as the secretariat for the **World Youth Forum of the United Nations System,** which held its first meeting in Vienna in 1991 and has scheduled a second in the same city in November 1996. At one of the planning sessions, 12 working groups were created, each to focus on issues relating to priorities of the World Programme of Action for Youth, as well as on such issues as human settlements—the subject of the next (and the century's last) major U.N. conference (Habitat II, June 1996). Co-chaired by a U.N. body and an NGO, this working group made plans to enlist the cooperation of the World Organization of the Scout Movement, the European Youth Homeless Group, and other "youth NGOs with specialized interest in youth and human settlement issues." A youth consultation held prior to 1995's World Summit for Social Development in Copenhagen had asserted that "the current involvement in the United Nations by young people needs to be improved, encouraged and maximized to ensure a situation which is more representative of the situation of young people and their role in modern societies throughout the world." It joined this with a call for a **U.N. Youth Rights Charter** [*Youth Information Bulletin*, Vol. 1/1995/No. 86].

The 1996 **Vienna Forum** (the host is Austria's Federal Youth Council) will report on the recommendations of the various working groups—on networking arrangements and joint action among U.N. system bodies, other intergovernmental organizations, and youth-related and youth NGOs, with a focus on youth policies, communications, and training. **Youth policies and programs are considered by the Assembly on a biennial basis,** and the findings of the Forum will be presented by the U.N. Secretary-General at the **52nd Session** of the General Assembly [A/Res/49/154 and A/Res/50/81]. The report will include an evaluation by governments and youth organizations of the youth programs established after the IYY, taking into account their success at implementing the World Programme of Action.

8. Aging
By Andrew H. Su

A population "is said to be ageing" (explains a U.N. publication concerned with "the world ageing situation") "when the share of people in the older age group increases and the share of children and youth decreases [United Nations, *The World Ageing Situation 1991*]. In fact, the world is graying so rapidly that the proportion of older persons in the population, approximately 1 in 14 only a few generations ago, will soon have risen to 1 in 4. A half-century ago there were 200 million people aged 60 or more—8 percent of the global population—and by 2025 the world's population of seniors is expected to be 1.2 billion 14 percent of the total, a sixfold increase. In 1992 the General Assembly declared **1999 the International Year of Older Persons** [A/Res/47/5]. The U.N. Secretariat's **Division for Social Policy and Development (DSPD)** in the **Development for Policy Coordination and Sustainable Development (DPCSD),** as the U.N. system's focal point for aging, has spearheaded preparations for the Year. Among the typical features of a U.N. Year are conferences, festivals, special projects, and new publications and studies. Hopes are that the Year will stimulate innovative national projects and the sharing of good practices, giving shape to effective programs on aging for the next century.

The decision to observe an International Year of Older Persons, the General Assembly said, was made "in recognition of humanity's demographic coming of age," and it noted the promise such a Year holds for "maturing attitudes and capabilities in social, economic, cultural and spiritual undertakings." The U.N. Secretary-General has since developed a **Conceptual Framework** for the preparations and observance. Its theme, **"Towards a Society for All Ages"** [A/50/114, 3/22/95], picks up on the discussion of "a society for all" at the 1995 World Summit for Social Development [A/Conf.166/9, Annex 1]. A "society for all ages," in the U.N.'s sonorous prose, is one that "adjusts its structures and functioning, as well as its policies and plans, to the needs of and capabilities of all, thereby releasing the potential of all, for the benefit of all" and encouraging respect for all [A/50/114, sec. V, par. 38]. The Secretary-General of the United Nations notes that such a theme has the additional effect of "open[ing] the Year wide for the participation of all generations and many sectors and organizations" [A/50/114].

The overall objective is to direct attention to the **"U.N. Principles for Older Persons"** adopted by the General Assembly in 1991 [A/Res/46/91], aimed at promoting the independence, participation, care, self-fulfillment, and dignity of this population. The "Conceptual Framework" for the Year's promotional efforts has four headings:

1. The Situation of Older Persons
2. Life-long Individual Development
3. Multi-generational Relationships
4. Development and the Ageing of Populations

In 1995 the General Assembly reviewed the Conceptual Framework and sought to enlist member states, U.N. bodies, and nongovernmental organizations (NGOs) in supporting "local, national, and international programmes and projects for the Year" [A/Res/50/141]. The same resolution requests the U.N. Secretary-General to report to the 52nd Session on preparations for that observance.

The Division for Social Policy and Development has already begun a broad-based dialogue with the **"key stakeholders" in the field of aging**—first to elaborate the Conceptual Framework for the Year's activities and afterwards to formulate an operational framework, in the interest of cooperation and efficiency. These stakeholders include both traditional actors in U.N. preparatory processes—other U.N. bodies (prominently, the United Nations Population Fund, the United Nations Development Fund for Women, and UNICEF), still other intergovernmental organizations, member states, and NGOs—and such nontraditional actors as the private sector, the academic community, and the media.

The "Aging Unit" of the DSPD, for its part, joined with the International Federation on Ageing in sponsoring in September 1995 an informal consultation of NGOs and governmental offices on the subject of preparations for the Year. Proposed at this Jerusalem gathering was the establishment of a collaborative international NGO network, "UN/NGO WEB-1999," to facilitate the sharing of plans and resources.

1995 also marked the fifth anniversary of the celebration of October 1 as International Day for the Elderly—henceforth **International Day of Older Persons,** final agreement on the "preferred term" having been reached at the 50th General Assembly [ibid.].

During 1995 the Division for Social Policy and Development of DPCSD published one single and one double issue of its *Bulletin on Age-*

ing, the former dealing with preparations for the upcoming Year and the latter (anticipating the Fourth World Conference on Women) with the situation of older women. The *Bulletin*'s first issue for 1996 will explore international and national programs for the Year, and the double issue will focus on "poverty and old age," in recognition of the International Year for the Eradication of Poverty. The same theme will be taken up at the October 1 observance of the Day of Older Persons [*Countdown to 1999*, newsletter of the DSPD, 7/95 (Rev. 1)]. In 1997 the *Bulletin* will explore various dimensions of the Conceptual Framework for the Year of Older Persons, and a third edition of *The World Ageing Situation* will come off press (a new edition appears every six years). The latest volume examines the aging factor "in countries at different stages of socio-economic and demographic development."

In January 1996, U.N. member states received a 20-page questionnaire about their progress in implementing the **International Plan of Action on Ageing** agreed to by governments at the **Vienna World Assembly on Aging** in 1982. This fourth quadrennial exercise [A/Res/37/51] looks at nine areas: infrastructure for aging, impact of aging on national development, health and nutrition, housing and environment, family, social welfare, income security and employment, education, and international cooperation. May 1996 was the deadline for filing, and findings will be reviewed by the intergovernmental Commission for Social Development in advance of presentation to the 52nd General Assembly [previous findings are recorded in E/1985/6 and Corr.1, E/1989/13, and E/CN.5/1993/7]. The 56th U.N. General Assembly will receive the fifth review and will evaluate the Year itself.

Member states are being encouraged to support the Year through contributions to the **Trust Fund for Ageing** (managed by DPCSD) or the **Banyan Fund Association** (an independent fund "under the patronage" of the United Nations). The Trust Fund (amounting to $50,000 in spring 1996, reports the Officer-in-Charge of the U.N. Programme on Ageing [interview with *A Global Agenda: Issues/51*, 3/96]), provides seed-money grants for "catalytic and innovative action related to ageing populations" by governments and by the nongovernmental community, "with concurrence of government(s) concerned." The types of action it has in mind are "promotion of greater interest and awareness of ageing of population structures, particularly in developing countries, including dissemination of the 'Principles for Older Persons'"; "assistance to governments on request in the formulation, implementation and evaluation of policies, strategies and programmes concerning ageing"; "applied research, evaluation, training, and advisory services in the field of ageing with emphasis on building national self-reliance"; and "technical exchanges of knowledge and information among developing countries" [U.N. Department of Policy Coordination handout].

The General Assembly voted no extra funds for the International

Year of Older Persons, determining that the international observance and DPCSD assistance to member states in launching their own observances and programs should come from the regular program budget for the 1998–99 biennium and voluntary contributions [A/Res/47/5]. **Belt-tightening at the United Nations** can shrink those limited budgetary resources even further—and has been felt already, in fact: Lack of resources is cited as the reason for the cancellation of a consultative meeting of the U.N. bodies promoting the Year, scheduled for Geneva in November 1995 [interview with the Officer-in-Charge, U.N. Programme on Ageing, 3/96]. The meeting had been called by the Division for Social Policy and Development in its capacity as focal point for the Year.

9. Disabled Persons
By Andrew H. Su

More than 500 million people throughout the world have some type of physical, mental, or sensory impairment, and an estimated 80 percent of them live in developing countries. The International Year of Disabled Persons in 1981 helped to publicize the needs of this population as well as the need for policies aimed at integrating disabled persons into the economic, political, and social life of their nations. An important outcome of the year was the drafting and adoption of the **World Programme of Action Concerning Disabled Persons** [A/37/351/Add. 1 and Add.1/Corr.1, Annex, sec. VIII, recommendations 1 (IV)], whose main themes are the equalization of opportunities, rehabilitation (physical and vocational), and the prevention of disabilities. The linkage of basic objectives with development concerns in the World Programme has been described as significantly ahead of its time.

When the General Assembly adopted the program in 1982, it proclaimed the period 1983–92 the **U.N. Decade of Disabled Persons.** As intended, the Decade served as a spur to implementation of the World Programme—by encouraging the development of new government-supported organizations of disabled people, of immunization and other disease-prevention programs, and of new legislation guaranteeing the rights of disabled people. It also proved to be a decade of learning for the U.N. agencies involved in these activities. In mid-Decade, when the United Nations undertook a review of the progress to date, it was revealed that many nations had adopted disability policies but that more resources—technical as well as financial—were needed to translate policies into programs [United Nations, *The U.N. Decade of Disabled Persons: A Decade of Accomplishment 1983–1992,* 1992]. Among the resources now available for meeting national needs are the **Standard Rules on the Equalization of Opportunities for Persons with Disabilities ("Standard Rules," 1994)** to guide legislation affecting every realm of national life—from education, employment, social security, and social services to recreation, sports, and culture [A/Res/48/96 Annex].

In 1992 the General Assembly undertook an end-of-Decade "review" of the implementation of the World Programme, and in 1994 endorsed a long-term strategy for achieving the program's goals in the light of lessons learned. These reviews will be conducted every five years; the third is to take place in 1997 during the 52nd Session.

The "core element" of the long-term strategy is a series of national plans supported by regional and global activities that aim at meeting the goal of "a society for all" [A/49/435]—a "conceptual innovation," notes a close observer of the process, and one that has found "application in other international instruments, such as the World Summit for Social Development's program of action." For the lead-in period (1995–96), governments are encouraged to establish a task force and "convene a broad-based national forum to obtain input and long-term commitment to a national disability strategy," with the aim of reviewing existing policies, matching needs and resources, and setting medium-term targets (i.e., for improvements in infrastructure and employment) [A/49/435].

In 1994 the Secretary-General appointed a **Special Rapporteur,** Bengt Lindqvist of Sweden, to monitor national progress in implementing the Standard Rules themselves. (Lindqvist's budget is being underwritten by member states.) One of the Special Rapporteur's early actions was to send a **questionnaire to governments inquiring about their progress in translating the Rules into policy and legislation.** Thirty-seven responded [A/50/374], and a second mailing, in 1995, garnered 73 responses by mid-1996 [communiqué from the Division of Social Policy and Development, 6/12/96]. The Special Rapporteur has been joined by a Panel of Experts—five men and five women with "different disabilities or experiences of disabilities" from all over the world—who will be meeting June 10–14, 1996, to consider, among other items, preliminary findings on the questionnaire.

The **U.N. Voluntary Fund for Disability** provides seed money for projects in the field that are helping governments and other players to implement the Rules and the World Programme. These projects range from pilot efforts in "disability aids" and technologies, to conferences for sharing technology and methodology, to workshops linking up overseas experts and resources with emerging national needs. In each case, disability is viewed in the perspective of economic and social development, and project proposals are examined for technical merit, realistic planning and budgets, and overall suitability [interview with Social Affairs Officers, Division for Social Policy and Development, 5/29/96]. Since 1980, the Fund has provided $3.6 million in co-financing grants to more than 200 projects [handout from Division of Social Policy and Development]. The 50th General Assembly encouraged member states to contribute to the Disability Fund and to respond to the Special Rapporteur's questionnaire [A/Res/50/144].

The **Division of Social Policy and Development,** as the **U.N.'s focal point on disabled persons,** facilitates these projects, coordinates the systemwide activities that affects its constituency, and works at developing partnerships with NGOs in disability-related fields. It was a sponsor of the Special Olympics World Games (New Haven, Conn., July 1995), and is currently preparing a **manual of national disability legislation, in historical perspective,** to guide developing countries (working title: *The First 50 Years*). The Division is also responsible for organizing at U.N. Headquarters the annual observance of the International Day of Disabled Persons (December 3), working closely with other U.N. bodies involved in disability issues, prominently UNICEF, the International Labour Organisation, and the Department of Humanitarian Affairs (DHA).

UNICEF, for its part, has distributed the Standard Rules to all its regional and country offices in more than 135 countries; and the Committee on the Rights of the Child, which monitors the Convention on the Rights of the Child, gives particular attention to provisions for children with disabilities when reviewing state party reports and in discussions with governments. The work of the **DHA De-Mining Team,** on the other hand, is aimed at *preventing* disabilities—in particular, those caused by antipersonnel mines, which have taken a high toll in lives and limbs (there are an estimated 250,000 amputees in 68 war-torn or recently war-torn countries, and exploding mines add 800 people to the amputee rolls each month [speech by data base consultant Andrew Cooper of the Mine Clearance and Policy Unit at the U.N. observance of International Day of Disabled Persons, 12/7/95]).

The Statistical Division of the U.N. Department for Economics and Social Information and Policy Analysis was responsible for developing the **International Disability Statistics Data Base (DISTAT)** in 1988 and the **Disability Statistics Compendium** in 1990. It is currently working on a "Manual for the Development of Statistical Information for Disability Programmes and Policies"—"in nontechnical language"—and "is seeking support for finalizing" a "Handbook on Census and Survey Methods for Development of Impairment, Disability, and Handicap Statistics" [speech by Herman Habermann, Department for Economics and Social Information and Policy Analysis, Statistical Division, 12/7/95].

Concerned with preventing injuries *and* with integrating disabled persons into the workforce is the **ILO,** which plays an important part in the implementation of the World Programme of Action. An estimated 5 percent of the global workforce suffers from some type of impairment or functional limitation, and there is an ILO Convention dealing explicitly with "vocational rehabilitation and employment of disabled persons" [No. 159, 1983; ratified by 55 states as of December 1995]. Each year this Specialized Agency offers governments advice on the development of rules for workplace safety and other matters, and in the course of 1995 supported activities aimed at integrating disabled persons into the labor market in 40 countries [statement by the ILO for International Day of Disabled Persons 1995].

Nongovernmental organizations too—international, national, and grass-roots—play an important role in the World Programme and in disseminating the Standard Rules and codifying its principles in various documents. Through NGO efforts, for example, the Rules are distributed not only in the U.N.'s six official languages but also in Czech, Danish, Estonian, Finnish, German, Hindi, Icelandic, Italian, Japanese, Korean, Slovak, Swedish, and Tamil. The World Blind Union makes available Braille versions in English, French, Italian, and Spanish, and there are plans for posting the Rules on the Internet. The Standard Rules likewise found their way into the final texts of both the World Summit on Social Development (Copenhagen, March 1995) and the Fourth World Conference on Women (Beijing, September 1995).

At **U.N. Headquarters** sites around the world the effort goes on to render buildings and facilities, as well as U.N. system documents and other sources of information, accessible to people with disabilities—a process initiated in 1980 [A/35/444, Annex]. In New York, a task force created at the initiative of the Department for Policy Coordination in January 1995 is reviewing suggestions for increasing the Organization's responsiveness to the needs of delegates, staff, and visitors with disabilities. (Sign language is available on request for some authorized meetings, for example, but not yet for regular meetings of the General Assembly and ECO-SOC [A/50/173].) The New York task force has taken the practical step of conducting a "walk-around" of the facilities [ibid.].

10. Habitat II
By Gail V. Karlsson

The **Second U.N. Conference on Human Settlements,** informally Habitat II or the City Summit, was held in Istanbul in June 1996. It was the last in a series of global conferences that began with the 1992 U.N. Conference on Environment and Development (UNCED, or Earth Summit) and has focused international attention on human rights, the needs and rights of women, population issues, and the challenges to social cohesion presented by widespread poverty and unemployment. A common theme of these conferences has been the need for just, equitable, and environmentally sustainable societies in a world where the human population is growing rapidly and natural resources are being depleted or destroyed.

Although some U.N. critics have questioned the usefulness of these global events, supporters have emphasized their importance in calling attention to long-term global crises and in building new partnerships among national governments, local authorities, and citizens and civic organizations around the world. In many cases, existing institutions have been unable to ameliorate the deepening conditions of unemployment, poverty, environmental destruction, and social disintegration that threaten communities and darken prospects for shared prosperity. New social and economic models may be needed to provide basic opportunities for meeting human needs without excluding vast groups of people or destroying the planetary ecosystems that we all depend on. U.N. conferences provide a forum and a focus for examining the root causes of these problems and potential avenues for corrective action. As Secretary-General Boutros Boutros-Ghali proclaimed in his opening statement at Habitat II: "I wish here, from this forum, to state, in the strongest possible terms: I consider the conferences of the United Nations central to the work of the Organization, essential to the fulfillment of its mandate, and critical for the determination of the future of life on this planet" [U.N. press release HAB/ISA/3, 6/3/96].

Habitat II was intended to focus on creating sustainable human settlements, particularly how to make cities more livable. Many of the discussions centered on the need for affordable housing and basic infrastructure—clean water, adequate food supplies, electricity, transportation, sewage systems, and waste disposal. But sustainable communities also require economic opportunities and political rights as well as education, health care, and social services. Because of the complex interconnections among all these factors, the conference attracted a wide range of participants.

The conference organizers characterized Habitat II as a "Partners' Conference," and actively encouraged representatives of local governments and grass-roots organizations to share their experiences together with academics, scientists, and business leaders. For the first time at a U.N. conference, members of local governments participated fully in the negotiation process and the meetings. They also held a separate **World Assembly of Cities and Local Authorities** in Istanbul just prior to the official conference, in order to discuss common issues and share experiences. Other Partners' Forums were convened for scientists, parliamentarians, labor unions, urban professionals, and business representatives.

As was the case with earlier U.N. conferences, nongovernmental and community-based organizations organized a parallel forum in Istanbul concurrent with the official conference. The NGO forum was located right next to the official conference to encourage cross-linkages through related workshops and panel discussions. Members of public interest groups from around the world attended the forum to inform each other and to present their recommendations to the Habitat II conference. An international trade fair on "Good Ideas for Better Cities" served as a showcase for innovative housing and construction technologies as well as other environmentally sound products and services.

U.N. Centre for Human Settlements

The first Habitat conference was held in Vancouver, Canada, in 1976 and led to the establishment of the **U.N. Centre for Human Settlements (UNCHS)** in 1978. Based in Nairobi, Kenya, UNCHS provides research and technical analysis to governments on community management and development. The current guideline for its work is the **Global Strategy for Shelter to the Year 2000,** adopted by the General Assembly in 1988, under which it coordinates national and international efforts to provide adequate shelter for all by the end of the century.

In the 20 years since the first Habitat conference, urbanization has increased dramatically. Almost half of the world's population lives in urban areas. Given rapid rates of migration and population growth, in another 30 years close to two-thirds of the world's people will be clustered in cities and towns. Especially worrisome is the uncontrolled spread of megacities, where the rural poor arrive to seek employment and opportunity but all too often find their hopes unrealized and their basic needs unmet. In 1995, UNCHS estimated that over a billion people worldwide had inadequate housing and that over 100 million were actually homeless [DPI/1730/Rev.1/HAB/CON, 1/96]. Although the urban poor are generally three to ten times better off than the rural poor, a *Global Report on Human Settlements* released by UNCHS warns that substandard housing, unsafe water, and poor sanitation in densely populated cities cause 10 million deaths worldwide every year [DPI/1788/HAB/CON, 1/96].

Is There a Right to Housing?

The most controversial issue during the preparations for Habitat II was whether there is a "right to housing" recognizable under international law. Many countries argued that there is such a right, as enumerated in the Universal Declaration of Human Rights (which has been accepted by all members of the General Assembly as an affirmation of common principles, though not as a treaty with the force of law). Article 25.1 of the Universal Declaration of Human Rights states that: "Everyone has the right to a standard of living adequate for the health and well-being of himself and his family, including food, clothing, housing and medical care and necessary social services, and the right to security in the event of unemployment, sickness, disability, widowhood, old age, or other lack of livelihood beyond his control." Similar language is contained in Article 11.1 of the 1966 International Covenant on Economic, Social and Cultural Rights, a treaty elaborating on the principles of the Universal Declaration that has the force of law but has not been universally adopted.

Some countries argued that it would be counterproductive to define the need for adequate housing as a universal human right. During the preparatory committee discussions, the U.S. delegate explained: "In the United States we have legally established rights. If at an international level we agree to housing as a right, this implies that a third party could be called in to adjudicate and intervene if such rights are being violated. What we are saying is that we should not confuse clearly established rights with needs and aspirations and goals" [DPI/1730/Rev.1/HAB/CON, 1/96].

During negotiations in Istanbul, the U.S. delegation eventually agreed to compromise language that affirmed governments' commitment to "the full and progressive realization of the right to adequate housing." Although the United States still does not recognize the right to housing as independent of the right to an adequate standard of living, some participants praised the compromise language as a major victory. While it does not mean governments are obligated to provide housing, it does mean they are committed to adopting policies to promote access to housing.

Building Effective Housing Markets

The proper role of governments in ensuring adequate and affordable supplies of housing was also much debated. Reports prepared for the Habitat II Preparatory Committee were unanimous in identifying lack of land and financing as major obstacles to housing availability: "The failure of markets and governments to deliver enough land and finance at the right price and time, and in the right places, is the most important factor in holding back progress in urban shelter. This requires strong government intervention; it cannot be rectified by markets alone, since markets care little for considerations of equity and sustainability" [A/CONF.165/PC.3/3/ Add.1, 11/15/95]. Another conclusion of the background reports was that economic inequality and social exclusion are increasing within cities in all parts of the world, "partly as a result (at least in the short-term) of economic liberalization, since markets always discriminate against those with less income and fewer assets" [ibid.].

In the **Global Plan of Action** adopted at Habitat II much emphasis is placed on the concept of "enablement." Governments by themselves cannot be expected to provide housing for all, but they have the responsibility to create an enabling environment for a well-functioning housing market, particularly through reforming policies, institutions, and legal frameworks. At the same time, they must be careful to avoid inappropriate interventions that stifle supply and demand. The plan also specifies policies and actions to ensure access to land, to mobilize sources of finance, to provide access to basic infrastructure and services, and to improve construction, maintenance, and rehabilitation of housing stock.

A recent World Bank policy paper on housing markets describes a number of major policy instruments governments can use to increase market supply and efficiency, as opposed to directly providing low-cost housing. Some of these policy measures address demand-side constraints on housing availability. For example, governments need to ensure that rights to own and transfer property are legally recognized and enforced. They also need to foster healthy mortgage-lending institutions to provide credit for home purchases. In order to increase the available supply of housing, governments could provide infrastructure (roads, water, electricity, and sewage systems) for residential and land development and stimulate greater competition in the construction industry. According to the report, improving the management of housing markets as a whole requires bringing together all the major public agencies, private businesses, and representatives of civic groups in the community, including the poor [*UNCHS Habitat Update,* Vol. 1, No. 4, 12/95].

Creating Environmentally Sustainable Cities

One section of the Global Plan of Action looks at the general requirements for developing sustainable human settlements in an urbanizing world. The challenge for cities is to support ever-growing numbers of people while avoiding destructive patterns of natural resource consumption and use. Many of these recommendations have evolved during the course of prior global conferences.

A number of communities have already begun to experiment with plans and designs for sustainable development. Agenda 21, the comprehensive international plan of action for sustainable development adopted at the Earth Summit, urged local governments around the world to work with community organizations, business groups, and other civic associations to create their own sustainable development plans. Since many of the environmental problems addressed in Agenda 21 are related to the demands and burdens placed on natural systems by urban populations, city governments and civic institutions can play a critical role in educating and mobilizing the public and in engineering new strategies for sustainable urban management.

In Sweden, for example, a youth network called Q2000, created by students following the Earth Summit, led a nationwide campaign to initiate sustainable development planning in all municipalities [*Countdown to Istanbul, Habitat II,* 11/95, Vol. 1, No. 5, UNCHS]. Almost all of the country's 288 municipalities are now participating. On the island of Gotland local authorities have started a major wind-power project, run by shareholder associations, to provide residents with clean, inexpensive electricity. In Falkenberg, oil consumption for heating and industry has been reduced by 75 percent due to the advice provided by a new Energy Information Bureau [ibid.].

Energy and transportation policies are particularly important for urban development. Emissions from burning fossil fuels contribute to air pollution, human health problems, global climate change, and other environmental damage. Governmental investments in infrastructure for public transportation and clean power generation are major elements of environmentally sustainable urban planning. The Habitat II Plan of Action recommends efforts to promote energy efficiency, to introduce nonpolluting renewable energy sources, and to discourage motor vehicle traffic.

Another important element of sustainable urban planning discussed in the Habitat II plan is the relationship between the central city and surrounding rural areas. The lack of infrastructure, services, and employment opportunities in rural areas contributes to urban migration. Regional planning designed to improve living and working conditions in small towns and rural areas can ease population pressures in the cities while at the same time preserving the environmental resources that provide the city with food, water, and other supplies. Rapidly expanding megacities are often forced to draw water from distant sources or from diminishing groundwater supplies. In many cases, freshwater sources are being contaminated by untreated sewage and industrial discharges. Scarcity of clean drinking water is one of the most dangerous of urban problems, according to Dr. Wally N'Dow, Secretary-General of the Habitat II conference: "With rapid urbanization and population increases, more and more people are competing today for diminishing supplies of freshwater. If we fail to address this challenge with full vigour now, we may soon witness major social and political conflicts in our societies" [UNCHS press release, 2/15/96]. Approximately 1 billion people currently lack access to safe drinking water and 1.7 billion people do not have access to adequate sanitation facilities [ibid.].

Economic and Political Sustainability

As centers of industry, services, communications, finance, and culture, cities are becoming the primary engines for economic growth. But many new jobs will be needed to provide adequate livelihoods for growing populations. Echoing the central themes of 1995's World Summit for Social Development, the Habitat II plan calls for poverty eradication through macroeconomic policies that support sustainable human development. Recommended actions to strengthen urban economies include improved access to education and health care, formation of new public and private sector partnerships, and support for increased employment opportunities in small businesses, microenterprises, and cooperative enterprises.

Good governance through shared decision-making is essential for economically, socially, and environmentally healthy cities. The Habitat II Plan of Action recommends decentralization and democratization of urban management to achieve a participatory process rooted in a shared vision. Participatory mechanisms like community-based planning boards give citizens and civic organizations an active role in formulating policies and projects that meet their particular needs and encourage socially responsible private activities.

Best Practices

All solutions to urban problems are essentially local, reflecting the particular cultural, economic, and political context of a given community. Nevertheless, there are common building blocks necessary to meet basic human needs as well as the long-term requirements of sustainable development. As part of the Habitat II conference preparatory process, UNCHS convened an **International Conference on Best Practices in Improving Living Environments,** held in Dubai, United Arab Emirates, in November 1995. The conference participants reviewed case studies of initiatives that have improved the quality of life and environments in urban communities in a sustainable way. Projects ranged from innovative waste disposal systems to effective poverty reduction programs. Selected examples of "best practices" were presented in an exhibit in Istanbul. In addition, reflecting the new importance of global information technology, UNCHS produced a database of 500 examples of best practices and made it available on CD-ROM and the Internet.

Habitat II went beyond previous U.N. conferences in promoting a more open and participatory process for approaching local as well as global problems. It encouraged open discussion of innovative ideas and advanced the vision of creative decision-making shared by national and local governments, citizens and community groups, in partnership with progressive business interests. In sum, the conference demonstrated that cities, despite their glaring deficiencies, represent opportunity and hope for billions of people seeking to make a living and to make a home. By providing a vehicle for exchanging local experiences and expertise, Habitat II sought to demonstrate that potential solutions are within reach.

VI
Legal Issues
By W. Andy Knight

For international law to develop as an instrument of world order it must be prepared to meet the requirements of international life and keep pace with the activities and demands of the state system. From this perspective, international law is a very weak instrument indeed, say many students of international organization, and they go on to list the many hurdles to overcome in strengthening it: the absence of a single court at the international level with compulsory jurisdiction; the underutilization of the International Court of Justice (ICJ) by U.N. member states and U.N. political organs; the states' propensity for attaching crippling reservations to their acceptance of ICJ judgments; the show of disrespect by some states for established principles and agencies of international law; the reluctance to treat individuals and international organizations as legal persons, the status accorded to states; the snail-like pace (and inefficiency) of the process of developing a comprehensive body of international law through custom, multilateral treaties, and conferences; and, most important perhaps, the inability to enforce international law given the absence of independent and permanent enforcement agencies at the international level [see A. Leroy Bennett, *International Organizations: Principles and Issues*, 6th ed., Englewood Cliffs, N.J.: Prentice-Hall, 1995, pp. 209–10].

Today we see a number of new and encouraging trends in the development of international law. One is the fact that non-state actors now have some role in shaping law and judicial processes at the international level. The U.N. Charter, of course, gives the General Assembly the responsibility for encouraging the development and codification of international law, and long ago the Assembly created the International Law Commission to serve as its proxy in recommending new areas to explore. Until recently the U.N.'s approach to legal issues could be characterized as "sober, cautious, conservative, and technical, and very, very slow moving" [Edward McWhinney, *United Nations Law Making: Cultural and Ideological Relativism and International Law Making for an Era of Transition*, New York: Holmes & Meier, 1984, p. 98], its work in the field mainly taking the form of studies, discussions, drafting, codification, revision, and the exercise of moral suasion to entice states into ratifying new conventions and bring them into force. But at the United Nations too we see subtle changes in the approach to the progressive development of international law and an indication that member states may be moving from rhetoric and platitudes to take on the difficult issue of the enforcement of international law.

1. The ILC, the International Criminal Court, and the Draft Code of Crimes

The need for an international criminal court was first noted by the General Assembly in 1948 [A/Res/260-III], in the aftermath of a war in which there were massive violations of human rights, not least Hitler's genocide of the Jews. That postwar discussion lasted five years, but it was not until the world witnessed the atrocities committed in Rwanda and the former Yugoslavia that the United Nations took up the subject again. After the establishment in 1992 of a highly controversial ad hoc international tribunal to try those accused of war crimes in the former Yugoslavia, the General Assembly instructed the 34-member International Law Commission (ILC) to elaborate a draft statute for a proposed International Criminal Court [see A/Res/47/33 and *A Global Agenda: Issues/50*, pp. 239–43].

Upon examining the ILC's draft statute, the General Assembly created an Ad Hoc Committee (open to all member states and nonmembers that, like Switzerland, have elected to join the specialized agencies) to review the major substantive and administrative issues arising out of the draft statute and consider arrangements for an international conference of plenipotentiaries to work through them [A/Res/49/53]. After four weeks of meetings, the Ad Hoc Committee reported that the participating states differed so markedly on the major substantive and administrative issues that it would be more effective to combine further discussions with the actual drafting of a consolidated text of a statute/convention for the court [see *International Documents Review*, 4/15/96, p. 3].

In November 1995 the Sixth Committee (Legal) of the General Assembly entertained the notion of establishing a Preparatory Committee (open to all states, as above) to take on the tasks of considering the issues arising out of the draft statute and of negotiating the final text of the statute/convention for an international criminal court [A/C.6/50/L.14]. The General Assembly voted its approval [A/Res/50/46] and the Preparatory Committee was instructed to base its work on the ILC's draft statute and to take into account the report of the Ad Hoc Committee on the Establishment of an International Criminal Court as well as documents and comments submitted to the Secretary-General by states and relevant organizations [A/C.6/50/L.16].

At the Committee's first session, March 25–April 12, 1996 (another is scheduled for August 12–30, 1996), Adriaan Bos of the Netherlands was elected Chairman; Cherif Bassiouni of Egypt, Silvia A. Fernandez de Gurmendi of Argentina, and Marek Madej of Poland as Vice Chairs; and Jun Yoshida of Japan as Committee Rapporteur. The participants had in hand the ILC's report of its 46th session [A/49/10], which contained the 60-article draft statute; the Ad Hoc Committee's report [A/50/22]; comments on the draft statute received pursuant to General Assembly Resolution 49/53 on the establishment of the court [A/AC.244/1 and Add.1–4]; the preliminary report of the Secretary-General on the provisional estimates of the staffing, structure, and costs for establishing and operating the court [A/AC.244/L.2]; and reports of the Secretary General relating to Security Council Resolutions 808 (1993) and 955 (1994) on the International Criminal Tribunals for the former Yugoslavia and for Rwanda [S/25704, Add.1 and Corr.1–2 and S/1995/134]. The final report of the Committee itself—consisting of a widely acceptable consolidated text, if all goes according to plan—will be submitted to the 51st Session of the General Assembly [U.N. press release L/2760, 3/22/96]. This will allow for a full discussion of the report cum text, leading to a call for convening an international conference of plenipotentiaries to finalize and adopt a statute/convention on the establishment of the court.

The **rationale for creating a single, permanent International Criminal Court,** the Ad Hoc Committee advised the 50th General Assembly, is to obviate the need for ad hoc tribunals for particular crimes [A/50/22]. The implication is that such a court is more likely to ensure stability and consistency in international criminal jurisdiction. But what will it look like? The Ad Hoc Committee envisages a **multilateral, treaty-established, independent judicial organ** that could remain in session permanently if its caseload required.

Administrative structure. The ILC draft statute calls for 18 judges, representing "the principal legal systems of the world," each elected to a nine-year nonrenewable term by an absolute majority of states parties to the statute of the court. It also calls for four main organs: a Presidency, the Chambers, a Procuracy, and a Registry. An absolute majority of the judges would elect the Presidency, to be composed of a President, first and second Vice Presidents, and two alternate Vice Presidents, each serving a three-year term. There would be two main Chambers—a six-member Appeals Chamber and a five-member Trial Chamber—and a special five-judge chamber to consider the application of the laws of pardon, parole, or commutation of the state in which the accused international criminal is being held. Decisions of the Trial Chamber could be reversed in Appeals (requiring a quorum of six and a majority vote). The Procuracy, intended as an independent investigative arm of the court, would be headed by a Prosecutor, assisted by one or more Deputies and supported by a qualified staff. Both the Prosecutor and the Deputies would be elected by an absolute majority of the states parties to the statute, the voting to be conducted by secret ballot. The Registry would consist of a Registrar, to be chosen via secret ballot (for a renewable five-year term) by an absolute majority of the judges. Support staff will be appointed, as necessary, to facilitate the work of the Registrar.

Jurisdiction. That the court was intended to complement national criminal justice systems, not replace them, is evident from the discussions of the Ad Hoc Committee and the ILC. The ILC made it clear from the outset that the proposed court would not replace national courts and that states have a vital interest in retaining responsibility for prosecuting violations of their own laws. But the discussions raised some sticky issues, including the need for a clearer definition of the principle of complementarity between the court and national criminal justice systems and a clearer determination of who will be responsible for deciding when the national court will be superceded. There were questions too about whether national courts should have priority over the international court and about whether the primacy of national jurisdictions might lead in some cases to the shielding of criminals.

Based on the draft statute, the court is deemed to have jurisdiction once a party to the statute files a complaint against the accused, and the state with custody of the suspect and the state on whose territory the crime occurred (or has received an extradition request relating to it) agree to accept the jurisdiction of the court. Acceptance of the jurisdiction of the court could take the form of a declaration of general application for a specified or unspecified period or of ratification of the statute by a declaration lodged with the depository or, at a later time, with the Registrar.

The draft statute also provides for jurisdiction over **crimes referred to the court by the Security Council,** acting under Chapter VII of the U.N. Charter. In the case of aggression, for instance, the Council would be the "trigger mechanism," since it is the only body authorized by the Charter to determine when an act of aggression has been committed. Under the terms of the draft statute, however, the Council would not normally refer a "case" against individuals to the court but, rather, would refer a "matter" or situation to which Chapter VII of the Charter applies. It would then be the court prosecutor's responsibility to determine which individuals will be charged with a crime against the peace and security of mankind [U.N. press release L/2760, 3/22/96].

With respect to the *court's* jurisdiction, participants in the debate generally supported giving it competence over **a "hard core" of crimes**— for example, genocide, war crimes, and crimes against humanity. Initially, there was some doubt about including aggression on the list of "core crimes," since under the U.N. Charter it is the Security Council that determines whether an act of aggression has been committed. In any event, it has become clear that the more focused the list of "core crimes" for the international court, the greater the number of states likely to accede to the statute.

There was also widespread agreement that the legal principles of *nullum crimen sine lege* and *nulla poena sine lege* (no crime without law, no penalty without law) ought to be followed in the drafting of the statute. Thus, the ILC and the Preparatory Committee are not simply enumerating the crimes to be dealt with by the court but are working to ensure that the statute defines them precisely. Several states suggested that definitions from the **Nuremberg Tribunal Charter** and the **statutes of the Ad Hoc International Criminal Tribunals for the former Yugoslavia and Rwanda** be incorporated into the final Draft Code of Crimes against the peace and security of mankind.

Opinion is still divided over whether, in the case of serious international crimes, the International Criminal Court should enjoy "inherent jurisdiction" that would allow it to proceed with the prosecution of alleged international criminals without a request from signatory states. Some states are of the view that inherent jurisdiction is incompatible with principles of complementarity and national sovereignty as articulated in the U.N. Charter; others argue that, given the magnitude of the "core crimes," the court should have as few restrictions as possible on its freedom to prosecute.

The debate between the advocates of complementarity and national sovereignty and the advocates of inherent jurisdiction over "core crimes" has led to serious discussion about **"trigger mechanisms"**—that is, about who will be responsible for determining when a "core crime" has been committed and is thus in a position to initiate the court's prosecution procedures [see discussion at the Ad Hoc Committee level in U.N. press release GA/8904, L/2737, 8/18/95]. Some states have argued that only states parties or the Security Council could be considered legitimate "trigger mechanisms," but many others contend that by limiting the court to prosecutions requested by states parties and the Security Council one would, in effect, be reducing the court's role to nothing more than that of executor.

The ILC and the Draft Code of Crimes

The 47th session of the ILC (Geneva, May 2–July 21, 1995) produced the 13th report on the Draft Code of Crimes Against the Peace and Security of Mankind [A/CN.4/466]. The draft statute itself creates two categories of crimes: those under general international law, such as genocide, aggression, serious violations of the laws and customs applicable in armed conflict, and crimes against humanity; and those covered by treaty provisions. The former can be considered "core crimes," while the latter— exceptionally serious crimes that are of international concern—are annexed to the statute under the heading "Crimes pursuant to Treaties," which includes the 1949 Geneva Conventions and the conventions on the hijacking of aircraft, on apartheid, and on "internationally protected persons," hostage-taking, torture, safety of maritime navigation, and illicit traffic in narcotic drugs.

In keeping with the spirit of the 12th report on the Draft Code [A/CN.4/460 and Corr.1], the ILC's Special Rapporteur for the 47th session proposed a strategy aimed at winnowing down the list of crimes to be included in the Draft Code to offenses whose characterization as crimes against the peace and security of humanity would be difficult to challenge. This was obviously an extremely difficult task, given the presence in the ILC of those who hold expansionist positions on this issue and those who hold restrictive ones. The expansionists favor the drawing up of a Code of Crimes with a list of offenses that is as comprehensive as possible; the minimalists argue for the narrowing of the scope of this Code.

The dilemma posed by these two extreme positions is clear: If the Special Rapporteur were to take the route advocated by the maximalists, the Draft Code could well be viewed as an instrument devoid of substance, with little chance of being applied in the "real world"; if the Rapporteur were to take the legal minimalist route, he could end up with a mutilated draft that is not only unacceptable to the victims of a variety of crimes but (even more to the point) to the vast majority of U.N. member governments. The "middle way" chosen by the Special Rapporteur produces a delicate compromise: For an internationally wrongful act to be listed in the Code as a crime against the peace and security of mankind, it must be an extremely serious act *and* there must be widespread agreement among the member governments of the international community that it is serious enough to be included on the "list." The basic problem with this compromise position is that the criteria for deciding what crimes are listed in the Code would still be highly subjective.

Further complicating the task of defining an international offense is the diversity of legal systems. And then there is the political problem. All such codifications in international law require the convergence of several political wills—something that has proved difficult to achieve on quite a few articles of the Draft Code, forcing the Special Rapporteur to **reduce the list of crimes** that had been proposed on the first reading. (The initial list of 12 read as follows: aggression; threat of aggression; intervention; colonial and other forms of alien domination; genocide; apartheid; systematic or mass violations of human rights; exceptionally serious war crimes; recruitment, use, financing, and training of mercenaries; international terrorism; illicit traffic in narcotic drugs; willful and severe damage to the environment.) Some U.N. member governments, for example, criticized the draft articles that sought to define the threat of aggression and intervention as crimes against the peace and security of mankind, citing their failure to meet standards of precision and rigor required by international law; some were unsatisfied with the draft articles on colonial domination and other forms of alien domination; and some members took issue with the articles dealing with willful and severe damage to the environment.

A number of draft articles were accepted by the ILC member governments with reservations: article 20 on apartheid; article 23 on the recruitment, use, financing, and training of mercenaries; article 24 on international terrorism; and article 25 on illicit traffic in narcotic drugs. With regard to article 20, for example, one government representative, claiming to have no objection to the substance of the article itself, proposed that the term "apartheid" be replaced by the term "institutionalized racial discrimination." Described in this way, the "crime" would apply not only to the racialist ex-regime of South Africa but in all places in which this form of systemic injustice is practiced. At the same time, there were those who saw no need for an article on apartheid because this specific discriminatory system had already been dismantled in the one country in which it was systematically applied. Still other governments argued that there was no need for a separate article on the crime of apartheid since draft article 21 dealing with "systematic or mass violations of human rights" already covered such acts. In the end, the Special Rapporteur made a solid case for keeping the article on apartheid within the Code of Crimes, arguing that, even if the word "apartheid" were to be dropped, "there would be no guarantee that the phenomenon to which it refers will not reappear" [A/CN.4/466, p. 5].

On the issue of recruitment of mercenaries, some governments pointed out that the convention on mercenaries itself had been signed by only a relative handful of countries and that this phenomenon is "neither widespread nor sufficiently serious to be included in the Code" [ibid., p. 6]. Observers have noted that such arguments raise the question of whether the international community must wait for an identifiable international crime against the peace and security of mankind to become widespread before taking action to codify it. (In fact, this sort of activity has been on the increase in many parts of the underdeveloped world as well as in such places as the former Yugoslavia and certain states of the Commonwealth of Independent States.) It is also noted, however, that the very existence of draft articles dealing with the crime of acts of aggression may make it unnecessary to have a separate article to address the problem of mercenaries.

The draft article on terrorism clearly needed amending, said some governments, since it is not only state agents that carry out this kind of criminal activity but private individuals acting as members of groups, movements, and associations as well. The Special Rapporteur proposed a modified version of article 24 for the second reading to take this fact into account.

Some other U.N. members have questioned the appropriateness of including in the Code an article on traffic in narcotic drugs; others would include one, citing the destabilizing effect that globalization of the illicit drug trade has already had on several countries, with repercussions for international peace and security [see the argument made by Switzerland in A/CN.4/488, chapter III].

In the end, for reasons of expediency more than anything else, the number of offenses addressed in **the new Draft Code was reduced from 12 to 6:** aggression, genocide, crimes against humanity, war crimes, international terrorism, and illicit traffic in narcotic drugs. These are considered "core crimes."

Work of the Preparatory Committee

As noted, the General Assembly asked the Preparatory Committee to resolve some of the issues that the states participating in the Ad Hoc Committee of the ILC could not settle and to combine these discussions with the preparation of a consolidated text of a convention for an International Criminal Court—all with an eye toward convening a conference of plenipotentiaries [see A/Res/50/46]. The following section indicates the complexity of several of the issues with which U.N. member states are struggling in their attempt to establish a permanent International Criminal Court. Covered below are application of national law as a source of law for the court; the principle of complementarity; the possibility of "opting-in," of "opting-out," and of developing "trigger mechanisms"; the power of the prosecutor; the principle of nonretroactivity; individual and corporate responsibility for international crimes; processes for "provisional arrest" of persons accused of committing serious international crimes; judicial assistance to the court; age of responsibility and possible defenses that might be raised; and recognition of the judgments of the court. The debate on these subjects also reveals that the international community may be some distance away from reaching consensus on the precise nature of this court.

Application of National Law as a Source of Law for the ICC

The issue of whether national laws of particular states should be applied by the proposed International Criminal Court—and, if so, *whose* national law?—was one that occupied the first session of the Preparatory Committee. It was pointed out by some delegates that if a prosecution involves offenses committed in one national jurisdiction by a person from another national jurisdiction, it would be difficult to decide which national laws should be applied by the international court—those of the country in which the crime was committed, those of the country of the nationality of the accused, or those of the country in which the accused was arrested?

This is not an easy matter to resolve. Colombia, the Netherlands, and the United Kingdom were among those who pushed for the elimination of any reference to national laws so as to avoid even the slightest possibility of confusion over legal jurisdiction. Others, like Canada, proposed the application of national law in cases of incidents not covered by the statute of the proposed court or by international treaty. In such event, the "national" law to be applied would be based on common, universal principles derived from the main international legal systems. Still other delegates argued, as did Sweden's, that the preference in terms of application should be for the law of the state in which the offense was committed as long as that law could be held to an acceptable international legal standard. Precedent for this can be found in Anglo-American tort law, which allows for the prosecution of civil suits in the jurisdiction in which the tort was committed.

In any event, the credibility of the court's decisions will depend largely on the consistency of its rulings, and to ensure such consistency it will be necessary for the statute of the International Criminal Court to make absolutely clear the circumstances under which the court would apply specific national laws. To ensure that there is no discrepancy between the applicable laws and the court's decisions, the statute's rules of procedure will also have to be clearly defined—not by the judges but by political agreement reached by the representatives of government [U.N. press release L/2767, 3/28/96].

The Principle of Complementarity

The issue of complementarity between national and international jurisdictions is an important one for state-based international institutions, and it is no surprise that the Preparatory Committee would spend a good deal of time and energy on the matter. The gist of its conclusion was that the proposed court should exercise jurisdiction over criminal cases only where national jurisdiction is either nonexistent or ineffective. This requires, however, that the statute provide a clear definition of what is meant by "unavailable" and "ineffective," and it raises the question of *who* determines unavailability and ineffectiveness.

The Tunisian delegate observed that, given the opportunity to pronounce a national court "ineffective," the international community could override the courts of some developing countries simply by claiming that they cannot be expected to do a good job of prosecuting particular cases. This was obviously the logic used to establish the ad hoc tribunals in Rwanda and the former Yugoslavia. India went on to advise that the International Criminal Court should not be the "first court of call" or an appellate court. Indeed, the majority of member states seem of the opinion that the proposed International Criminal Court should not be allowed to override—or erode—national jurisdictions [U.N. press release L/2773, 4/2/96].

The representatives of Malaysia, Argentina, and Colombia asserted that, to be consistent with the principle of sovereignty enshrined in the U.N. Charter, national courts would have to have priority over the proposed court [U.N. press release L/2772, 4/2/96]. Malaysia suggested that the question of international jurisdiction should arise only when decisions at the national level were taken in bad faith, when prosecutions were improperly delayed, or when no internationally recognized national jurisdiction remained in place. In this view, the court would play a residual role, entering the picture only after the failure of national jurisdiction. (This does not necessarily imply that the court would be reduced to a subservient role.)

The New Zealand delegate pointed out that "complementarity" is *not* an established legal principle and should not be used by states to shield their nationals from the court's jurisdiction [ibid.]. Finland's representative noted that too much emphasis on safeguarding national jurisdictions might render the court somewhat useless, and went on to argue—in opposition to the U.S. delegate—that the International Criminal Court should be able to decide for itself whether national courts were handling prosecutions adequately [U.N. press release L/2771, 4/1/96]. The delegate of the Netherlands added that, although it was important to "draw the line" between concurrent national and international jurisdictions as carefully as possible, the International Criminal Court should be given the benefit of the doubt, since it was better to risk infringing on national jurisdiction than it was to allow perpetrators of crimes against humanity to go unpunished when protected by national authorities. It is for this reason that many states believe the proposed court should be permitted to pursue a case in which there is some pretence of pursuing it at the national level. Certainly in the case of genocide, no one would expect either an aggressor state or the victim of aggression to be able to prosecute that crime in adequate fashion [U.N. press releases GA/8902, L/2735, 8/17/95; and GA/8904, L/2737, 8/18/95].

The principle of complementarity set out in the preamble of the proposed court's draft statute, however, implies that **neither the international nor the national jurisdiction is meant to be subservient to the other** [see U.N. press release GA/8897, L/2730, 8/14/95, for discussion of this in the Ad Hoc Committee]. Citing the relative vagueness of the definition of complementarity in the preamble to the draft statute, the Egyptian delegate noted that lack of precision could give rise to conflicts that might threaten the court's authority, and the French delegate called for a description in the statute of the means by which the court would note the absence of a verifiable national trial. For these reasons, many delegates felt that the statute should define the minimum standard of conduct required for the court to exercise or assume jurisdiction. Another reason for spelling out the jurisdictional criteria is to ensure that the court will not be allowed too much latitude.

The representative of China was notably concerned about the circumstance under which representatives of the court would be allowed to conduct national on-site inspections. Other delegates made clear their wish that the court be prevented from re-prosecuting crimes already prosecuted by national juridical bodies, except in cases in which the prosecution is deemed not to have been conducted in good faith [U.N. press release L/2772, 4/2/96]—requiring, of course, a clear definition in the statute of exactly what constitutes an "act of bad faith" [L/2773, 4/2/96]. Absent from the discussion has been the (hypothetical) case of the national court that prosecutes an act that constitutes murder at the national level but genocide at the international level.

It is generally agreed that the task of deciding which cases are to be brought before the International Criminal Court should not be left up to individual states, and that it is necessary to establish some sort of multilateral mechanism for determining the admissibility of cases to the court. One suggestion envisions a kind of "grand jury" system [see U.N. press release L/2777, 4/4/96].

Opting-in, Opting-out, and Developing Trigger Mechanisms

At the 14th meeting of the first session of the Preparatory Committee on Establishment of an International Criminal Court, there was heated discussion about matters related to **state consent to the proposed court's jurisdiction,** about which crimes would fall under the court's competence, about acceptance of court jurisidiction through a system of "opting-in" and "opting-out," and about which states must accept the court's jurisdiction for the purpose of bringing a complaint. This last point raised the seminal issue of **which actors could initiate a court proceeding by "pulling the trigger"**—states parties, the Security Council, or the prosecutor of the court?

Within the Committee there was considerable support for the inherent jurisdiction of the court over all "core crimes" against humanity. The major opponents were China, Algeria, and Malaysia, citing the overriding nature of the sovereignty clause in the U.N. Charter. The Chinese delegate argued that inherent jurisdiction should be replaced by jurisdiction based on consent. Pushing for the opting-in approach, he argued that the court would be unable to carry out its prosecution effectively without the cooperation of both the territorial state (the state in which the crimes were committed) and the custodial state (the state with custody of the accused). The Algerian representative bluntly informed the Preparatory Committee that, without a system of opting-in *and* opting-out, his government simply would not accept the court's exercise of jurisdiction. Furthermore, he said, any judicial tribunal must be independent of the Security Council, and went on to propose the deletion of the draft statute's article 23 (b), which provides that the court will not take action without the Council's go-ahead in any situation the Council has determined to be a threat to or breach of the peace in accordance with Chapter VII of the U.N. Charter.

The U.S. delegate on the Preparatory Committee supported the opting-in, opting-out approach on the grounds that this would maximize the chances of **universal participation in the court.** The Finnish delegate, for his part, asserted that this approach would only "derogate from the idea that the court should take over jurisdiction where national jurisdictions had failed."

On the issue of state consent, it was suggested that the list of states whose consent was required for the court to prosecute—the custodial state, the territorial state, and so forth—should be strictly limited so as not to paralyze the court. Italy's representative suggested focusing on the territorial state, and the U.S. representative expressed concern about including the custodial state in the list of those whose consent would be required for the court to proceed with prosecution. The actual location of the defendant was of little importance, she maintained, and the role of the state in which the defendant happened to be located would be simply to cooperate with the court [U.N. press release L/2774, 4/2/96].

The representative of India remained unconvinced by the argument that the court should have inherent jurisdiction when it comes to the crime of genocide, or any other crime for that matter. Accusing the Preparatory Committee of developing international law through the "back door," he asserted that inherent jurisdiction is not in line with the concept of complementarity or with the principle of state sovereignty. Israel's delegate, for his part, found the term "inherent jurisdiction" contradictory: The jurisdiction of the court would arise out of its statute—a contractual instrument creating the court—and acceptance of the statute should not mean automatic acceptance of the court's jurisdiction. An opting-in arrangement would be in accordance with the contractual nature of the court, he said, leading to broader acceptance of that body.

The delegate of Pakistan spoke of the need for putting strict limits on "trigger mechanisms." Rather than inherent jurisdiction, he said, the court should have consensual jurisdiction [U.N. press release L/2775, 4/3/96]. Chile pointed out that inherent jurisdiction does not have to mean exclusive jurisdiction for the court but can be designed to remove certain pre-consent requirements. Consideration of state sovereignty is important, said Sweden, but when a state ratifies the statute, it should be bound by the jurisdiction of the court. Both the Nuremberg and Tokyo tribunals enjoyed this kind of inherent jurisdiction, noted Switzerland.

The Israeli delegate maintained that prosecution by the court should require the consent not only of the territorial and custodial states but also of the country of which the suspect is a national. Seeing some potential for abuse of this requirement, he went on to advocate "the inclusion of a provision to the effect that prosecution by the court could not begin unless the national jurisdiction concerned had failed to investigate and prosecute properly." Guatemala's delegate pointed out that if there is no state of detention, the requirement of consent of the custodial state is redundant and that such an eventuality should be addressed. He suggested adding to the provision regarding the state of detention the words "if there is such a State." Japan's delegate argued that since each investigation would require a trigger mechanism to establish the court's jurisdiction, there could be no investigation without one.

Indonesia commented that, in order to avoid frivolous cases, only states with a direct interest in a particular matter should be able to lodge a complaint at the court. He added that, once a complaint is lodged, the court's jurisdiction should be invoked only after a thorough investigation. Moreover, the complaining state should be a contracting party of the statute and have accepted the jurisdiction of the court [ibid.].

Some states suggested the prosecutor as a trigger mechanism. The delegates of Jamaica and Denmark, for example, supported the idea that the prosecutor be allowed to initiate an investigation on his own on the basis of any sort of information received from any source. Others proposed regional organizations as trigger mechanisms, although Austria favored having these organizations channel matters to the court indirectly, through the Security Council.

Obviously it has been difficult for states to acknowledge the proposed court's inherent jurisdiction over all core crimes, particularly when some of those crimes are not yet clearly defined. It is equally obvious that without inherent jurisdiction, an international criminal court loses much of its potential value. In the words of France's delegate: Care should be taken to avoid reducing this international jurisdiction into a "supermarket court" in which states can pick and choose (by opting-in and opting-out) the cases that the court may and may not prosecute.

Role of the U.N. Security Council as a Trigger Mechanism

A number of opposing views were expressed on the Preparatory Committee concerning the role of the Council in triggering prosecution by the proposed International Criminal Court. Discussion centered on three paragraphs of article 23 of the draft statute: paragraph 1, allowing the Council to refer matters to the court involving the "core crimes" listed in the statute; paragraph 2, prohibiting the bringing of complaints related to aggression unless the Council has determined that an act of aggression was committed; and paragraph 3, barring the commencement of prosecution in relation to a situation that the Council determines to be a threat to or breach of the peace under Chapter VII of the U.N. Charter until the Council gives its go-ahead.

Several speakers expressed concern that the jurisdiction of the Council and the court should be kept separate and that, in fact, the Council should not have the power to refer matters to the court. The Mexican representative, for instance, saw no reason to involve the Council in the work of the court at all, especially a court that was intended to be permanent, universal, impartial, and independent. The primary concern of Mexico and some others seems to be the potential for Council manipulation of the court, with the effect of politicizing the court's work and reducing its authority. The Libyan representative, for his part, appeared certain that the political nature of the Council would erode the effectiveness of the court and called for the deletion of article 23. **The Council has been a "sword in the hand" of the hegemonic great powers,** he said, and is known to have **applied its own powers selectively;** the great powers should not be allowed to extend their vetoes to the court. Argentina's delegate, agreeing with this sentiment, asked why any government would choose to become party to a treaty that applied to all states parties except the permanent members of the Council.

Still other member states upheld the right of the Council to refer matters to the court but, expressing the belief that the court should never be forced to seek the Council's approval to initiate a prosecution, questioned the need for and desirability of article 23's paragraphs 2 and 3. Greece noted that if the court could act only when the Council decided that aggression had occurred, then the court would be paralyzed in situations in which the Council, for whatever reason, failed to act. Sweden concurred, drawing attention to paragraph 3, with its potential for delaying the action of the court while the Council is seized of a particular matter, and recommending deletion. The implication of paragraph 3, as currently worded, is that the court would be subordinate to the Council in some areas [see U.N. press release L/2777 4/4/96].

The Council's five permanent members emphatically endorsed the draft statute provision for referral by the Council, arguing that the court's statute should not limit the powers of the Council in any way and reminding members of the Preparatory Committee that decisions of the Council, taken on behalf of the international community under Chapter VII, were legally binding. France went so far as to recommend **strengthening the referral provision,** suggesting that the Council be allowed to state its views prior to the initiation of *any action* by the court. The U.S. delegate stated quite bluntly that the Preparatory Committee was not in a position to amend the U.N. Charter and that the Council would continue to exercise authority in matters related to international peace and security. She added that states parties are political entities, that they will remain political entities, that any state lodging a complaint with the court would have some political reasons among its reasons for doing so, and that these would not necessarily be aimed at securing justice. Concluding, she suggested that "the fears of certain delegations regarding the role of the Council under the powers conferred by the draft statute were misplaced" [U.N. press release L/2776, 4/4/96]. This assertion is contested by a number of scholars, who have confirmed that the fears expressed by the great majority of states (largely unrepresented in the Council) about the potential for misuse of power by the Council are probably valid [for a discussion of this issue see José E. Alvarez, "Judging the Security Council," *American Journal of International Law*, 1/1/96].

Powers of the Prosecutor

At the Preparatory Committee, many delegations were in agreement that the prosecutor should be granted the power to initiate investigations based on information received from whatever source, to request national judicial assistance, and to enter into ad hoc arrangements with nonparties that would allow for exchange of information when needed. It was generally felt that the granting of such powers to the prosecutor would enhance the effectiveness of the court. Some others argued that the prosecutor should not be able to initiate prosecutions on his own behalf or without a complaint being lodged by a state party. The representative of Slovenia pointed out that it was hardly possible for any prosecutor to play the role normally played by police in the pre-trial investigations that traditionally launch the prosecution of criminal cases. The prosecutor, he went on to say, should not in any event fill the possible gap in the trigger mechanism [U.N. press release L/2778, 4/4/96].

Participants in the Preparatory Committee were nearly unanimous in opposing the notion of granting the prosecutor power to initiate **on-site investigations** without the participation of relevant national authorities. The United Kingdom, for instance, urged that the prosecutor not be given the power to act on his own initiative within the territory of states and that the prosecutor's investigations be carried out by the national executive or judicial authorities operating under national law. It was widely held, however, that the prosecutor could be allowed to participate in a state-approved on-site inspection [U.N. press release L/2782, 4/9/96].

Observers have noted that there are circumstances under which national authorities might not be required, e.g., when nationals are willing to volunteer evidence to the court. And the statute would have to make provision for situations in which national authorities were no longer functioning (as in the case of **"failed states"**) [U.N. press release L/2781, 4/9/96].

The Nonretroactivity Principle

Another controversial issue debated by the Preparatory Committee was the need for an explicit statement of the principle of nonretroactivity in the statute of the proposed International Criminal Court. The International Law Commission's draft statute did not include one. Some state representatives on the Committee noted that there can be criminal responsibility for an act only if such an act was a crime at the time it was committed. Further, this principle of nonretroactivity is akin to the universal concept of *nullum crimen sine lege* (no crime without law) and should be clearly fixed in the statute of the proposed International Criminal Court *and* applied the very moment the statute enters into force [U.N. press release L/2769, 3/28/96].

Individual and Corporate Criminal Responsibility

There was also near-unanimity in the Preparatory Committee on the need to include in the statute a clause about individual responsibility, and some participants pointed out that certain provisions of article 7 of the International Criminal Tribunal for the Former Yugoslavia and some provisions of article 6 of the Rwanda Tribunal could guide the drafting of such a clause. The inclusion of an individual responsibility clause would mean, in effect, that **no one could use the fact that he or she occupied an official position to avoid being assigned responsibility for the crimes committed.** An issue yet to be resolved is whether assigning individual responsibility for a crime means that the state in which the individual holds citizenship has been absolved from responsibility. At the Preparatory Committee, the delegates of several states, including those of the United States and India, called for a fuller explanation of the principle of individual responsibility in the statute, to serve as a guide for the court and avoid giving it the job of determining those elements.

It became clear, though, that most participants in the preparatory process would not grant immunity from prosecution by the court to any official alleged to have committed one of the core crimes against humanity. Just because a person holds an official government position, said India, does not mean that he or she is absolved of responsibility for the crimes committed [U.N. press release L/2769, 3/29/96].

This discussion led to others about whether the court should allow a **statute of limitations,** about whether the court would be allowed to **prosecute corporations,** and under what circumstances, if any, individuals should be granted **immunity from prosecution.** On the statute of limitations issue, several delegates expressed the view that, given the exceptional gravity of the suggested "core crimes" to be adjudicated by the proposed International Criminal Court, "no statute of limitations should be allowed." France agreed that there should be no statute of limitations for such crimes as genocide but insisted on one for lesser crimes. Japan rejected this position, arguing that statutes of limitation were an important principle of criminal law in all cases—and even more so in cases of exceptional gravity: The graver the crime, the more important the role of due process. Typically, the Canadian delegate suggested a compromise: The court would declare no fixed statute of limitations but would allow accused persons to appeal to the court if they thought that the passage of time might prejudice their right to a fair trial. The court would thus be empowered to make a determination on a case-by-case basis.

Even more contentious was the Preparatory Committee debate over the issue of corporate criminal responsibility. Portugal felt that the court should be free to pursue the prosecution of corporations, while South Africa and Israel were strenuously opposed to allowing the proposed International Criminal Court to do any such thing. Canada pointed out the unlikelihood of the court ever handling a case in which a corporation was accused of committing any of the crimes envisaged in the draft statute. Even if a corporation were somehow involved in one of the "core crimes," it was more likely that the individuals who ran it would be deemed liable in their individual capacities. The U.S. delegate noted that it was still important to consider including the criminal liability of corporations in the area of restitution, since some corporations could indeed benefit from crimes in the jurisdiction of the court and might well be assessed a certain liability [ibid.].

Processes for Provisional Arrest of Persons Accused of Serious International Crimes

The need for draft statute articles concerning arrest, pre-trial detention or release, cooperation and judicial assistance, and the transfer of accused persons was emphasized at the 20th meeting of the First Session of the Preparatory Committee on Establishment of an International Criminal Court.

According to a paper by Canada outlining such articles, the court prosecutor would transmit a warrant to the requested state along with practical information regarding the accused person's identity and location. If the arrest took place before indictment, then the prosecutor would transmit the indictment to the requested state as soon as possible. States receiving a warrant or pre-indictment would act on the warrant or initiate equivalent national procedures. The authorities of **custody states** would be expected to respect the rights of accused persons and determine the issue of "interim release" pending indictment. Once a person surrendered to the jurisdiction of the court, the court itself could make determinations with regard to interim release pending trial. States would be obliged to surrender individuals—either by transfer or by extradition—upon request by the International Court. States deciding between the competing requests of national courts and the International Court would take into account the relative seriousness of the offenses, the relative strength of the case, the time and place of the commission of the offenses, the respective dates of the requests, the nationality of the person sought, and the ordinary place of residence of the person concerned. In situations in which the requested state was a party to the court, it would give priority to the court's request for extradition over the requests of other states [U.N. press release L/2780, 4/9/96].

The need for a balance between the court's ability to carry out its mandate and the need for **protection of accused individuals from abuses and/or errors** was highlighted by France's representative on the Committee. He expressed a preference for a 40-day limit on provisional arrest pending transfer, as opposed to the 90 days proposed in the statute; and he argued that, when it came to applying the court statute on arrest and surrender, states should apply their laws within the framework of their own constitution. In France, for example, judges would have to verify the procedural legality of an extradition request. What might prohibit transfer in the French case were manifest error on the part of the court and a statute of limitations in indictments for war crimes [ibid.].

The U.S. representative suggested that when it came to issuing "provisional arrest" and post-indictment warrants, the statute should insist that evidentiary support be provided along with requests for transfer and extradition; and countries should advise the court in advance of what these evidentiary requirements will be. Accused persons have the basic right to be advised of the reason why they were being pursued by the court, but states should be able to waive evidentiary and other requirements, if permitted to do so under national law. The evidentiary requirements of requested states should be no more stringent than they are for any partner in an extradition treaty. If persons other than the accused (witnesses, for example) are required by the court, the court should have flexibility to receive testimony from outside its seat. *Pace* the draft statute, however, the United States maintained that detention prior to surrender—including bail and provisional release—should be determined by national authorities, not the International Court.

Thailand noted the importance of making the **request for extradition** in writing and transmitting it through diplomatic channels; such a request might include a description of the accused and a brief description of the offense. It was also deemed important that, **once arraigned,** the accused is sent before a proper court without delay, and if the arraignment itself does not take place within a certain period, the accused should be set free. Australia insisted that pre-indictment arrest be undertaken only if a formal request for extradition was expected to follow. It was suggested that **witnesses** who did not wish to appear in person before the court be given such options as a video or telephone link-up, and that all persons other than the accused be compelled to appear before the International Criminal Court only in exceptional cases (although indirect compulsion, such as the threat of fine or imprisonment, could be utilized as a prod).

Finland suggested the incorporation of a **"rule of specialty"**—to the effect that persons transferred to the court could be prosecuted only for the crimes for which they were transferred—into the procedural rules governing arrest and pre-trial detention [ibid.]. Some other delegates argued that this rule is sound but should be more flexible: There may be some good reasons why the prosecution has decided to shift the charge from the crime for which the person was transferred to another, and the statute should make provision for that eventuality [see Brunei's position in U.N. press release L/2781, 4/9/96].

Since the International Criminal Court would have neither territory nor police force, the Japanese delegate pointed out, the court would require the cooperation of states and would have to acknowledge and respect the constitutional requirements of those states. Given the uniqueness of the court, Slovenia added, existing systems of cooperation would not operate automatically, and it would be idealistic to expect that states whose constitutions proscribed extradition, for instance, would amend their constitutions to accommodate the court. For all such reasons, several delegates agreed, it would be necessary for the statute to set out, clearly and comprehensively, its **expectations of cooperation by the states.** Any exceptions to the requirement to cooperate with the court would also be set out in the statute—although this obviously could not include the argument that the state is prevented by its constitution from delivering its nationals. Argentina would allow only one basis for noncooperation: inadmissibility of the evidence against the accused [U.N. press release L/2780, 4/9/96], subscribing to the belief that the greater the number of reservations to cooperation with the court, the greater the likelihood of defeating the purpose for which the court was set up.

Judicial Assistance to the Court

Consensus emerged in the Preparatory Committee about the obligation of states parties to provide judicial assistance to the court. Several delegates suggested that the statute itself should offer a detailed listing of the types of judicial (and other) assistance that states might be expected to render, allowing them to preview their obligations under the statute and, as required by some states, signaling the need for domestic legislation to make such assistance possible. The list would not have to be exhaustive, since there is no anticipating all future needs [U.N. press release L/2782, 4/9/96], and it is quite possible that the proposed International Criminal Court would be requesting judicial assistance of a kind different from that which states provide to each other. In the meantime, minimum standards could be established in an exemplary manner in the statute (e.g., regarding search, seizure, surrender, and interviews of witnesses). And it would be useful, said a number of delegates at the Preparatory Committee, if parties to the statute of the proposed International Criminal Court were to designate particular national authorities to receive the court's requests for judicial assistance, streamlining the handling of requests from the court.

There might be some reasons for states to limit the provision of assistance—for example, in cases in which the national judicial system was currently investigating the same matter and in cases involving essential national security interests. But such exceptions would have to be circumscribed and should be stated, up front, in the statute [U.N. press release L/2781, 4/9/96]. What of the case in which a state simply refused to provide judicial assistance to the court? In such situations, said France, a special chamber of the court could decide whether the refusal was justified and, if found to be otherwise, the prosecutor would be empowered to act on his own initiative [U.N. press release L/2782, 4/9/96].

Acts of Omission, Negligence, and Conspiracy

Many participants in the Preparatory Committee stressed the need to ensure that the statute reconciles common law concepts, such as intention, gross negligence, and conspiracy, with their analogous civil law concepts, *culpa, dolus eventualis, and complot.* Such reconciliation would guarantee that omissions, negligence, and conspiracy that result in crimes falling within the jurisdiction of the proposed International Criminal Court would be punishable under its statute. Debate on the issue of **whether causation should be a factor in international criminal liability,** however, proved contentious. Some delegates felt that it was unnecessary to include provisions on causation and, in fact, that these might burden the statute: Since criminal responsibility would exist only if traceable to a defendant, a provision on causation was unnecessary. In response to calls for a clear definition of intention, the Canadian delegation offered one that attempts to deal with civil and common law concepts of intent and implies that knowledge is a cornerstone of criminal liability. There were suggestions too that the statute provide for the prosecution of "willful blindness"—that is, cases in which a defendant's knowledge is clearly manifest but he or she has simply turned a blind eye. Switzerland argued that special intention must be determined in such cases as genocide but that a determination of intention may not be required when it comes to prosecuting other grave breaches of international law [U.N. press release L/2770, 3/29/96].

Consideration of Age of Responsibility and Possible Defenses

There was near-unanimity in the Preparatory Committee that an age of responsibility should be specified in the statute, although there was disagreement over what that age ought to be. Each country's suggestion of a specific age for criminal responsibility seemed to coincide with the age noted in its own penal codes: Switzerland, for instance, opted for 16 as the age of responsibility for the purpose of mitigation and 18 as the age of full responsibility; France made a case for assigning 13 as the age of criminal responsibility.

The United States asserted that **"relationship crimes"**—such as complicity, aiding, abetting, soliciting, and acting as an accessory—could all be combined in one article, the overriding rules being that all participants have the intent and purpose of committing a crime, that they share equal responsibility, and that the type of activities giving rise to that responsibility is specified [ibid.].

Regarding the **type of defenses** that might be mounted before the proposed International Criminal Court, it was generally agreed that any listing of such defenses in the statute should include a note to the effect that the list is not exhaustive or exclusive, which would permit the court to allow others in the future. Malaysia, Germany, and China registered objections to this, arguing that to allow an inexhaustive list would be to give the court legislative powers. Such matters as self-defense and the use of intoxication as a defense were also addressed, with different conclusions reached in each case. There appeared to be general agreement that the issue of self-defense should be dealt with in the statute but that the use of intoxication as a defense should be left to the court.

Recognition of International Criminal Court Judgments

Most participants in the work of the Preparatory Committee took the position that states that become parties to the statute automatically recognize the decisions and judgments of the proposed International Criminal Court. The representative of the Netherlands went further: The judgments of the court, he said, should be treated as judgments rendered by the states' own judiciaries, and he asked that the statute provide a rule of **"burden-sharing,"** obliging states to carry out the verdict of the court. Other delegations were of the opinion that the sentences handed down by the International Criminal Court should not be considered as "foreign statements" that have to be translated into national law but should be recognized automatically by states parties.

The French representative pointed out that some difficulties might arise with sentences involving **fines and restitution.** And how will the international community address questions related to **parole and par-**

don? In certain countries the head of state has a constitutional right to pardon convicted prisoners (if France, for instance, accepted an international criminal convicted by the court, the President of France would be expected to reserve the right to pardon the incarcerated individual). With regard to **parole,** the Jamaican delegate recommended that the states parties to the statute create a body to deal with this and other questions that normally involve extralegal considerations.

Other constitutional concerns were raised by the delegates of Ireland and the United States. Under Irish jurisdiction, it was noted, murder is punished by life imprisonment but the punishment for manslaughter makes provision for parole. How would such constitutional issues be settled? Indeed, could one consider pardoning perpetrators of such "unpardonable" international crimes as genocide? Decisions about the type and length of punishment, it seemed to many delegates, should not be left to the individual incarcerating state [U.N. press release L/2783, 4/10/96]. It will also be important for state prison systems to comply with international norms of incarceration.

2. War Crimes and U.N. Ad Hoc Tribunals

The precedent for creation of war crimes tribunals was the Nuremberg trials of 1945–46—218 days of hearings that sought to assess the responsibility of individual government officials for initiating acts of war that resulted in massive abuses of human rights. Hermann Göring, Rudolf Hess, and Albert Speer, among others, achieved their notoriety in the process. The trial produced 12 death sentences, 3 acquittals, and 7 prison terms ranging from 10 years to life [see Kenneth Anderson, "Nuremberg Sensibility: Telford Taylor's Memoir of the Nuremberg Trials," 7 *Harvard International Law Review* (1994)].

Germany was the loser of the war, the vanquished, and it had been relatively easy for the international community to gain access to those accused of war crimes [see "War's Crimes and Punishments, Then and Now," *New York Times*, 11/20/96]. This has proven more difficult today, as witness the attempts of the Ad Hoc International War Crimes Tribunals for the former Yugoslavia and for Rwanda to bring to trial some of the alleged perpetrators of war crimes in these arenas. At the same time, a number of questions are being raised about the legitimacy—and lasting value—of ad hoc judicial bodies established by the U.N. Security Council [see José E. Alvarez, "Nuremberg Revisited: The Tadic Case," scheduled for publication in the *European Journal of International Law*, 1996]. The U.N. Secretary-General admits that expediency or "urgency" was behind his decision to bypass the normal treaty route in establishing the two tribunals [see Secretary-General's Report Pursuant to Paragraph 2 of the Security Council Resolution 808, S/25704, 5/3/93].

Former Yugoslavia

Security Council Resolution 808 of February 23, 1993 called for the establishment of an international tribunal for the prosecution of persons responsible for serious violations of international humanitarian law committed in the territory of the former Yugoslavia since 1991. Resolution 827 of May 25 created the tribunal itself. At the same time, the Council adopted a **statute for the tribunal,** in accordance with which the General Assembly elected (on September 17) 11 judges to serve a four-year term.

Financing the work of the tribunal was estimated at $31.2 million for the first full year and $33.2 million for the 1994–95 biennium, to be financed through assessed contributions of U.N. member states outside the regular U.N. budget. Members were encouraged to make voluntary contributions to the tribunal both in cash and in kind as well, and a trust fund was set up to receive them [United Nations reference paper, "The UN and the Situation in the Former Yugoslavia," 3/15/94, and Add.1, 2/23/95]. In February 1996, after considering the report of the Secretary-General on the financing of the International Tribunal for former Yugoslavia [A/C.5/50/41] and a related report by the Chairman of the Advisory Committee on Administrative and Budgetary Questions [A/C.5/50/SR.42], the General Assembly decided to appropriate to the Special Account for the International Tribunal the amount of $8,619,500 gross ($7,637,500 net) for the first quarter of 1996, allowing the tribunal to continue its activities. It also decided to waive, as an ad hoc and exceptional arrangement, member states' respective shares in the remaining credits arising from previous budgets of the U.N. Protection Force (UNPROFOR) in the amount of $4,309,750 gross ($3,818,750 net) and accept an equivalent increase in the assessment for a future budget period of the Force in the same amount, to be transferred to the Special Account for the International Tribunal from the Special Account for UNPROFOR, as established in General Assembly Resolution 46/233 (1992). Further, the Assembly apportioned the amount of $4,309,750 gross ($3,818,750 net) for the period January 1–March 31, 1996, among member states in accordance with the scale of assessments for the year 1996, and decided, with respect to Assembly Resolution 973 X of 1955, to set off against the apportionment among member states their respective shares in the Tax Equalization Fund of the estimated staff assessment income of $491,000 for the International Tribunal for the same period [A/Res/50/212].

The **first trial** by the War Crimes Tribunal opened in The Hague on October 9, 1995, **without the defendant present.** He is Dragan Nikolic, a Bosnian Serb commander at the Susica prison camp charged with the murder and torture of 10 prison inmates as well as with the illegal detention and mistreatment of 500 of the estimated 8,000 Bosnian Muslims held at that camp between April and September 1992. Serb authorities refused to hand him over to the tribunal despite mounting evidence against him, including evidence produced by a Serbian guard at the Susica prison camp [*New York Times*, 10/10/95].

Also **indicted by the tribunal but still at large** is General Ratko Mladic, commander of the Bosnian Serbs, who is accused of some of the worst atrocities seen in Europe since World War II, including the deaths of literally thousands of Bosnian Muslims. Troops of the U.S. Army's First Armored Division have avoided the Han Pijesak area, Mladic's base of operations, just as NATO forces have failed to effect the capture of Croatian militia leader Ivica Rajic, indicted by the tribunal for killing 16 Muslim civilians in an "ethnic-cleansing" campaign in 1993. As of June 28, 1996, the tribunal had indicted for war crimes in the former Yugoslavia 75 people, the vast majority of whom are Serbs. Only seven were being held [*New York Times*, 6/28/96] in the court's 24-cell detention center in The Hague [*Washington Post*, 5/8/96], despite repeated vows by, prominently, the President of the United States that American forces would help to bring them to justice [see, for example, "G.I.'s in Bosnia Shun Hunt for War-Crime Suspects," *New York Times*, 3/2/96]. And one Bosnian Serb, Goran Lajic, suspected of war crimes at the Keraterm prison camp, has been freed by the tribunal because of possible mistaken identity [*New York Times*, 6/18/96].

Indicted too but at large are Dario Kordic, a Bosnian Croat political leader and accused mass murderer, who has been living openly in southwestern Bosnia, near the Croatian border, within reach of local authorities and the European police officers in the area; General Tihomir Blaskic, who was promoted to a top position in the Croatian army by President Franjo Tudjman on November 14, 1995, the day after he was indicted by the tribunal; and Bosnian Serb civilian leader Radovan Karadzic, who on several occasions passed right under the noses of some of NATO's 60,000 troops without being arrested. The head of the Danish peacekeeping troops in Bosnia, General Finn Saermark-Thomsen, has been quoted as saying that his troops would not be involved in such arrests, despite the Clinton administration's insistence that NATO troops are under orders to arrest suspected war criminals.

The **reluctance of the U.S. contingent of NATO forces to arrest those indicted for war crimes** seems to have much to do with fear of **"mission creep"**—the notion that U.S. peacekeepers could be dragged into a situation similar to the one they faced in Somalia, when 18 American soldiers were killed during the pursuit of faction leader General Mohammed Farah Aidid [*Economist*, 2/17/96]; and defense officials confirm that "the spectre of Somalia hangs over this place." The Pentagon is also concerned that the arrest of major Bosnian Serb leaders suspected of war crimes could result in NATO troops being tagged anti-Serbian, a label that could jeopardize not only the safety of the troops but also the entire peace effort [*New York Times*, 3/2/96]. Underlying this public show of weakness by U.S. and NATO forces too is a certain skittishness—of European countries in particular about strengthening the Muslim regime of Bosnia.

The effect of such attitudes—especially in the absence of an international enforcement capability—is to render certain aspects of international law quite meaningless. To ignore the indictments also goes against the belief, expressed by historians, jurists, and other close observers of the human scene, that there can be no meaningful peace without justice. If individuals charged with mass murder are not brought to justice, the cycle of violence is very likely to repeat itself, said Chief War Crimes Prosecutor Richard Goldstone not long after the first trial began [cited by Anthony Lewis in *New York Times*, 11/20/96].

The lawyers and researchers in the Office of the Prosecutor of the International Criminal Tribunal for the Former Yugoslavia have estimated that 200,000 people have been killed in the Balkan conflict and that the cases of murder, rape, torture, and kidnapping can be counted in the many thousands [Franke Wilmer, "Fragmented Self/Fragmented Society: Identity, Conflict and Civil Society in the Balkans," paper presented at the International Studies Conference, San Diego, 4/96, p. 1].

Also mostly honored in the breach have been the **provisions of the Dayton peace accord of December 1995 calling on the signatories to turn over to the international tribunal all indicted persons found within their borders.** Back in December 1995, in fact, Bosnian Croat authorities *released* from jail military commander Ivica Rajic, the first Croat to be charged by the tribunal and the first person to be held accountable for the October 23, 1993, massacre in the Muslim village of Stupni Do during fighting between the predominantly Muslim government forces and the Croat militias for territorial control in central Bosnia. U.N. troops and Western reporters, arriving on the scene shortly after the fighting ended, witnessed the gruesome aftereffect: mutilation, death, and destruction. Based on the U.N.'s investigation, Rajic "knew or had reason to know" that his troops were about to attack the village, had done nothing to stop them, and had failed to punish those responsible for the massacre. For that, the tribunal has indicted him on three counts: willful killing, destruction of property, and "deliberate attack on the civilian population and wanton destruction of the village." Rajic was arrested by Bosnian Croat authorities on separate murder charges of killing five fellow members of the Croat Defense Council but was acquitted on these charges by a Bosnian Croat judge because of a lack of evidence and allowed to go free—this even after a post-Dayton promise by the leader of the Bosnian-Croat Frederation, Kresimir Zubak, that Rajic would be turned over to the U.N. War Crimes Tribunal [*New York Times*, 12/8/95].

On June 9, 1996, the Croatian police announced the arrest of Zlatko Aleksovski, one of six Bosnian Croats charged by the tribunal with killing

Muslims in Bosnia's Lasva valley three years before. Four of the men indicted with him, notes the *New York Times* [6/10/96], continue to live openly in Croatia and one is under house arrest in The Hague. The *Times* report of the arrest suggests that the Croatian government reluctantly threw the tribunal a relatively small fish after it was denied membership in the Council of Europe, which cited its failure to arrest people charged with war crimes.

Meanwhile, on January 30, 1996, the Muslim-led Bosnian government arrested eight Bosnian Serbs, including a general (Djordje Djukic) and a colonel (Aleska Krsmanovic) suspected of war crimes, who were on their way to a meeting with NATO officers in a suburb of Sarajevo to discuss the transfer of certain buildings to the NATO peacekeeping force [*New York Times*, 2/6/96]. The suspects were flown to the Netherlands for questioning by members of the tribunal [ibid., 2/13/96]. The indictment on June 27, 1996 of eight other Bosnian Serb military and police officers in connection with rapes of Muslim women marks the first time in history that sexual assault has been treated separately as a crime of war [ibid., 6/28/96].

It was not until June 13, 1996, that the Bosnian government sent to The Hague to stand trial two "Muslim prison camp officials accused of murdering and raping Bosnian Serb inmates," Hasim Delic and Esad Landzo, **the first time that a signatory to the Bosnian peace accord has extradicted nationals already indicted for war crimes** [Associated Press, 5/13/96; *New York Times*, 6/14/96].

Early in 1996 there had been indications that NATO would begin to provide **security for human rights investigators looking into evidence of war crimes** throughout the former Yugoslavia. Under the terms of the Dayton accord, the 60,000-member force was expected only to supervise the marking of cease-fire lines and ensure that the rival forces drew back from those lines. The investigators believe that exhumation of the graves—containing the bodies of up to 2,700 Muslim civilians, U.S. intelligence sources say—is crucial to finding out what happened after the fall of Srebrenica and to prosecute successfully those responsible for this mass slaughter [*Christian Science Monitor*, 12/14/95].

On January 12, 1996, citing reports that Bosnian Serbs were using a vast open-pit mine in northern Bosnia as a grave for thousands of Muslim and Croat victims of "ethnic cleansing," U.S. Defense Secretary William Perry announced that NATO-led troops would secure all suspected mass graves in Srebrenica so that bodies could be exhumed in the spring for use as evidence. Those who had been exploring the site were being arrested by Bosnian Serbs, and the Perry announcement noted that human rights investigators would be provided with military escorts as they went about their tasks. There are 15 or 20 such sites in Bosnia to be examined by the human rights investigators who are gathering the evidence that will indicate whether or not the Bosnian Serbs carried out a deliberate policy of genocide against Muslims and Croats [*New York Times*, 1/13/96].

A week after Perry's announcement, however, NATO appeared to back away from this commitment to aid the U.N. War Crimes Tribunal investigation. The senior NATO commander, General George A. Joulwan, and NATO Secretary-General Javier Solana, while maintaining that the primary mission of NATO forces was to create an overall secure environment for the tribunal, nonetheless **ruled out the possibility (envisioned by Judge Goldstone) of having NATO troops guard suspected sites.** This brought into the open the deep divison between the needs of the War Crimes Tribunal—to enforce international law—and the core responsibilities of the NATO forces in Bosnia—to keep the peace and secure the cease-fire arrangement [ibid., 1/28/96].

The International Tribunal investigating war crimes in the former Yugoslavia (and the tribunal for Rwanda) is also facing a time of transition—from one **Chief Prosecutor, Judge Goldstone,** who has been credited with making the war crimes prosecutions a cornerstone of the Dayton peace accord [ibid.], to another. His replacement is a relatively unknown, respected Canadian jurist, **Louise Arbour,** a judge of the Ontario Court of Appeals and an expert in criminal law [S/Res/1047, 2/29/96]. Judge Goldstone had made it clear from the time of his appointment that he would eventually return to his post on the newly created South African Constitutional Court. His resignation is effective October 1996.

Whether the **U.N. financial crisis** will be an ongoing factor in the work of the ad hoc tribunals remains to be seen. In September 1995 a temporary freeze on traveling and hiring imposed by the U.N. Secretary-General had the effect of imposing limits on the tribunals' ability to investigate dozens of cases, including the charges against two men near the top of the Yugoslavia tribunal's "most-wanted" list: Radovan Karadzic, de facto political leader of the self-proclaimed Serbian Republic, and General Ratko Mladic, its military commander. This budget crunch was linked directly to the failure of the United States and other U.N. members to pay their dues in full and on time [see *Boston Globe*, 9/29/95, and *New York Times*, 10/4/95].

On July 11, 1996—the first anniversary of the massacres in Srebrenica in which the two are accused of having played a part—the tribunal issued an international warrant for the arrest of Karadzic and Mladic. This provides additional legal backing for their arrest and extradition, and puts pressure on the international community to assist in bringing them to trial in The Hague.

Rwanda

In late 1994 the Security Council created a similar ad hoc tribunal for Rwanda, officially "the International Criminal Tribunal for the Prosecution of Persons Responsible for Genocide and Other Serious Violations of International Humanitarian Law Committed in the Territory of Rwanda and Rwandan citizens responsible for genocide and other such violations committed in the territory of Neighbouring States between 1 January and 31 December 1994" [S/Res/995, 11/8/94]. **Arusha, Tanzania,** was chosen as its seat. The inauguration of the tribunal for Rwanda, on June 27, 1995, was accompanied by an appeal to the world to help bring to justice those responsible for the deaths of hundreds of thousands of Rwandans. Judge Laity Kama of Senegal and Judge Yakov Ostrovsky of Russia were elected President and Vice President, respectively [*New York Times*, 6/28/95].

To **finance the work** of this tribunal, the General Assembly appropriated $7,609,900 gross ($7,090,600 net) for the first quarter of 1996 [A/Res/50/213]. The same resolution approved an ad hoc arrangement, similar to the one approved for the Yugoslav tribunal—in the Rwandan case, allowing member states to waive their respective shares of the credits arising from previous budgets of the U.N. Assistance Mission for Rwanda. Here, too, member states were encouraged to make voluntary contributions to the tribunal. In early June the General Assembly allotted an additional $32.5 million to the tribunal for 1996 [A/50/852/Add.2].

On February 19, 1996, the U.N. War Crimes Tribunal for Rwanda indicted two Rwandans in jail in Zambia on charges of genocide. The indictments were **the first to be handed down against people who, because they were already under arrest, seemed likely to be extradited and to stand trial** [*New York Times*, 2/20/96]. One of these men, Georges Rutaganda, was vice president of the Interahamwe, a Hutu militia that carried out the mass killings of Tutsis in Kigali and Nyanza. He had been a high-ranking official in the majority Hutu government and a major investor in RTLM Radio, which broadcast messages of hate against the Tutsi minority in the period before the outbreak of ethnic slaughter. The second suspect is Jean Paul Akayesu, a former mayor of Tapa in the Gitarama prefecture, who is believed to have encouraged the murder of a Tutsi teacher in Tapa in April 1994, which itself set off widespread killings of Tutsis. Akayesu is also thought to have ordered the killings of several people near his office and to have supervised the torture and beatings of Tutsi residents. The indictment of these two men set the stage for the first trial to stem from the 1994 massacres in Rwanda, in which an estimated 500,000 (the majority of them Tutsi) died. Tutsi forces eventually drove out the Hutu government (as well as hundreds of thousands of Hutus, fearing reprisals for the massacre of Tutsis) and formed a new government [ibid.].

The Zambian, Belgian, and Swiss governments have detained at least a dozen people suspected of leading the genocide in Rwanda, but the **tribunal investigators have received little help from the governments of neighboring states,** prominently Kenya and Zaire, where many of the leaders of the former Rwandan Hutu government are now living. One of them, François Karera, a former mayor of Kigali, is considered a key figure in the genocidal attacks [ibid., 12/31/95].

Human rights officials tracking the whereabouts of Rwandans involved in the genocide have noted that some 10,000 Rwandan refugees now live in Kenya and that the country undoubtedly benefits financially from the presence of a good number of wealthy and powerful members of the former Hutu government. Kenyan President Daniel T. arap Moi's offer of protection to these people not only undermines the work of the tribunal but also undercuts the long-term viability of the new Rwandan government, not to mention the prospects for peace in the region [ibid., 10/6/95]. Indeed, President Moi has stated openly that he will reject any summonses from the tribunal body and will arrest any members of that body who enter the country. He claims he is not against the tribunal and would cooperate if its mandate was broadened to include an investigation into the deaths of President Cyprien Ntaryamira of Burundi and President Juvénal Habyarimana of Rwanda in an as-yet-unexplained plane crash in April 1994—the event that was followed by the Hutu orgy of violence—and an investigation into the invasion of Rwanda in October 1990 by a Tutsi-dominated rebel force backed by President Yoweri Museveni of Uganda. Said President Moi: "To ignore this vital aspect and to concentrate on the period after the deaths of the two presidents would be superficial and a miscarriage of justice" [ibid., 10/8/95]. Some U.N. officials have suggested that the international donor community's suspension of desperately needed financial and technical aid could help to bring Kenya around [ibid., 10/6/95].

By the first week of June 1996, the U.N. War Crimes Tribunal for Rwanda had in custody 18 Rwandans suspected of genocidal activities in 1994, the majority of them Hutus [Associated Press, 6/5/96]. Three of this number were being held at the tribunal's headquarters in Tanzania; ten were under detention in Cameroon but expected to be transferred to the tribunal's care; and five had been arrested in Europe. Among those detained in Cameroon is Theonest Bagosora, a former defense minister and camp commander suspected of the torture and murder of ten Belgian U.N. peacekeepers by Rwandan presidential guards. He is wanted by Belgium as well [ibid.]. It should be noted that the two-year-old Rwandan government has 76,000 people in squalid jails throughout the country—most of them arrested on genocide charges [*New York Times*, 6/24/96].

3. The International Court of Justice

On April 18, 1996, at its seat in The Hague, the International Court of Justice (ICJ, or World Court) held a Special Sitting in the presence of Her Majesty the Queen of the Netherlands to commemorate **the Court's 50th**

anniversary. The body's President, Judge Mohammed Bedjaoui, delivered a commemorative address, and there were statements by General Assembly President Diogo Freitas do Amaral and Netherlands Minister of Foreign Affairs Hans van Mierlo.

The ICJ, principal judicial organ of the United Nations (replacing in 1946 the Permanent Court of International Justice), has been given a dual mandate: to settle in accordance with international law the legal disputes referred to it by states and to give advisory opinions on legal questions submitted to it by duly authorized international organs and agencies. The Court is composed of 15 judges (no more than one judge per nationality) elected to nine-year terms by the U.N. General Assembly and the Security Council. Elections are held every three years for a third of the seats; retiring judges may be reelected. At the **death of Judge Andreas Aguilar Mawdsley of Venezuela** on October 24, 1995, the Security Council initiated the process of electing a replacement to serve the remainder of the Judge's term [U.N. press release SC/6121, 11/7/95]. The position went to fellow-countryman **Gonzalo Parra-Aranguren.**

Eight contentious cases and two requests for an advisory opinion are currently before the Court. The **pending cases** are Maritime Delimitation and Territorial Questions between Qatar and Bahrain (**Qatar v. Bahrain;** see *Issues/50*); Questions of Interpretation and Application of the 1971 Montreal Convention arising from the Aerial Incident at Lockerbie (**Libya v. United Kingdom,** and **Libya v. United States;** see *Issues/47*); Oil Platforms (**Iran v. United States;** see *Issues/48*); Application of the Convention on the Prevention and Punishment of the Crime of Genocide (**Bosnia and Herzegovina v. Serbia and Montenegro;** see *Issues/48* and *Issues/49*); Gabcikovo-Nagymaros Project (**Hungary v. Slovakia;** see *Issues/49*); Land and Maritime Boundary between Cameroon and Nigeria (**Cameroon v. Nigeria;** see *Issues/49*), and Fisheries Jurisdiction (**Spain v. Canada;** see *Issues/50*).

A public sitting was held on September 11, 1995, in the case of **New Zealand v. France,** regarding France's nuclear tests on the Mururoa and Fangataufa atolls in the South Pacific. New Zealand had approached the Court once before, in 1973, to request legal protection from France's intention to conduct nuclear tests, but in December 1974, France announced that it no longer intended to conduct those tests. When a new French government under Jacques Chirac had a change of heart, New Zealand requested that the Court declare the tests a violation under international law of the rights of New Zealand and other states, since these tests introduce radioactive material into the marine environment. The Court was also asked to declare it unlawful for France to have conducted those tests before undertaking a proper environmental impact assessment according to accepted international standards. Subsequent to New Zealand's application, Australia, Samoa, Solomon Islands, Marshall Islands, and Federated States of Micronesia filed similar applications with the Court [U.N. press release ICJ/540, 9/11/95].

The Court dismissed the requests of the above states on the grounds that they did not fall within the provisions of paragraph 63 of the Judgment of the Court of December 20, 1974, in the Nuclear Test case (New Zealand v. France). The 1974 judgment, the Court said, was made on the basis on France's undertaking not to conduct any further atmospheric nuclear tests, and only a resumption of nuclear tests in the atmosphere would have affected it. Because the 1995 tests were not atmospheric nuclear tests, the requests of New Zealand and the others could not be acted upon [U.N. press release ICJ/541, 9/22/95].

The 21 **advisory opinions** handed down by the ICJ in its 50-year history have had to do with such matters as admission to U.N. membership, reparation for injuries sustained in the service of the Organization, the territorial status of South-West Africa (now Namibia), expenses of certain U.N. operations, and the applicability of the U.N. Headquarters Agreement. Of the two recent requests for advisory opinion currently pending, one, made by the World Health Organization (WHO), concerns the Legality of the Use by a State of Nuclear Weapons in Armed Conflict—"would the use of nuclear weapons by a state in war or other armed conflict be a breach of its obligations under international law, including the WHO Constitution?"—and the other, by the U.N. General Assembly, asks about the Legality of the Threat of Nuclear Weapons [ICJ, *Communiqué* No. 96/14, 4/2/96; and see *Issues/50*].

The Court's unanimous finding, which delighted disarmament lobbyists when reported in the press in early July 1996, was that "a threat or use of force by means of nuclear weapons . . . is unlawful" if it contravenes U.N. Charter provisions for the protection of territorial integrity and political independence [*Financial Times*, 7/9/96]. On the threat or use of nuclear weapons in the case of self-defense, where the very survival of the state is at stake, the advisory opinion was less clear cut. "After a seven-seven split," wrote the *Financial Times*, the tie-breaking vote of presiding judge Mohammed Bedjaoui of Algeria "carried a recommendation that 'the threat or use of nuclear weapons would generally be contrary to the rules of international law applicable in armed conflict, and in particular the principles and rules of humanitarian law' " [ibid.]. Noted Judge Bedjaoui, "The Court cannot conclude definitively whether the threat or use of nuclear weapons would be lawful or unlawful in an extreme circumstance of self-defense" [*New York Times*, 7/9/96].

4. Space Law

The General Assembly established the **Committee on the Peaceful Uses of Outer Space** in the late 1950s, following the Soviet Union's launch of the first earth satellite. The Committee's 1995 annual report [A/50/20] describes its continuing efforts to ensure that the exploration and use of outer space will be only for the betterment of mankind and will benefit states whatever their stage of economic or scientific development. The document also reviews the reports of the Committee's Scientific and Technical Subcommittee and Legal Subcommittee and addresses questions relating to some of the spin-off benefits of space technology (affecting, for example, industrial measurement and control, image and data processing, medicine, computer systems, robotics, power generation, special materials and chemicals, water treatment, public safety, consumer goods, manufacturing, and refrigeration). And the report offers another chapter in the continuing saga of **Unispace III**—the would-be third U.N. Conference on the Exploration and Peaceful Uses of Outer Space, the holding of which is opposed by the United States and some other major industrial countries, citing U.N. budgetary constraints.

The Committee plays an important role in strengthening the international basis and norms for the consideration of the peaceful exploration and use of space, taking into account the particular needs of developing countries. And it is responsible for preparing international agreements governing various practical, peaceful applications of space science and technology and strengthening international cooperative regimes in the area of peaceful exploration of outer space. Outer Space Committee Chairman Peter Hohenfeller, in introducing his Committee's annual report to the General Assembly's **Fourth (Special Political and Decolonization) Committee,** noted that "international cooperation in space technology could contribute substantially to economic and social development, and could also be a key to the future prosperity of developing countries [U.N. press release GA/SPD/72, 11/6/95; see also draft resolution A/C.4/50/L.9 and A/Res/50/27].

On the agenda of the **Scientific and Technical Subcommittee,** for example, are issues related to the implementation of recommendations made at the second Unispace conference in 1982 (Unispace '82); remote sensing and its application for developing countries; the use of nuclear power sources in outer space; space debris and space transportation systems; the use of the geostationary orbit; and life sciences and space medicine. Also on the agenda were national and international space activity relating to the Earth's environment, to planetary exploration, and to astronomy.

A major impediment to implementing the **recommendations of Unispace '82** has been the limited financial resources made available by U.N. member states for carrying out the **U.N. Programme on Space Applications.** At the present stage, funds are needed to support workshops and training courses for educators and others who can help develop national capabilities in space science and technology and develop new appli-

cations. "Seminars of the U.N. Programme on Space Applications" [A/
AC.105/584] and "Highlights in Space: progress in space science, technology
and applications, international cooperation and space law" [A/AC.105/583]
offer a review of developments to date. Even with funds so limited, the
International Space Information Service has managed to develop "limited
database capability" and to create a home page on the Internet offering a
wide range of information regarding the space-related activities of the
United Nations [U.N. press release GA/SPD/72, 11/6/95].

Conferences too are a means by which the Vienna-based **U.N. Office
for Outer Space Affairs** helps to promote the widest possible use of space
technology in tackling national economic and social problems. The use of
space technology, especially satellites, in drawing up sustainable development strategies and improving national and regional communication capacities was the theme of one such regional conference—this one organized jointly with the European Space Agency in fall 1995. The ability of
space technology to provide repeated observations over large or inaccessi-
ble areas makes it a unique tool for monitoring and managing the environment and for studying global change. Communication satellites are
now playing an important economic and social role in most countries.
They are used for improving telephone communications as well as for
transmitting entertainment, health, and educational programs, particularly to rural areas. Mobile communications and global positioning systems can have a strong impact on countries' economies over the long run;
and the use of data from Earth-observation satellites, communication satellites, and Seismic Alert systems is helping to prevent or mitigate the
effects of natural disasters.

Based on the report of the **Outer Space Committee's Legal Subcommittee,** the primary issues to be addressed in this area are the possibility of an early review and even revision of the **Principles Relevant to
the Use of Nuclear Power Sources in Outer Space** [see A/Res/47/68], in light
of changing technology; the definition and delimitation of space—
especially the consideration of a conventionally defined boundary between airspace and outer space; ways of ensuring the rational and equitable use of the geostationary orbit; and the legal aspects of the principle
that space should be used for the benefit of all states, taking into particular
account the needs of the developing countries [U.N. press release GA/SPD/72, 11/6/
95]. Also of special concern to the Outer Space Committee and the Fourth
Committee are the **prevention of an arms race in outer space** [see U.N.
press release GA/SPD/74, 11/9/95] and the **conversion of military industries to
productive civilian uses** (noting that such conversion would help to facilitate the transfer and use of space technologies and their spin-off benefits
and provide, as in the case of micro-satellite technologies, substantial benefits to developing countries at low cost) [U.N. press release GA/SPD/72, 11/6/95].

When the Legal Subcommittee of the Outer Space Committee held its 35th session in March 1996, it continued the consideration of three topics taken up at earlier sessions: (1) the need to review or revise the principles adopted by the General Assembly in 1992 governing the use of nuclear power sources in outer space in light of subsequent technological developments; (2) the means of arriving at a commonly agreed definition and delimitation of outer space and of ensuring the rational and equitable use of the geostationary orbit, without prejudice to the role of the International Telecommunication Union (ITU); and (3) the drafting of principles aimed at ensuring that all states share the benefits of space exploration and research.

On **sharing the benefits of space exploration and research with developing countries,** the Legal Subcommittee was successful in formulating a new, compromise text, reconciling the concerns of North and South—a major breakthrough in the debate on this subject. These differences were aired in rival working papers prepared for previous sessions of the Subcommittee. A proposal by Brazil and 11 other developing countries had stressed the need to develop indigenous space capabilities and likewise the need for technology transfers. A counterproposal sponsored by Germany and France stressed the freedom of states to determine the level and kind of cooperation, guided by the need to allocate resources efficiently. The compromise text notes that "states are free to determine all aspects of their participation in cooperation in the exploration and use of outer space *on an equitable and mutually acceptable basis*" and that modes of cooperation, whether governmental or nongovernmental, commercial or noncommercial, would "be tailored to suit the countries concerned" [U.N. press release OS/1722, 4/3/96]. This text was submitted to the Outer Space Committee for consideration at its June 3–14, 1996 meeting.

At a day-long symposium co-sponsored by the Paris-based International Institute of Space Law and the European Centre for Space Law, the Legal Subcommittee heard presentations by several countries on **ways to protect the space environment, with an emphasis on space debris.** The Subcommittee felt that the question of elaborating appropriate legal strategies for dealing with space debris would have to await further progress in the Scientific and Technical Subcommittee on such matters as debris measurement techniques. The Institute proposed some **new agenda topics** for the Legal Subcommittee, including the status of the five outer space treaties; commercial aspects of space activities, such as property rights, insurance, and liability; and a comparative review of international space law and international environmental law.

Reform of the Subcommittee's work session was debated at the March session, where some delegates pushed for a cut in the length of the body's annual sessions, from three weeks to two, and others cautioned that such a cost-saving measure might preclude the possibility of introducing new issues on the Subcommittee's agenda. In fact, said one speaker, even if space activities are driven by "market forces," the development of space law will continue to be of major importance for the world community and the Subcommittee should be strengthened and its meetings lengthened [ibid.].

5. Other Legal Developments

The United Nations proclaimed 1990–99 the Decade of International Law to promote acceptance, respect, and "the progressive development" of international law as well as to "encourage" the peaceful settlement of disputes and the teaching and dissemination of international law. The following section highlights the contributions to the development of international law by various bodies and programs that fall within the U.N. ambit, whether members of the U.N. system, other international organizations, or nongovernmental organizations (NGOs).

A Working Group on the United Nations Decade of International Law, headed by Peter Tomka of Slovakia, held five meetings between November 6 and 21, 1995, and gave an oral report to the Sixth Committee [A/C.6/50/SR.45]. The Sixth Committee's draft resolution, endorsed by the General Assembly, recalled the main purpose of the Decade and invited member states and international organizations to provide or update information on activities they have undertaken in implementing the goals of the Decade [A/Res/50/44]. (Specifically included in the 50th Assembly's request for information were such NGOs as the International Committee of the Red Cross.)

The International Maritime Organization (IMO) has made substantial contributions to the progressive development and codification of international law. Some of its recent contributions can be found by examining the outcomes of important diplomatic conferences held under its auspices, e.g., the May 1994 Conference of Contracting Governments to the International Convention for the Safety of Life at Sea, which adopted additional chapters (IX and XI) of the Convention Annex; the November 1994 Conference of Parties to the International Convention for the Prevention of the Pollution from Ships (1973) as modified by the Protocol of 1978, which adopted amendments to Annexes I, II, III, and V of the Convention; the June 26–July 7, 1995, Conference of Parties to the International Convention on Standards of Training, Certification and Watchkeeping for Seafarers (1978), which adopted amendments to the Convention's Annex as well as an associated Seafarer's Training, Certification and Watchkeeping Code; and the concurrent International Conference on Standards of Training, Certification and Watchkeeping for Fishing Vessel Personnel, which adopted a convention of the same name.

This progressive evolution and codification of international law has continued in the IMO through the efforts of its Legal Committee, which in April 1995 concluded work on a **draft convention that establishes a system for liability and compensation in connection with the carriage at sea of all types of hazardous and noxious substances (HNS**—defined by reference to existing lists of substances, such as those found in, for example, the International Maritime Dangerous Goods Code and Annex II of the International Convention for the Prevention of Pollution from Ships). This draft, which was expected to be adopted at a diplomatic conference in the spring of 1996, is much wider in scope than is the previously agreed-upon oil-pollution compensation regime, since it covers not only pollution but the risks of fire and explosion as well. It also introduces strict liability for the shipowner, higher limits of liability than exist under the current general limitation regimes, and a system of compulsory insurance and insurance certificates. At the same time, it establishes a link to the extant general limitation regimes in order to avoid unnecessary costs for the shipowner and make the best possible use of the limited capacity of the insurance market. It is generally felt that it is impossible to provide sufficient coverage simply through the shipowner's liability for damage that may be caused in connection with the carriage of HNS cargo. Such liability, which forms a first tier of the draft convention, would therefore be supplemented by a second tier—**the HNS Fund**—to be financed by cargo interests. The IMO's Legal Committee has also proposed for consideration at the spring 1996 HNS Conference a draft protocol to **amend the 1976 Convention on Limitation of Liability for Maritime Claims** [see A/50/368/Add.1].

The progressive development and codification of international law has also been the central focus of the **Committee of Legal Advisers on Public International Law (CAHDI) of the Council of Europe**—a body that reports directly to the Committee of Ministers of the Council of Europe. CAHDI examines many different questions relating to public international law, including: the work of the ILC; state succession in Europe relating to treaties; jurisdictional immunities of states and their property; the law and practice with respect to reservations, particularly in the case of human rights treaties; the U.N. Decade of International Law; debts of embassies and diplomats; and the International Ad Hoc Tribunals for the former Yugoslavia and for Rwanda [see ibid.].

The Council of Europe, through CAHDI, set up in 1990 a Group of Specialists on publications concerning **state practices in the field of public international law,** who considered the feasibility of a pilot project on documentation concerning European practices relating to state succession and issues of recognition. The pilot project—a highly useful contribution to the U.N. Decade—was approved in March 1994 and launched in May

1994. If this project works at the European level, a similar one might be entertained at the global level.

In 1994 the General Assembly had asked the **Secretariat** to update a 1994 study, **"Survey of State practice relevant to the topic of international liability for injurious consequences arising out of acts not prohibited by international law"** [A/Res/49/51], and the Secretariat complied, completing the work in July 1995. The update reviewed existing international conventions, international case law, and other forms of state practice as well as domestic legislation and/or court decisions that had any bearing on the issue of liability. Judicial decisions, arbitral awards, and documents exchanged between foreign ministries and government officials were also considered because they constitute important sources of state practice in the area of liability. Considered too were settlements through nonjudicial methods, since these could represent a new trend in resolving substantive issues in dispute.

The main difficulty in evaluating state practice with respect to issues of liability has to do with the fact that different policies may motivate the conclusion of treaties or decisions; some may be the result of compromise or of accommodation for extraneous reasons. Despite this difficulty, it was felt that continuous similar behavior, regardless of motivation, may lead to the creation of a customary norm and demonstrate a trend in expectations concerning the evolving principles of liability. Examination of actual practice in this area may also expose ways in which competing principles, such as "state sovereignty" and "domestic jurisdiction," are being reconciled with the new norms.

The outline of the study was formulated on the basis of functional problems that appear relevant to liability issues. It begins with a description of the general characteristics of liability regimes, reviews the historical development of the concept of strict liability in domestic law, and goes on to provide an overview of the evolution of the concept of liability in international law. Among the issues covered are the polluter-pays principle, operator liability, state liability, compensation, compensable injuries, limitation on compensation, statute of limitations, requirements of insurance and other anticipatory financial schemes that guarantee compensation in case of injury, and enforcement of judgments in respect to compensation to injured parties [A/CN.4/471].

The **United Nations Industrial Development Organization (UNIDO),** for its part, is not only contributing to the development of international law but has taken steps to encourage the **wider acceptance of multilateral treaties**—in particular, the Convention on the Privileges and Immunities of the United Nations. In December 1995 this Specialized Agency indicated that all future agreements with member states concerning the establishment of UNIDO industrial-cooperation and investment-promotion services would include a clause confirming the applicability of the above-named convention to various aspects of the legal relationships contemplated in those services agreements. UNIDO also reported that it had encouraged the incorporation, in the **Basic Cooperation Agreement concluded with member states,** of a standard dispute-settlement clause that provides for an arbitration procedure. Furthermore, in the interest of encouraging the teaching, study, and dissemination of international law, UNIDO has **registered with the U.N. Secretariat the treaties to which it is a party,** in accordance with Article 102 of the Charter, and notes that some of those treaties were subsequently published in the U.N. *Treaty Series* [A/50/368/Add.3]. UNIDO also contributes annually to the *United Nations Juridical Yearbook.*

The Work of the Sixth Committee

During its 50th Session the General Assembly adopted a baker's dozen of resolutions based on reports of the Sixth Committee about matters as various as the U.N. Commission on International Trade Law's new convention on independent guarantees and standby letters of credit [A/Res/50/47], on amending the statute of the U.N. Administrative Tribunal [A/Res/50/54], and on the future of the Trusteeship Council [A/Res/50/55].

The **U.N. Commission on International Trade Law (UNCITRAL),** established in 1966 and with a membership representing the various geographic areas and principal legal and economic systems of the world, is charged with the progressive harmonization and unification of international trade law. The hope is to reduce legal obstacles to the flow of international trade, especially those that affect the developing states. The normative bases for such activity are universal economic cooperation among states, equality, equity, and a common interest in the eventual elimination of discriminatory practices in international trade [A/50/17].

The reality, however, is that there have been few experts from developing countries at recent sessions of UNCITRAL, and particularly the sessions of its working groups. The main reason for this is the lack of funds to underwrite the travel of such experts and not any paucity of experts. Nevertheless, UNCITRAL has some important achievements under its belt. In addition to the completion and adoption of its draft **Convention on Independent Guarantees and Stand-by Letters of Credit**—this was opened for signature on November 6, 1995 [for full text see A/Res/50/48 Annex]—it has made excellent progress in the preparation of a draft **Model Law on Legal Aspects of Electronic Data Interchange and Related Means of Communication** and in the preparation of draft **Notes on Organizing Arbitral Proceedings.** And it has begun looking into such matters as receivables financing and cross-border insolvency, and the feasibility and desirability of undertaking work on negotiability and on the transferability of EDI transport documents. UNCITRAL continues to organize seminars and briefing missions in places as various as Armenia, Botswana, China, Colombia, and the Czech Republic. Both the continuation of these seminars and the participation of experts from the developing world are threatened by financial cutbacks and bureaucratic downsizing at the United Nations. An appeal was made to member states for an increase in voluntary contributions to the **Trust Fund for Travel Assistance** [A/C.6/50/L.4; A/Res/50/47].

Regarding the **future of the Trusteeship Council**, the delegate of Malta drafted, the Sixth Committee recommended, and the General Assembly approved a resolution requesting the Secretary-General to invite member states to submit by May 31, 1996, written comments on this subject and to report before the end of the 50th Session [A/C.6/50/L.6; A/Res/50/55]. That report is expected to note the recommendation of the Commission on Global Governance, an independent panel of experts, that the Trusteeship Council be given a new mandate as **trustee of the "global commons"** [*Our Global Neighbourhood*, Oxford and New York: Oxford University Press, 1995].

The Sixth Committee also considered the Report of the Special Committee on the Charter of the United Nations and on the Strengthening of the Role of the Organization [A/50/33] about the proposed deletion of the "enemy State" clauses in Articles 53, 77, and 107 of the Charter, and the 50th General Assembly "agree[d] to initiate the procedure . . . at its earliest appropriate future session" [A/C.6/50/L.8; A/Res/50/52]. The "Report of the Special Committee" will be taken up again at the 51st Assembly.

Another draft resolution of the Sixth Committee submitted to the 50th General Assembly dealt with issues arising out of the Report of the **Committee on Relations with the Host Country** and the Secretary-General's report on **diplomatic indebtedness** [A/AC.154/277]. The resolution made clear that such indebtedness reflects badly on the entire diplomatic community and tarnishes the image of the United Nations itself—and that noncompliance with contractual obligations cannot be condoned or justified at all [A/C.6/50/L.8; A/Res/50/49]. The resolution also urged the host country—the United States—"to consider lifting travel controls with regard to certain missions and staff members of the Secretariat of certain nationalities," and called on "the host country to review measures and procedures relating to the parking of diplomatic vehicles as a means of responding to the growing needs of the diplomatic community" in New York [ibid.].

Also among the resolutions recommended by the Sixth Committee was one on the **U.N. Programme of Assistance in the Teaching, Study, Dissemination and Wider Appreciation of International Law**, the implementation of which had been the subject of a report by the Secretary-General [A/50/726]. The encouragement of these activities is one of the primary goals of the U.N. Decade of International Law, and Ghana's draft resolution called on the General Assembly to authorize the Secretary-

General to carry out in 1996 and 1997 the activities specified in his report: creating a number of international law fellowships in 1996 and 1997, to be determined in light of the overall resources for the program and awarded at the request of governments of developing countries; awarding a minimum of one scholarship in both years under the Hamilton Shirley Amerasinghe Memorial Fellowship on the Law of the Sea, subject to the availability of new contributions earmarked for the fellowship fund; providing assistance in the form of a travel grant for one participant from each developing country to attend regional courses organized in 1996 and 1997; and financing the above activities from provisions in the regular budget, when appropriate, as well as from voluntary contributions earmarked for each activity [A/C.6/50/L.9; A/Res/50/43]. The subject will be taken up again at the 51st General Assembly.

The General Assembly also adopted the Sixth Committee's draft resolution on the U.N. Decade itself, as proposed by the Chairman of the **Working Group on the Decade** [A/C.6/50/L.10; A/Res/50/44]. The resolution, among other things, welcomed recent advances by the Treaty Section of the Office of Legal Affairs in computerizing the **Multilateral Treaties Deposited with the Secretary-General** and the **United Nations Treaty Series,** and it expressed the hope that these documents will be available to U.N. member states and other users on the Internet. The Decade of International Law will be taken up again during the 51st Session.

Continuing its interest in measures to eliminate **terrorism,** the Sixth Committee offered a draft resolution on the subject to the 50th Session. The draft and the Assembly resolution [A/C.6/50/L.12; A/Res/50/53] recalled a similar resolution adopted by the Assembly in 1994 [A/Res/49/60] and recognized the need for strengthened cooperation between and among states, the U.N. system, regional organizations and arrangements, and international agencies. States are encouraged to take the "necessary steps to implement their obligations under existing international conventions, to observe fully the principles of international law, and to contribute to the further development of international law on this matter" [A/Res/50/53]. This matter will be taken up under the item "Measures to eliminate international terrorism" at the 51st Session.

Another subject commanding the attention of the Sixth Committee was the **implementation of Charter provisions relating to assisting third states affected by the application of sanctions.** The draft resolution on the subject was proposed by the Chairman of the Working Group on implementation of these provisions and adopted by the 50th General Assembly [A/C.6/50/L.13; A/Res/50/51]. Article 49 of the U.N. Charter obligates all member states to assist and cooperate with the Council in carrying out Chapter VII sanctions against any state, but any other state has the right, according to Article 50, to consult with the Security Council about addressing special economic problems that might result from such cooperation. (The Secretary-General's *Agenda for Peace* and *Supplement to An Agenda for Peace* demonstrated awareness of this problem [A/47/277-S/24111 and A/50/60-S/1995/1].) The resolution on this subject emphasizes the importance of early consultations with states that may be faced with the abovementioned problem; invites the Security Council to consider appropriate ways to increase the effectiveness of its working methods and the procedures applied in considering requests for assistance; and recommends immediate steps the Secretariat can take to accomplish this, through collating and assessing information; recommending adjustments to the administration of the sanctions regime to mitigate some adverse effects on third states; and exploring innovative and practical measures of assistance.

Although the activities of the Sixth Committee, of the International Law Commission, and of the myriad other U.N. bodies that contribute to the development of international law demonstrate the seriousness with which U.N. member states view the process, further efforts may be jeopardized by the Organization's financial crisis. To keep up this work—including the work of developing an International Criminal Court—will require a substantial amount of money, not least a renewed commitment by U.N. members to pay up their assessed contributions to the Organization's regular budget in full and on time. Most member governments will be looking to the U.S. government for leadership in this regard.

VII
Finance and Administration
By Deborah Scroggins

1. U.N. Finance

The United Nations teetered so perilously close to bankruptcy in 1995–96 that Secretary-General Boutros Boutros-Ghali called for a Special Session of the 51st General Assembly to come up with a comprehensive plan to restore the Organization to financial health. As in previous years, the problem was the refusal of the United States and a growing number of other member states to pay their dues both to the U.N. regular budget and to its peacekeeping operations. By the the end of April 1996, the United Nations had spent all the money in its regular budget balance. At the same time, the Organization was owed $2.8 billion, with the United States responsible for more than half the total. Unless the United States and its fellow debtor nations paid up, the United Nations would have to close its doors by the end of 1996, the Secretary-General wrote [*New York Times*, 4/8, 30/96].

To cope with its financial straits, the United Nations adopted a number of belt-tightening measures in 1995–96, including some long advocated by Washington. In 1995 the General Assembly adopted the **first zero-growth budget** in the Organization's history, forcing the U.N.'s top financial official, Joseph Connor, to cut some $250 million from its operating expenses by the end of 1997 [ibid., 4/2/96]. Connor, the Under-Secretary-General for Administration and Management, also announced plans to cut the 10,000-member staff in New York City and seven other cities by 10 percent over the next two years [ibid., 2/6/96]. In October, the **Under-Secretary-General of the new Office of Internal Oversight Services, Karl Paschke,** delivered his first report to the General Assembly, identifying $16.8 million in misappropriated funds [*International Documents Review*, Vol. 6, No. 38].

In a series of reports and press releases throughout the year, Boutros-Ghali also proposed a number of innovative and even radical changes in the way the Organization raises its money. The U.N. chief called for a

reduction in the assessment of the United States from 25 percent to 15 or 20 percent. He proposed creating a kind of bond that would assign debts of member countries in arrears to member countries who were owed money. He suggested that a tax to fund the United Nations be imposed on international financial transactions or on international airline tickets. "I regard the financial situation as my top priority in the period ahead," the Secretary-General told the **High-Level Working Group on the U.N. Financial Situation** in February 1996 [SG/SM/5892].

Yet the Secretary-General himself acknowledged that few member states showed the political will in 1996 to make the tough political trade-offs that a thorough reform of the U.N.'s financing would require. "Throughout the past four years we have tried again and again to win support for measures that enable the United Nations to overcome these problems," he reminded the High-Level Working Group. "I have taken the decisions that fall within my authority. I have repeatedly called for decisive action by the Member States. Yet today, four years later, the United Nations is still afflicted by these problems. And time is running out."

Many member states were particularly reluctant to consider measures that would reduce the financial responsibilities of the single largest debtor, the United States. During the U.N.'s 50th Anniversary celebrations, some of the closest allies of the United States lined up day after day to castigate the host nation for its failure to pay its dues. Britian's Foreign Secretary called Washington's unilateral withholdings "representation without taxation," while the Nordic countries complained that the United States was setting a "deplorable" example for the world. Australian Foreign Minister Gareth Evans warned that the United States could lose its U.N. voting rights. And in a bitter retort to American charges of organizational bloat, Evans noted that the New York City police department had a annual budget $600 million higher than the $1.2 billion needed to run the U.N. regular budget. He went on the say that the entire U.N. system, including all the Specialized Agencies, employed 4,000 fewer people than three Disney amusement parks [*New York Times*, 3/10/96].

Though **President Clinton** pledged in his address to the 50th General Assembly to work with Congress on a plan to meet the U.S. obligations to the United Nations, he also followed in the footsteps of his Republican predecessors in criticizing the United Nations for inefficiency. "The U.N. must be able to show that the money it receives supports saving and enriching people's lives, not unneeded overhead," Clinton said. "Reform requires breaking up bureaucratic fiefdoms, eliminating obsolete agencies, and doing more with less" [*Washington Weekly Report*, XX-33].

Despite the President's words, the **hostility of the Republican-controlled Congress toward the United Nations** showed no sign of abating. The day before the U.N.'s 50th Anniversary, Rep. Joe Scarborough (R-

Fla.) announced he was introducing legislation to require the United States to withdraw over a four-year period from the world body [ibid., XXI-34]. In February a spokesman for the Senate Foreign Relations Committee said there was a strong argument to be made that the U.N. system of assessing member nations is unconstitutional. Marc Theissen said assessing nations a percentage of the U.N. budget based on each country's share of world income "allows the U.N. General Assembly to make commitments of the U.S. taxpayer. Congress is the only body permitted to do that under the U.S. Constitution" [*Washington Times*, 2/7/96].

Washington's niggardly stance aroused a resentment among other member states that boded ill for the five-year plan the Clinton administration unveiled in March for paying off $1.5 billion in debts to the United Nations. Dubbed "the grand bargain," the plan calls for a reduction in the U.S. assessment to 20 percent and a host of U.N. reforms in return for the payment of this year's dues and the repayment of American arrears. But the plan depends on congressional approval, and after a decade in which the Congress has repeatedly reneged on presidential promises to pay U.S. debts if the United Nations would reform its bureaucracy, it met with a cool reception at the world body. By contrast, the second largest debtor, the Russian Federation, was lauded when it produced a five-year plan to pay back about $400 million, including its regular assessment of $46 million [*New York Times*, 4/8/96].

Assessed at 25 percent, the United States contributed only about 12 percent of the regular budget in 1995, noted Under-Secretary-General Connor [Inter Press Service, 2/7/96]. As of March 31, 1996, the United States owed the United Nations a total of $1.58 billion, including its 1996 assessment. (In 1982 the Reagan administration unilaterally decided to start paying U.S. assessments at the beginning of Washington's fiscal year in October; under the U.N. system, assessments are due in January.) The U.S. debt included $879 million in peacekeeping dues, $699 million toward the regular budget, and $2 million in payments to the international tribunal system. As shown in Table VII-1 the other top debtors were the Russian Federation, Ukraine, Japan, Belarus, Germany, the United Kingdom, Iran, Brazil, and Italy.

Indeed, even as the administration was proposing its plan, Congress continued to add new restrictions to some U.N. funding and to cut others. Under the long-awaited budget agreement the administration and Congress negotiated in April, the United Nations would receive $304 million in overdue payments for 1995 operating expenses and $359 million in peacekeeping assessments. The legislation made payment contingent on continued zero-growth U.N. budgets and the enhanced effectiveness of the newly created Inspector General's office [*Washington Weekly Report*, XXII-7; *New York Times*, 4/30/96]. The funds fell far short of Clinton's original request

Table VII-1
Top Debtor Nations*

	Total Debt (in millions)
United States	$1,580
Russian Federation	$426
Ukraine	$244
Japan	$129
Belarus	$63
Germany	$61
United Kingdom	$37
Iran	$26
Brazil	$25
Italy	$22

*Includes arrears and 1996 assessments for the U.N. regular budget, peacekeeping operations, and international tribunals as of March 31, 1996.
Source: United Nations.

Table VII-2
Top Debtors to the Regular Budget

	Debt (in millions)
United States	$699
Japan	$128
Ukraine	$53
Germany	$49
United Kingdom	$37
Brazil	$18
Belarus	$13
Iran	$12
Yugoslavia	$12

for $934 million and were not expected to be available until June. At the end of 1996 the United States would still owe $1.3 billion.

A foreign appropriations bill passed in January designated a total of $285 million for U.N. voluntary programs in fiscal year 1996, $140 million less than the administration request. By press time, the State Department had not yet decided how to divide this reduced amount among dozens of U.N. programs, such as the United Nations Development Programme, the United Nations Children's Fund, and the United Nations Environment Programme [ibid.]. In December 1995 the United States announced a decision to withdraw from the United Nations Industrial Development Organization on the grounds of budget austerity [*Washington Weekly Report*, XXI-38].

Under-Secretary-General Connor said the "total level of unpaid assessments has increased to unprecedented levels" in 1995–96. The total of $2.3 billion owed to the United Nations at the end of 1995 represented a jump of $500 million over the previous year [*New York Times*, 2/6/96]. Connor kept the Organization going in the face of the shortfall by **raiding payments earmarked for peacekeeping to pay salaries and other routine bills.** This meant postponing reimbursements to the countries that charged $985 per month for each soldier sent to a danger spot. By the end of 1996, the United Nations owed these nations a total of $1 billion. Connor also used new peacekeeping payments to work off some of the U.N.'s most pressing debts. To finance the $20 million International Tribunal in The Hague that is investigating crimes in Bosnia, he dipped into the regular budget. "In the textbooks, it's called a Ponzi scheme; use the current cash to pay past bills," said Connor, a former chairman of Price Waterhouse. "We had to shout from the rooftops, 'This is what we're doing,' and no one said 'Stop' " [ibid.].

Connor tried to borrow from the World Bank in the fall of 1995, but the Bank refused on the grounds that it is only allowed to lend to sover-

Table VII-3
Top Debtors to Peacekeeping Operations

	Debt (in millions)
United States	$879
Russian Federation	$425
Ukraine	$199
Belarus	$49
Italy	$22
Poland	$16
Iran	$14
Germany	$12
France	$11
Spain	$10

Table VII-4
Countries Owed the Most by the United Nations for Peacekeeping Contributions

	Owed (in thousands)
France	$216,181
Pakistan	$60,446
India	$49,472
United States	$47,119
United Kingdom	$40,717
Norway	$40,414
Malaysia	$39,167
Sweden	$38,445
Bangladesh	$35,612
Denmark	$33,744

Source: A/50/666/Add.4.

eign states. (The United Nations is not allowed to borrow on the financial markets.) At Connor's suggestion, the Secretary-General floated the bond-issue idea at the Group of Seven meeting of wealthy, industrialized nations in Halifax, Nova Scotia. "The proposal met with silence," the *New York Times* reported [ibid.].

The Secretary-General's outspoken advocacy for some form of fee on international transactions to fund the United Nations prompted Sen. Bob Dole (R-Kans.) to introduce a bill in February that would cut off U.N. funding if it persists in seeking **"global taxes"** [*Washington Times*, 2/7/96]. But the opposition of the Republican presidential candidate failed to inhibit Boutros-Ghali. In the March/April 1996 issue of *Foreign Affairs,* he reiterated his proposal:

> It is reasonable to contemplate the creation of some procedure by which the organization could regularly collect a relatively small amount from one of the many daily transactions of the global economy. Measures for consideration could include a fee on speculative international financial transactions or a levy on either fossil fuel use or the resulting pollution; the dedication of a small portion of the anticipated decline in world military expenditures or the utilization of some resources released by the elimination of unnecessary government subsidies; a stamp tax on international travel and travel documents or an assessment on global currency transactions. Finding the right formula that will enable funds to flow automatically while keeping expenditures under control is a project the secretary-general must bring to fruition in the next century.

Even the Secretary-General pointed out that financial reform on the scale he envisioned would have to coincide with the reform of the intergovernmental machinery of the United Nations, and particularly the composition of the Security Council. And few observers predicted that member states would be willing or able in the 51st Session of the General Assembly to pass the kind of rehaul of obligations under the U.N. Charter that Boutros-Ghali saw as essential to place the Organization on a sound financial footing. A spokeswoman for the Assembly said the members were not likely to take any action on his call for a Special Session devoted to finance until the **High-Level Group on the U.N. Financial Situation** delivered its recommendations in the summer. Those recommendations were scheduled to be placed before another, overarching group, the **High-Level Group on Strengthening the U.N. System,** which was not expected to offer its suggestions until the General Assembly opens in the fall, at the earliest [interview with Leona Foreman, General Assembly press secretary, 4/24/96].

Scale of Assessments

Though the Fifth Committee (Administration and Budget) is not due to consider a new scale of assessments until 1997, representatives to the 50th

General Assembly spent a great deal of time discussing ways to reform it. The **Committee on Contributions** decided to undertake over the next two sessions a comprehensive review of the methodology used in calculating national assessments [A/50/11]. The questions of what factors should be taken into account in determining assessments and whether the ceiling or the floor on assessments ought to be moved provoked hot debate within both committees.

Outside the United Nations, the Secretary-General's call for a reduction in the ceiling on assessments received wide publicity, as did Washington's demand that its regular budget and peacekeeping dues be reduced. In his February report to the High-Level Group on the U.N. Financial Situation, the Secretary-General said the issue of the scale of assessments was at the heart of any approach to addressing the long-term dimensions of the financial crisis. "A ceiling of 20 percent or even 15 percent on the assessed contribution of any member state to the regular budget of the United Nations would provide for a more even distribution of the assessed contributions, and would better reflect the fact that the United Nations is indeed the instrument of all nations," he said [SG/SM/5892].

In March 1996, U.S. Permanent Representative Madeleine K. Albright announced that she would ask the United Nations to lower America's assessment for the regular budget from 25 percent to 20 percent, and for peacekeeping from 31.7 percent to 25 percent. Albright described the shift as part of Washington's "grand bargain" to pay its U.N. arrears. (Congress voted in 1994 to unilaterally decrease the U.S. peacekeeping assessment to 25 percent, but the other U.N. member states have not agreed to accept this reduction.) Privately, U.N. officials were skeptical of the U.S. commitment to pay an assessment of even 15 percent, noting that Washington was currently paying only 12 percent. They speculated that a change was likely to mean the newly industrialized countries of Asia, such as Malaysia, Singapore, Thailand, Indonesia, and South Korea, would pay more [*IPS Daily Journal*, Vol. 4, 2]. The proposals to reduce the ceiling are not likely to win many supporters during the 51st General Assembly within either the Advisory Committee on Administrative and Budgetary Questions (ACABQ) or the Committee on Contributions.

Expressing implicit and sometimes explicit criticism of the United States, nearly every representative who addressed the Fifth Committee in 1995 noted that no reform of the assessment system could solve the financial crisis unless member states resolve to pay their U.N. bills on time. The representative of Marshall Islands said it was extremely difficult to understand how the broader question of arrears had become so serious. All states had a treaty obligation to pay their assessments in full and on time. They had ample opportunity to discourage excessive demands on the Organization. Once an expenditure was agreed upon, however, delegations must pay up [A/C.5/50/SR.4].

The representative of Australia took up the theme when he stressed that while reform of the scale of assessments was necessary, it was not itself sufficient to resolve the financial crisis brought about by the widespread failure of member states to pay their assessed contributions in full, on time, and without conditions. Like other representatives to the committee, the Australian delegation showed some sympathy for the debtor countries among the 22 that resulted from the breakup of **the Soviet Union, Yugoslavia, and Czechoslovakia.** Australia agreed that their assessments were too high. Australia also joined Canada and New Zealand in proposing the elimination of the floor rate of 0.01 percent, arguing that it puts too heavy a burden on smaller developing states. But the Australian representative maintained that the current ceiling of 25 percent conferred a considerable advantage on the wealthiest member state, which had to be subsidized by other states. Even when assessed at 25 percent, the United States pays considerably less per capita than many other member states, he added.

Only the representative of Ecuador expressed any interest in reducing the U.S. assessment, arguing that it was neither prudent nor in the interest of the Organization to rely on just one member state for a quarter of the regular budget [A/C.5/50/SR.8]. The Committee on Contributions resolved to consider the issue of moving the ceiling at its next meeting in June [A/50/11].

The representative of Ukraine, the third biggest debtor, told the committee that nearly a quarter of total outstanding contributions were owed by states whose assessments were too high. He said that Ukraine had contributed nearly $30 million to the United Nations since gaining its independence and was about to contribute a further $10 million. If Ukraine had been assessed in accordance with its ability to pay, the $30 million would have been sufficient for his country not to have a single dollar of U.N. debt.

The representative from Bangladesh agreed with the Secretary-General that the United Nations was technically bankrupt and must, as a matter of urgency, be put on a stable financial footing. Its financial difficulties stemmed primarily from the failure of certain member states to pay their contributions in full and on time. Review of the scale would neither add to the Organization's income nor guarantee it the necessary minimum resource base, he said.

The representative from Nepal noted that, paradoxically, the majority of the 70 member states that had paid their contributions for 1995 in full were developing countries, as were most of the troop-contributing countries to which the United Nations owed considerable sums [A/C.5/50/SR.7].

The 1995–96 session saw growing support for **lowering the floor rate of 0.01 percent,** if not for lowering the ceiling of 25 percent. The

Committee on Contributions recognized "the apparent distortions in the capacity to pay inherent in the current system," saying that it was the belief of the committee that the anomaly could be rectified in part by lowering the floor [A/50/11].

In the Fifth Committee, the representative from Marshall Islands spoke for many developing countries when he complained that the principle of capacity to pay was not applied to all member states on an equal basis. Many smaller developing countries were assessed at disproportionately higher rates. He also said that the committee was taking too long to resolve various issues. For example, he said, it was absurd that Yugoslavia was being assessed when the state in question had ceased to exist. He called for forgiving the arrears accrued by the former apartheid government of South Africa so as to allow the current democratic government to use its resources for nation-building. And he said the former Communist countries should be assessed more fairly, taking into account their current difficulties.

The representative of Singapore noted that almost a quarter of the members were assessed at the floor rate of 0.01 percent although their share of global income was far less than that figure. That anomaly should be corrected by lowering the floor rate, a step that could be facilitated by using more than two decimal points in quantifying the scale of assessments.

The representative of the United States said his delegation was among those that favored revising the scale of assessments for the regular budget and for peacekeeping operations. He admitted that revision would not solve the Organization's financial problems, but said it would create a fairer and more transparent system. He said the United States also supported the recommendation of the Ad Hoc Working Group on the Implementation of the Principle of Capacity to Pay that GNP be used to calculate assessments. He also called for the phase-out of the **scheme of limits**—a 1970s budget innovation that limited the degree to which assessments could be changed in any one year.

Iraq formally asked the committee to release it from its obligation to pay under Article 19 of the Charter, on the grounds that circumstances beyond its control made it impossible for Iraq to meet its U.N. obligations. Iraq's representative noted that the United Nations had refused its request to release $300,000 of its frozen assets to enable it to pay part of its debt to the regular budget or to accept payment in local currency. Iraq's representative remarked that the increase in Iraq's rate was unjustified, since it ignored the country's economic situation and the adverse consequences of the embargo imposed on it by the Security Council. He said the embargo had deprived Iraq of any source of income and rendered it unable to respond to the humanitarian and vital needs of its population.

The Chairman of the Fifth Committee summarized the discussions by saying that some issues clearly required further consideration, such as the length of the base period, the debt-burden adjustment, and the low per capita income adjustment. He said there was a convergence of views regarding the possibility of using market exchange rates for the conversion of national income statistics, the need to study adjustments to be applied in special cases, and the taking into account where appropriate of other indicators of income to measure capacity to pay. He said attention should be given to phasing out the scheme of limits in the context of the new scale methodology [A/C.5/50/SR.10].

Program Budget for the 1996–97 Biennium

The 50th General Assembly adopted the **first no-growth budget in U.N. history,** a plan to spend $2.61 billion over the two-year period 1996–97 that involved **$250 million in cost reductions.** The budget represented a victory for the United States, which had long fought to replace the policy of zero real growth in place since 1986 with a regimen of zero nominal growth [*Washington Weekly Report,* XXII-2]. To adjust to the smaller budget, Secretariat officials planned to cut some 800 staff posts and various services. Nevertheless, managers had only identified about $140 million in cuts by April [*International Documents Review,* Vol. 7, No. 12]. Nor did the budget include the additional $100 million the Secretary-General has estimated it will cost to continue a number of political and human rights operations whose mandates were due to be renewed in 1996. In April the Assembly extended the **human rights missions in Guatemala and Haiti** and asked the Secretary-General to absorb them into the existing budget. The action prompted Boutros-Ghali to warn that the U.S.-backed programs might end up on the chopping block [*New York Times,* 4/12/96].

The U.S. Representative for U.N. Management and Reform, David E. Birenbaum, called the no-growth budget "a sharp and welcome departure from business as usual." But in remarks to the Assembly in December 1995, Birenbaum said the United States could not give its full support to a budget that remained higher than Washington had recommended. Still, he said that "although this budget is not as lean as my government proposed, it is perhaps the most austere ever adopted by the General Assembly. It should be viewed by the Secretariat, and by the world, as a mandate for change" [*Washington Weekly Report,* XXII-2].

Madeleine Albright had told the Fifth Committee in October 1995 that the United States would not approve a budget package exceeding $2.51 billion. Albright said that even though budgets had been maintained at or near zero real growth, the U.S. regular assessment had grown by more than 80 percent over the last decade. She reminded the Assembly that Congress had recently lowered President Clinton's request for $923 million in U.N. funding and denied the administration's request for $672 million to pay off peacekeeping arrears. She recommended cutting the Department of Public Information, reducing paperwork, and denying a 9.2 percent pay raise sought by the International Civil Service Commission [A/C.5/50/SR.10].

Albright's exclusive focus on budget-cutting contrasted with statements of other representatives to the Fifth Committee in discussing the program budget. Once again the debate was marked by a North-South split over whether the United Nations ought to direct more of its resources toward political and humanitarian work, as the wealthier countries generally saw it, or toward economic and social problems, as the poorer countries tended to agree. In 1995, North-South disagreement over how much weight should be given to U.N. auditing and oversight added a special twist to the familiar arguments.

For example, the representative from Norway endorsed the four areas earmarked for special attention in the 1996–97 program budget. He said these include the strengthening of political and peacekeeping activities; the reinforcement of international and regional cooperation for development; the enhancement of support for humanitarian affairs and human rights; and an increase in the capacity for internal oversight. He added that Norway shared the view of the European Union that the overall proportion of the budget dedicated to human rights remained inadequate [A/C.5/50/SR.4].

On the other hand, the representative of the Philippines, speaking on behalf of the Group of 77 and China, complained that cost-cutting and productivity gains were not the objectives of the Organization. "It should be the committee's constant endeavor to provide the United Nations with the financial provisions to fulfill all the mandates laid out by the General Assembly in pursuit of the organization's goals," he said [ibid.]. The representative from Egypt added that the current emphasis on peacekeeping and humanitarian assistance should not divert attention from established priorities, such as economic development, economic revitalization programs in Africa, environmental protection, and control of narcotic drugs. He said the program budget attempted to reduce the ability of the United Nations to respond to the needs of the majority of its membership. The delegate of Iran echoed several developing countries when he criticized the Secretary-General for making oversight a priority when the General Assembly had never named it as such [A/C.5/50/SR10].

The final budget approved by the General Assembly in Resolution 50/215 requires the Secretary-General to find $154 million in savings over the $98 million already included in his program budget submission [A/C.5/50/57]. The budget is shown in Table VII-5. The Assembly sought to cut $50 million by increasing the vacancy rates recommended by the Secretary-General from 6 percent for professional staff and 0.8 percent for general service staff to 6.4 percent for all staff. It then asked the Secretary-General to find $104 million in unspecified reductions.

In his subsequent report to the General Assembly on the proposed program budget, the Secretary-General concluded that "a resource reduction of the magnitude mandated . . . could not be achieved while implementing the full program of work as initially envisaged; nor could overall savings be achieved without a significant reduction in staff costs" [ibid.]. Overall, Boutros-Ghali proposed to begin with **three savings measures:** (1) An estimated average vacancy rate of 9 percent for professional posts and 7 percent for general service posts; (2) delays and postponements in program delivery and services; (3) efficiency gains related to procedural simplification [ibid.,].

To arrive at specific recommendations, the Secretary-General said he relied on a two-track approach. First, program managers in every depart-

Table VII-5
1996–97 Program Budget, U.S. dollars

Expenditure section	Secretary-General's estimates	ACABQ recommenda-tions	Appro-priation
Part I: Overall policy-making, direction, and coordination			
Overall policy-making, direction, and coordination	$39,885,600	$39,885,600	$40,348,200
Part II: Political affairs			
Political affairs	$59,330,500	$59,330,500	$60,989,500
Peacekeeping operations, special missions	$90,394,100	$88,149,400	$102,868,200
Outer Space affairs	$4,447,600	$4,447,600	$4,705,500
Part III: International justice and law			
International Court of Justice	$21,575,000	$20,369,600	$21,339,600
Legal activities	$31,107,300	$31,107,300	$31,605,400
Part IV: International cooperation for development			
Department for Policy Coordination and Sustainable Development ...	$43,032,100	$43,032,100	$44,318,700
Africa: Critical economic situation, recovery, and development	$4,020,400	$4,020,400	$4,305,100
Department of Economic and Social Information and Policy Analysis	$48,364,300	$48,233,700	$48,612,100
Department for Development Support and Management Services	$25,832,700	$25,832,700	$26,556,000
U.N. Conference on Trade and Development (UNCTAD)	$116,783,100	$116,783,100	$121,925,300

Table VII-5 (continued)

Expenditure section	Secretary-General's estimates	ACABQ recommenda-tions	Appro-priation
International Trade Center (UNCTAD/GATT)	$21,642,000	$21,642,000	$21,642,000
U.N. Environment Programme (UNEP)	$9,986,100	$9,986,100	$9,512,200
U.N. Centre for Human Settlements	$14,800,400	$14,800,400	$13,059,600
Crime Control	$4,913,400	$4,913,400	$5,254,600
International Drug Control ...	$16,409,400	$16,307,400	$17,344,100
Part V: Regional cooperation for development			
Economic Commission for Africa	$79,524,800	$79,524,800	$87,845,600
Economic and Social Commission for Asia and the Pacific	$67,720,600	$67,720,600	$66,379,300
Economic Commission for Europe	$50,792,700	$50,792,700	$52,883,100
Economic Commission for Latin America and the Caribbean	$90,645,800	$90,645,800	$88,327,200
Economic and Social Commission for Western Asia	$38,457,400	$38,457,400	$37,791,200
Regular program of technical cooperation	$49,227,400	$49,227,400	$44,814,700
Part VI: Human rights and humanitarian affairs			
Human rights	$49,717,700	$49,597,400	$52,987,600
Office of the U.N. High Commissioner for Refugees (UNHCR)	$52,057,200	$52,057,200	$54,318,500
U.N. Relief and Works Agency for Palestine Refugees in the Near East ..	$23,611,700	$23,611,700	$22,643,000
Department of Humanitarian Affairs	$20,300,200	$19,912,800	$21,039,300
Part VII: Public information			
Department of Public Information	$137,911,700	$137,911,700	$137,658,000
Part VIII: Common support services			
Department of Administration and Management	$952,683,500	$943,373,800	$960,885,100
Part IX: Jointly financed activities and special expenditures			
Jointly financed administrative activities	$27,447,400	$27,447,400	$28,915,000
Special expenditures	—	—	$41,701,700

Table VII-5 (continued)

Expenditure section	Secretary-General's estimates	ACABQ recommenda-tions	Appro-priation
Part X: Internal oversight services			
Office of Internal Oversight Services	$15,821,800	$15,689,600	$15,716,500
Part XI: Capital expenditures			
Technological innovations	$21,876,500	$21,876,500	$21,999,600
Construction, alteration, improvement, and major maintenance	—	—	$31,585,400
Part XII: Staff assessment			
Staff assessment	$368,603,200	$367,510,400	$369,080,100
Part XIII: International Seabed Authority			
International Seabed Authority	$776,000	$776,000	$1,308,200
Total estimated expenditure	$2,687,067,800	$2,668,566,900	$2,712,265,200
Less: Anticipated reductions to be confirmed by the General Assembly			($103,991,200)
Grand Total			$2,608,274,000
Estimates of income			
Income from staff assessment	$373,607,000	$372,514,200	$384,306,000
General income	$81,832,400	$81,832,400	$86,209,200
Services to the public	$5,982,000	$5,982,000	$886,500
Total estimated income	$461,421,400	$460,328,600	$471,401,700
Total Net Expenditure	$2,225,646,400	$2,208,238,300	$2,136,872,300

Source: GA/AB/3017 and A/50/842.

ment except the Joint Inspection Unit and the Office of Internal Oversight Services produced plans to implement proposed savings targets. (The Joint Inspection Unit refused to suggest any reductions in its budget, arguing that it had system-wide oversight functions and budgetary independence. Internal Oversight Services was not asked to produce any cuts.) Second, the Secretary-General put in motion a series of efficiency reviews designed to find still other, less costly ways of doing work and improving services. He reported that he expected to realize the staff reductions through the full use of attrition; strict enforcement of the retirement age; a freeze in recruitment, subject to limited exceptions; an early separation program, if funds were made available; and a program for the lateral deployment of staff. He said he would fire staff as a last resort.

With cuts of $44 million to $48 million, the **Department of Administration and Management's** $960 million budget took the single largest hit. The report said the reductions would result in the deferral of energy lighting conservation measures, upgrades of telecommunications equipment, the enhancement of the budget information system, and the full automation of conference services in Vienna, among other items. They would involve the reduction of a training program and of the capacity of the conference services division to service meetings and produce publications. But it also stated that some of the savings would be accomplished through such efficiencies as the development of a database; the creation of a guidelines document for capital improvement projects; the reallocation of maintenance staffs; and a consolidation of U.N. procurement activities. It also suggested the implementation of a correspondence-tracking scheme; the elimination of tracking rental subsidies by hand; streamlining the procedures for verifying dependency status, references, and termination for reasons of health; the suspension of regular weekend duty to reduce overtime costs; the restriction of document availability and circulation; and other management measures.

The **Department of Public Information** came next, with cuts of between $7.2 million and $8 million from a budget of $138 million. The report said the department planned to use greater selectivity in the frequency of its radio programs; to reduce its press coverage; to integrate its information centers with those of the United Nations Development Programme; and to postpone a plan to upgrade exhibitions along the guided tour route at U.N. Headquarters. It said the department intended to achieve some other efficiencies by using advanced information technologies; by merging the publication *Development Business* with the World Bank's International Business Opportunities service; and through better promotion and marketing efforts.

Among the U.N.'s substantive programs, the **economic and social sectors were hit hardest,** with cuts totaling between $40 million and $44 million out of an overall budget of some $691 million. The Secretary-General proposed that the **U.N. Conference on Trade and Development (UNCTAD)** absorb a cut between $6 million and $7 million. The report said UNCTAD could find efficiencies by reorganizing to create a visibly leaner organizational structure and through the streamlining of administration and management. From the $45 million budget of the U.N.'s regular program of technical cooperation, the Secretary-General proposed a cut of over $7 million. The five regional economic commissions each took budget reductions of several million. With the largest budget, the Economic Commission for Latin America and Caribbean was recommended for the biggest cut, between $4 million and $5 million, while the commission with the smallest budget, the Economic and Social Commission for Western Asia, was recommended for the smallest cut, between $200,000 and $2 million.

For other social and economic programs the report proposed cuts of about $2 million from the $44 million budget of the Department for Policy Coordination; about $3 million from the Department for Economic and Social Information and Policy Analysis; over $2.6 million from human rights programs budgeted at $53 million; about $1 million from international drug control programs; some $500,000 to $600,000 from the Department for Development Support and Management Services; about $500,000 from the U.N. Environment Programme's $9.5 million budget; and smaller cuts in the areas of crime control and human settlements.

The U.N.'s **political and humanitarian departments** were spared such bloodletting. The Secretary-General called for a reduction of $5.8 million to $6.4 million from $103 million appropriated for the **Department of Peacekeeping Operations and Special Missions.** The report tersely noted the impact of the cuts as an "increase in workload." It said the department was reviewing greater delegation of authority; expanded use of information technology; a cheaper but fast way of transporting staff on field missions; and the development of an integrated electronic network between field missions and Headquarters.

From the **Department of Political Affairs** $61 million budget, the U.N. head suggested a $3.1 million to $3.5 million cut. The report said the department planned to save the funds partly by reducing travel expenses and disarmament fellowships and by limiting the Advisory Board on Disarmament Matters and the Standing Committee on Security Questions in Central Africa to two meetings each.

In the humanitarian field, the report recommended a reduction of between $3.3 million and $3.6 million from the $54 million budget of the **United Nations High Commissioner for Refugees (UNHCR).** It proposed cuts of about $1 million from the **Department of Humanitarian Affairs** budget of $21 million and over $1.2 million from the $23 million allocated to the **United Nations Relief and Works Agency in Palestine (UNRWA).**

The report said the **International Court of Justice** planned to slim its $21.3 million budget by about $1 million. The Department of Legal Activities planned a cut of $1.6 million to $1.8 million in its budget of $32 million, while the Department of Outer Space Affairs was to see its annual $4.7 million reduced by over $200,000. The report said the Secretariat could save nearly $3 million more by deferring construction and maintenance projects and by implementing technological innovations. Finally, the Secretary-General proposed a cut of between $1.2 million and $1.4 million from the $40 million set aside for the **Department of Overall Policy-making, Direction and Coordination,** which includes his own office.

The Budgets of Peacekeeping Operations

The 51st General Assembly will be a time of reckoning as scaled-down U.N. peacekeeping missions no longer generate enough money to repay funds borrowed to finance the regular budget. "The expedient financial improprieties that we progressively adopted [will] come home to roost," Under-Secretary-General Joseph Connor predicted in December [*New York Times*, 12/8/95]. The highly publicized failure of missions in Bosnia, Rwanda, and Somalia in 1995–96 led the Security Council to sharply curtail an explosion of operations that saw annual peacekeeping assessments grow nearly tenfold over five years, from $384 million in 1990 to about $3 billion at the end of 1995 ["Financing the United Nations," UNA-USA; DPI/1634/Rev.2, 3/96]. The cost of peacekeeping is expected to be less than half that in 1996, or between $1.4 billion and $1.5 billion [DPI/1634/Rev.2, 3/96].

The end of the huge Bosnia operation heralded an especially big decline in the collection of peacekeeping monies—and a corresponding cash crunch at the Secretariat [*Economist*, 2/10/96]. While the yearly cost of the U.N. Protection Force in the Former Yugoslavia (UNPROFOR) ran at around $1.6 billion, its latest replacement, the U.N. Mission in Bosnia and Herzegovina (UNMIBH), was expected to spend only about $53 million in the first six months of 1996 [ibid.].

The shrinking of the Bosnia operation left the U.N Angola Verification Mission III (UNAVEM III) the most costly of the Organization's current peacekeeping ventures, with a rough annual price tag of $254 million. Behind UNAVEM III came the U.N. Mission in Haiti (UNMIH) at $243 million annually, the U.N. Assistance Mission for Rwanda (UNAMIR) at $199 million, and the U.N. Interim Force in Lebanon (UNIFIL) at $135 million. The yearly bill for a dozen smaller peacekeeping operations authorized for 1996—ranging from the U.N. Mission for the Referendum in Western Sahara (MINURSO) to the U.N. Mission of Observers in Tajikistan (UNMOT)—was expected to total less than $350 million.

The drop in peacekeeping assessments was not necessarily likely to translate into a drop in peacekeeping debts to the United Nations (see table VII-3). Peacekeeping assessments represented the fastest-growing portion of unpaid dues to the United Nations in 1995, totaling $1.8 billion by March 1996 [ibid.]. The U.N.'s top three peacekeeping debtors were the United States, Russia, and Ukraine, which together owed $1.5 billion. Its top three creditors were France, Pakistan, and India, which were due a total of $326 million.

In the discussions of the Advisory Committee on Administrative and Budgetary Questions (ACABQ) on funding peacekeeping operations, a number of representatives expressed deep concern about a report released in October 1995 by the new **Office of Internal Oversight Services (OIOS)** [A/C.5/50/SR.12]. In its first annual report, the OIOS said: "The United Nations does not have in place proper arrangements for the maintenance of institutional memory or policies requiring the assessments needed to learn systematically from recent experience in peacekeeping" [A/50/459]. Overall, the report recommended that the Peacekeeping Financing Division speed up the filling of its vacant posts, start sending budget officers to their related field missions, and maintain ongoing dialogue and coordination with the Field Administration and Logistics Division. It was sharply critical of the Field Administration Division, saying it does not function in an environment that facilitates operational efficiency, promotes effective internal controls, or promotes effective management. It found the United Nations in danger of wasting considerable sums of money and risking third-party liability because of uncertain insurance policies where troops are deployed. It also said that the controls in peacekeeping operations over the deployment of international contractual personnel were not as strict as those normally exercised over the deployment of U.N. staff members, leading to higher staff costs.

Audits of specific missions found cases of excessive compensatory time off by military observers, civilian police, and military staff officers, overpayment of mission subsistence allowances, instances of unauthorized use of aircraft for non-official purposes, inadequate budgetary and accounting controls, and other irregularities. For example, a shortage in the delivery of fuel resulted in a loss of $540,000, the report said.

Two audits of UNPROFOR uncovered "unnecessary, excessive and extravagant expenditures." These included the purchase of uniforms for civilian personnel, snow scooters that were never used, luxurious heavy buses, and 1,400 more generators than were needed. The report said many of the generators were found intact in their boxes.

Perhaps the most serious losses were found in an audit of the U.N. Operation in Somalia (UNOSOM II). After the audit, the management of UNOSOM II agreed to recover $909,000 in overpayments made to a fuel distribution contractor. The management also failed to recover $1.5 million worth of food rations transferred to a food rations contractor until the resident auditor pointed it out. UNOSOM II procured water on the open market at a cost of 25 cents per liter when it could have bought the water from the food contractor for 10 cents per liter, at a savings of $1 million. (The OIOS made a separate investigation in 1995 of the theft of $3.9 million from UNOSOM II.)

Finally, the report said an OIOS audit of MINURSO exonerated the mission's Deputy Special Representative of charges of mismanagement and irregularities. "The complaints were triggered primarily by frustration as a result of non-extension of contract and personal animosity," it concluded.

In Resolution 49/233, the General Assembly had requested the Secretary-General to review the entitlements of staff assigned to peacekeeping missions, including the basis for and establishment of mission subsistence allowances. The report presented to the 50th General Assembly concluded that the entitlements of staff assigned to peacekeeping missions are dictated by the temporary and short-term mandates of the operations

[A/50/797]. It said that mission subsistence allowances provide a relatively simple and cheap mechanism to meet the costs of living in the field. The study added that the U.N. allowances were in many cases lower than those given to U.S. civil servants working in the same locations.

2. U.N. Administration

The election of a Secretary-General and the ongoing staff reductions and management reforms forced by the U.N.'s financial crisis are the administrative issues likely to dominate at the 51st General Assembly. When Boutros Boutros-Ghali was elected in 1991 he pledged to step down after one term. By early 1996, however, there was "a near unanimous belief" among U.N. diplomats that the Egyptian-born Secretary-General planned to seek another five years in office [*Washington Post,* 2/21/96]. The reelection of Boutros-Ghali will not help relations with the United States. The Clinton administration has clashed with him frequently over U.N. reform and peacekeeping ventures in Somalia and Bosnia. Among the Republican conservatives controlling Congress, Boutros-Ghali is regarded as "radioactive," according to the *Washington Post.*

Some possible candidates for Secretary-General whose names have been been mentioned in Washington are Mary Robinson, the president of Ireland; Sadako Ogata, the Japanese head of the Office of the U.N. High Commissioner for Refugees (UNHCR); Kofi Annan, the Ghanaian former Under-Secretary-General for Peacekeeping Operations; and Richard Goldstone, the South African judge and prosecutor at the U.N. War Crimes Tribunal.

With at least $110 million in additional budget cuts yet to be identified for 1996–97 and the staff vacancy rate already set to rise substantially, U.N. staff were said to be "agog with expectation and fear" at the end of the 50th Assembly [*International Documents Review,* Vol. 7, No. 3]. The transfer of three senior officials, including Annan, his deputy, Assistant Secretary-General Iqbal Riza, and Under-Secretary-General for Humanitarian Affairs Peter Hansen, was interpreted as a harbinger of the changes to come as the Secretariat adjusts to the drawdown of big, complex peacekeeping operations. Annan was moved to Zagreb to coordinate the transition from UNPROFOR to the NATO-led implementation force. Riza, a Pakistani, became the U.N. Coordinator in Bosnia Herzegovina. Hansen, a Dane, was transferred to the Vienna-based U.N. Relief and Works Agency for Palestinian Refugees (UNRWA). Joseph Connor has recommended that the Department of Peacekeeping go on to cut 40 percent of its posts, though France and some other countries argue that the department needs to retain some of the institutional memory it has developed.

U.N. diplomats and staff began to feel the constraints of the new budget in early 1996 as services were cut back and staff levels began to shrink. The United Nations reduced the number of documents it distributes. It refused to provide translation services for some meetings. It even cut out the freshly sharpened free pencils delegates were accustomed to picking up by the handful at every meeting [ibid.]. The Secretary-General offered a worldwide early separation program for 1996, with the expectation that voluntary buy-outs would significantly reduce staff levels [A/C.5/50/57]. The hiring of professional staffers was frozen in September 1995, and a freeze on hiring clerical staff followed in January 1996. The Secretariat also cut travel and slashed overtime spending [Associated Press, 2/5/96].

The hiring freeze is not likely to help the United Nations meet its **target for improving the status of women in the Secretariat.** The 50th Assembly received the report it had requested in Resolution 49/167 on the Secretariat's progress in appointing or promoting women to higher levels. The 20-page report says the percentage of women in posts subject to geographical distribution rose from 32.6 percent to 34.1 percent [A/50/691]. Women's share of posts above the D-1 level increased by 2 percentage points in the year ending June 30, 1995, rising from 15.1 percent to 17.1 percent. No women were among the four D-2 (Director) appointments during the year. Women made up 29.2 percent of those promoted to the D-1 (Deputy Director) level, and 58.9 percent of promotions to the P-5 level. At the Under-Secretary-General and Assistant Secretary-General level, the percentage of women remained the same: 11.8.

The Secretary-General submitted a **progress report on the Integrated Management Information System** [A/C.5/50/35]. Six years in the making, the computerized administration system now provides U.N. managers with instant access to information about how many staff are where and doing what, according to the report. Next it will make financial information available. The report does not mention how much the project has cost so far, but insiders estimate the price tag at $70 million [*International Documents Review*, 12/11/95].

The United States continued to push for other administrative reforms. On February 21, Madeleine Albright submitted a 33-page document detailing proposed changes to Diogo Freitas do Amaral, President of the General Assembly and the Chairman of the **High-Level Group on Strengthening the U.N. System.** Reiterating earlier Albright comments, the U.S. text recommended that the annual agenda of the General Assembly be greatly shortened. It suggested that the Assembly serve primarily as "the forum for addressing major issues of the sort that have been the subject of proposals for separate international conferences," such as human rights, housing, environment, and women's rights. It proposed that U.N. reform and funding "constitute the main thematic debate for the 51st Session" [*Washington Weekly Report*, XXII-5].

The United States also wants to merge such committees as the Committee on Program Coordination, the Special Committee on Decolonization, and the Palestinian Committee with other parts of the U.N. system. It wants the Second Committee (Economic and Social) to combine its separate annual resolutions into one omnibus resolution. And it wants to make the Fifth Committee (Administrative and Budget) and the ACABQ more accountable by opening ACABQ meetings to all member states and making its data available to them.

The document said continued public and financial support of the Secretariat depends on "early, visible, and continuing signs of improvement in four areas: restructuring, oversight, personnel, and system coordination." On restructuring, it recommends that the Secretariat be organized into a smaller number of departments with fewer Under-Secretaries and Assistant Secretaries-General, though it does advocate the creation of a new Deputy Secretary-General to assist the U.N. head with "routine responsibilities." It said the U.N. Trusteeship Council should be abolished and a number of departments phased out, such as the Department of Development Support and Management Services (DDMS), the Department of Economic and Social Information and Policy Analysis (DESIPA), and the Department of Policy Coordination and Sustainable Development (DPCSD). It advises making the Administrative Committee on Coordination (ACC), a coordinating committee of top personnel within the United Nations and its Specialized Agencies, "the functional equivalent of a 'cabinet' for the U.N. system."

The paper highlights the role of the Office of Internal Oversight Services (OIOS) as the U.N.'s Inspector General. It calls for "ongoing U.N. efforts to inculcate a management culture of accountability and responsibility among U.N. personnel," including "performance appraisals, new procedures for grievances and internal justice and financial disclosure requirements." It pushes for the development of a "sunset policy," arguing that it should become "the standing practice throughout the U.N. system for programs to end after a specified period of time unless they have conclusively demonstrated their continuing relevance and value according to established criteria."

Washington's proposals for economic and social matters focus mainly on the role of the Economic and Social Council (ECOSOC). The document says the number of ECOSOC subsidiary bodies should be reduced significantly by consolidations and terminations. It suggests that the Commission on Sustainable Development (CSD) "take the lead in reviewing and overseeing the integrated implementation of the results of recent U.N. conferences on sustainable development and related issues." The United States is adamantly opposed to the United Nations planning any more major conferences until the results of the most recent series, including the World Food Security Summit in Rome and Habitat II in Istanbul, are "fully applied and absorbed." It also recommends that five regional and economic commissions in the U.N. system focus on "services or assistance to countries in their region, leaving economic studies and the like to other bodies."

The United States would like to see the U.N. Development Programme (UNDP) act as an umbrella structure for integrating the work of other agencies and activities concerned with development. It proposes the enhancement of U.N. organizations involved with humanitarian relief, advising the Department of Humanitarian Affairs to "concentrate its efforts on developing blueprints." It also recommends that the World Food Programme (WFP) discontinue its role in agricultural development and that the U.N. Children's Fund (UNICEF) "concentrate its activities on the transition from relief to development." Within the other Specialized Agencies, Washington proposes the elimination of one of the World Health Organization's (WHO) six regional offices, the dismantling of the country offices of the Food and Agriculture Organization (FAO), and the reduction of publication and meeting expenses by the International Labour Organisation (ILO).

"By setting a high standard for U.N. management and by restructuring the organization to meeting changing needs, we can ensure the continued relevance, productivity and improved performance of the U.N. as it begins its second fifty years," Albright wrote in a cover letter to Freitas do Amaral. "That is a goal toward which all nations must work and from which all nations will benefit."

Audit and Control

The Fifth Committee considered a number of reports in 1995–96 from all three of the U.N.'s auditing bodies, including the Joint Inspection Unit, the Board of Auditors, and the Office of Internal Oversight Services. The major reports of both the JIU and the OIOS concentrated on improving U.N. administration and management, while the Board of Auditors produced a financial report for the U.N. Institute for Training and Research.

The JIU published a two-part study in October entitled "Accountability, Management Improvement and Oversight in the United Nations System" [JIU/REP/95/2]. Its top two recommendations were that: (1) each organization in the U.N. system establish a single focal point under its executive head dedicated to strategic planning, performance management, and maximally effective accountability and management improvement; and (2) each organization use its strategic planning unit to report to its oversight governing body in a concise and integrated way. The report found that with only 272 professional-and-above oversight posts, representing about 0.5 percent of the staff, the U.N. system needs more auditors. It argued that few U.N. organizations have yet seized on the dynamic opportunities offered by modern information technologies. It said the United Nations is only slowly developing human resource management programs and recommended that the organizations strengthen their training programs.

At the same time, the JIU presented the Assembly with another report called "Management in the United Nations: Work in Progress" [A/50/507]. In its executive summary, the report compared changing the U.N.'s entrenched bureaucracy to changing the course of an ocean tanker. "The enormous process of change is being done with modest resources, against entrenched habits of mediocre management, and in the midst of continuing financial and operations turbulence for the United Nations." It recommended: (1) the creation of a "command post" to head up the strategic planning units that the other JIU report recommended each organization establish; (2) that specific objectives, including dates for their completion, be inserted in all unit work plans in the Secretariat; (3) a series of measures to make Secretariat management and performance reporting more understandable, timely, action-oriented, and focused; (4) that the Fifth Committee systematically reassess its workflows and annual calendar and establish small, professionally qualified subcommittees to focus more clearly on management and oversight issues.

Interestingly, "Management" also offered what it called "non-recommendations." It said these were oft-mentioned recommendations that, if implemented, would improve U.N. management, but in fact do not stand a chance of becoming a reality in the politicized climate of the world body. For example, the report said it would do no good to recommend that the next Secretary-General be a better manager, since it can be reliably assumed that the politicians and diplomats who choose Secretaries-General will continue to select politicians and diplomats for the post, rather than individuals chosen for their managerial competence. It dismissed on the same grounds the pet U.S. project of creating a position for a Deputy Secretary-General to manage the Organization. "This is a non-recommendation because it is unlikely that a Secretary-General could find a Deputy to whom he or she would be willing to entrust the requisite managerial powers," the report said. Finally, it scoffed at the suggestion that an Executive Secretariat could assure the horizontal and vertical communication "so sadly lacking in the present United Nations": "A political Secretary-General and the top echelons of the Secretariat would be unwilling to risk a loss of personal power should the Organization's information flow be routinely controlled by the Executive Secretariat's Director."

The representative of the United States called the report "a valuable contribution" and said the JIU should focus on systemwide issues, leaving the OIOS to study peacekeeping operations [A/C.5/50/SR.36/par. 19–22]. The representative of Japan commended the JIU for taking steps to ensure systematic follow-up on its reports, but he said the unit should listen to the executive heads about why they were reluctant to respond to its recommendations [ibid., par. 2–5]. Finally, the delegate from Norway agreed with the report that the Fifth Committee itself should set an example by undertaking a serious review of its working methods and setting its own house in order [ibid., par. 11].

The first annual report presented to the General Assembly by the OIOS dealt with some of the same issues. In a preface to the report, Under-Secretary-General Karl Theodor Paschke said many of the U.N.'s problems could be traced to the lack of internal oversight, and he made the case that OIOS needs more staff. "The bureaucracy has grown without pruning for many years; procedures and structures have become too rigid, frustrating creativity and individual initiative; overlapping and duplication of responsibilities have not been adequately addressed, let alone eliminated," he wrote.

Paschke summarized the main substantive findings of the report in his preface. First, U.N. "rules and regulations are too complicated and simply too numerous to serve as clear guidance for staff." The personnel system is too cumbersome; "hiring new talent is as difficult as the termination of non-performers." Management and administrative skills are not well distributed. The different departments do not know enough about each other's work, creating the danger of overlapping and a preoccupation with "turf." Vertical communication also needs to be improved. The staff, even in key positions, has a tendency to shun responsibility and accountability. The United Nations has no central approach to the recording of actions and the maintenance and indexing of files, as some well-run governments do. The geographic spread of the Organization adds to its fragmentation and communications problems, so that the duty stations away from Headquarters "clearly lead a life on their own."

The report said that from November 15, 1994 to June 30, 1995, OIOS identified and recommended the recovery of $16.8 million it felt the United Nations was entitled to collect. Of that amount, $3.98 million had actually been collected [*International Documents Review,* Vol. 6, No. 38].

Speaking for the European Union, the delegate from Spain said the Union was encouraged by the fact that despite the short time OIOS had been in existence, its work had resulted in considerable savings, though it realized that the recoverable costs did not necessarily represent the total amount of waste that existed in the Organization [A/C.5/50/SR.31, par. 17–19]. The U.S. representative endorsed the recommendation calling for the adoption of a set of internal control standards and hoped it would be implemented promptly. His delegation noted with satisfaction that the report had addressed concerns over operational independence, whistle-blower protection, adequacy of resources, and access to and authority over other funds and programs. Though the resources allocated to OIOS had been adequate to address current needs, his delegation agreed that increased resources should be allocated to ensure its future effectiveness [ibid., par. 25–28]. The representative of Norway wanted to know why the Secretary-General had not commented on the very rich substance of the OIOS report. She was particularly disturbed by the lack of information on how the Secretariat intended to follow up [ibid., par. 42]. The representative of the Russian Federation warned that the report was no cause for complacency.

As in previous years, the General Assembly passed several resolutions ordering U.N. bodies to comply with the findings of the auditors. For example, Resolution 50/204 deplored the delays encountered in the implementation of recommendations found in the Board of Auditors' report on UNITAR. It expressed "serious concern" about "continuing problems of the lack of adequate managerial control" at the Office of the U.N. High Commissioner for Refugees. And it requested the Secretary-General to submit a report on the measures taken in response to a 1994 Board of Auditors' report on the U.N. Transitional Authority in Cambodia.

Human Resource Management

The Fifth Committee is scheduled to decide between two proposals to revamp the U.N. Secretariat's internal system of justice in 1997. The committee voted at its 40th meeting to postpone consideration of reforming the justice system after the Secretary-General and the ACABQ could not agree on whether to replace the current system, in which volunteers serve on a Joint Appeals Board, with a professional Arbitration Board [A/C.5/50/SR.42, par. 17].

The ACABQ has been complaining about the internal justice system since as far back as the 1986–87 Session. At that time, the advisory committee indicated "an urgent need to simplify administrative procedures with a view to achieving a significant reduction in the number of cases requiring a full-scale formal review' [A/50/7/Add.8, par. 3]. In 1995 the Secretary-General presented the committee with a plan that Under-Secretary-General Connor said "would seek more informal resolution of disputes, more professional and expeditious appeal and disciplinary machinery, and a much simpler and more cost-effective justice system overall" [A/C.5/50/2 and Add.1]. The ACABQ endorsed the report's recommendations for additional training and for the creation of a post of coordinator for new ombudsman panels. It also approved new posts for administrative review and for a panel of counsel. But it recommended that more work be done on what Connor called "the cornerstone of the proposed reform," the establishment of a professional Arbitration Board [A/C.5/50/SR.40, par. 38].

Connor said the advisory committee's partial approach could only be marginally effective, since none of the partial measures addressed the root cause of the problem, "namely, the volunteer nature of the current justice system." He said there were no longer enough volunteers to serve and those who were available did not have the required technical knowledge to deal with cases. He added that the substantial expenditure required by the "piecemeal reform" recommended by ACABQ could hardly be justified [ibid., par. 39–41].

Describing the proposal to replace the Joint Appeals Board and the Disciplinary Board as "radical and controversial," the chairman of the advisory committee concluded that the time was not ripe to implement the proposed changes [ibid., par. 44]. The president of the U.N. Staff Committee also said the union could not support the Secretary-General's plan. He accused the Secretariat of deleting agreements from the final plan that the Staff-Management Coordination Committee had reached in June 1995. He said the resulting proposal lacked due process and equity [ibid., par. 69].

The staff union's fears about an internal justice system that gives management more power seemed vindicated when an independent panel in January found that the United Nations erred in two cases in which employees were punished. An international panel found that a Canadian employee who took responsibility and resigned in 1994 after $3.9 million was stolen from a U.N. office in Somalia was made a scapegoat for the theft even though he was never accused of complicity. In their decision on November 22, the three judges on the Administrative Tribunal awarded the official, Douglas Manson, $10,000 plus accrued interest for "moral injury" and asked the Secretary-General to clear his record. In another case, four U.N. officials had been suspended when a U.S. company alleged that a competing Canadian company, Skylink, had won contracts to supply aircraft to the U.N. mission in Cambodia through "irregularities" in a secretive bidding process. The tribunal noted that a U.N. disciplinary committee had already exonerated the men. It asked the Secretary-General to rescind all disciplinary orders in the case and erase them from the men's files. If that was not done, the tribunal ordered the United Nations to pay the men $20,000 each [*New York Times*, 1/4/96].

The Secretary-General also reported to the Fifth Committee on the composition of the Secretariat in 1995 [A/50/540]. The deputy to the Assistant Secretary-General for Human Resources told the committee that the number of states underrepresented on the Secretariat staff had been reduced from 28 to 25. She said that 40 percent of the 135 appointments made had been candidates from developing countries, and 45 percent had been female.

The Common System

The Fifth Committee's most emotional debate at the 50th General Assembly concerned the 9.2 percent raise for professional staff proposed by the International Civil Service Commission (ICSC). A 15-member panel, the ICSC is responsible for the regulation of the U.N. common system's salaries, allowances, and other conditions of service. Backed by the Secretary-General, the Commission argued in 1995 that a 9.2 percent raise was needed to keep the U.N. competitive under the Noblemaire principle [A/C.5/SR.28, par. 1–30]. Meanwhile the staff unions accused the ICSC of being intolerably politicized, insisting that staff deserved a 25 percent across-the-board raise. Though some European and developing countries supported the smaller salary increase recommended by the ICSC, the United States, Russia, and China were vehemently opposed, and they carried the day. The General Assembly denied the raise in the program budget for 1996–97.

In Resolution 47/216, the General Assembly had asked the ICSC to study the application of the Noblemaire principle and a series of related remuneration issues. In its resulting report, the Commission defined the principle to mean that the conditions of service of international staff should be such as to attract staff from the country with the highest-paid national civil service. Historically, the United Nations had always based its salaries on comparison with the U.S civil service. For this report, however, the Commission studied not only U.S. salaries but those of the civil services of Germany and Switzerland as well as at the World Bank and the Organization for Economic Cooperation and Development (OECD). The studies found that conditions in the German civil service were superior to those in the United States. While the Commission did not come out in favor of making Germany the new, official comparator, it decided to continue monitoring the compensation of German civil servants.

The ICSC said a 9.2 percent raise phased in over the spring and summer of 1996 was necessary to bring the ratio of U.N. and U.S. salaries in line with the ratio approved by the General Assembly in 1985. U.N. and U.S. salaries are compared according to a ratio that reveals the difference between U.N. pay and that received by U.S. civil servants in similar jobs. U.S. salaries are given the numerical value of 100. In 1985 the General Assembly approved a range of 110 to 120 for the remuneration of professional and higher U.N. officials. The "margin" of 10 to 20 points between the pay of U.N. and U.S. officials is supposed to compensate for the expatriation, the insecurity of tenure, and the fewer opportunities for career development allegedly available to U.N. officials. In a study of the financial implications of the ICSC report, the ACABQ found that the average pay of a professional or higher U.N. official in New York is $87,980. The study concluded that the proposed raise would cost the U.N. regular budget $38 million [A/50/7/Add.7].

The Secretary-General opened the discussion of the Commission's proposal, arguing that increasing the salaries of professionals was an essential step in the process of reforming the United Nations and its Specialized Agencies. "Whatever their field of activity—telecommunications, atomic energy, patent law, education, agriculture, health, aviation, postal services, or trade—the shared concern of the organizations of the common system was the loss of competitiveness in relation to other international organizations and national civil services. . . . By taking action on conditions of service, the General Assembly had a unique opportunity to advance the overall reform effort." The representative of the International Atomic Energy Agency added that the current system of remuneration did not provide sufficient incentive to entice enough specialists to interrupt their careers to come to Vienna.

The president of the Coordinating Committee for International Staff Unions and Associations of the U.N. system took the floor next. He denounced the ICSC for failing to name Germany's civil service as the official new comparator for U.N. salaries. "The Commission's politically motivated refusal to recommend a change of comparator was tantamount to reneging on its technical mandate and had allowed the views of a minority of its members to prevail," he said. The approach was all the more regrettable, he added, given the Commission's six-year delay in carrying out a study of the best-paid civil service: While many national civil service salaries were keeping pace handsomely with inflation, U.N. remuneration had been frozen because of the financial crisis.

The president of the Federation of International Civil Servants' Associations attacked the work of the ICSC even more ferociously. He said the Commission in its current form was "too unresponsive, too political and too expensive." He pointed out that the Federation had submitted a resolution to the Secretary-General requesting a 25 percent raise in professional salaries "justified by hard evidence." He went on to say that "far too many of his constituents faced the grim prospect of being laid off at very short notice, the innocent victims of the domestic policies of one major donor country." He said that while staff were willing to continue their cooperation in management reforms, there was a limit, and that limit had been reached in Geneva on November 9, 1995. On that day more than 2,000 international civil servants demonstrated against the politicization of the common system, the politically inspired budget cuts, and the delays in paying contributions on the part of a single member state. The demonstrators also asked for the immediate abolition of ICSC and firmly intended to strike if the General Assembly accepted the totality of the recommendations contained in the ICSC report.

The representative of the Russian Federation said his delegation had difficulty accepting the Commission's recommendation for a raise. Not only did the proposal have unprecedented financial implications, he said, but there also was no sound justification for such an increase. He criticized the methodology used to calculate the margin. His delegation did not believe the United Nations was not a competitive employer. And since the U.S. federal civil service remained the U.N. comparator, he considered any reference to other potential comparators completely unacceptable. He said the only proposal his delegation could accept would be an adjustment of U.N. salaries to reflect the 3.22 percent raise given to U.S. civil servants in January 1995.

The representative of Norway spoke up in favor of the 9.2 percent raise. He said the ICSC recommendations could not be viewed in isolation. The necessary investment for a more efficient organization must be made; that meant investing in human resources with a view to attracting and keeping qualified staff and setting apart financial resources for training programs and career planning. The delegate from India also supported the raise, though he disapproved of studying other civil services to determine whether U.N. pay scales remained competitive. "That would lead to endless revisions and confusion," he said. U.S. salaries, broadly speaking, were still among the best.

The representative of the United States said his government was strongly opposed to the pay increase. He said the ICSC had overstated the salaries of U.S. civil servants. He pointed out that the Commission itself had noted the absence of any widespread or acute recruitment problems, adding that agencies could use special occupational rates to address particular recruitment and retention problems. Finally, he said the proposal came at the worst possible time, when both the United Nations and other international organizations were in the midst of a financial crisis.

"It would be difficult to tell the hard-working people of the U.S. that their tax dollars were being used to increase the compensation of U.N. staff," who already made more money than comparable employees in any civil service in the world, the U.S. representative said.

Index

Abdul Amir al-Anbari, 53
Abi-Saab, George, 89
Abkhazia, 68–73
Abortion, 160, 166, 226
Abrahamsohn, Carin, 233–37
Abuja Agreement, 46, 201
Abuse of women, 204
Accra Agreement, 45
Acquired immunodeficiency syndrome
    (AIDS), 160, 234–35
Ad Hoc International War Crimes Tribu-
    nals, 214
Addis Ababa agreements, 39–40
Aerial incidents, 290
Afghanistan, 3, 6, 200–201, 209; displaced
    persons, 218–19; food production, 153;
    Tajikistan and, 65–68
Africa, debt adjustment, 117; desertification,
    146; economy, 105, 114; education, 165;
    food production, 153; health care, 165;
    infectious diseases, 236–37; nuclear
    weapons, 83; overview, 30; poverty re-
    lief, 147; privatization, 117; trade, 149;
    see also names of specific countries; Sub-
    Saharan Africa
Agenda 21, 138, 140, 143, 169, 257
Agenda for Peace, 7, 8, 100, 183
Aggression, 265, 266, 270
Aging, 247–50
Agribusiness, 154, 158
Agriculture, 150–52, 154; Caribbean is-
    lands, 139; China, 157; practices, 135,
    141–42, 144; subsidies, 126; sustainable,
    151–52, 156–57; see also Food issues
Ahmed Yousif Mohamed, 63
Aidid, Mohammed Farah, 37–42, 284
AIDS. see Acquired immunodeficiency syn-
    drome (AIDS)
Air strikes, 12–13, 15
Airbus Industries, 124

Ajami, Fouad, 23
Ajello, Aldo, 74
Akashi, Yasushi, 14, 16, 19
Akayesu, Jean Paul, 288
Akosombo Agreement, 45
al-Assad, Hafez, 59–60
Albright, Madeleine K., 53, 54, 61, 63, 309,
    312–13, 322, 324
Alday, Ricardo, 24–30
Aleksovski, Zlatko, 285–86
Algeria, 163–64, 271, 272
Ali Mahdi Mohammed, 37–38, 41
Aliyev, Heydar, 73
Al-Kidwa, Nasser, 57
Allen, Patricia, 156
Alliance of Small Island States, 139
American Society of International Law, 218
Amir, Yigal, 56
Amnesty International, 206
Andean Group, 128
Angola, 30, 33–37, 200; disarmament, 10;
    elections, 7–8, 35–36; human rights
    abuses, 212; peace-building, 195; peace-
    keeping operations, 8, 200; repatriated
    refugees, 215; UNAVEM, 2, 4, 35–37,
    319
Annan, Kofi, 11, 19, 321
Anstee, Margaret, 35
Antarctic Treaty, 84
Antarctica, 167, 171–72
Anti-Ballistic Missiles (ABM) Treaty, 91
Antipersonnel mines. see Landmines
Anti-Semitism, 185
Aouzou Strip, 3, 6
Apartheid, 180, 266
Arab League, 37–38
Arab-Israeli conflict, 55–57
Arabs, 185
Arafat, Yasser, 55–58, 62, 64
Arbitrary detentions. see Detentions

Arbour, Louise, 287
Ardzinba, Vladislav, 71, 72, 73
Argentina, 125, 128, 168; economy, 121; ICC, 270, 274, 279; trade, 128
Aristide, Jean-Bertrand, 25–27
Armed conflicts, 6–7, 265; children and, 209, 243–44; human rights and, 195–206; post conflict peace-building, 195–96, 198–99; UNHCR and, 212; *see also* Refugees
Armed Forces of Liberia (AAFL), 43
Armenia, 73–75, 125, 208
Arms, 240; conventional, 93–103; embargo, 43, 49, 51, 100; outer space, 293; suppliers, 98; trade, 10; transfer of, 86, 93–103; *see also* Disarmament; Nuclear weapons
Arrests, 202
Arusha Peace Agreement, 48
Asia, AIDS, 235; children, 245; economy, 105, 122–23; foreign direct investment, 116; foreign exchange, 132–33; UN assessments, 309
Asia Pacific Economic Cooperation (APEC), 128–29
Assassinations, 56, 62–63, 64
Assessments, 304–10
Asylum, 78, 211, 215–16, 221
Atmosphere, 135–36, 137
Aung San Suu Kyi, 205
Australia, 168, 290, 310
Austria, 103, 168, 273
Automakers, Japan, 108
Automobiles, 129
Axworthy, Lloyd, 197
Ayala Lasso, José, 80, 174, 175
Azerbaijan, 73–75, 125, 208
Aziz, Tariq, 52

Bacteria, drug-resistant strains, 235
Bagosora, Theonest, 289
Bahrain, 290
Balkans, peacekeeping operations, 8
Ballistic missiles, 54, 91
Bangladesh, 30, 163, 168, 310
Bank of France, 110
Bank of Japan, 108
Banks and banking, 26, 106, 108, 109, 110, 111; *see also* International Monetary Fund (IMF); World Bank
Banyan Fund Association, 249
Barak, Ehud, 61
Baranja, 2, 4
Barre, Mohammed Siad, 37–38

Basel Convention, 150
Bassiouni, Cherif, 263
Bedjaoui, Mohammed, 290, 291
Beijing Conference, 219–22, 224–25, 227, 229
Beijing Declaration, 160–61
Belarus, arms control, 90–91, 125, 305–306
Belgium, 98, 99, 226
Bellamy, Carol, 242
Berlin Mandate, 136
Bernadotte, Count Folke, 5
Bhutto, Benazir, 94
Bicesse Accords, 35, 36
Bildt, Carl, 18, 20
Biodiversity, 144–45, 148, 167
Biological weapons, 54, 83, 87, 88, 97–98
Biosafety, 145
Biotechnology, 145
Birenbaum, David E., 312
Bíró, Gáspár, 201
Bizimungu, Pasteur, 50
Blacks, 185
Blaskic, Tihomir, 284
Blind, 253
Blondin Beye, Alioune, 36–37
Boeing jetliners, 124
Bolin, Bert, 137
Bolivia, economy, 119
Bolshakov, A. A., 72
Bonner, Raymond, 14
Border disputes, 64–68
Bos, Adriaan, 263
Bosnia and Herzegovina, 1, 11, 14–24, 100, 290; civilian affairs officers, 198–99; displaced persons, 218–19; human rights abuses, 195, 198, 283–84; peacekeeping mission, 2, 4; peacekeeping operations, 319, 321; refugees, 213–14; war crimes tribunal, 307
Bosnian Serbs, 11, 12–16, 20, 283–87
Bosworth, Stephen, 87
Bota, Liviu, 71–72
Boutros-Ghali, Boutros, 176, 254; Angola and, 35; Bosnia, 1; drug trafficking, 230; gender issues, 221–24; global taxes, 308; Haiti policy, 25–29; human rights and, 174; Iraq and, 53; Israel and, 61; Liberia and, 45; nuclear weapons, 96; peacekeeping, 5; population conference, 164; poverty and, 147; role in Balkan crisis, 23–24; Tajikistan and, 68; terrorism summit, 58; trade, 149; UN administra-

tion, 321, UN budget, 312–21; UN financial health, 303; war crimes tribunals, 282; Yugoslavia and, 19, 23; *see also Agenda for Peace*

Brahimi, Lakhdar, 29

Brazil, 168; economy, 121; trade, 128; UN debt, 305–306; WTO, 127

Bread for the World, 151

Bretton Woods, 222

Briquemont, Francis, 24

Brookings Institution, 185, 218

Brown, Frederick Z., 75–81

Brunei, 84

Brunner, Edouard, 71–72

Buchanan, Pat, 127

Budget deficits, France, 110–11; Germany, 110; United States, 107–108

Bundesbank, 109

Bunly, Thun, 80

Burke, Helmut, 233

Burundi, 30, 46–52, 209, displaced persons, 219; elections, 47–48; human rights abuses, 48, 195, 197, 219; refugees, 213–14

Buyoya, Pierre, 47–48

Byrd, J. Lee, 210–19

Cairo Conference on Population and Development, 221

Cairo Programme of Action, 160, 162–65

Calcetas-Santos, Ofelia, 245

Cambodia, 5, 328, advance mission, 3; economic issues, 76–77; elections, 7, 80–81; human rights abuses, 78, 79–80, 195, 212; justice system, 239–40; nuclear weapons, 84; overview, 75–76; peace-keeping operations, 8; politics, 77–78; UNTAC, 3, 75, 78, 79, 199–200, 327

Cambodian People's Party (CPP), 77–78, 80–81

Cambodian Red Cross, 78

Cameroon, 168, 290

Canada, 58, arms exports, 98; economy, 111; fisheries, 290; foreign exchange, 132; Haiti mission, 29–30; human rights contribution, 197; ICC, 269, 277, 277, 280; UN debt, 310; UN personnel, 328

Canberra Commission on the Elimination of Nuclear Weapons, 90

Capital development, 115–17

Capitalism, 105–106

Cardoso, Fernando Henrique, 121

CARE-USA, 39

Caribbean area, 107, 139, 317

Carlson, Stan, 1

Caspian Sea, 74

CD-ROM, 259

Cease-fires, 2, Angola, 35–36; Armenia, 73–75; Azerbaijan, 73–75; Bosnia, 286; Georgia, 68–70; Lebanon, 61–62; Liberia, 42–46; Rwanda, 47–48; Somalia, 37–42; Tajikistan, 64–68; Western Sahara, 30, 32

Centers for Disease Control, Atlanta, 237

Central America, 3, 6, 10, 121

Central American Common Market, 128

Central Intelligence Agency, U.S., 86, 96

Centre for Human Rights, 79–80, 175–80, 182, 183, 191–95, 227, 244

Chad, 208

Chechnya, 75, 209, 236

Chemical weapons, 54, 83, 87, 88, 96–97

Chemical Weapons Convention (CWC), 96–97

Chhon, Keat, 76

Chicago Board of Trade, 158

Child labor, 207, 244

Children, 241–47; armed conflicts, 209, 243–44; Asia, 245; child soldiers, 243; deaths, 233, 244; diseases, 234, 236, 244; education, 244; girl child, 228, 245; heath care, 160; hostages, 225; hunger, 158; immunizations, 236–37, 244; Latin America, 245; malnutrition, 244; needs of, 241–45; pornography, 207, 209, 225; prostitution, 79, 207, 209, 225; refugees, 217; rights of, 207, 242–45, 252; sale of, 225; sexual exploitation of, 245; sub-Saharan Africa, 245; trafficking, 201, 241; unaccompanied, 243; violence against, 245

Chile, 107, 168, economy, 114–15, 120, 121; NAFTA, 127–28

China, 60, 62, 163–64, 168, 203, 209, aid to, 148; economy, 123–24, 130–31; food issues, 153, 157; foreign direct investment, 116; grain imports, 157; Haiti mission, 29–30; HIV/AIDS, 234–35; human rights abuses, 124; ICC, 271, 281; nuclear testing, 83, 92–95; nuclear weapons, 84, 85, 89; Russia and, 18; Taiwan and, 124; trade, 129, 130–31; UN budget, 313; UNFPA, 166; United States and, 123–24, 130–31; WTO, 126

Chirac, Jacques, 290

Christopher, Warren, 22, 57, 59–61, 64
Cities and towns, 254–55
Civil law, 280
Civil service, 329–31
Clean Air Act, 149–50
Climate, change, 257–58; human effects on, 135–36; treaties, 136–37
Clinton administration, 58; arms transfer, 86, 100; Balkan settlement, 19; Bosnia war crimes, 284–85; chemical weapons treaty, 96–97; Dayton Accord, 21–22; economic policy, 107–108; Haiti policy, 25, 28; Israel and, 60, 64; landmine policy, 103; Middle East peace talks, 62; Somalia and, 41; trade policy, 127–33; UN budget, 312–13; UN obligation, 304–306; UN relations, 321; UNFPA funding, 166
Coastal resources, 140, 145
Coastal zone management, 140
Cocaine, 230
Colombia, 163, 205, 219, 269, 270
Colonialism, 31
Commission on Population and Development, 164
Common law, 280
Commonwealth of Independent States (CIS), 65, 69–73, 267
Communications, 293, 294, 298–99
Communism, 105
Competition, 128
Complementarity, 269–71
Comprehensive nuclear test-ban treaty (CTBT), 83–84, 94–96
Computers, 208, 322
Condoms, 235
Conference on Disarmament (C.D.), 83, 89–91, 92–96, 100
Confidentiality, 208
Congo, peacekeeping operations, 3
Congress, U.S., peacekeeping budget, 6; PLO, 57; UN obligation, 304–305
Connor, Joseph, 303, 307–308, 319, 321, 327–28
Conservation of marine life, 140–41
Conservation of natural resources, 144, 146, 148
Consultative Group on International Agricultural Research (CGIAR), 150, 154
Consultative Group to Assist the Poorest (CGAP), 152
Consumerism, 142

Consumption patterns, 142–43, 153, 154
Contraception, 226
Convention on the Elimination of All Forms of Discrimination against Women (CEDAW), 224–27
Convention on the Rights of the Child, 242–45
Convention to Combat Desertification, 145–46
Conventional Forces in Europe Treaty (CFE), 99
Conventional Weapons Convention (CWC), 101
Cooraswamy, Radhika, 187
Coordinating Committee for Multilateral Export Controls (COCOM), 101
Coral reefs, 139
Cotonou Agreement, 43–45
Council of Europe, 286, 296–97
Crime and criminals, 237–41; accessories, 281; arrest of accused, 277–79; Asia, 77; corporate, 276–77; custody states, 277–78; Draft Code of Crimes, 265–68; extradition, 278–79, 286, 288; fines and restitution, 281–82; judgments, 281–82; liability, 280; parole, 281–82; punishment, 282; *see also* Legal issues
Crimes against humanity, 174, 265, 270, 271
Croatia, 3, 14–24, 198
Cruel and unusual punishment, 202, 204
Cuba, 34, 168, 179, 184, 205, 209, 226
Currencies, 107, 108, 112–14, 130–32
Custody states, 277–78
Cyprus, 3, 6, 209, 226
Czech Republic, economy, 124, 125
Czechoslovakia, 98, 310

Dayton Accord, 11, 16–21, 198, 285
de Charette, Hervé, 93
Debt, 189; development and, 117–18; food role in, 152, 154; Uganda, 120
Decade of International Law, 295–301
Declaration of Principles, 55
Decolonization, 30, 31–33, 47
Defense Department, U.S., 97
Deforestation, 141–42
Delic, Hasim, 286
Deng, Francis, 185, 219
Denmark, 273
Desai, Nitin, 143
Desertification, 145–46
Detentions, 23, 80, 188, 202, 209, 283–84
Deutch, John, 54

Deutsche mark, 109–10, 131–33
Developed countries, economy, 105–16;
UN debts, 310; WTO membership, 131
Developing countries, aid to, 148; capital,
131; children's deaths, 233; consumption
patterns, 142; debt, 117–18; economy,
105, 114–15; energy supplies, 137; food
supply, 153; foreign aid, 118–19; foreign
direct investment, 115–17; foreign ex-
change, 132–33; population assistance,
163; space exploration, 294; UN assess-
ments, 311; UN budget, 313; WTO
membership, 131
Development, right to, 189–91, 209, 223
Dieng, Adama, 200
Diplomatic indebtedness, 299
Disabled persons, 250–53
Disappearances, 23, 188, 204, 209
Disarmament, 10, 291; Georgia, 69–70; Li-
beria, 44–45; Somalia, 39–40; *see also*
Arms; Nuclear weapons
Disasters, 10, 139
Discrimination against women, 186–87,
224–27
Diseases, 235–37
Displaced persons, 185–86, 209, 211, 212,
215, 217–19; Armenia, 74–75; Azerbai-
jan, 74–75, Bosnia, 218–19; Burundi, 48,
219; Cambodia, 79; Georgia, 69, 70, 75;
Liberia, 45; number of, 7; Rwanda, 49,
219; Sudan, 201; UN policy, 218–19
Djukic, Djordje, 286
Doe, Samuel, 42–43
Dole, Bob, 21, 308
Dollar, 107, 130, 131–32, 314–16
Domestic violence, 221
dos Santos, José Eduardo, 35, 36–37
Dracunculiasis, 234
Driftnet fishing, 170–71
Drought, 146
Drug trafficking, 230, 240, 266, 268
Drugs, 229–33, 237
Due process of law, 204

Earth Summit, 138, 143, 151, 253, 257
East Asia, 117, 123, 148, 149
East Timor, 206, 209
Eastern Slavonia, 2, 4, 20
Ebola hemorrhagic fever, 236
Economic Community of West African
States (ECOWAS), 42–46
Economic development, 76–77
Ecosystems, 139, 141–42, 146, 253–59

Ecuador, 310
Education, Africa, 165; children, 244; HIV/
AIDS, 234–35; human rights, 192, 196
Egypt, 60, 63, 168, arms imports, 99; ICC,
270; population programs, 163; UN
budget, 313
Ekeus, Rolf, 54, 55
El Salvador, elections, 7; human rights
abuses, 7, 195; justice system, 239–40;
observer mission, 3, 212
Elaraby, Nabil, 63
Elderly. *see* Aging
Elections, Angola, 7–8, 35–36; Burundi,
47–48; Cambodia, 7, 80–81; El Salvador,
7; Gaza Strip, 55–57; Haiti, 24–28,
Human Rights Com- mission, 209–10;
Israel, 63–64; Liberia, 42–44; Palestin-
ians, 181; self-determination, 182;
United States, 127; West Bank, 56–57;
Western Sahara, 8, 32–33, 181
Electricity, 257
Electronic Data Interchange and Related
Means of Communications, 298–99
Eliasson, Jan, 39
Embargoes, Angola, 36; arms, 10, 22, 100;
Burundi, 51; Liberia, 43; Rwanda, 49, 51
Emissions, 135, 138, 139, 257–58
Employment, 228–29
Energy, 144, consumption, 123, 142–43,
257; renewable, 137–38; sources, 137,
138, 143; sustainable, 137; uses, 138
Energy Department, U.S., 95
Engström, Jenny M., 241–47
Enron, 120
Environmental issues, 10, 253, 257–58, 259;
Antarctica, 171–72; Asia, 123; food is-
sues and, 156; human rights and, 191;
nuclear weapons, 89; ocean protection,
140–41; overview, 135–36; poverty; re-
lief, 147–48; space debris, 292, 294; trade
and, 149–50; UN role in, 136
Environmental Protection Agency, U.S.,
149–50
Equatorial Guinea, 209
Ethiopia, 226
Ethnic cleansing, 13, 14, 184, 214, 284, 285,
286–87
Europe, 106, 109–14
European Institute for Crime Prevention
and Control, 238
European Monetary Union (EMU), 109,
110, 112–14

European Parliament, 103
European Union, 18, 51, 58, 109, 112, 125–26, 198, arms transfers, 103; currency, 131–33; currency unification, 112–14; human rights contribution, 197; UN budget, 313; UN oversight, 326–27; UNDCP funding, 232–33
Evans, Gareth, 304
Evictions, 191
Exchange rate mechanism (ERM), 112, 131–33
Executions, 23, 202, 203, 204, 209
Exports, arms, 98–99; Cambodia, 77; China, 123, 130; control of, 101; debts and, 118; European Union, 125; food, 152, 153–54; France, 110; grain, 157, 158; hazardous wastes, 150; Japan, 107, 108; Mexico, 107, 122; Russia, 125; Turkey, 112; Uganda, 120
Extradition, 278–79, 286, 288

Fall, Ibrahima, 175, 176
Family planning, 160–61, 162–64, 166, 226, 244
Family reunification, 78, 189
Family values, 243
Famine, 10, 153
Fangataufa Atoll, 290
Federal Republic of Yugoslavia, 198
Federal Reserve Bank, U.S., 107
Federated States of Micronesia, 290
Fernandez de Gurmendi, Silvia A., 263
Fertility rates, 162
Financial aid, 147
Financial Times, 291
Finland, 279
First U.N. Emergency Force (UNEF I), 3
Fish stocks, 140–41, 167, 172
Fisheries, 140–41, 144, 170, 290
Fishing, 167, 170–71
Fissile material, 91–92
Food and Agriculture Organization (FAO), 150, 151, 153, 156, 167, 171, 244, 324
Food issues, 212, 217; access to food, 154; China, 157; demand for, 154; economics and, 158–59; global food production, 152–54; hunger, 151–52; overview, 150–51; supply, 154; United States, 157–58; WFP, 38–39, 78, 150, 212, 219, 229, 324; World Food Summit, 150–52, 155–56, 157; *see also* Agriculture
Forced labor, 23, 204
Ford Foundation, 229

Foreign Affairs, 308
Foreign aid, 118–19; debt and, 189; Haiti, 28
Foreign direct investment (FDI), 115–17, 133, Cambodia, 76–77; China, 123; India, 120; Mexico, 121; transitioning nations, 124–25
Foreign exchange, 131–33, *see also specific currency*
Forensic science, 188
Forests and forestry, 141–42, 145
Fossil fuels, 135–36, 137, 257–58
Franc, 110, 112
France, 58, 60, 61, 62, 168, agricultural subsidies, 126; arms exports, 98; budget, 162; chemical weapons treaty, 96–97; currency, 110, 113; economy, 110–11; foreign aid, 118; foreign exchange, 132; ICC, 270–71, 273, 274, 278, 280; nuclear testing, 83, 84, 92–95, 140, 290–91; nuclear weapons, 89, 90; peacekeeping debt, 319
Freedom of religion. *see* Religious intolerance
Freedom of the press, 185, 204
Freedom of travel, 189
Freitas do Amaral, Diogo, 290, 322, 324

Gabcikovo-Nagymaros Project, 290
Gabon, 236
Gálvez, Sergio González, 90
Gambari, Ibrahim, 50
Gambia, 42
Gaza Strip, 55–57
Gender equality, 175, 186–87, 219, 228
Gender issues, 221
Gender-based persecution, 216
General Agreement on Tariffs and Trade (GATT), 126, 127, 149, 150, 153
General Assembly, 5; First Committee, 93; Second Committee, 139, 148, 163–64, 179, 323; Third Committee, 175, 176, 179, 180–81, 184, 189, 201, 209; Fourth Committee, 180–81, 292; Fifth Committee, 178, 308–12, 323, 324–29; Sixth Committee, 189, 262, 295, 298–301; secretariat, 228–29, 322; women, 228–29
Genital mutilation, 216, 226
Genocide, 10, 196, 197, 243, 262, 264, 265, 270, 277, 280, 282; Bosnia, 290; Rwanda, 49, 51, 287–88, 289
Georgia, 68–73, 75, economy, 125; human

rights abuses, 69, 70, 75; observer mission, 3, 69–73
Germany, 58, 60, 168, 282, arms exports, 98, arms transfers, 103; Bosnia and, 14; civil service, 329–31; currency, 113, 109, 131–33; economy, 109–10; foreign aid, 118; foreign exchange, 132; ICC, 281; population assistance, 162–63; UN debt, 305–306
Ghana, 42, 119
Ghose, Arundhati, 92, 95
Giacomelli, Giorgio, 231, 232–33
Girls, empowerment of, 186; girl child, 228, 245; persecution of, 216
Glèlè-Ahanhanzo, Maurice, 184–85
Global Biodiversity Assessment, 144–45
Global economy, 105–106
Global Environment Facility, 144, 167
Global Programme of Action, 229–33
Global warming, 137–38, 148
Golan Heights, 59, 64
Goldstein, Gordon M., 11–24
Goldstone, Richard, 229, 285, 287, 321
Gomes, Pericles F., 34–35
Gordon-Somers, Trevor, 44
Gore, Al, 26–27
Göring, Hermann, 282
Gotland Island, 257
Goulding, Marrack, 199
Grain, 153, 157–58
Greece, 126
Green, Rosario, 221–22
Greenhouse gases, 135, 136–37, 138–39
Gregg, Donald P., 87
Gross domestic product (GDP), 112, 117; Cambodia, 76–77; Mexico, 121; OECD members, 106; Russia, 124
Groth, Carl-Johan, 205
Group of 77, 163–64, 313
Group of Seven, 92, 308
Guarantees, 298
Guatemala, 195, 200, human rights, 312; ICC, 273
Guinea-Bissau, 60
Guinea-worm disease, 236–37

Habitat II, 143, 161–62, 240, 253–59, 323
Habyarimana, Juvénal, 47, 49, 289
The Hague, 23, 286, 287, 289, 307
Haiti, 5–9, 24–30, 200, elections, 24–28; human rights, 312; human rights abuses, 195; justice system, 239–40
Hamas, 56–57

Hamilton Shirley Amerasinghe Memorial Fellowship, 300
Hammarberg, Thomas, 200
Hansen, Peter, 321
Hashimoto, Ryutaro, 129
Hassan, King of Morocco, 31
Hatfield, Mark, 103
Hazardous substances, 150, 296
Health care, 257–58, Africa, 165; AIDS, 235–37; WHO, 233–37, 244, 291, 324
Hebron, 55, 56, 64
Hertel, Shareen, 219–29
Hess, Rudolf, 282
Highly enriched uranium, 91–92
Hijacking of aircraft, 266
Hiroshima, 83, 88
HIV. *see* Acquired immunodeficiency syndrome (AIDS)
Hohenfeller, Peter, 292
Holbrooke, Richard, 16–19
Holum, John, 85, 91–92, 95–96
Honduras, 60
Hong Kong, 122–23, 130
Host countries, 299, 304
Hostages, 188, 266, children, 225; Liberia, 46; women, 225
Housing, 254–57
Howe, Jonathan, 40
Human resources, 327–28
Human rights, Afghanistan, 200–201; Angola, 200; Cambodia, 199; China, 203; Colombia, 205; contributions to, 196–97; Cuba, 205; development and, 189–91; education, 196; environment and, 191; Georgia, 71; Guatemala, 200, 312; Haiti, 26, 200, 312; indigenous people, 182–83; Indonesia, 206; Iran, 204; Iraq, 202; law and legislation, 174; Liberia, 201; migrant workers, 191; minorities, 183–84; Myanmar, 204–205; overview, 173–75; politics of, 175–80; promotion of, 191–95; Rwanda, 195–97; self-determination, 180–82; Sudan, 201–202; UN budget, 313; women hostages, 225; women's rights, 186–87; workers' rights, 191; Yugoslavia, 22–23
Human rights advocates, 203, 209
Human rights field operation in Rwanda (HRFOR), 195–97
Human rights violations, 6, 282, abuse of women, 199, 204–205; Afghanistan, 218–19; Angola, 212; arbitrary deten-

tions, 188; Armenia, 74–75; arrests, 202; Azerbaijan, 74–75; Bosnia, 195, 198, 218–19, 283–84, 290; Burundi, 48, 195, 197, 219; Cambodia, 78, 79–80, 195, 212; Chechnya, 75; China, 124; confidentiality of, 208–209; Croatia, 198; cruel and unusual punishment, 202, 204; detentions, 23, 80, 188, 202, 209, 283–84; development obstacle, 190; disappearances, 23, 188, 204, 209; displaced persons, 7, 45, 48, 49, 69, 70, 74–75, 79, 185–86, 201, 209, 211, 212, 215, 217–19, 293; El Salvador, 7, 195; ethnic cleansing, 13, 14, 184, 214, 284, 285, 286–87; evictions, 191; executions, 23, 202, 203, 204, 209; forced labor, 204; genocide, 10, 49, 51, 196, 197, 243, 262, 264, 265, 270, 277, 280, 282, 288, 289, 290; Georgia, 69, 70, 75; Haiti, 195; hostages, 188, 225, 266; Iran, 204; Iraq, 202; Israel, 181; kidnapping, 285; Liberia, 45; mass exodus, 23, 186; massacres, 11, 12–13, 14–15, 49, 285, 288; mercenaries, 181, 209, 267; missing persons, 198; Montenegro, 198, 209; murder, 283, 285, 289; mutilations, 202; Myanmar, 204–205; Nigeria, 203, 203–204; political intimidation, 80; prevention of, 191–92; racial discrimination, 185, 209, 225; racism, 184–85, 216, 267; rape, 23, 187, 199, 285, 286; refugees, 7; religious intolerance, 185, 204; relocations, 204; Rwanda, 49, 51, 195–97, 219, 243, 262, 287–88, 289, 290; sale of children, 201; Sarajevo, 14–15; Serbia, 198; sexual slavery, 187; slavery, 201; Somalia, 195; Sudan, 201; terrorism, 56, 58–59, 188–89, 238, 240–41, 267–68, 300; Togo, 194; torture, 187–88, 202, 204, 206, 209, 266, 283, 285, 288, 289; toxic wastes dumping, 191; violence against women, 186, 187, 220, 223, 225, 226, 227, 228, 241; xenophobia, 184, 185, 209, 216; Yugoslavia, 7, 23, 24, 197, 209, 212, 262, 285; *see also* Refugees
Humanitarian assistance, 5, 7, 312–13, Armenia, 74; Azerbaijan, 74; coordination of, 211–13; emergencies, 216–17; Liberia, 44; Rwanda, 48; Somalia, 2, 37–42; UN budget, 318
Humanitarian law, 174
Hun Sen, 77, 76, 78
Hungary, 125, 226, 290
Hunger, 150, 151–52, 155, 158

Hurricanes, 139
Hussein, Saddam, 53, 54, 55
Hutus, 46–52, 196, 288–89

Iceland, 226
Illegal arms, 240
Immigration, 216
Immunizations, 236–37, 244
Implementation Force (IFOR), 20
Imports, arms, 99; grain, 157; semiconductors, 129–30
India, 168, chemical weapons, 96; economy, 120–21; ICC, 272, 276; nuclear testing, 94, 95; nuclear weapons, 85; observation mission, 3; peacekeeping debt, 319; peacekeeping operations, 3
Indigenous people, 182–83, 209
Indonesia, 60, 84, 163–64, 168, 206; economy, 122; population programs, 163; UN assessment, 309
Industrialized countries, aid to developing countries, 148; budgets, 162; consumption patterns, 142–43; emissions control, 139; energy demands, 138; food exports, 152; greenhouse gases, 136–37; overconsumption, 153, 154; women's issues, 222
Indyk, Martyn, 56–57
Infant mortality, 234
Infectious diseases, 10, 244; *see also* Acquired immunodeficiency syndrome (AIDS)
Inflation, Cambodia, 77; China, 123; foreign currencies and, 133; Italy, 111; Latin America, 121; Mexico, 121–22; Russia, 124; transitioning nations, 124; Turkey, 111; Uganda, 120; United Kingdom, 111
Information, 10, crime and justice, 238–40; disability data base, 252; electronic data interchange, 298–99; management systems, 322; retrieval systems, 208
Ingushetia, 236
Intellectual property, 131, 145
Inter-American Development Bank (IDB), 26
Interest rates, 107, 109, 110
Intergovernmental Panel on Climate Change (IPCC), 135–36, 139
Interim Government of National Unity (IGNU), 43–45
Internally displaced persons. *see* Displaced persons
International Atomic Energy Agency (IAEA), 85, 330

International Civil Service Commission (ICSC), 329–31

International Committee of the Red Cross (ICRC), 38–39, 205, 212

International Conference on Population and Development (ICPD), 159 66

International Council on Voluntary Agencies (ICVA), 212–13

International Court of Justice (ICJ), 89, 261, 289–91, 318

International Covenants on Human Rights, 206

International Criminal Court (ICC), 262–65, 268–82, 301

International Development Association (IDA), 118, 119, 147

International Disability Statistics Data Base (DISTAT), 252

International Federation of Red Cross, 78

International Federation on Ageing, 248

International Finance Corporation (IFC), 119

International Fund for Agricultural Development (IFAD), 146, 150–52, 155

International Human Rights Law Group, 218

International Labour Organisation (ILO), 165, 174, 252 53, 321

International law, 218, 261–62, 272, 280, 283, 287, 288, 290, 295–301; codification of, 296; education, 299–300; jurisdiction, 297; state practices, 296–97

International Law Commission (ILC), 262–68, 276, 301

International Maritime Organization (IMO), 295–96

International Monetary Fund (IMF), 26, 77, 111, 114–15, 117–18, 120, 121, 124, 148

International Narcotics Control Board (INCB), 231

International Organization for Migration (IOM), 74, 217

International Police Task Force (IPTF), 198

International Red Cross, 44

International Seabed Authority (ISA), 167, 168

International Telecommunication Union (ITU), 294

International Training and Research Institute for the Advancement of Women (INSTRAW), 186–87, 222–23, 227, 229

International Tribunal in The Hague, 307

International War Crimes Tribunal for the Former Yugoslavia, 23, 229, 263, 265, 269–70, 276, 283, 283–87

International War Crimes Tribunal for Rwanda, 51–52, 226, 229, 263, 265, 269–70, 276, 282, 283–87

International Youth Year (IYY), 245–46

Internet, 239, 248, 259

Iran, 58, 65, 65, 179, 209, arms transfer, 100; human rights abuses, 204; nuclear weapons, 85; oil platforms, 290; UN budget, 313; UN debt, 305–306; UNIMOG, 3, 6

Iraq, 52–55, 58, 202, 209, food production, 153; human rights abuses, 202; nuclear weapons, 85–86; oil sanctions, 86; oil-for-food deal, 52; UN assessment, 311; UNIMOG, 3, 6; weapons of mass destruction, 53–55

Ireland, 103, 126, 282

Isenberg, David, 83–103

Islamic Conference, 38

Israel, Arab-Israeli conflict, 55–57; elections, 63–64; human rights abuses, 181; ICC, 273, 277; Lebanon and, 60–62; nuclear weapons, 85; Syria and, 59–60

Italy, 58, 60, 168, budget, 162; currency, 112, 132; economy, 111; ICC, 272; UN debt, 305–306; UNDCP funding, 232 33

Ivanko, Alexander, 15

Izetbegovic, Alija, 18–19

Jamaica, 273

Janvier, Bernard, 12–13

Japan, 58, 168
  currency, 108, 130, 132
  economy, 108–109, 129–30
  exports, 107, 108
  foreign aid, 118
  foreign exchange, 132
  ICC, 273, 277, 279
  population assistance, 162
  trade, 129, 129–30
  UN debt, 305–306
  United States and, 129–30

Japan International Cooperation Centre, 79

Johan, James, 38

Johnson, Philip, 39

Joint U.N. Programme on AIDS (UN-AIDS), 234–35

Jonah, James, 48

Joulwan, George A., 287

Journalists, 203–204

Judgments, 281–82
Judiciary, independence of, 209
Justice, administration of, 187–89, 238
Juvenile justice, 188

Kagian, Jules, 52–64
Kama, Laity, 288
Kamil, Hussein, 54, 86
Karabakh, Nagorno, 73
Karadzic, Radovan, 14, 22, 23, 284, 287
Karlsson, Gail V., 135–50
Kaunda, Kenneth, 35
Kayibanda, Jouvénal, 47
Kazkhstan, arms control, 90–91
Kennedy, John F., 158
Kentucky Fried Chicken, 120
Kenya, 163, 168
Keting, Paul, 90
Khmer Rouge, 76, 80, 200
Kidnapping, 285
Kinigi, Sylvie, 48
Kirby, Michael, 199–200
Kjellen, Bo, 146
Knight, W. Andy, 261–301
Knin, 13–14
Kodak, 243
Kohl, Helmut, 110
Kordic, Dario, 284
Korean Energy Development Organization
    (KEDO), 87
Kouyate, Lansana, 41
Krajina, 11, 13–14
Krona, 132
Krsmanovic, Aleska, 286
Kurdish provinces, 52, 53
Kuwait, 52, arms imports, 99; observation
    mission, 3, 6

Lajic, Goran, 284
Lake, Anthony, 27
Land use, 135–36, 141–42, 157
Landmines, 10, 83, 101–103, 201, 252; Libe-
    ria, 44; Rwanda, 48; Somalia, 40
Landzo, Esad, 286
Laos, 84
Lasers, 102
Lasher, Craig, 159–67
Latin America, aid to, 148; children, 245;
    economy, 105, 120–21; nuclear weapons,
    84; privatization, 116–17; UN budget,
    317
Law of the Sea, 140–41, 167–72, 300
Lebanon, 58, 59, 209, Israel and, 60–62;

peacekeeping operations, 2, 3, 6, 12–13,
    15–24, 60–62, 319, 320
Legal issues, Draft Code of Crimes, 265–68;
    ICC, 262–65, 268–82; ILC, 262–65, 268;
    jurisdiction, 264, 269–74; outer space,
    292–95; overview, 261–62; *see also*
    Crime and criminals
Leprosy, 234
Li Juan-zu, 28
Liberia, 30, 42–46, 201, disarmament,
    10; elections, 42–44; human rights abuses,
    45; observer mission, 3, 44–46
Liberian National Transitional Government
    (LNTG), 45
Libya, 58, 62, 63, chemical weapons, 88, 96;
    Lockerbie aerial incident, 290
Light water reactors, 87
Lindqvist, Bengt, 251
Lockerbie, Scotland, 290
Logging, 77
Los Angeles Times, 60, 100
Low-enriched uranium, 92
Lusaka Protocol, 36
Lynch, David A., 105–33

Maastricht treaty, 109, 110, 112, 113
Macedonia, 20–21
Machel, Graça, 244
Madej, Marek, 263
Madigan, Elizabeth K., 229–33
Madrid Accords, 31
Mail, 208
Malaria, 237
Malaysia, 84, 168, currency, 132; economy,
    122; ICC, 270, 271, 281; trade, 129; UN
    assessment, 309
Mali, 42
Malnutrition, 150, 244
Mandela, Nelson, 149
Manhattan Project, 90
Manson, Douglas, 328
Marine environment, 140, 145, 167, 170,
    172, 290, 296
Marine resources, 172
Maritime claims, 296
Maritime delimitation, 290
Maritime navigation safety, 266
Maritime safety, 295
Marks, Stephen P., 173–210
Marshall Islands, 137, 290, 309, 311
Martin, Ian, 196
Mass exodus, 186
Mass expulsions, 23

Massacres, 11, 12–13, 49, 285, Rwanda, 288; Sarajevo, 14–15; Yugoslavia, 24
Maternal mortality, 244
Mauritania, 31
Mawdsley, Andreas Aguilar, 290
Mayugi, Nicolas, 47
Mazowiecki, Tadeusz, 23, 197–98
McKinney, Cynthia, 103
McKinnon, Don, 93
McLaughlin, Martin M., 150–59
Measles, 234, 244
Medical assistance, 212
Megacities, 161
Men, AIDS, 235
Menon, Bhaskar, 1–11
Mercenaries, 181, 209, 267
Mercosur, 128
Mexico, currency, 131–32; economy, 105, 106, 115, 116, 119, 120–22, 127–28; exports, 107; foreign exchange, 132–33; ICC, 274; NAFTA, 107, 122, 127–28; population programs, 163
Michel, Smarck, 26–27
Middle East, biological weapons, 96; chemical weapons, 96; economy, 114; foreign direct investment, 116; nuclear weapons, 85, 86; peace process, 180–81; *see also names of countries*
Migrant workers, 184, 186, 187, 191, 207, 227
Migration, 123, 184, 217
Military Observer Group (ECOMOG), 42–46
Milosevic, Slobodan, 16–20
Minorities, 183–84, 204, 225
Minsk Group, 73–75
Missing persons, 198, 209
Mission of the Representative of the Secretary-General in the Dominican Republic (DOMREP), 3
Mladic, Ratko, 13, 14, 284, 287
Moi, Daniel T., 289
Moldova, economy, 125
Monetary policy, 106, 107, 109–11
Money laundering, 22, 230
Monrovia, 42
Montenegro, 198, 290
Montgomery, Thomas, 41
Montreal convention, 290
Montreal Protocol, 148, 150
Morocco, 8, 31, 99, 163, 184
Moscow Agreement, 69

Most favored nation (MFN), 131
Mozambique, 30; disarmament, 10; peacekeeping operations, 3, 39–40, 8
Mubarak, Hosni, 58, 62–63, 64
Multinational companies, 142
Murder, 283, Rwanda, 289; Yugoslavia, 285
Mururoa Atoll, 93, 290
Museveni, Yoweri, 289
Muslims, 12–14, 20, 60, 185, 283–87
Mutilations, 202
Myanmar (Burma), 84, 89, 204, 209

Nagasaki, 83, 88
Nairobi Conference, 219–20
Nakajima, Hiroshi, 235–36
Namibia, 8, 10, 34, 168, 291
Nandan, Satya N., 168
National Front for the Liberation of Angola (FLNA), 33–35
National Institute of Justice (NIJ) of the United States, 239
National laws, 268–69
National Patriotic Front of Liberia (NPFL), 42–44
National Unified Front for an Independent Peaceful, Neutral, and Cooperative Cambodia (FUNCINPEC), 77–78, 80–81
National Union for the Total Independence of Angola (UNITA), 6, 34–37, 215
Nationalism, 57
Ndadaye, Melchior, 47–48
N'Dow, Wally, 258
Negrophobia, 185
Nepal, 208, 310
Netanyahu, Benjamin, 63–64
Netherlands, 168, arms exports, 98; ICC, 269, 270, 281–82; population assistance, 162–63;
Neto, Agostinho, 33
New Guinea, peacekeeping operation, 3
New York City, 161
New York Times, 12–13, 286
New Zealand, 290–91, economy, 111; ICC, 270; UN debt, 310
Nigeria, 42, 168, 203–204, 209, 290
Nikolic, Dragan, 283–84
Nobel Prize for Peace, 90
Noblemaire principle, 329
Non-Aligned Movement (NAM), 83–84, 88–89, 163–64
Nongovernmental organizations (NGOs), 2, Agenda 21 progress, 143; aging pro-

grams, 248; Cambodia, 76, 79, 81; children's rights, 245; Colombia, 205; development right and, 189–90; disability related programs, 252–53; food issues, 155–56; human rights and, 173, 174, 176, 180, 191–93, 195, 205, 209–10; humanitarian assistance, 74–75, 212–13; indigenous issues, 183; Indonesia, 206; international law, 295; landmines ban, 102; Liberia, 201; religious intolerance, 185; Somalia, 39; women's issues, 220–21, 224; youth and, 246
Non-Proliferation Treaty (NPT), 83, 85, 88–92
North American Free Trade Agreement (NAFTA), 107, 122, 127–28
North Atlantic Council, 20
North Atlantic Treaty Organization (NATO), 11, 15–22, Bosnia, 284–87; nuclear weapons, 90
North Korea, 87, 98
Norway, 93–94, 313, 327
Norwegian Radiation Safety Institute, 94
Norwegian Seismological Service, 94
Ntaryamira, Cyprien, 48–49, 50, 289
Ntibantunganya, Sylvestre, 50–51 Nuclear testing, 83, 84, 92–93, 140, 290–91
Nuclear weapons, 83, accidents, 10; control of, 88–92; proliferation of, 84–88; use of, 88
Nuclear weapons-free zones (NWFZs), 83, 84–86, 89
Nucleonics Week, 86
Nuremberg tribunal, 265, 273, 282
Nuri, Abdullo, 65–66

Occupied Arab territories, 179, 180
Ocean affairs, 169–171, 290
Odom, William E., 21
Ofuatey-Kodjoe, W., 30–52
Ogata, Sadako, 211, 321
Oil consumption, 257
Oil platforms, 290
Oil spills, 172, 296
Oil trade, Azerbaijan, 74; Iraq, 52–53; Mexico, 116
Oman, 99, 168
Operation Restore Hope, 39
Operation Retour, 51
Operation Turquoise, 49–50
Organization for Economic Cooperation and Development (OECD), 106, 109, 111, 116, 119, 329

Organization for Security and Cooperation in Europe (OSCE), 71, 73–75
Organization for the Prohibition of Chemical Weapons (OPCW), 97–98
Organization of African Unity (OAU), 31–32, 37–38, 47, 48, 49, 51, 63, 243–44
Organization of American States, 8, 9, 26–29
Organized crime, 238
Oslo Accords, 55, 57
Ostrovsky, Yakov, 288
Ould-Abdallah, Ahmedou, 50
Outer space, peaceful uses of, 292
Oxfam, 117–18
Ozone depletion, 148, 150

Pacific affairs, 84, 93, 137, 139–40, 290, 309, 311
Pakistan, 65, 94, Haiti mission, 30; ICC, 272; nuclear weapons, 85; observation mission, 3; peacekeeping debt, 319; peacekeeping operations, 3
Palestine, Arab-Israeli conflict, 55–57; relief, 318
Palestine Liberation Organization (PLO), 56
Palestine National Council (PNC), 57–58
Palestinians, 181
Papua New Guinea, 140
Paraguay, 128, 168, 226
Paris Agreements, 75, 78, 79, 81
Parra-Aranguren, Gonzalo, 290
Partners in Action (PARINAC), 212–13
Paschke, Karl, 303, 326
Patarroyo, Manuel, 237
Pathfinder International, 166–67
Peace-building, post conflict, 195–96, 198–99
Peaceful nuclear explosions (PNEs), 95
Peacekeeping operations, Angola, 8, 35–37; assessments, 309; Balkans, 8; Bosnia, 20–22; budget, 4, 6; Cambodia, 8; costs, 75; dangers of, 8; financing, 305–308; Georgia, 68–73; history, 5; human rights abuses and, 7; Liberia, 42–45; Mozambique, 8; Namibia, 8; NATO, 286; overview, 2–4; personnel deployed, 4; police functions, 72; power, 4–6; safety of personnel, 8, 12; Somalia, 38–42; staff, 1; table, 3–4; Tajikistan, 65–68; troop support, 9–10; UN budget, 313, 318–321
Pelindaba, Treaty of, 84–85
Peres, Shimon, 56–58, 59, 62, 63–64

Pérez de Cuéllar, Javier, 32, 42
Perlez, Jane, 14
Perry, William, 22, 62, 87, 96, 286–87
Persecution, 218
Persian Gulf War, 85–86
Peru, 219
Peseta, 132
Peso, 131–32
Philippine Islands, 84, 168, 184, 313
Piot, Peter, 234–35
Piriz-Ballon, Ramiro, 65–67
Poland, 60, 168, arms exports, 98; economy, 124, 125
Poliomyelitis, 234, 236, 244
Political intimidation, 80
Political prisoners, 203, 205
Politics, conflict resolution and, 8–9; foreign aid, 118–19; United States, 128; unpredictability of, 11
Pollution, 257–58, marine, 140, 295–96; transitioning nations, 124
The Pope, 51
Popular Movement for the Liberation of Angola (MPLA), 33–35
Population, 253–59, Africa, 158; aging of, 247–50; China, 157; conference, 159–66; growth of, 153, 254; Habitat II, 161–62; mass movements of, 10; projections, 159–60; UN awards, 166–67; urban areas, 161
Pornography, 207, 209, 225
Portfolio investment, 116
Portugal, 33–35, 126, 277
Pound, 131–32
Poverty, 155, 190, 223–24, 253–59, Africa, 147; Cambodia, 77; China, 123; health care, 233; Iraq, 53; reduction programs, 259; rural areas, 146, 152, 255; Uganda, 120; urban areas, 255
Preval, René, 27–28
Preventive deployment, Macedonia, 20–21
Prevlaka, observer mission, 2, 4
Price Waterhouse, 177
Prison administration, 79
Prisoners of war, 13, 284
Privatization, 26, 116–17, 124
Procurement, 11
Prostitution, 79, 207, 209, 225
Psychotropic substances, 230, 231
Public office holders, code of conduct, 241

Q2000, 257
Qatar, 290

Quadripartite Agreement, 70–72
Quality of life, 259

Rabin, Yitzhak, 56
Racial discrimination, 185, 209, 225
Racism, 184–85, 216, 267
Radio broadcasts, 10
Rain forests, 141
Rajic, Ivica, 284
Rakhmonov, Emomali, 65–67
Rakhmonov, Zafar, 67–68
Ramaker, Jaap, 94
Ramos, Fidel, 84, 166
Ranariddh, Norodom, 76, 78
Rand, 132
Rape, 23, 187, 199, 285, 286
Rarotonga, Treaty of, 84–85
Rawlings, J. J., 45, 46
Recessions, 111, 114
Red Crescent Societies, 78
Refugee Policy Group, 185, 218
Refugees, 20, 184, 212, Armenia, 74; asylum, 215–16; Azerbaijan, 74; Bosnia, 213–14; Burundi, 51, 213–14; Cambodia, 78–79; camps, 243; Chechnya, 75; children, 217; definition, 213; food, 217; Georgia, 70–72, 73; Hutus, 196; Liberia, 43; militarization of camps, 214; number of, 7; repatriation, 70–71, 78, 79, 196, 214–15; Rwanda, 48, 49, 51, 213–14, 289; status of, 211, 213–14; Western Sahara, 32
Rehn, Elisabeth, 198
Religious intolerance, 185, 204
Reproductive health, 160–61, 162–64, 166
Republic of Korea, 168
Resolution *435*, 34
Resolution *808*, 263, 283
Resolution *827*, 283
Resolution *878*, 41
Resolution *955*, 263
Resolution *986*, 52, 53
Resolution *1044*, 63
Resolution *1056*, 33
Resolution *1960*, 55
Ricupero, Rubens, 149
Rieff, David, 12
Rio Summit, 169
Ritalin, 231
River blindness, 236–37
Riza, Iqbal, 321
Robinson, Mary, 321
Rockefeller Foundation, 163
Rodley, Nigel, 188

Romania, arms transfers, 103
Rotary International, 236
Rotblat, Joseph, 90
Royal Cambodian Government (RCG), 76–81
Rural areas, 146, 152, 186, 255
Rushdie, Salman, 204
Russia, 58, 62, 65, 168, arms exports, 98; Chechnya and, 75; chemical weapons treaty, 96–97; China and, 18; economy, 124; nuclear testing, 92, 93–95; nuclear weapons, 85, 89, 91, 92; peacekeeping debt, 319; polio, 236; United States and, 18; WTO, 126, 127
Russian Federation, 60, 68–69, 70, 73–74, U.N. budget, 10, UN debt, 305–306; UN oversight, 327; UN salaries, 330–31
Rutaganda, Georges, 288
Rwanda, 6, 7, 30, 46–52, 209, assistance mission, 3, 49–51; displaced persons, 219; human rights abuses, 49, 51, 195–97, 219, 243, 262, 287–88, 289, 290; justice system, 239–40; observer mission, 3, 6; peacekeeping operations, 319; refugees, 213–14; troop support, 10; troop withdrawal, 11; war crimes tribunal, 51–54, 214, 226, 229, 263, 265, 269–70, 276, 282, 283–87; women's issues, 226
Rwandan Patriotic Front (RPF), 47–51

Sadik, Nafis, 162, 164, 165
Saermark-Thomsen, Finn, 284
Safe havens, 11, 12–13, 15, 24
Saharan Democratic Arab Republic (SDAR), 31
Sam Rainsy, 78, 81
Samoa, 290
Sanchez, Oscar Arias, 103
Sanctions, 300–301, Angola, 36; economic, 53; Iraq, 53, 86; oil, 86; Serbia, 18; Sudan, 62, 63; Yugoslavia, 22
Sanders, Kanya D. Tampoe, 210–19
Sarajevo, 14–24, 286, human rights abuses, 14–15; NATO air strikes, 15–16; UN-PROFOR, 15–24
Saro-Wiwa, Ken, 203
Saudi Arabia, 99, 208
Savimbi, Jonas, 35, 36
Scarborough, Joe, 304–305
Schroeder, Oskar, 231
Schultz, Kathryn R., 83–103
Sea level rise, 137, 139
Seabed mining, 168

Seafarers, 295
Second U.N. Emergency Force (UNEF II), 3
Secretary-General. *see* Boutros-Ghali, Boutros
Security Council, Angola and, 35–37; Bosnia air strikes, 18; Burundi, 48–52; crimes referred to ICC, 264; Georgia and, 69–73; Haiti and, 29–30; judicial bodies, 282; members, 2, 274–75; peacekeeping dangers, 8; role in ICC, 273–75; role in peace operations, 5–6; Rwanda and, 46–48, 50–51; Somalia and, 37–42; Sudan and, 62–63; Western Sahara and, 31–33
Self-determination, 31, 180–82
Semiconductors, 129–30
Senegal, 168
Serbia, 14–24, 198, 290
Sexual exploitation, 245
Sexual harassment, 229
Sexual health, 160, 166
Sexual slavery, 187
Shahani, Letitia Ramos, 166
Shamgar Commission of Inquiry, 56
Sharipov, Mufti Fatkhulla, 67
Shevaardnadze, Eduard, 72
Shiddo, Abdel Aziz, 202
Shinrikyo, Aum, 96
Shuttle diplomacy, 14, 74
Sierra Leone, 208
Sihanouk, Norodom, 199
Singapore, 84, 122–23, 311
Sirivudh, Norodom, 78
Skylink, 328
Slavery, 201
Slovakia, 124, 125, 290
Slovania, 208, 275, 279
Small island states, 138–40
Smallpox, 234
Smith, Harold, 88
Smith, Rupert, 12
Social services, 164–65
Solana, Javier, 287
Solar energy, 137, 138, 143
Solomon Islands, 290
Somalia, 5, 6, 30, 37–42, 284, disarmament, 10; human rights abuses, 195; humanitarian aid, 2; justice system, 239–40; peacekeeping operations, 2, 3, 38–40, 319, 321; troop withdrawal, 11; UN staff, 328; United States and, 41; UNO-SOM II, 1–2, 3, 320

Son Sann, 78

South Africa, 168, 204, 267, currency, 132; foreign exchange, 132; ICC, 277; Namibia and, 34; nuclear weapons, 84, 85; UN assessment, 311

South America, economy, 121

South Asia, 84, 86, 96

South East Asia Nuclear Weapon-Free Zone (SAENWFZ), 84

South Korea, 122–23, 129, 309

South Pacific, 84, 93

South West Africa. *see* Namibia

Southeast Asia, 83

Sovereignty, 7, 182, 270, 271, 272, 297

Soviet Union, grain imports, 157; UN debt, 310; *see also names of specific countries*

Space debris, 292, 294

Space law, 291–95

Space science, 292–93

Spain, 58, budget, 162; currency, 132; fisheries, 290; Western Sahara and, 31

Special Olympics World Games, 252

Specter, Arlen, 57

Speer, Albert, 282

Speth, Gus, 146

Spratly Islands, 84

Srebrenica, 11, 12–13, 15, 24, 198, 286

Sri Lanka, 218–19

Stand-by letters of credit, 298

START treaties, 83, 90–91

State Department, U.S., 59, 80, 101, 306

State of the World's Children, 243, 245

State Parties to the LOS Convention, 167, 168–69

Stockholm International Peace Research Institute (SIPRI), 98, 99

Su, Andrew H., 247–50

Sub-Saharan Africa, 146, aid to, 148; children, 245; food issues, 158; foreign direct investment, 116, 117

Sudan, 58, 62–63, 168, 201–202, 209

Summit of the Americas, 128

Sustainable agriculture, 151–52, 156–57

Sustainable development, 157, 165, 167–68, 169–72, biodiversity, 144–45; climate issues, 137–39; consumption patterns, 142–43; desertification, 145–46; financing, 147–48; forests, 141–42; ocean protection, 140–41; program implementation, 143; small islands, 139; threats to, 144; trade role in, 149–50; UN role, 142–43

Sustainable energy, 137

Sustainable human settlements, 253–59

Sweden, 132, 272, 274

Switzerland, 280, 281, 329–31

Syria, 58, 59–60, 64

Taba Agreement, 55

Tabatabai, Zuzu, 222

Taiwan, China and, 124; economy, 122–23; human rights, 131; trade, 129

Tajikistan, 64–68, economy, 125; observer mission, 65–68, 319

Talbott, Strobe, 25, 86–87

Taylor, Charles, 42–43

Technology, 142–43, 154, biotechnology, 145; outer space, 293

Technology transfer, 294

Teheran Agreement, 65

Telecommunications, 330

Temperature, changes in, 135–36

Ter-Horst, Enrique, 29

Terrorism, 56, 188–89, 238, 240–41, 267–68, 300, campaign against, 58–59; counterterrorism, 62

Tetanus, 234, 244

Thailand, 84, 163, 208, AIDS, 235; currency, 132; ICC, 278; UN assessment, 309

Theissen, Marc, 305

Third World countries, 182

Tierra del Fuego, 120

Tlatelolco Treaty, 84

Tobago, 168

Togo, 42, 194

Tokyo war crimes tribunal, 273

Torture, 187–88, 206, 209, 266, 283, Iran, 204; Iraq, 202; Rwanda, 288, 289 Yugoslavia, 285

Tourism, Antarctica, 171–72; Caribbean islands, 139

Toxic substances, 191, 209

Trade, Africa, 149; bilateral, 129–31; developing countries, 149–50; food system, 153–54; forest exploitation, 142; GATT, 126, 127, 149, 150, 153; global taxes, 308; hemispheric, 128; intellectual property, 145; international law, 298–99; NAFTA, 107, 122, 127–28; regional nature of, 127–29; trends, 126–27; UNCTAD, 317–18; WTO, 124, 126–27, 130, 131, 149–50, 222

Trade union leaders, 203

Transitioning nations, 105–106, 124–25, 126

Transparency in armaments, 98–103

Transportation, 144, 257–58
Treaties, acceptance of, 297–98; Antarctica, 84; Anti-Ballistic Missile, 91; children's rights, 242–43; climate change, 136–37; computerization of, 300; Conventional Forces in Europe, 99; desertification, 146; drug, 231; human rights, 206–208; indigenous issues, 183; Maaschrict, 109, 110, 112, 113; nuclear test ban, 83–84, 94–96; Pelindaba, 84–85; Rarotonga, 84–85; START, 83, 90–91; Tlatelolco, 84
Triple Seven Agreement, 45
Trust Fund for Ageing, 249
Trust Fund for Travel Assistance, 299
Tuberculosis, 235–36
Tudjman, Franjo, 18–19, 284
Tunisia, 163, 168, 269
Turajonzoda, Ali Akbar, 67
Türk, Danilo, 176
Turkey, 58, 111–12, 132
Tutsis, 46–52, 288–89
Twagiramungu, Faustin, 50

Uganda, 47, AIDS, 235; debt payment, 118; economy, 120; observer mission, 3, 6
Ukraine, 168, arms control, 90–91; economy, 125; peacekeeping debt, 319; UN debt, 305–306, 310; women's issues, 226
U.N. Advance Mission in Cambodia (UNAMIC), 3
U.N. Advisory Committee on Administrative and Budgetary Questions (ACABQ), 309, 314–16, 319, 323, 327–39
U.N. Angola Verification Mission I (UNAVEM I), 34–37
U.N. Angola Verification Mission II (UNAVEM II), 3, 35–37
U.N. Angola Verification Mission III (UNAVEM III), 2, 4, 36–37, 200, 319
U.N. Aouzou Strip Observer Group (UNASOG), 3, 6
U.N. Assistance Mission for Rwanda (UNAMIR), 3, 49–51
U.N. Centre for Human Settlements (UNCHS), 139, 255
U.N. Charter, 4–5, 6–7, 181, 182, 186, 209–10, 271, 291, Article *102*, 298–301; Chapter VI, 49, 195; Chapter VII, 6, 39, 49, 55, 195, 264–65, 272, 274–75; costs share, 10; enforcement powers, 7
U.N. Children's Fund (UNICEF), 39, 150,

207, 212, 217, 219, 229, 233, 234, 236, 241–45, 248, 252, 306, 324
U.N. Commission on Human Rights, 75, 79–80, 207–208, 209–10, 223, 225
U.N. Commission on International Trade Law (UNCITRAL), 298–99
U.N. Commission on Narcotic Drugs (CND), 231–32
U.N. Commission on Sustainable Development (CSD), 137–50, 167–68, 169–72
U.N. Commission on the Status of Women (CSW), 220–28
U.N. Committee on Contributions, 309, 311
U.N. Committee on New and Renewable Energy and on Energy for Developpment, 137–38
U.N. Conference on Environment and Development (UNCED), 138, 143, 151, 253, 257
U.N. Conference on Human Settlements, 240, 253–59
U.N. Conference on Trade and Development (UNCTAD), 115, 125, 139, 147, 149–50, 317–18
U.N. Confidence Restoration Operation (Croatia) (UNCRO), 3
U.N. Convention Against Illicit Traffic in Narcotic Drugs and Psychotropic Substances, 230
U.N. Crime and Justice Information Network (UNCJIN), 238–40
U.N. Decade of Disabled Persons, 250
U.N. Department for Policy Coordination and Sustainable Development, 222
U.N. Department of Administration and Management (DAM), 222, 316–17
U.N. Department of Humanitarian Affairs (DHA), 211–12, 216–17, 252, 318
U.N. Department of Overall Policymaking, Direction and Coordination, 318
U.N. Department of Peacekeeping Operations (DPKO), 1–2, 11, 318
U.N. Department of Policy Coordination and Sustainable Development (DPCSD), 139
U.N. Department of Political Affairs, 318
U.N. Department of Public Information, 317
U.N. Development Fund for Women (UNIFEM), 187, 222–23, 227, 229, 233, 248

U.N. Development Programme (UNDP), 79, 119, 121, 144, 146, 148, 166, 200, 212, 223, 233, 234, 236, 238, 306, 317, 324

U.N. Disarmament Commission, 100–101

U.N. Disaster Relief Organization (UNDRO), 212

U.N. Disengagement Observer Force (UNDOF), 3, 6

U.N. Division for Social Policy and Development (DSPD), 247, 252

U.N. Division for the Advancement of Women (DAW), 222, 227

U.N. Drug Control Programme, 230

U.N. Economic and Social Council (ECOSOC), 164, 165, 170, 174, 184, 206–208, 223–25, 227, 231–32, 238, 239, 323–24

U.N. Educational, Scientific and Cultural Organization (UNESCO), 138, 150–51, 193, 234

U.N. Environment Programme (UNEP), 135, 137, 139, 144–45, 146, 148, 150, 170, 229, 306, 318

U.N. Framework Convention on Climate Change (FCCC), 136–37

U.N. Good Offices Mission in Afghanistan and Pakistan (UNGOMAP), 3, 6

U.N. High Commissioner for Human Rights, 71, 175–80, 190, 205, 212

U.N. High Commissioner for Refugees (UNHCR), 7, 20, 70–73, 78–79, 150, 174, 186, 210–19, 229, 244, 318, 327

U.N. India-Pakistan Observation Mission (UNIPOM), 3

U.N. Industrial Development Organization (UNIDO), 297–98, 306

U.N. Interim Force in Lebanon (UNIFIL), 3, 6, 60–62

U.N. International Drug Control Programme (UNDCP), 230–33

U.N. International Police Task Force, 20

U.N. Iran-Iraq Military Observer Group (UNIMOG), 3, 6

U.N. Iraq-Kuwait Observation Mission (UNIKOM), 3, 6

U.N. Military Observer Group in India and Pakistan (UNMOGIP), 3, 6

U.N. Mission for the Referendum in Western Sahara (MINURSO), 3, 6, 32–33, 329, 320, 32

U.N. Mission in Bosnia and Herzegovina (UNMIBH), 2, 4, 198–99

U.N. Mission of Observers in Tajikistan (UNMOT), 65–68, 319

U.N. Mission of Observers in Prevlaka (UNMOP), 2, 4

U.N. Observation Group in Lebanon (UNOGIL), 3

U.N. Observer Group in Central America (ONUCA), 3, 6

U.N. Observer Mission in El Salvador (ONUSAL), 3, 212

U.N. Observer Mission in Georgia (UNOMIG), 3, 69–73

U.N. Observer Mission in Liberia (UNOMIL), 3, 26–30

U.N. Observer Mission Uganda-Rwanda (UNOMUR), 3, 6

U.N. Office for Outer Space Affairs, 293

U.N. Office of Internal Oversight Services (OIOS), 303–304, 319 20, 323, 324–27

U.N. Operation in Mozambique (ONUMOZ), 3, 39–40

U.N. Operation in Somalia I (UNOSOM I), 2, 3, 38–40

U.N. Operation in Somalia II (UNOSOM II), 1–2, 3, 320

U.N. Operation in the Congo (ONUC), 3

U.N. Peacekeeping Force in Cyprus (UNFICYP), 3, 6

U.N. Population Fund (UNFPA), 162, 163, 165–66, 229, 233, 234–35, 248

U.N. Preventive Deployment Force (former Yugoslavia) (UNPREDEP), 2, 4

U.N. Programme on Space Applications, 292–93

U.N. Protection Force (UNPROFOR), 2, 12–13, 15–24, 319, 320, 283

U.N. Register of Conventional Arms, 83, 98–103

U.N. Relief and Works Agency in Palestine (UNRWA), 318

U.N. Security Force in West New Guinea (UNSF), 3

U.N. Special Commission (UNSCOM), 86, 96

U.N. Transition Assistance Group (UNTAG), 3, 6

U.N. Transitional Administration for Eastern Slavonia, Baranja and Western Sirmium (UNTAES), 2, 4

U.N. Transitional Authority in Cambodia (UNTAC), 3, 75, 78, 79, 199–200, 327

U.N. Truce Supervision Organization (UNTSO), 3, 5, 6

U.N. Trusteeship Council, 299
U.N. Unified Task Force (UNITAF), 2, 39
U.N. Voluntary Fund for Disability, 251
U.N. Yemen Observation Mission
    (UNYOM), 3
U.N. Youth Unit, 246
Undernutrition, 158
Unemployment, 253–59, Argentina, 121;
    France, 110; Germany, 109, 110; Italy,
    111; Japan, 108–109; OECD members,
    109; transitioning nations, 124
Unispace III, 292
United Arab Emirates, 99
United Kingdom, 58, 60, 168, arms exports,
    98; chemical weapons, 96; currency, 112,
    113, 131–32; economy, 111; ICC, 275;
    Lockerbie aerial incident, 290; nuclear
    testing, 95; nuclear weapons, 84–85, 89,
    90; population assistance, 162; UN debt,
    305–306; UNDCP funding, 232–33
United Liberation Movement for Democ-
    racy in Liberia (ULIMO), 43–46
United Nations, administration, 321–24;
    aging funding, 249–50; AIDS program,
    234–35; assessments, 304–307, 308–12;
    audits, 320, 324–27; Board of auditors,
    324–27; budget, 229, 312–21; crime bud-
    get, 239–40; Dayton Accord, 20–22; dis-
    ability fund, 251; dues of members, 303–
    307; economic commissions, 317–18;
    financial health, 287, 299, 303–10, 321;
    funding appeals, 217; Headquarters, 253,
    317; hiring freeze, 321–22; human re-
    source management, 327–28; humanitar-
    ian departments, 318; Integrated Man-
    agement Information; System, 322; Joint
    Inspection Unit, 324–27; Legal Office,
    167, 169–72; Office for Special Political
    Affairs, 2; oversight, 303–304, 313, 316,
    319–20, 323, 324–27; peacekeeping
    costs, 10; peacekeeping dues, 305–308;
    political departments, 318; population
    awards, 166–67; procurement, 317; pro-
    gram budget, 314–16; relief workers, 38;
    role, 5; safety of personnel, 8, 12, 38, 45,
    69–70; Secretariat, 2, 187, 200, 222, 229;
    sexual harassment, 229; social commis-
    sions, 317–18; staff, 228–29, 321–22; Su-
    dano-Sahelian Office, 146; UNAIDS
    budget, 234; UNDCP financing,
    232–33; UNICEF budget, 242, 244–45;
    UNPROFOR budget, 283; U.S. involve-
    ment, 166; voting rights, 304; war crimes
    tribunal funding, 283, 288; women, 228–
    29, 322; youth unit budget, 246
United Nations Association of the USA,
    208
United Nations Border Relief Organization,
    78
United States, 60, 62, 168; aid to developing
    countries, 147; Angola and, 34; arms ex-
    ports, 98, 99; arms transfer, 100; Bosnia
    and, 14; budget deficit, 107–108; chemi-
    cal weapons treaty, 96–97; China and,
    123–24, 130–31; civil service, 329–31;
    Cuba and, 205; currency, 130, 131–32,
    314–16; domestic violence, 221; econ-
    omy, 106–108, 130–31, 157–58; elec-
    tions, 127; foreign aid, 118–19; foreign
    exchange, 132; grain exports, 158;
    human rights covenant, 207; ICC, 272,
    274–75, 276, 278, 282; Iran and, 290;
    Japan and, 129–30; landmine policy, 103;
    Lockerbie aerial incident, 290; monetary
    policy, 106, 107; NAFTA, 107, 122,
    127–28; nuclear testing, 95; nuclear
    weapons, 84–85, 89, 90, 91, 92; peace-
    keeping assessment, 309; peacekeeping
    debt, 319 population assistance, 163;
    Russia and, 18; Somalia and, 41; trade,
    128–31; UN assessment, 304–11; UN
    budget, 10, 312–16; UN involvement,
    166; UN obligation, 303–306; UN over-
    sight, 326; UN programs, 323; UNDCP
    funding, 232–33; WTO, 126, 127
U.N.-OAS International Civilian Mission to
    Haiti (MICIVIH), 26–29
Urban areas, crime, 240; development, 144,
    257–58; population, 161; poverty, 255
Urbanization, 161, 162, 255, 257–58
Uruguay, 128
Uruguay Round, 126, 149, 150, 153
Uzbekistan, 208

van der Stoel, Max, 202
van Kappen, Franklin, 60–61
van Mierlo, Hans, 290
Venezuela, economy, 121; trade, 128; WTO,
    127
Vetere, Eduardo, 239, 240
Vienna Declaration and Programme of Ac-
    tion, 179–80
Vienna World Assembly on Aging, 249
Vietnam, 84
Vietnam War, 12

Violence against children, 245
Violence against civilians, 7
Violence against women, 186, 187, 220, 221, 223, 225, 226, 227, 228, 241
Visegrad nations, 125–26
Vulnerability index, 139

Wages, Asia, 122–23; Japan, 108; UN personnel, 329–31
War crimes, 174, history, 282–83; rape, 22; Srebrenica, 12
War crimes tribunals, 6, 214, 307; Nuremberg, 265, 273, 282; Rwanda, 226, 229, 263, 265, 269–70, 276, 282, 283–87; Tokyo, 273; Yugoslavia, 20, 22–23, 29, 229, 263, 265, 269–70, 276, 282, 283–87
Washington Declaration, 140
Washington Post, 321
Waste disposal systems, 259
Water supply, 144, 148, 154
Water-related diseases, 236–37
Weapons of mass destruction, 53–55, 83, 86
Werleigh, Claudette, 27
West Bank, 55–57
Western Bekaa, 209
Western Sahara, 30, 31–33, 180; elections, 8, 32–33, 181; referendum mission, 3, 6, 32–33, 319, 320
Western Sirmium, 2, 4
Winder, Cristian B., 237–41
Wolfensohn, James, 147
Women, 210; abuse of, 199, 204; advancement of, 222; AIDS, 235; character of, 223; conference, 219–22, 224–25, 227, 229; discrimination against, 186–87, 224–27; empowerment of, 186, 221–23; gender equality, 175, 186–87; hunger, 158; persecution of, 216; reproductive health, 160–64, 166, 244; status of, 175, 186–87, 219–29, 322; trafficking in, 241; UN, 228–29; *see also* Violence against women
Women's rights, 186–87, 253–59
Workers' rights, 191
World Bank, 26, 77, 115, 117–18, 144, 153, 165, 190, 233, 234, 238, 307–308, food issues, 150–52; housing, 256–57; loans to developing countries, 147–48; population programs, 163; wages, 329

World Blind Union, 253
World Court, 31, 89
World Food Council, 152
World Food Programme (WFP), 38–39, 78, 150, 212, 219, 229, 324
World Food Summit, 150–52, 155–56, 157
World Health Organization (WHO), 78, 89, 212, 233–37, 244, 291, 324
World Meteorological Organization (WMO), 135, 137
World Programme of Action Concerning Disabled Persons, 250–53
World Programme of Action for Youth to the Year 2000 and Beyond, 245–47
World Solar Summit, 138
World Summit for Children, 244–45
World Trade Organization (WTO), 124, 126–27, 130, 131, 145, 149–50, 222
Worldwatch Institute, 151
Wye Plantation conference, 59

Xenophobia, 184, 185, 209, 216

Yamoussoukro IV Accord, 43
Yellow fever, 237
Yeltsin, Boris, 18, 97, 124
Yemen, observation mission, 3
Yen, 108, 130, 132
Yokota, Yozo, 205
Yoshida, Jun, 263
Youth, 188, 241–47
Yugoslavia, former, 5, 6, 7, 209, 267, arms embargo, 22; human rights abuses, 7, 23, 24, 197, 199, 209, 212, 262, 285; Implementation Force, 20; justice system, 239–40; massacres, 24; overview, 11–12; peace-building, 195; sanctions, 22; troop reduction, 11; troop support, 10; UN assessments, 311; UN debt, 310, UNPRE DEP, 2, 4; war crimes, 214; war crimes tribunal, 23, 229, 263, 265, 269–70, 276, 282, 283–87

Zaire, 209, 236, 243
Zambia, 168
Zedillo, Ernesto, 122
Zepa, 13, 15, 198
Zimbabwe, 163
Zubak, Kresimir, 285
Zur, David, 61

An Invitation...

TIRED OF MERE TALK about post-Cold War cooperation while global problems such as international drug trafficking, human rights abuses, ageing and health issues, and atmospheric pollution cry out for attention? Wish you could do something positive to help translate all that talk into global action?

There is something you can do! Join with thousands of your fellow citizens who have already discovered the vital work of the United Nations system—and who have lent their support by joining the United Nations Association of the USA!

UNA-USA is a nonprofit, nonpartisan organization working in Washington, D.C., at U.N. Headquarters in New York, and in hundreds of communities across the country to build public understanding of — and support for — greater international cooperation. That cooperation can only be achieved through the United Nations.

Hear and be heard

Founded a half-century ago by Eleanor Roosevelt and other concerned Americans, UNA-USA today boasts a national membership of more than 20,000 people — people who, like you, want to know about the global issues that affect their lives. And who want to know what's being done to address them.

As a UNA-USA member, you will receive the Association's acclaimed journal, *The InterDependent*, with expert analysis that takes you beyond daily newspaper headlines and into the halls where global policy is made. In fact, as a UNA-USA member you can actually help develop such policy! Each year you will be invited to take part in the Association's

unique Global Policy Project — a program designed to find answers to specific international problems, and which reaches the highest levels of decision-makers, both at U.N. Headquarters and in our nation's capital.

Be a part of it all

In addition to the benefits that come with being a national member (listed below), you are also invited to participate in your local UNA-USA Chapter to whatever degree you wish. Many of our members enjoy the opportunity to come together with like-minded citizens in their immediate community to discuss current events, participate in various projects and programs, to plan the observance of U.N. Day (October 24), or to attend a lecture or conference — often featuring senior U.N. officials and representatives of foreign governments. It's like having a small piece of the United Nations right in your town! But remember, participation is strictly voluntary.

Sign on and receive . . .

■ A subscription to the highly acclaimed UNA-USA journal, *The InterDependent*.

■ A new membership kit, full of insider information on global issues and the many parts of the U.N. system that address them.

■ Discounts on all UNA-USA materials.

■ An opportunity to become active in your local UNA-USA Chapter (if you wish).

■ The knowledge that you are a part of the decision-making process that affects you, your family, and your world.